Desk Copy

Mrs. Wallace

Child Development

and Parenting

Consultants

Mamie Hardy
Director, Professional Services
Changing Times Education Service

Melinda S. Lassiter
Home Economics Education Consultant
North Carolina Department of Public Instruction
Raleigh, North Carolina

Jeanne Warren Lindsay
Educator and Author
Buena Park, California

Joyce Miles
Home Economics Supervisor
Duval County Public Schools
Jacksonville, Florida

Judy Wall
Home Economics Coordinator
Fort Worth Independent School District
Fort Worth, Texas

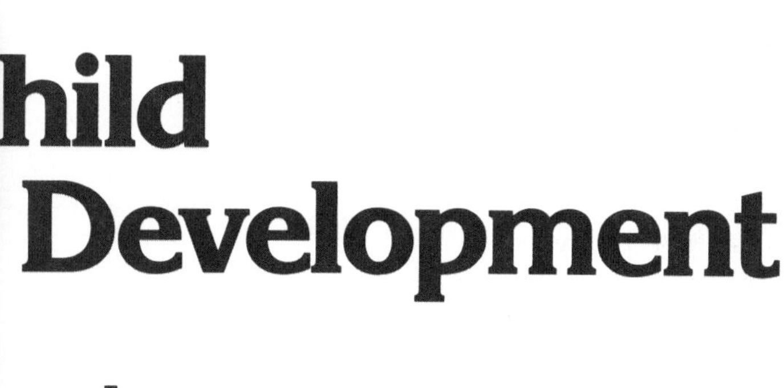

Child Development and Parenting

Helen Gum Westlake, M.S.

Home Economics Department Chairperson

York Community High School

Elmhurst, Illinois

Donald G. Westlake, Ph.D.

Senior Scientist

Argonne National Laboratory

Argonne, Illinois

Changing Times Education Service
EMC Publishing
Saint Paul, MN 55101

Editor Eileen C. Slater

Feature Writer Carol Walsh

Design, Production (DTP), and Cover
Slater Studio, Minneapolis, Minnesota

ISBN 0-8219-0490-6

Published by EMC Publishing
300 York Avenue
St. Paul, Minnesota 55101

Printed in the United States of America
0 9 8 7 6 5 4 3 2

Introduction

Child Development and Parenting was written to give insight into the many phases of childhood and the corresponding phases of parenthood. Children's needs change with growth. Parents and caregivers need to understand stages of child development so that they can best meet the needs of children. This book is divided into six units to help you understand parenting and children including their physical, intellectual, emotional, social, and moral development.

Unit 1, "Introduction to Parenting," discusses parenthood as it relates to the roles, theories, and society's responsibility for children. It stresses the great importance of the parenting role for all of us.

Unit 2, "Becoming Parents," covers prenatal development and the importance of proper prenatal care. The unit ends with the birth of the child.

Unit 3, "Infancy," stresses the needs of the infant. The first few months of life are of extreme importance because they are the foundation upon which the new life will be built. Physiological development and psychological growth of the infant are examined.

Unit 4, "The Preschool Child," emphasizes that these early years lay the foundation for the child's personality, lifestyle, philosophy, and character. The self-concept that a child perceives from the early environment will be carried with him or her into maturity. Focus is on the relation of concepts and on the individuality of each child.

Unit 5, "The School-Age Child," spotlights the importance of the peer group, the development of values and goals, plus cementing of character traits.

Unit 6, "Guiding Children Through Change," recognizes that childhood is filled with challenges and crises. These crisis situations demand different resolutions depending on the individual child, the child's age and stage, and the type of crisis.

Also, throughout this book you will find features that highlight related facts and issues in each of the chapters. These features include:

"A Matter of Fact"—Offering practical tips and hints, these features help you develop useful skills such as teaching a child how to tie a shoe, planning a birthday party, and even playing games that encourage cooperation rather than competition.

"A Closer Look"—Providing a personal look at the chapter material, these case studies help you better understand the chapter concepts.

"Look, Listen, and Learn"—Through the practice of observation, you can learn about child development first-hand. These features tell you what to look for at each stage of development.

"Life's Work"—What careers are available if you want to work with children? Learn about 15 different careers involving children by reading about real people and their jobs.

Finally, the artwork at the beginning of each chapter was done by children whose ages range from 2 years to 8 years. The artists' names and ages are listed in the back of the book. By comparing the various pictures, you can gain an appreciation for the individuality and creativity of children. You also may be able to see how children's stages of development are expressed in their art.

Table of Contents

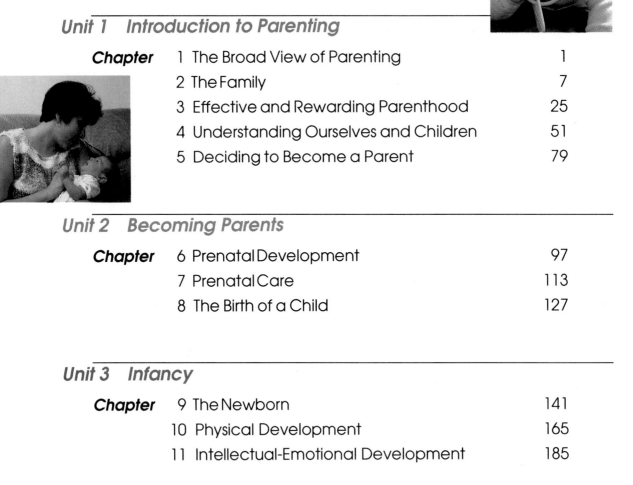

Unit 1 Introduction to Parenting

Unit 2 Becoming Parents

Unit 3 Infancy

Unit 1
Introduction to Parenting

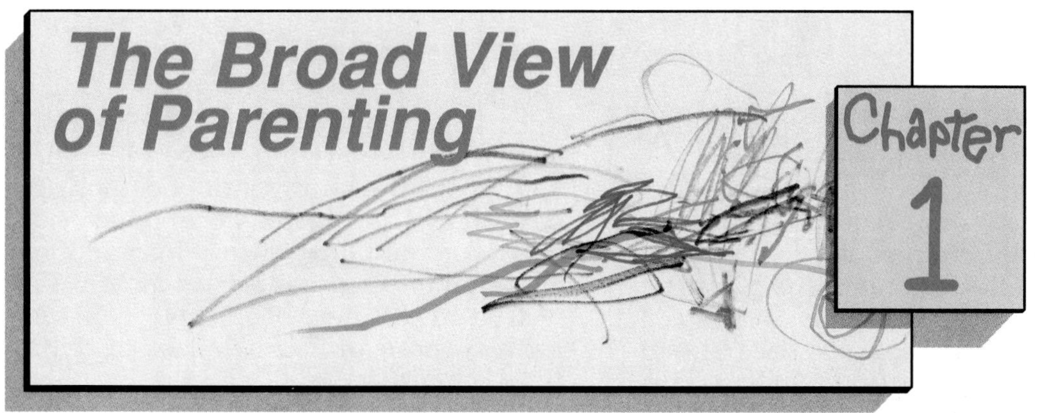

This chapter will help you:

- ✎ understand the full scope of the meaning of "parent"
- ✎ describe the influence of school on children's development
- ✎ recognize the importance of families and schools working together
- ✎ identify the responsibility that accompanies parenthood

We Are All Parents

Who is a parent? The Webster's dictionary defines "parent" as "one who begets or brings forth offspring." Obviously, that is a narrow definition because it includes only the parents who give birth to a child. Left out of the definition, for example, are people who become parents by marrying someone who has children or who become parents through a legal process, such as adoption.

A broader definition of "parent" might be "guardian" or "one who is responsible for the welfare of a child." Therefore, according to this definition, we are all parents. Even if we have not had children or are not legal guardians, we are all responsible for the next generation. Almost every decision we make in our communities, our states, our nation, and the world affects, or will affect, our children. If the welfare of children is ignored, the future of society is ignored.

Some of the responsibility for children's welfare is assumed by public employees. For example, firefighters risk their own lives to save children trapped in burning houses. Police officers come to classrooms and warn young children of "Stranger Danger." Crossing guards and school bus drivers maintain safe conditions for children. There are other people who assume responsibilities for the welfare of children even though they are not paid for it. Volunteers take leadership roles in religious youth groups, Scouts, 4-H, FFA, FHA/HERO, boys' clubs, girls' clubs, family service groups, and

> **A Matter of Fact**
>
> Children are our country's most valuable resources. The hope of a better, secure tomorrow, free from fear lies with the children of today. When someone sees a child in danger, do you suppose this races through the rescuer's mind? Most anyone would respond to the cries of a child for help.
>
> Children's safety has become a concern to American business as well. Many are doing something about it. For example, the employees of Commonwealth Edison, an Illinois utility, created the E-Team. The purpose of the E-Team is to help children who are hurt or scared when there's no one else nearby.
>
> Jason Jerde suffered a head injury in a bicycle accident in DeKalb. Mark Minnihan, a lineman for Commonwealth Edison, radioed for help and remained with Jason until an ambulance arrived.
>
> Minnihan's actions earned the E-Team a citation from former President Ronald Reagan for "finding innovative private solutions to public problems."

many others. In the broadest sense, all of these people are acting as parents.

Even in totally unstructured situations, we see people playing **parenting roles.** Think of the neighbor who told you to go home because it was getting dark, or the older brother of a friend who drove you home when you cut your knee falling off your bicycle. Think of your friend who reminded you to wear your coat on a sunny, but cool, spring day. All of these people were concerned with your welfare. Their interaction with you affected your development or well being. Some people, of course, have a more profound effect on you than others.

In the broadest sense, we can even be a parent to ourselves. When we give ourselves a pat on the back, or when we scold ourselves, we are accepting the responsibility for our own behavior. Having learned self-discipline, mature persons are able to take the parenting process and apply it to themselves. Making these parenting tasks a part of personal behavior moves us from childhood to adulthood.

Home and School—Working Together

The school is second only to the home in its importance to the development of children. For the welfare of future generations, we need to provide excellent teachers, to upgrade courses, to build outstanding school facilities, etc. We also must have parents who understand children in all their ages and stages, who love them, who support them, and who work with the schools to meet common objectives for them. Some of those objectives for both parent and schools should be the following:

1. Children should feel "good" about themselves.
2. Children should feel confident about the **competence** of their caregivers. Competence means having

adequate ability.

3. Children should develop morally and socially as well as physically and intellectually.

4. Children should have achievable goals.

5. Children should acquire the knowledge and the skills that allow them to reach their goals and full potential.

The family and the school must work together in reaching those objectives and in the education of children. **Cooperation** (working together for common benefit) is the key. Children need to respect their schools and their teachers as well as their homes and parents. Parents need to have a positive attitude toward education. They need to encourage their children to study. Parents can become a part of this process if they appreciate learning.

In addition, there must be mutual respect if parents and teachers are to cooperate and communicate effectively. Teachers will have to respect the ideas, ideals, and hopes of parents. Parents will have to respect the objectives, efforts, and philosophy of teachers.

Better communications can be established between school and home if teachers take the time to explain their own concerns, hopes, and dreams for the children. In order for the school and the home to be supportive of each other, they will need to speak a common language. Children who come to school from homes where they are encouraged to study, where they experience love and care, and where they do not experience emotional stress have the greatest opportunity for academic achievement.

Even children can play parenting roles. Caring for a sick parent is a sign of this ability.

Preparing for Parenthood

In today's rapidly changing world, parenting is not easy, but then it never was. For society to meet the challenge, we must all recognize that parenthood, like marriage, needs to be a decision based on knowledge and responsibility. The responsibility that accompanies parenthood is immense, and the parent-child relationship is not temporary, it is for life. This book will help you realize what responsibilities parenting involves. It will also help you learn good parenting practices.

Researchers have been able to show that good and bad parenting practices are perpetuated. That is, people tend to

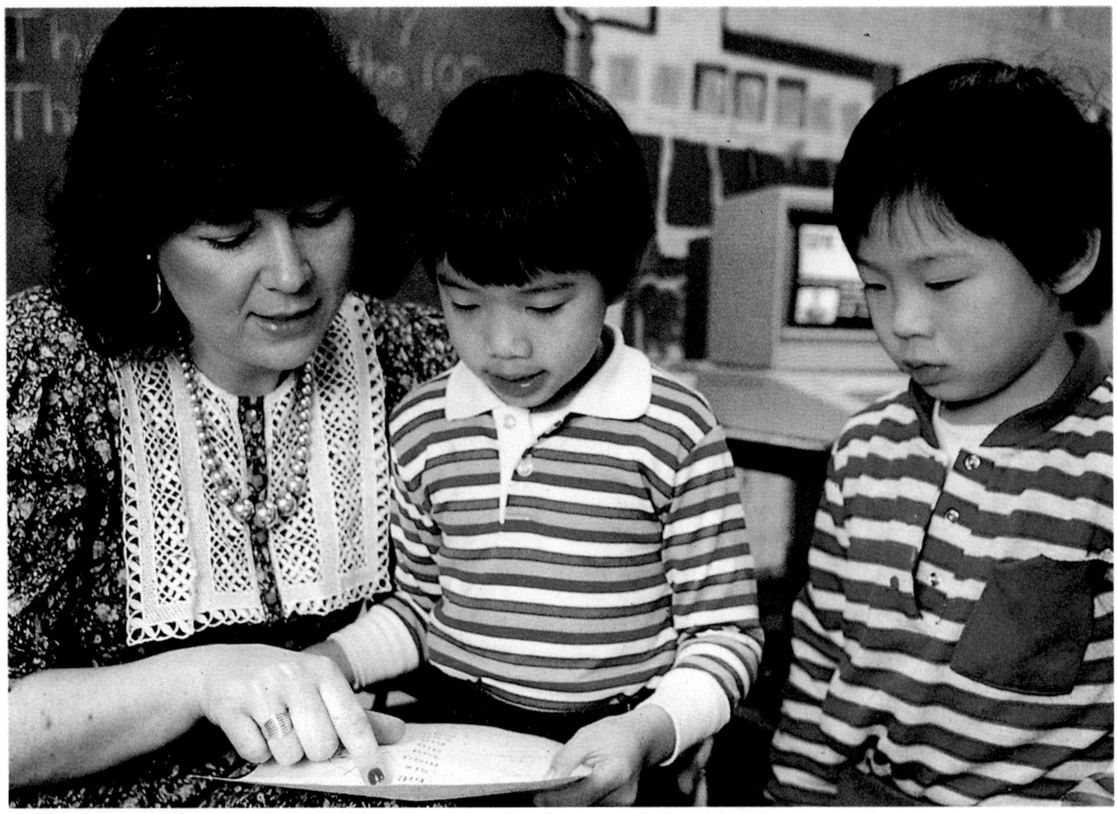

Teachers have a great impact on children's lives. Teachers can motivate learning and help develop self-esteem.

treat their children as their parents treated them. We do not inherit an instinct that makes us good parents. We need to work at being good parents. We can become good parents by studying the concepts of child development and parent-child relationships and putting those concepts into practice. Even if you choose not to become a parent, you can benefit from studying child development. For instance, if you choose a career in child care, you'll find this study invaluable. Remember, too, we are all responsible for the future generation. Finally, studying about children—how they grow, why they act certain ways, and how they develop—can help you understand yourself and others. After all, we all started out as children.

In the chapters that follow, among the questions we'll explore are parental responsibility, the birth rights of babies, children's stages of development and parental roles at the various stages, the function of the family and school, children's crises, and sources of professional help. Such information will provide you with a basis for the kind of serious thought and consideration that is essential to quality parenthood and caregiving.

In Review

Vocabulary

parenting roles
competence
cooperation

Summary

- ✓ In the broadest sense of the word, we are all "parents."
- ✓ Cooperation between home and school provides maximum opportunities for children to realize their potential.
- ✓ Parenthood, like marriage, needs to be a decision based on knowledge, because the parent-child relationship is for life.
- ✓ Good parenting is not instinctive. Good parenting comes from putting into practice the concepts of child development and parent-child relationships.
- ✓ The study of child development helps us to understand ourselves. It also makes us better prepared to meet our adult responsibilities to the younger generation, whether or not we become parents.

Questions

1. Give five examples of people, other than your own parents and teachers, who have touched your life in some way because they are interested in the welfare of children.
2. What examples can you give that demonstrate your ability to be a parent to yourself?
3. Parents, school administrators, and teachers should have many goals in common. Can you list four examples?
4. Why is it important for teenagers to study the principles of being a good parent?

Activities

1. Give two examples of situations in which you have shown your concern for the welfare of children.
2. Find organizations that need volunteers to work with children. Are there ways you could help as an individual or as a class project?

This chapter will help you:

- recognize that each child is unique and that uniqueness needs to be accepted by the parents
- understand that the family is responsible for the physical and mental well-being of children
- interpret the statement "parenting is not an action, it is an interaction"
- describe the responsibilities of a smoothly functioning family
- define a society
- describe the different types of family life today
- assess how working parents and single parents can coordinate family and work-oriented goals

The Child as an Individual

Parents often have ideas of how their children should be. Many of these ideas are based upon how parents view themselves. The parents' likes and dislikes, however, may center on characteristics that their children do not have. One parent wants a certain look, certain personality, or certain intellectual or physical abilities. One parent wants a boy. The other wants a girl. A perfectly normal child is born, but sometimes the baby does not fit the parents' ideal. When a child is born, there is no return and no exchange. Parents cannot reject some part of the child. Each child needs to be accepted completely. Total acceptance means that we accept the child's sex, physical characteristics, personality, intellectual abilities, and limitations.

Each newborn infant is unique, and parents should recognize that fact. We need to understand that children

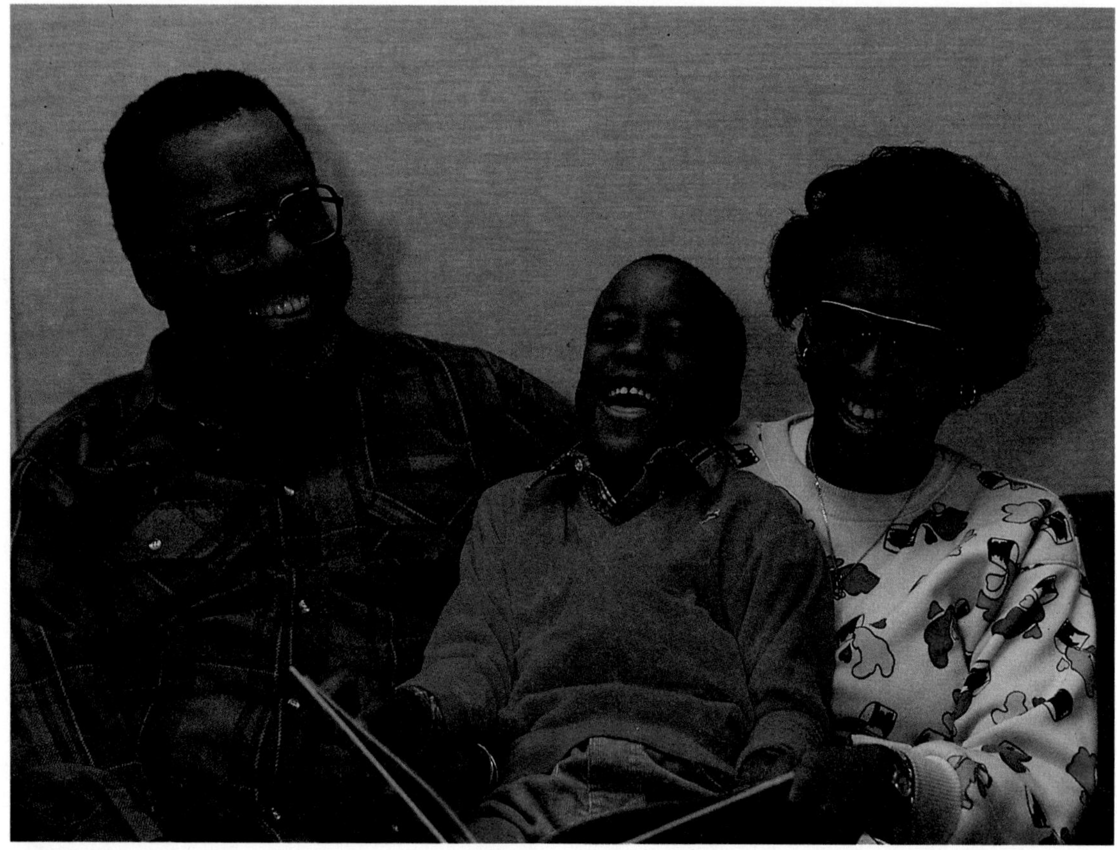

The types of relationships children experience in the family will affect their relationships all through life.

should not be compared with other children or with either of their parents. Each child has a unique heredity and a unique environment. **Heredity** includes the physical characteristics passed on by parents, such as brown eyes or small bones. **Environment** includes surroundings—people, places, and things.

One might think that a four-year-old girl and her two-year-old brother have the same environment. They have the same parents, they live in the same house, and they eat the same food. In fact, however, their environments are quite different. The girl has a younger brother. He has an older sister. She started her life as an only child. He started his life in a family of two children. Even before birth they experienced different environments. Their mother did not eat exactly the same food throughout both pregnancies. She did not exercise exactly the same, nor did she experience all the same emotions.

As children grow through their various stages, their environments become increasingly diverse. Because they are unique in both their heredity and environment, it is understandable that children within one family can have personalities as different as those of unrelated children.

The Child as a Member of a Family

We cannot discuss the development of children without considering the family. Children are dependent on the family for their existence; their food, clothing and shelter; and their general well-being. The family must provide for the basic needs of children for them to be physically and mentally healthy. Also the most influential and lasting relationships that children experience are within the family. The types of interactions children experience within their family will form the basis for their relationships with other people in later years.

A child can no more flourish in a home stripped of love and care than a green plant can flourish without sun and water. In order for children to learn to love others and accept themselves, they must develop in an atmosphere in which there is love and acceptance. Children need to know there are adults in their life who care. The adults need to interact with the child. For example, when children draw pictures, they need adults who say, "Tell me about your picture. I like the colors you used." Children need encouragement. "I like the way you put away your toys." "I saw you throw the ball high into the air." "I enjoy hearing about your day at school." Statements such as these make children feel their efforts are really appreciated.

Parents also must make every effort to know and understand their children. Open **communication** is vital. Communication is a two-part exchange. It involves someone sending a message and someone receiving it—a speaker and a listener. In turn, the listener may become the speaker, and the speaker, the listener.

One of the main reasons there is conflict between the generations is the lack of communication. Parents must

A Matter of Fact

Good communication is a skill that can improve relationships between parents and children and even between friends. Follow these guidelines.

- **Good communication takes listening. Think about what the other person is saying, not what you will say next.**
- **Good communication takes time. Don't try to get ideas across in a hurry.**
- **Good communication involves different viewpoints. People don't have to agree to get along and to communicate.**
- **Look for the right words to express a feeling or an idea.**
- **Go back over what was said so you know you understand each other. Repeat what was said using your own words.**
- **Don't make fun of other people's ideas or feelings.**

Babies quickly learn that their cries will help them get what they want—food, comfort, and love.

sort through many issues with their children. Some important questions that both parents and children need to consider include: Do we accept ourselves? Are we capable of loving and receiving love? Do we dare to face ourselves? Can we face both joy and sorrow? Do we relate well to others? Do we know how to relax? Do we know how to express ourselves with sensitivity and use our imagination?

Parent-Child Interaction

Parenting is not one-sided. That is, parenting is not something we do *to* children, it is something we do *with* children. Parenting is not an action, it is an interaction. Parents can strongly influence the behavior of children, but children strongly influence the behavior of parents as well.

Even in the first few days of life, babies learn that they have a degree of control over their environment. Babies cry when they are hungry or wet. The parents or caregivers respond by feeding or changing them. Babies quickly learn to cry out for food or comfort. They also learn to cry when they are in need of the even more important hugging and comfort of a loving caregiver. This is a simple conditioned response and requires no complicated thought process on the part of the baby.

In the same way, most of us go

through life behaving intentionally, but subconsciously, so as to influence the behavior of those around us. For example, some children can intentionally infuriate their parents without trying to understand their own behavior or the parents' response that follows. That is, the child does not consciously think, "If I do this, I'll make them really mad." Nevertheless, the child intentionally does something that irritates the parents. Moreover, if parents have no knowledge of child development, psychology, and the fundamentals of interpersonal relationships, their own responses may be equally instinctive and inappropriate.

A Closer Look

For example, Kim Lee's parents have been ignoring her all afternoon. They have been watching a football game on TV and no matter how many times Kim Lee tried to talk to them or get them to play, they told her, "Be quiet. Go play by yourself." Kim Lee decides to stuff some of her toys in the toilet. Next time one of them comes into the bathroom, they'll notice—and notice her, too. Sure enough, her father comes in during a commercial, sees the plugged up toilet, and yells, "Kim Lee, what have you been doing?" Kim Lee says, "Nothing." "Well, it looks like you've been doing *something,* " he replies. "Dear, the game's back on. What are you doing?" Kim Lee's mother calls from the living room. Kim Lee's father says to Kim Lee, "I don't have time to deal with you now. You go to your room and don't come out until I tell you." Crying, Kim Lee runs off. Now Kim Lee, her father, and her mother (once she finds out) are all unhappy.

Behavior can be changed. People are more likely to change their behavior when knowledge helps them to see change as desirable. How would different behavior have changed Kim Lee's situation? Kim Lee's parents could have invited her to sit on the couch with them and watch the game. Maybe they could suggest that she quietly play in the living room so they could all be together. Then they could play after the game. Those responses probably would have changed the situation to a desirable outcome.

Families are dynamic. As children mature, the parents' own attitudes and behavior also evolve. The roles parents and children play in each others lives change with each level of maturity. For example, parents of a newborn baby provide for the baby's every need. How does that compare to parents' caregiving of a 10-year-old?

Obviously, the roles of both parents and children are affected by other factors as well. As just two of many possible examples, consider the following. The youngest child or "baby of the family" must assume a different identity when a new baby is born. After a divorce, both parents assume new roles in the lives of their children.

Parental Responsibilities

Just as you learned in Chapter 1 that there are many different meanings to "parent," there are a wide variety of

Children enjoy new experiences such as this community class in candlemaking.

parental responsibilities. However, all families do share some basic responsibilities. The parents in a smoothly functioning family need the stability to provide the following:

1. financial support.
2. physical and emotional care for the children.
3. mutual acceptance of mother and father roles.
4. an atmosphere that allows for the parents' own professional and personal growth.
5. a companionable partnership that is mutually supportive.
6. a problem-solving process that allows all family members to interact.
7. opportunities for the children's development (within the family's resources).
8. family routines to meet the changing needs of growing children.
9. work and recreation schedules to suit the needs of all the family members.
10. opportunities for all family members to identify with organizations such as youth groups, religious groups, or clubs, etc.
11. an atmosphere in which children can sense that they are a joy to their parents, and that the rich satisfaction of parenthood has enhanced their marriage.
12. an atmosphere that helps children learn responsiblity, values, moral behavior, etc.

The Family in Today's Society

Any group that lives according to its own generally accepted code of behavior can be classified as a **society**. Over long periods of time, a society and its set of rules evolve because the needs of the society change. The society exists only because it is essential to the survival of its individual members.

A family is a segment of society. In fact, it is a fundamental building block of society. It is a basic unit. The family developed in prehistoric times because it was essential to survival. Some experts who study prehistoric society have proposed that the family emerged out of the need for cooperative hunting techniques and protection of the young. Obviously, those roles are practiced in only a few societies of the world today. In more technically developed cultures, the roles of family members may be quite varied. In fact, those roles have evolved so rapidly in recent years that it might almost be termed revolution, instead of evolution. For example, the mother used to stay at home to care for the family. In recent years, over 60% of women with children under 18 years old are in the workforce. In turn, fathers take a more active parenting role than they did 20 years ago.

Even with all the changes, the family is still just as essential, but in different ways and for different reasons. The basic human needs for nourishment of the body and nurturing of the mind remain unchanged. The modern family, in each of its many forms, must provide those needs or the children cannot develop into healthy adults. At the same time, the family, which is the basic building block of the society, must teach children the rules by which the society is governed. If children grow up not understanding those rules, or if they fail to respect them, then the society cannot be perpetuated.

Families Yesterday and Today

For several generations of American history, the typical family consisted of a husband, wife, and their children. The husband was a farmer, a tradesman, or a businessman, while the wife was a homemaker. Early in their childhoods, boys worked with their fathers. Girls worked with their mothers. Quite often, grandparents

In the majority of families today, no one is a full-time homemaker.

lived in the same household or very nearby.

Families today are only half as large as they were when the United States was young. In 1790, the average household had nearly seven members. Today, the average household has fewer than three members. Since "average household" is a census category that includes people who live alone, here is a more family-based way to look at it. In 1800, the average woman had seven children, five of

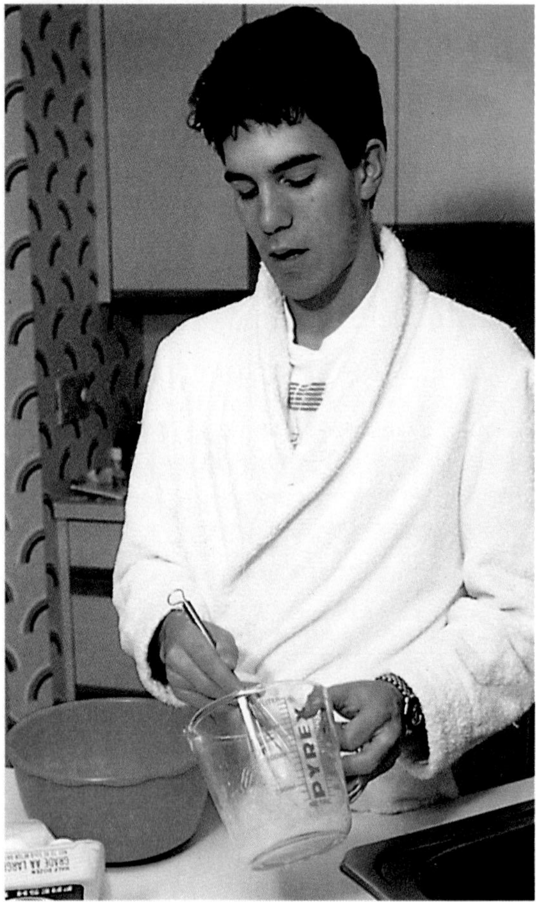

In today's family, everyone needs to have flexible roles and pitch in at home.

whom survived to adulthood. Today, the average woman has two children, both of whom survive.

In the primarily farming society of the 1800s, it was economically advantageous to have many children. They provided free labor. In today's primarily urban and suburban society, however, there is little opportunity for children to contribute to the family's financial gain. Furthermore, the high costs of feeding, clothing, and schooling children tend to discourage parents from raising large families. Apparently, there is a spin-off benefit of this family-size reduction. Psychologists agree that children from small families live up to their potential mentally, emotionally, socially, and physically better than children from large families. Seemingly, children in small families get more time and attention from parents. This extra advantage results in higher verbal skills.

Family Life Today

In recent years, it has become difficult to define a "typical" family. There are unmarried couples performing the functions of a family presented earlier in this chapter. There are husband-wife-children combinations that do not perform the functions of a family. It seems that all possibilities exist in society today. For example, let us examine the following real case.

A Closer Look

A 65-year-old widower lives in a five-room, urban apartment. He sleeps on a hide-a-bed in the living room. His 92-year-old mother sleeps in the smallest bedroom. His married daughter and her husband sleep in the second bedroom. Their six-year-old son shares the third bedroom with his unmarried aunt. The aunt has a good job and is the sole support of all the others. When the boy is not in school, he plays on the sidewalks in the neighborhood, and his grandfather watches over him. The boy's mother spends her days and evenings watching television.

Her husband does all the cooking and cleaning. The boy has extraordinary verbal skills and seems to be very well-adjusted. While the arrangement is far from traditional, this extended family is apparently satisfied with its own style of functioning.

A majority of families today do not fit the traditional mold. Of the American mothers with children under the ages of 18, almost 60% are in the workforce according to the Bureau of Labor Statistics. That number is expected to increase to 80% in the early 1990s. Other evidence of the rapid changes in family life is revealed by comparing statistics provided by the U. S. Census Bureau for the years 1970 and 1980. Over the 10 year period, the total number of married couples in the United States increased by only 7%, while the number of unmarried couples living together increased by 15%. The number of marriages performed per year increased by only 7%. The number of divorces per year increased by 65%. The total number of children living with only one parent increased by 40%.

In addition to divorce, teenage motherhood is another social phenomenon that is an important factor contributing to the number of children living with only one parent. Each year over one million unwed, teenaged girls become pregnant. Of those adolescents who have been pregnant once, three out of every 10 become pregnant again within two years. Further education is ruled out for almost all teenage mothers. Only 49% received a high school degree as reported by the National Center for Health Statistics in its National Survey of Family Growth.

Single parents face the challenge of earning an income as well as taking care of a family.

Single parents face virtually all the same problems of child-rearing as couples who both work, and they face some additional problems as well. Single parents have no one (except maybe older children in the family) with whom they can share parenting responsibilities such as taking the child to the doctor or reading bedtime stories as well as decision-making and homemaking chores. In addition, they must support the family on only one paycheck.

According to the U.S. Census Bureau, in 1979 there were 18.3 million people living in families that included women who were divorced, separated, remarried, or never married. Twenty-seven percent of those people were living below the poverty level compared with only eight percent of all other people living in family units.

As mentioned, contributing to that statistic is the fact that most women who became mothers during adolescence never acquire the education necessary to receive higher level incomes.

Whatever the causes, by 1984 more than 25.7% of all American families with children were headed by a single parent. That number was 21.5% in 1980 and only 12.9% in 1970. Equally significant is the fact that even by 1978 **traditional families** (children, biological mother who is the homemaker, and biological father who is the sole support of the family) constituted only 13% of all family units. Thus, a vast majority of today's family units do not fit the traditional pattern.

The Blended Family

The problems of single parents are not necessarily resolved when they remarry. In addition, other serious problems can arise. As we all know, there are times in any relationship when some degree of conflict occurs. The possibility for conflict is multiplied when the number of family bonds increases. Let's look at Susan's situation.

A Closer Look

Susan has two children and is divorced from their father, Robert. At this stage of her life she is strongly affected by her bonds or relationships with at least seven different people: her two children, the children's four grandparents, and her ex-husband. Yes, she is divorced from Robert, but he is the children's father.

Now, let's suppose that Robert marries a divorced woman who has two children. Susan's two children must establish relationships with these three new people in their father's life. Susan will be affected by her children's interaction with their father's new family. Susan might become jealous of her children's affection, or she might feel that the children's new stepmother is too lax about discipline.

Now, let's suppose that Susan remarries. Her new husband is John. He has three children from his first marriage. Besides her bond with John, Susan also must establish relationships with his children and his ex-wife, because John's children stay with him several weeks a year. The relationships established between Susan's children and John, and between Susan's children and John's children could be strongly influenced by Susan. Conversely, the nature of those relations will greatly affect Susan and her relationship with her new husband.

Let us suppose, further, that Susan and John begin having children of their own. Not only will Susan be forming still more bonds, but she will be tangled in the web of bonds formed by the "second" family with her "first" family and with John's "first" family. By considering this **blended family** from the perspective of Susan, we realize that she and probably all the other mem-

Look at Susan's blended family. Can you determine the number of relationships?

bers are being pushed and pulled in many directions. Each individual is somewhat like a juggler who is trying to keep many objects in the air at the same time. Such situations can be very stressful, and it requires a great deal of understanding, patience, and cooperation on all sides to maintain the delicate balance.

Even in the traditional family, a good deal of cooperation is necessary if most of the interactions are to be pleasing. It is important to recognize that the number of relationships increases rapidly as the family size increases. The mathematical formula is:

$$r = \frac{1}{2}p\,(p - 1)$$

In this equation, r is the number of relationships, and p is the number of people in the family. Thus, we can set up the following table:

P	2	3	4	5	6	7	8	9	10
r	1	3	6	10	15	21	28	36	45

In a family of a father (f), a mother (m), a boy (b), and a girl (g), the six bonds are f-m, f-b, f-g, m-b, m-g, and b-g. If the parents have two more children, the number of relationships in the household will increase from six to 15. In Susan's blended family, let's assume that Susan has two children with her present husband, John. Then, when John's three children are visiting their father, there is a household of nine people. There are then 36 relationships, all of which affect Susan's life. For a more complete picture, consider adding Susan's first husband, his second wife and her children, John's first wife, Susan's parents, Robert's parents and John's parents to the mathematical formula. It becomes mind boggling.

Working Parents

In today's society when both parents work, there is an urgent need to coordinate the time and effort devoted to achieving family- and work-oriented goals. Just as for single parents, when both parents work suitable arrangements must be made for child care. Good daycare can provide wonderful experiences for children, but they are not inexpensive. Some children are cared for by older people or homemakers in their homes. The cost may be less than a daycare center, but it still means an expense for the family. Older children often face the problems of coming home from school to an empty home. These children are called **latchkey children,** a term used because many of them carry their own key.

Naturally, an important contributing factor is the number of working mothers with children under 18 years of age. In the United States, in 1986 there were nearly 20 million mothers in the labor force according to the Bureau of Labor Statistics. That means that over 34 million children had working mothers. More than 50% of the mothers of preschool children are working outside the home.

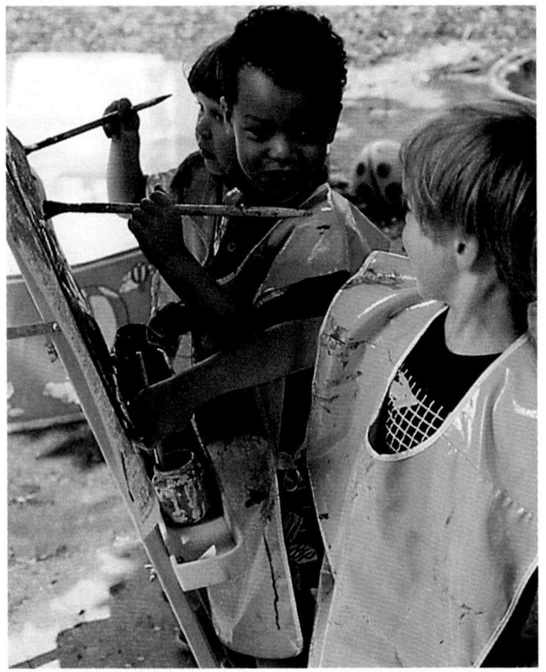

Daycare centers provide working parents a safe environment for their children and new experiences for the children.

Many companies are now recognizing the importance of family time and have introduced a program called **flex-time.** This allows employees to choose their daily work hours, within certain limits. Some parents use the plan very effectively to provide them more time with their children. For example, a father chooses to start work at 9:30 in the morning so he can eat breakfast with his wife and their children. In another family, the mother chooses to go to work early, so she can be home by 3:30 in the afternoon when the children's school bus arrives. Some companies also have job sharing programs. Two people share one job,

A Matter of Fact

The switchboards of companies across North America become overloaded about the same time children arrive home from school. What's the connection between the two? Many children have been instructed to check in with their parents each day after arriving home from school. The number of children who spend a portion of their day without adult supervision and companionship is increasing. In our society, the trend is toward two working parents whose workdays don't end when school gets out. Latchkey children are responsible for letting themselves into their homes and taking care of themselves until the parents come home.

When parents or caregivers can't be around, there are some ways to provide for the safety and comfort of the child.

- Don't let the child become a couch potato. Organize activities. The child can start on homework, care for a pet, or do chores, or work on a hobby.
- Prepare a first-aid kit and teach the child basic first-aid. Make sure the child knows what to do in case of a medical emergency. Post emergency numbers by the phone.
- Find a neighbor the child can call upon in case of an emergency.
- Give an extra key to the home to a neighbor. Don't hide a key around the house.
- Caregivers and parents should tell the child when they expect to return. They should call if they are going to be late.
- The child should walk home everyday with other children from the neighborhood and take the same route.
- Tell the child never to open the door to strangers or give out information over the phone.

When leaving a child home alone, there are many things to consider. Open communication is the place to start. If the child appears to be nervous or afraid about being left alone, the caregiver or parent should consider making other arrangements. If the child has shown responsible behavior, the caregiver or parent may try leaving the child for 15 minutes at first, then increasing the time away gradually. It is not a good idea to leave a child home alone more than two hours.

each working only part of the day. Some companies also provide child care at the company or assist with the cost of child care.

When both parents work, questions arise among all the family members as to how cooking, cleaning, and other household chores should be divided or shared. If there are grandparents living nearby who require a certain amount of care, suitable arrangements are necessary for them, also. Each of these situations would be the assumed responsibilities of the homemaker in

Even with all the changes families are undergoing today, they still fulfill a vital part in our society.

the traditional family. When both parents work outside the home, however, both are contributing to the financial support of the family. For harmony, both must agree on a mutually acceptable division or sharing of homemaking responsibilities.

The Family in the Future

We have seen that today's family is under great stress. Only a minority of families fit the description of the traditional family. One might wonder whether families will still serve a useful function in the years ahead. According to Dr. Urie Bronfenbrenner, a noted authority on the family and a professor at Cornell University, the answer is "Absolutely." He feels that the family is essential in creating competent and compassionate members of society. Some of his other thoughts, which appeared in *Forecast for Home Economics*, January 1983, can be paraphrased as follows.

- The family is much better qualified than any institution to keep human beings human.
- Society should provide whatever is necessary to encourage the family in its efforts.
- Above all, society must ensure that parents have time for parenthood, and all adults have time to fulfill parenting roles.

The following verses are selected from a song composed by Mike Nobel of Gorham, Maine. Reprinted with permission.

State of the Family

From the heart of a ghetto, to a carpeted condo,
to anywhere you care to name,
Families are trying to keep love from dying
in the high tension world of today.

The numbers are scary for folks who marry,
five outa' ten fall apart,
And our kids hang on while we fight,
or we run, for a place to make a new start.

The strains of a nation will bring desperation
to many a family abode,
And children will bear the pain of their parents
when anger and tension explode.

And how can a country be strong,
with weakening family bonds...
In the world of priorities
time after time, will families wait
at the end of the line,
There are so many falling behind
in the race to survive....

Our children grow up, and take on the job
of gaining a handle on life,
With days of defiance, depressions, and highs,
and unraveling family ties.

Society changes, and time rearranges
our image of husband and wife,
Traditions are breaking, and hearts are aching,
to keep emotions alive.

But to those who thrive in family life,
I offer my praise, and my prayers,
Like a safe embrace for the human race, you offer a reason to care.

And every society lives on the vision our families give,
To see the beauty in children's dreams, to celebrate people who share their needs,
To summon the heart to believe in the power of love....

From the heart of a ghetto, to a carpeted condo,
to anywhere you care to name,
Families are trying to keep love alive
in the high tension world of today.

In Review

Vocabulary

heredity
environment
society
traditional family
blended family
latchkey children

Summary

- ✓ Every child is unique in his or her heredity and environment.
- ✓ Parents should recognize and accept their children's abilities and limitations.
- ✓ The family is the fundamental building block of society. It provides the basic needs to maintain a child's physical and mental health.
- ✓ The most influential and lasting relationships that children experience are within the family.
- ✓ Children learn to love by being loved.
- ✓ The parent-child interaction requires good communication. Parenting is not something we do *to* children, it is something we do *with* children.
- ✓ There are many different types of families, but the smoothly functioning family needs stability to accept certain basic responsibilities.
- ✓ It is the family's responsibility to teach children the rules by which society is governed.
- ✓ Family life has evolved rapidly in recent years. Today, fewer than 15% of American families fit the "traditional" mold.
- ✓ Divorce and teenage motherhood are two important factors contributing to the number of children living with only one parent.
- ✓ The number of interpersonal relationships increases rapidly as family size increases.
- ✓ The success of blended families depends strongly on the willingness of all family members to cooperate in the network of interpersonal relationships.

Questions

1. What is the meaning of the word "unique"? Explain why "unique" is truly descriptive of all children. Why should we expect every parent-child pair to have a unique relationship?

2. What is the fundamental building block of society? Why?

3. How can parents help their children learn to love others and accept themselves?

4. Explain the statement, "Families are dynamic."

5. In this chapter are listed 12 of the characteristics of a smoothly functioning family. Which of these must prospective parents be prepared to provide even *before* they make the decision to become parents? Is it safe to assume that any of the other characteristics can be developed later if they are lacking when a baby is conceived?

6. What is meant by the "traditional family"? About what percentage of families in the United States are traditional?

7. Explain the statement, "Parenting is not unilateral."

8. List some problems faced by single-parent families.

9. Can you think of situations in which a child might be better off in a single-parent family than a traditional family?

10. List some problems faced by families in which both parents work outside the home. How are these similar to problems of single-parent families? How do they differ?

11. Why is it important for society as a whole to encourage families in the performance of their functions?

Activities

1. Assume that you are married and that you and your spouse both work outside your home. Prepare a plan by which all the household tasks might be accomplished in a mutually agreeable way. Remember to allow recreational time. Now, alter the plan to include the additional responsibilities of parenting an infant.

2. Team up with another classmate. Pick a "problem" to discuss, such as one person not helping out with a project or borrowing a personal item without first asking. Using the communication tips in "A Matter of Fact" in this chapter, work through your problem.

Popsicle

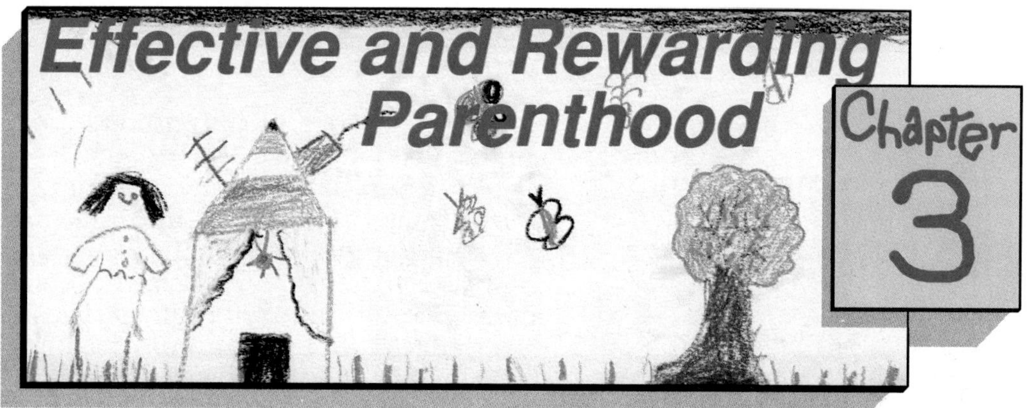

This chapter will help you:

- ✎ describe the three different styles of parenting
- ✎ recognize good parenting practices
- ✎ define child abuse and determine ways an abused child can be helped
- ✎ understand why trust is an important part of a child's development
- ✎ describe how parents meet children's emotional and physical needs
- ✎ understand the purpose of discipline and give examples of positive approaches to discipline
- ✎ assess how good relationships develop by families spending quality time together

The Importance and Creativity of Child Care

Child care and home care can be more creative, make a greater contribution to the world, and bring more pleasure to family members than any other job. A family is very fortunate when the parents think of their marriage, children, and home as their primary career, whether one or both of them have outside jobs in addition. They realize that enduring satisfaction does not come from position and money, but from loving relationships and shared activities.

In the past, typically it was mothers who stayed home. Today many mothers work outside the home. Some fathers now decide they would like to be homemakers, at least while their children are young. Both mothers and fathers are entitled to a career outside the home if they want one. Fathers and mothers are both responsible for the care of the children and the home.

Parenthood is a very creative career because the parent shapes the character of the child.

The career of parenthood is truly creative. Both mother and father shape the characters of their children just as definitely as the sculptor shapes the statue, the architect designs the building, or the author writes the novel. It is not just their manners and interests that parents transmit to their children. It is every aspect of their own characters, their ideals, their lovingness, their steadfastness, their honesty, their ambition, their intelligence, even their sense of humor—as well as some of their problems.

The experience of parenthood also can be a constructive one because it is a step in maturation and personality growth for the adult. Child-rearing presents parents with many new and exciting challenges. It also presents many difficult and trying times. These experiences influence parents' feelings and insights about themselves and the world around them.

Existing Styles of Parenting

The parent who recognizes the importance and creativity of child care will try to develop a style of parenting that works well for all of the family. Just as every child is unique, so is every parent. As a result, every parent-child pair has a unique relationship. Nevertheless, it is possible to divide parenting styles into three very broad categories: strict, permissive, and democratic.

- **Strict parents** take an authoritarian posture regarding their responsibility as guardians of children. Strict parents make and enforce the rules. The children are punished when they disobey. Rigid standards of behavior, performance, and achievement are set, and children must conform. The ways strict parents enforce the rules are highly predictable. For example, a strict parent would probably expect a child to greet guests a certain way, such as saying, "It's nice to meet you." If the child failed to meet expectations, the parent would be likely to discipline the child immediately, even at the risk of embarrassing the guest. For example, if the child said, "Hi there," the parent would respond, "Is that the way you're supposed to greet a guest? What did I tell you? Now say it right."

- **Permissive parents** are often not predictable. They expect children to exhibit rather independent behavior and to be responsible for the consequences of their own decisions. Thus, when parental control is required, it is apt to be formulated differently for each set of circumstances. For example, a permissive parent might be very tolerant of a child's interruptions during conversations with neighbors and grandparents, but intolerant during conversations with business associates. No consistent demands for performance are made on the children.
- **Democratic parents** believe that children should be allowed to have a voice in making the rules and choosing the limits for their behavior. When changes become necessary, they are negotiated by the parents and the children. Democratic parents feel that children will learn self-control by being a part of the decision-making process.

Not every family fits neatly into just one of these styles. In some families, one parent is strict while the other is permissive. Families may move through stages, too. Strict parents may become democratic parents as their children grow older.

Researchers who have studied the various parenting styles have concluded that none of the styles can be said to work well for every family in which it is practiced. In turn, none of the styles fails for every family in which it is practiced. Remember, every family is unique, so they need to decide which style best suits them. For any of the styles to be effective, however, the children have to sense that their parents truly love them and provide them with all the support they need.

Good Parenting Practices

The overall concern of parents should be to help their children to develop in normal ways through all the ages and stages so they arrive at adulthood ready to assume adult responsibilities. Intellectually, emotionally, socially, and morally, children should be ready to meet life's challenges when they set out on their own.

Being good parents depends heavily on the concepts the parents have of themselves. If parents feel loved by their own parents, spouses, relatives, and friends, it is much easier for them to share those feelings of love with their own children. It is extremely important to children that their parents are emotionally stable and, at the same time, strong and decisive. Child-rearing brings on many surprises, even crises, and parents must be flexible and resilient enough to cope. They also must know the ages and stages of normally developing children and be willing to make the necessary adjustments in their own expectations and behavior.

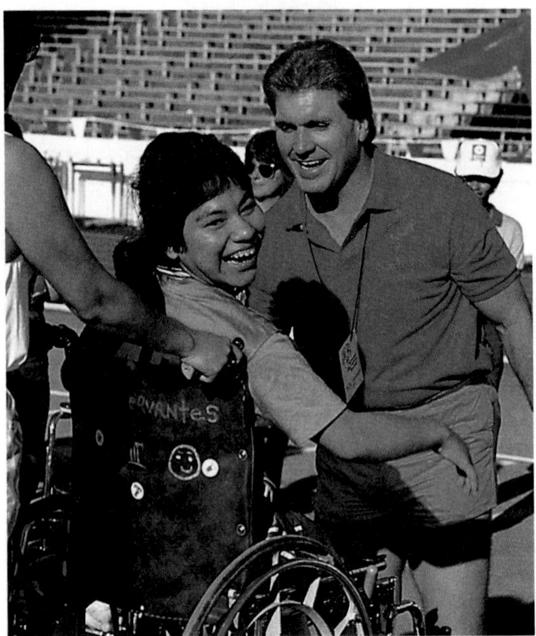

All children need the opportunity to learn how to meet life's challenges.

Good parents find the antics of children amusing, and their sense of humor should include the ability to laugh at themselves.

We must recognize that all parents make mistakes, but they don't need to be repeated. Children, also, make mistakes, and they learn from them. It takes a lot of patience on the part of parents to allow that process to occur. For example, some parents don't want to see their children struggle or fail. To avoid this, the parents try to do everything for their children. These actions prevent the children from developing their own skills and abilities. Parents need to let their children try. Then parents can convey their love and support to their children with hugs, words of love, kind acts, and encouragement. Good parents not only provide for all the basic needs of children, they also offer guidance that fosters growth.

Trust is also important to children. From the moment children are born, they need to be able to trust their parents. They need the security of knowing they will not be dropped and that parents are on hand to provide for all of their needs.

At the same time, it is important for both parents and children to recognize that even trusted children require supervision. The parent can best judge how much supervision is appropriate when there is a good relationship between parent and child.

Sometimes, when unsupervised, children make mistakes—just as parents do. The consequences of such mistakes may range from serious to minor. The parents' initial response might be to scold a child after a mishap. However, they should be aware that the child needs support and encouragement to overcome and learn from the consequences of the mistake. Discipline needs to educate. The child should be aware of how to correct the mistake without hurting the child's self-esteem. (Discipline will be covered more thoroughly later in this chapter.)

Poor Parenting Practices

Unfortunately, not everyone is a good parent. Some individuals who have legal responsibility for the welfare of their children fail to perform their duties. This may occur because of willful mistreatment, ignorance, alcoholism, drug addiction, or many other reasons.

Some people do not know how to be good parents. Ignoring children can lead to misbehavior as they try to gain a parent's attention.

Neglect and Rejection

Two extremes of poor parenting are **neglect** and **rejection.** There are parents who do not provide the food, clothing, shelter, and safe conditions necessary for the normal physical development of their children. This is neglect. Just as importantly, there are parents who do not provide an atmosphere of love, caring, and sharing in which children can develop intellectually, emotionally, and socially. Many cases of "failure to thrive" have been reported. In such situations of gross neglect, the babies actually die because they sense no reason to live. It also is considered neglect when parents do not make children aware of society's moral and ethical codes, or if they do not help their children to develop a value system.

Rejection may occur at any time in a child's life. One or both parents may accept no responsibility for a child's welfare at the time of birth. In another situation, a pregnant adolescent may be ordered out of her home by an angry parent. In many cases, rejection can be the result of low self-esteem on the part of parents. If the parents feel inadequate to cope with the problems of parenthood, they reject parenthood by rejecting the child. Children suffer emotionally, socially, and psychologically from rejection.

A Matter of Fact

Although many people say they don't understand how anyone could hurt or neglect a child, the National Committee for the Prevention of Child Abuse reports that child abuse has reached epic proportions throughout the world. Just in the United States, five children per day are hurt so badly that they die.

Who are the abusers? They look just like you or me. They may seemingly live a very comfortable, normal life in the eyes of the outside world. You cannot tell a person is an abuser just by looking at him or her. Basically, an abuser is caught up in his or her own emotional problems and lacks self-esteem. The abuser may have an obsessive need for control or think that responsible parenting means harsh discipline. Is there help for an abusive parent?

Yes, there are many services available to families suffering from child abuse. Parents Anonymous, for example, is an international self-help organization that offers support groups and information on other family resources to abusive parents or those who feel at risk of being abusive. There are chapters throughout the United States. Parents Anonymous also has a 24-hour Parents' Hotline. An abusive parent can call to discuss problems and troublesome emotions.

There are time-out shelters, called crisis nurseries, where parents can leave their infants or small children for a limited period of time. The services available at crisis nurseries vary depending on the facility and the location.

Some families may have grandparents or other relatives take care of the children while the abusive parent gets counseling or treatment. Of course, because our society is highly mobile, many families in the United States do not have a family support system.

The important point is for these people to look for help to stop their destructive behavior. Help is available if they look for it.

Child Abuse

One of the worst poor parenting practices is **child abuse.** Among the forms are physical abuse, psychological abuse, and sexual abuse. Sexual abuse might be thought of as a combination of physical and psychological abuse. All three forms tend to be perpetuated. That is, many people who were abused as children have a tendency to abuse their own children.

Physical abuse takes every imaginable form, from beating to burning. It may be administered by anyone, but usually the abuser is some member of the family: mother, father, stepmother, step-father, uncle, or grandparent. Often abusers feel they are disciplining children, but their expectations of children and their reactions to children's behavior are obviously irrational. For example, there are actual cases of babies being

Loving caregivers let a child know they can be counted on to help them through the rough times.

thrown against walls or dropped out of windows because they would not stop crying. Some parents try to toilet train their toddlers before the children are physically able to control those bodily functions. The parents then become abusive when "accidents" occur. Very often, a little knowledge of the ages and stages of children would help parents to see the inappropriateness of their own behavior and to deal kindly, patiently, and lovingly with their children.

Similarly, if parents' expectations are unreasonable, they may abuse their children psychologically. A girl doing poorly in school may be called "dummy" when she brings home her report card. An eight-year-old boy drops a fly ball causing his team to lose the baseball game, and his father says, "You clod! You'll never learn to catch the ball!" Such remarks hurt badly enough if they are used only once, but when used repeatedly, they can do serious damage to the child's self-esteem. When children don't feel good about themselves, when they feel they have little chance of success, they stop trying. When they stop trying, life is not much fun.

In very recent years, the subject of sexual child abuse has been brought to everyone's attention by the newspapers, magazines, and television. It is not a new problem. It

A Matter of Fact

What can an abused child do? Where can she or he turn for help? Some children confide family abuse problems to a friend, then the friend tells a caring adult who takes action on behalf of the abused child. The abused child may choose to confide in grandparents, aunts or uncles, and older cousins. In school, teachers, school social workers, and school nurses can help. The Child Protection authorities are very helpful. In the city or town, babysitters, daycare workers, doctors, nurses, and neighbors may also be able to give comfort and advice to an abused child.

Placing abusive parents in jail does not solve the problem; it only offers temporary protection for children. Depending on the family situation, an abused child may be placed in a foster home or in the home of a relative until the time when the abusive parent has come to terms with the abusive behavior and has sought counseling or treatment.

has been going on through all of history. Today, we may read reports of sexual abuse in school settings, childcare centers, or neighborhoods, but researchers agree that by far the greatest number of cases occur in family units. This type of abuse may begin in infancy or at any other age of the child. It may persist through adolescence. Girls are abused more often than boys. The abuser may be an older brother, a stepfather, the boyfriend of a single mother, an uncle, or, quite often, the girl's own father.

Such abuse is psychologically traumatic for youngsters. Usually, they are sworn to secrecy by the threats of various dire consequences, including violence. In addition, for example, a girl being abused by her father may feel that she would lose her father's affection if she rejected him or "told on" him. She might fear that her family would split up if she told her mother what was happening. She also might assume that no one would believe her, and she would be punished severely for telling what they think is a lie. There are also cases in which the mother does believe the girl, but the mother has such a poor self-concept that she does nothing. She fears a confrontation with her husband would break up the family. This leaves the girl feeling totally hopeless. In such a situation, a girl may not escape such abuse until she is old enough to become aware of agencies outside the home that can help. Otherwise, the abuse may persist until the girl moves away from the home. The psychological scars of child abuse in any form are often permanent.

Older, abused children may actively avoid interacting with the abusive parent. They may withdraw from a situation when violence might erupt. Some abused children will take on "model child" behaviors as they keep attempting to win the approval and love of the abusive parent.

Unfortunately, younger children have no resources for protection from parental abuse, and the children may

Teachers not only have the responsibility of educating their students but of watching out for their welfare as well.

be forced to endure these circumstances for extended periods. They must rely on others to help them.

In 1984, more than 30 states had made it illegal not to report suspected child abuse or neglect. Abused infants or very young children have no resources to protect themselves from parental abuse. In general, young children rely on society-at-large to keep an eye out for their best interests.

Neighbors, teachers, doctors, or others who suspect child abuse need to take on this responsibility. Sometimes, though, other people are afraid to get involved. Perhaps they fear they may infringe on the family's right to privacy. The children can get no relief from their predicament until outsiders exercise the parenting role and realize there is no way the children can help themselves. In other words, these persons are willing to get involved because they feel a moral obligation for the welfare of children. They accept the premise that we are all parents.

Children don't always fit the "mold" that their parents have set out for them.

Other Poor Parenting Practices

Poor parenting practices are not limited to neglect and abuse. Anything that parents do to detract from helping their children to become independent and responsible adults is a poor parenting practice.

The use of "put-downs" should be discouraged at all of the child's ages. Even when these are not severe enough to be classified as abusive, they detract from children's self-concept. Put-downs discourage. Children need to be encouraged. For example, Jamie's parents watched her try to tie her shoes. She could not manage the bow. Her mother said, "You're a clumsy idiot." Jamie was hurt and discouraged. She didn't want to try again. It would have been better if her mother said, "I'll show you how to do it, Jamie," and then encouraged Jamie the next time she tried. Parents should not put each other down, either. Children learn by example.

As children mature, parents who break promises or reveal children's secrets destroy their trust. Just as importantly, children need to be trusted. Parents who place no trust in their children help to destroy their self-confidence. How can children gain confidence in their ability to perform a task, if the parents do not trust them to try it on their own?

A lack of trust can be related to another poor parenting practice called overindulgence. Overindulgent parents try to anticipate every want and need of their children, as if the youngsters cannot be trusted to know what they might want or need. Because all the children's wants and needs are satisfied without any effort, thought, or creativity on their part, they are apt to remain highly dependent and be poorly prepared for adulthood. Overindulgence can lead children to become very demanding. Indulgent parents only compound their problems if they submit to these demands out of fear that the children won't like or love them unless the demands are met. When parents are submissive toward demanding children, they lose the respect of the children and their own self-respect, as well.

Demanding rigid conformity is another parental practice that severely limits children's development. (Conformity is acting or behaving like others.) In some ways, children enjoy conformity. They may like having clothes, toys, records, etc., that are similar to those of their friends. But, all too often, parents' codes of behavior for children are not understood by the children. The children find conforming to those codes restrictive or even demeaning. For example, a parent says, "No, Sandy, you're not going to that party with Bill or anyone else. Don't ask why! I'll tell you when you're ready to date. You're not going, and that's final!" Obviously, there has been little, if any, communication or understanding. In addition, Sandy has been given no chance to develop a reasonable approach to making judgments and decisions on her own. In this case, also, she has been given no cause to feel that her parent trusts her. Such concerns and questions are much better resolved through discussion and **compromise** based on mutual respect. Compromise, of course, does not mean submission. Compromise means people agree to a solution based on ideas from both sides. Each side gives in a little to reach an agreement.

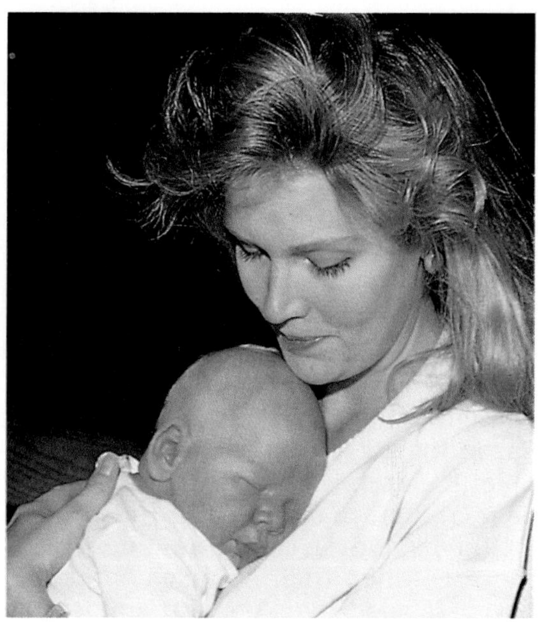

Babies need love.

Parenting Guidelines

Basic Need for Love

The most important ingredient for an effective parent is love. When parents love and care, children have a sense of security, belonging, and support. Parental love should be unconditional and constant. Children need to understand that when they misbehave, their parents do not dislike them, but only their misbehavior.

A household in which love is openly expressed is a household in which children flourish. Parents must let their children know they are appreciated for their own special qualities by making open expressions of love. Verbalizing love to children is not enough. Hugs and kisses are needed. Parents also should make every effort to let children see warmth and tenderness in their marriage. Parents should let their children know how delighted they are when their spouses enter the house. A good-bye kiss in the morning and a warm greeting when a spouse comes home at the end of the day set examples that encourage affection in children. A husband and wife are more apt to be very successful parents when they give their marriage high priority. Happy parents whose roles are clearly and lovingly defined are more apt to have happy children. Child-centered households produce neither happy marriages nor happy children.

Basic Physical Needs

Children of all ages need balanced diets. Children need good diets for growth, development, and health. Without proper amounts of proteins, carbohydrates, fats, vitamins, and minerals as supplied by eating the variety of foods required for sound nutrition, children will not prosper. Substituting sweetened drinks, candy, and pastries for a balanced diet is detrimental to the child's physical, emotional, and intellectual development. Children need regular mealtimes, too. You cannot expect maximum performance in school from a child who does not eat breakfast or skips lunch. Breakfast is an important start to the day, and a nutritious lunch helps children get through the afternoon.

Children of all ages require adequate sleep and periods of rest. Parents of young children need to arrange their schedules so these needs are met. For example, if a child needs a nap in the afternoon, the parent should not go out shopping. Children also are dependent on parents for the provision of suitable clothes for all seasons and for housing. For their physical and mental health, children need to be taught neatness, cleanliness, and general health habits.

Handicapped and special needs children may require more care. They should be encouraged to try to do things for themselves, as much as possible. This will help build their self-esteem.

Discipline: Acceptable and Unacceptable Forms

Discipline is setting and adhering to standards of behavior. Discipline should be used to educate children, not punish or hurt them. The ultimate goal should be **self-discipline.** Self-discipline is children's ability to guide and control their own behavior. It is important that parents make the rules and set the limits that are necessary, and only those that are necessary. Too many rules and limits may seem op-

Some rules are necessary for family safety. By knowing the reason for rules, children better understand why they must follow them.

pressive to children at any age. Rules that are not meant to be followed or enforced should never be made. Say what you mean, and mean what you say.

As children develop, unnecessary rules should be discarded and more appropriate ones adopted. For example, older children may want to have some input in the rule-making process. Parents should welcome this as a sign of their maturing toward independence, responsibility, and self-discipline. Some flexibility is also appropriate.

A Closer Look

Cindy had been taught by her parents not to play in mud puddles in the street because then she tracked mud into the house. One hot summer day, though, it started to rain. It had not rained for more than a month and the neighborhood children were thrilled. Laughing, they all ran through the rain and jumped in the puddles. Cindy could not resist the fun and joined in. Cindy's mother watched from inside the house. When the rain stopped and the fun ended, Cindy went home. Cindy said, "I'm sorry. I know I'm not supposed to get muddy. I couldn't help it though. It was such fun." Smiling, Cindy's mother said, "I understand," and gave her a towel to dry off.

It is most helpful to children for caregivers to use a positive approach to discipline. In other words, support and encourage children in their good behavior rather than remembering and dwelling on misbehavior. Small differences in words and tones are important to a child who is trying to please. For example, compare the statement, "You're such a good boy. I like the way you have picked up your toys," with an alternative statement, "I see you have picked up your toys, for once!"

When discipline for misbehavior becomes necessary, it should never be done in anger or with malice. There should be the sort of communication that allows children to realize they are being treated fairly and with love. Children who have experienced the warmest type of relationships with parents usually have a strong desire to behave in ways that are acceptable to the parents.

The punishment should be based on natural and logical consequences. That type of discipline teaches children to be responsible for their own behavior. A logical consequence permits children to learn from reality.

A Closer Look

John always forgot to bring his toys in after playing outside. His parents reminded him time after time. Sometimes they became angry and sent him to his room. John didn't correct the problem. His parents picked up the toys. Then his parents learned about natural consequences. When John left his toys out the next time, his parents didn't scold him, or pick them up themselves. Instead, they left the toys outside. The next day when John went outside, his toys had been chewed up by a dog in the area. When John complained to his parents, they explained that's one thing that can happen to toys left behind. John cried and asked for new toys. His parents said, "No. You'll just have to play with your other things." John learned an important lesson—responsibility. Basing discipline on logical and natural consequences motivates children to make responsible decisions, not just follow orders.

Experts agree that physical punishment should be avoided, not only because of the possible harm to children, but also because it is not effective. Research has shown that physical punishment usually does not cause children to refrain from misbehavior. Instead, they try harder to avoid being caught while misbehaving. In addition, parents who physically punish their children discover that the last punishment did not work, so they use greater and greater force each time. Thus, parents who had no intention initially of being abusive may find themselves beating their children in a frustrated attempt to make them obey.

By far the most effective way to avoid this syndrome is to love children, to understand children, to understand ourselves, and to develop a warm parent-child relationship from the moment of birth. This can be done when we recognize that children are "real people" with as much, and quite possibly more, sensitivity than we adults. The thoughts of an abused nine-year old have been expressed touchingly in lyrics written by Mike Nobel, a songwriter and performer from the state of Maine.

The Main Thing You Have Over Me

I am only nine years old,
But I have a mind and a soul.
I have needs and dreams that
I can't deny....

And I know, in your eyes,
That I am not very wise.
You tell me, what do I know
About trouble and life....

But I have brains and my blood runs red,
And when I climb outa bed,
I know there's a hard time ahead
Every day of my life....

Other people do me wrong,
My mamma and daddy don't get along,
And nobody knows the pain
I'm hiding inside....

I am only nine years old,
But I have a mind and a soul.
I have needs and dreams that
I can't deny....

And I know, in your eyes,
That I am not very wise.
Still, I think the

Main thing you have over me
Is your size.

Even with a hectic lifestyle, families need to plan time to spend together.

Family Time Together

As mentioned in Chapter 2, it is often difficult to coordinate efforts in work- and family-oriented activities. It is essential, however, that all family members plan their lives so they can spend time together. Good relations cannot be developed without time.

The importance of eating meals together cannot be stressed enough. Even today when family members' schedules are so different, taking the time to share a meal is important. Breakfast is the ideal time to hear everyone's plans for the day, and there is no better time than dinner to share the joys and problems of the day. While sharing a balanced meal, so essential to the well-being of all, parents can show their interest and support for the activities of all family members. Nothing can do more for children's sense of security and belonging. Just as importantly, children can become aware of their parent's activities. By having a feeling for the kind of work their parents do, children can gain an appreciation and respect for their parents' talents and character. Mealtime is also the perfect setting for sharing humorous moments and the jokes of the day.

It is important to spend lots of time together, but time is not enough. There must be communication—talking and listening. For example, watching a good television program together is enjoyable, but if that is all that people do during their time together, they are not going to establish meaningful relationships.

Parents should plan to spend part of their time with children showing them how to accomplish everyday tasks such as cleaning, laundering, cooking, mowing the lawn, making small

A Matter of Fact

Children who are encouraged to participate in food preparation and clean-up tasks will develop an active interest in food. The main ingredient for success is having the time and the patience to work one-on-one in the kitchen. Caregivers who want children to learn food preparation skills should remember to:

- **Keep sturdy stools nearby. Children will need to stand on them to perform some tasks.**
- **Manage all activities closely.**
- **Match the skill to the abilities of the child.**
- **Give detailed and clear instructions, demonstrate the task, and provide plenty of practice time.**
- **Repeat the instructions before the child begins the task.**
- **Make clean-up a part of each job.**

Here are some activities preschool children can learn to accomplish.

Two- and three-year-olds can:

- Clear own place setting.
- Peel bananas (caregiver should cut the top first).
- Place waste in the trash.
- Shape hamburgers and meatballs.
- Shuck corn.
- Snap beans.
- Tear lettuce.
- Wash vegetables.
- Wipe the table.

Three- and four-year-olds can:

- Break eggs into a bowl.
- Knead and shape dough.
- Make sandwiches.
- Mix ingredients.
- Open packages.
- Pour cereal, milk, and water.
- Toss salads.
- Wash baking utensils.

Five-year-olds can:

- Load the dishwasher with help.
- Make cakes and cookies using baking mixes with help.
- Make pancakes with help from caregiver.
- Set and clear the table.

repairs, maintaining the automobile, and budgeting their allowances. Children who know how to do these things can take pride in their ability to make valuable contributions to the family work load. Furthermore, they will master the skills they'll need when they have homes of their own. (Remember, the children's independence is the final goal of parents.)

One very important skill children can learn from parents is the ability to resolve problems. Some parents believe that children should never hear them argue. Experts agree, however, that children are not harmed by parents' arguments. In fact, children can benefit from occasional conflict, if the parents follow the rules of constructive arguing. Watching parents come to a

Can children learn from their parents' arguments?

mutually acceptable resolution of a disagreement is a very valuable experience for children.

It is good for a child to recognize that parents can disagree and then reach agreement by discussion and compromise. The time spent in such discussions should be minimal, however, compared with the time spent in more enjoyable activities.

Family Activities

Family spirit and a sense of belonging are developed by doing things together as a family. Children do not need material things nearly as much as they need enjoyable activities with their parents. Families need to:

- Have regular family outings and special dinners including relatives who live in the area.
- Spend holidays together.
- Maintain family traditions and develop new ones. They'll mean a great deal to children now and in the years to come.
- Go to religious, social, or sporting events together.

Games are wonderful for children to learn that their parents are fun to be around, and for parents to help children learn good sportsmanship. The nature of the game is unimportant. It could be Ping-Pong, checkers, hopscotch, softball, or cards.

A Matter of Fact

How to argue in front of children.

- Do make children aware that they have not caused the argument. That way the argument does not make the children feel guilty.
- Do make children aware that they are not expected or allowed to take sides.
- Don't quarrel about money in front of children. This can make them feel insecure.
- Don't discuss marital problems. Marital problems are private concerns and can only frighten children.
- Do not fight about relatives. This can affect children's relationship with those relatives.
- Children should be absent, also, when parents disagree about how to raise children.
- The use of name-calling or any other verbal abuse is taboo.
- The worst experience for a child observing a quarrel is for one or both parents to give up on a reasonable resolution and resort to physical violence.
- Chronic fighting, even without physical violence, is also very harmful to children.

The possibilities for family outings are unlimited. There are picnics, museums, bike rides, lectures, swimming, libraries, movies, high school plays and concerts, hiking, camping, etc. The entire family can watch the local newspapers for announcements of special events in the community and make room on their calendar. An additional bonus is that caregivers and children can discuss the activity both before and after the event.

What activities does your family enjoy doing together?

Family vacations can create some of the most enjoyable memories of a childhood. The event will be more meaningful if the children are involved in the planning stage. They can create or find games to play while traveling. Children can have certain responsibilities, such as packing and carrying small luggage, watching for road signs, navigating for the driver, calculating the gas mileage, etc. Children can learn money management on vacation by having an allowance each day for their meals and souvenirs. Vacations don't need to be expensive for families to have fun. Camping or going to the state fair are enjoyable for many.

Family activities practiced on a regular basis are important, too. Two of these—singing and reading to children at bedtime—can start when the children are babies. Both give parents the ultimate opportunity to establish mutually satisfying relationships. The coziness of nestling in a parent's arms, while hearing the sound of a loving voice, gives children the sense of security that is one of their basic needs. In addition, children who have been read to regularly usually are eager to learn to read. They learn a respect for books that can last throughout their lives.

Teaching Basic Concepts

Caregivers need to actively teach children right from wrong. Children should be made aware of proper values—behavioral, social, moral, ethical, and financial. Children can learn through the assignment of chores and responsibilities at home. Children need to be taught to treat others with kindness, respect, and honesty. Table manners and other social graces can be emphasized in the home. Caregivers can set personal examples of moral courage and integrity. Parents need to discuss moral values with children. (See also Chapter 19.) When children stray, parents should communicate in a manner that encourages them to listen. Children need to know where their parents stand. Children have to be taught right from wrong, respect for others and their property, and respect for older people. While vocalizing basic values is extremely important, children will be most influenced by their parents' own examples.

Mutual Respect

All family members need to treat each other with respect. This respect can be shown by politeness. Apologize to a child when you are wrong. Show an active interest in children's books, TV shows, and activities. Be interested in a child's friends. Be honest and sincere with children at all times. It is very important to follow through on any promises made. It is also important to show basic trust in a child's character and judgment. A child feels respected when thought of as an individual. Never compare one child to another child.

Parents have a right to individuality and should cultivate their own interests and talents. It is very important for children to have a parent who handles parenting tasks, but children also need to see the parent as a person. For example, a child might say, "My mom (or dad) reads stories to me, cooks for our family, plays the piano, sells real estate, and likes to play golf in the city competitions."

Caring for a pet helps children develop responsibility.

Guidance that Fosters Growth

When children come to you for guidance about their problems, you can help by thinking through the problem with them. Children need to understand that you are willing to discuss problems. However, before offering them solutions, expect them to think about the problem. Ask them to come up with some possible solutions. For example, suppose three-year-old Andy comes home crying because Lim Chi and Rosa won't play with him. When you ask Andy what he would do, he says, "Tell them I hate them," or "Take all their toys," You could say, "Will that make them want to play with you?" By discussing it, you can help Andy realize that a good solution would be to invite Lim Chi and Rosa to his home to play. In order to involve Andy in the decision-making, ask him to suggest games they could play.

Children need gradual growth toward independence. As they grow up, they need more and more freedom to make their own decisions so they will develop into responsible adults. They need to learn that they will have to live with the consequences of their actions. For example, children who steal may be punished by the law. Allow children to make decisions regarding minor matters first. Then gradually expand the areas of decision-making.

Empathy—The Way to Understanding

We recognize that the family's degree of success in raising responsible children influences the future of our society. The question now is, "How does a family successfully perform this essentially psychological function?" In other words, under what circumstances can we give our children the sense of well-being and security they so desperately need? The answer lies in our ability to empathize.

We define **empathy** as the ability to sense, appreciate, and understand the feelings of another person. When we empathize, we imagine ourselves projected into the situation of that other person. It is not, however, an emotionally based condition. Rather it is one in which a person actually knows, often through experience, the feelings of another. To empathize is to bring to bear a real insight into the problem of someone else. It is not merely an emotional tenderness devoid of understanding or knowledge.

Empathy is similar to sympathy, but whereas the sympathizer "feels as you do," the empathizer "knows how you feel." Empathy enables you to use your head rather than just your heart. When you sympathize with someone in trouble, you catch and reflect some of his or her suffering. Your anxiety, in turn, may increase the other person's distress. But when you empathize, you bring to bear a detached insight, which may be of far greater help. Empathy does not exclude sympathy, but uses insight rather than emotion as its guide.

Empathy in the Parent-Child Relationship

The family may be likened to a team of mountain climbers. On a climbing expedition, all the climbers are roped

Knowing how it feels to lose the big game can help a parent empathize.

together. Let us suppose that one climber loses his or her footing, slips, and falls to the ledge below. The rest do not help by jumping down after the fallen person. Rather they make their footing more secure and haul that person back up. This is the kind of effect that is involved in empathizing. It means understanding someone else's position and using your own knowledge and experience to help the troubled one. Feeling sorry for other persons or going down with them in despair does not fulfill their needs. As an empathizing person, you have the advantage of objectivity, in spite of your ability to partake of another's feelings. It is these two seemingly differing conditions that make empathy such a vital part of any relationship.

Many support groups recognize and use empathy in helping people cope with life's challenges. For example, members of a support group for parents who have suffered the death of a child can certainly empathize with newer members who have only recently lost a child. They can help the newer members by sharing those experiences that helped them through their own periods of grieving.

Importance of Listening

If one has not experienced or does not have knowledge of another's situation, perhaps the next best course to

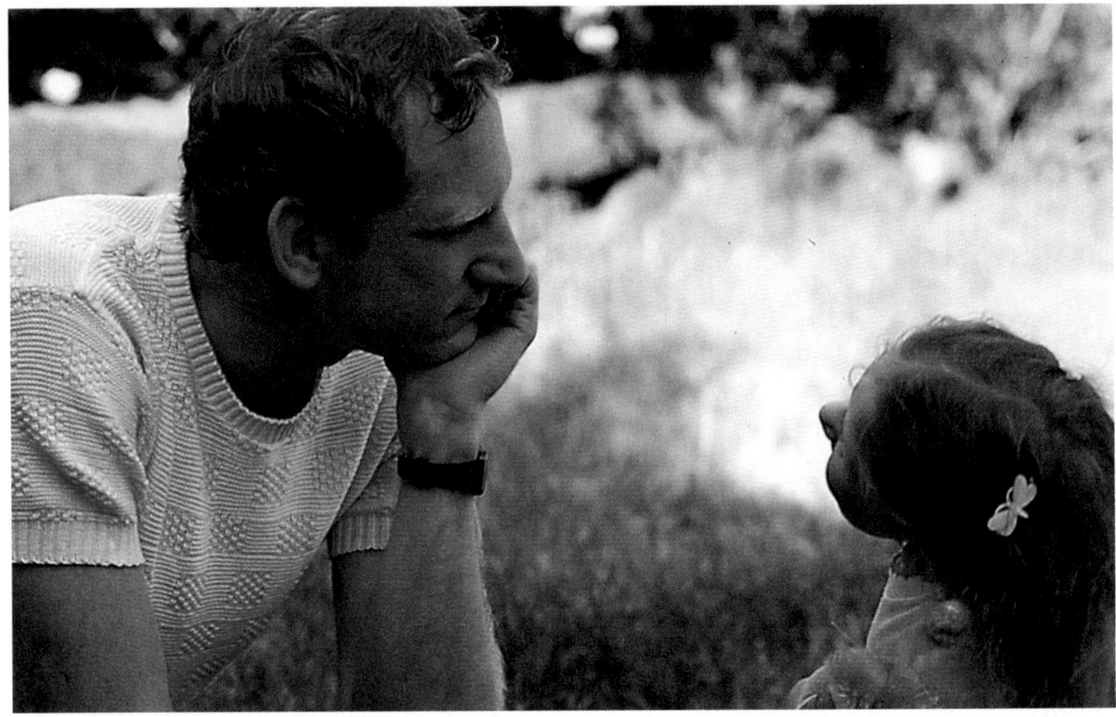

Communication is a two-way street. In order to be heard, you have to listen.

empathic understanding is good listening. We all desire human communication. Often, when we communicate our day-by-day thoughts and concerns, the talk is an effort to rid ourselves of an emotion that has been plaguing us. As good listeners, however, we must be absolutely selfless. Listening is the one way for us to achieve at least some degree of empathy for another person's situation and not a way for us to air our own problems—even though it may be a great temptation.

Some parents often complain that their misbehaving child"—just won't listen!" But it is important for parents to *listen* if they want their children to hear. That may sound backward, but consider this. We listen because we respect the person who is speaking. If parents don't respect their children enough to listen to them, the children will not only stop talking to their parents, but they will stop listening to them, too. As mentioned, mealtimes are great times to listen, but often families need to set aside other times, as well. With smaller children, as bedtime approaches, the time just before reading or singing is an excellent time for listening.

For true listening, distractions such as television and loud music need to be shut out. The best listening is done when your eyes are used along with your ears. Sit down so that it is comfortable to make eye contact. As a listener, you need to let speakers know they are getting their messages across. You can do this by telling them how their message sounds to you. For example, suppose Donna says to her mother, "Sandy's father won't let her go to the party with Bill or anyone else. He said she's not old enough to date." Donna's mother might respond, "It sounds as if you feel Sandy's father is being rather unfair." By doing so, she has demonstrated her interest and opened the door for further communication.

If parents make quick judgments, preach sermons, or postpone listening, children eventually decide not to reveal their concern. Suppose Donna's mother had said, "I don't have time to hear about that. I have to be at the bowling alley in 45 minutes!" or if she had answered, "That's Sandy's family's business. You keep your nose out of it." What would the result be? The conversation would be over. Communication would be finished.

A Closer Look

In a high school class studying family relationships, students were asked to develop techniques for improving family relationships. One high school boy handed in the following example:

"Last Saturday, Dad and I were cleaning the garage. He was really grouchy. Everything I did was wrong. Finally, I stopped and said, 'Dad, you must be feeling awful! What's wrong?' Then he loosened up and told me about an accident for which he felt he was responsible. After he had finished telling me what happened, he decided it actually hadn't been his fault. He became a lot more cheerful, and we finished the garage in record time."

A girl wrote:

"I was going home with Mother after work. She seemed very upset. I could tell by the way she drove the car. She'd really step on the gas and then she'd slam on the brakes. I kept quiet until we got home, but then I said, half jokingly, 'What's wrong, Mom? Had a fight with the boss?' She surprised me by saying, 'Yes. How did you know?' I decided I had better not try to explain, so I just said, 'Oh, I don't know.' She then told me all that had happened while we fixed dinner. By the time dinner was ready and Dad came home, she was calmer."

For deeply troubled people, good listeners can provide important outlets and may actually be modifying forces. When people are upset, they build things up in their mind to an unreasonable degree. Their imagination and emotions get the best of them. It is one thing for someone to say to himself or herself, "I'd like to kill him," and quite another to say it out loud to another person. When people get to the point of actually verbalizing whatever is bothering them, they have a tendency to modify their thoughts. As a listener, then, we can have a modifying or calming effect on a troubled person. In addition, the troubled person may gain more insight into the nature of his or her problem and may find some new solutions.

In Review

Vocabulary

permissive parents
democratic parents
neglect
rejection
child abuse
compromise
discipline
self-discipline
empathy

Summary

- ✓ Effective parenthood is a challenge requiring creativity.
- ✓ Every parent-child pair has a unique relationship.
- ✓ There are at least three styles of parenting: strict, permissive, and democratic. None of these is ideal for *all* families, and none can be effective in any family that is not loving and supporting.
- ✓ Good parenting practices are those offering guidance that fosters growth.
- ✓ Neglect, rejection, and child abuse in any form are all poor parenting practices.
- ✓ Parental love should be unconditional and constant. A parent can dislike a child's behavior without disliking the child.
- ✓ Parents must supply children with open expressions of love, an appreciation for truth and trust, the basic physical needs, and appropriate discipline.
- ✓ Effective family time includes listening, resolving disagreements, working cooperatively, playing together, sharing common interests, and maintaining family values and traditions.
- ✓ Children's values are most strongly influenced by the example of their parents.
- ✓ In every parent-child relationship there should be mutual respect—respect earned by each of the individuals.
- ✓ Understanding child development helps parents to empathize with children. As a good listener, a parent can help children find solutions to their own problems. In this way, parents give guidance that fosters growth.

Questions

1. Name the three styles of parenting and the characteristics of each. What factor is common to all effective parents?
2. Who should take the major responsibility for tending to the needs and the character development of children?
3. What are the three worst parenting practices you know about?
4. Which is more apt to stimulate children to improve their performances—reminding them of their failures or their successes? Why?
5. What behavior might one expect from children of indulgent parents?
6. Why is trust important in a parent-child relationship?
7. What are the basic physical needs of children?
8. What are the basic psychological needs of children?
9. What is the purpose of discipline?
10. What is self-discipline?
11. When should one not discipline children, even if they have misbehaved?
12. Why is physical punishment an ineffective mode of discipline?
13. Why is it important for families to eat together?
14. How can one make family conflict a valuable experience for children?
15. What is the difference between empathy and sympathy?
16. Why must we be able to empathize to be good parents and caregivers?

Activities

1. Describe how you might be able to empathize with a person even if you have never experienced the troubling problem.
2. Brainstorm what you can do yourself to become a better listener. Illustrate some of your ideas in a "guide to listening" or a cartoon.
3. Talk to a police officer in your area, or invite one to class to discuss what happens to shoplifters, drug users, and other law breakers.

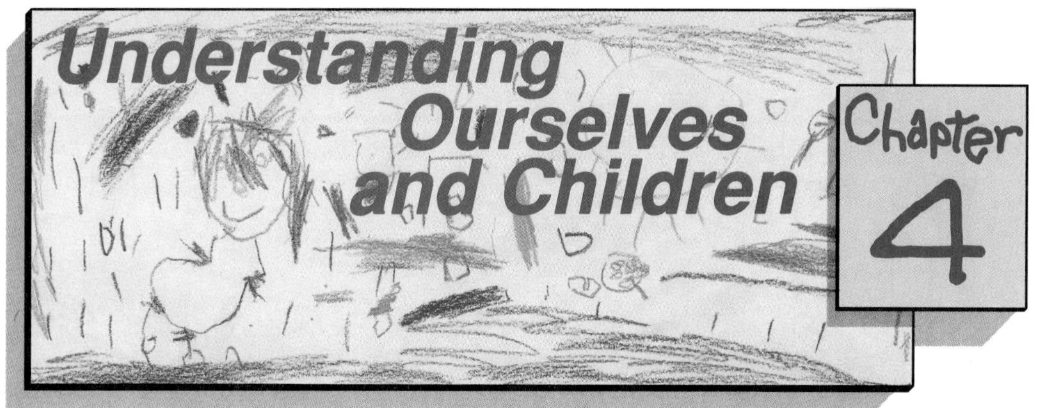

This chapter will help you:

- to gain an appreciation for the responsibilities and commitment inherent in parenthood
- to identify the objectives and purposes of parent education and training programs
- to understand the necessity for parents to maintain self-control
- to identify the principles of Parent Effectiveness Training, the Parent Involvement Program, and the Responsive Parent Training Program
- to understand Rudolf Dreikur's approach to parenting
- to become familiar with three of the historically important theories of child development

Parent Education

Life with children can be very challenging and rewarding. The object of child development and parent education programs is to enhance the parent-child relationship so that it will become more rewarding for all.

There has always been a need for parents to know more about children and about themselves in order to meet their parental responsibilities more effectively. Unfortunately, in the past, far too many parents have believed that parenting is instinctive. As mentioned in the preceding chapters, parenting practices tend to be handed down from one generation to another. The only way a chain of poor parenting practices can be broken is for parents to gain the knowledge that allows them to see the need for change.

For teenagers, one of the most important objectives of a course in parenting and child development is to gain an appreciation for the never-end-

Good family relationships require cooperation and teamwork.

ing commitment parenthood brings. Teens need to be aware of the magnitude of responsibilities. Those subjects will be considered in the next chapter along with factors to consider before becoming parents. A study of parenting also can help teenagers gain an appreciation for the trials and tribulations of their own parents. With increased understanding, the student can initiate steps to better relationships.

In addition to the objectives above, child development and parent education should:

a. help potential parents to become aware of their own values and how these can affect their relations with children.

b. help us to understand how children are influenced by other children.

c. alert us to the fact that various techniques are available for guiding children's behavior.

d. provide the opportunity to interact with children and practice communication skills.

Having learned some principles of good parenthood, we can reflect on our childhood to understand our own development. How does it happen that we are as we are, or that we believe as we believe? Knowing the answers to these questions is very important if we are going to be able to exercise child care wisely.

Many teenagers don't have the op-

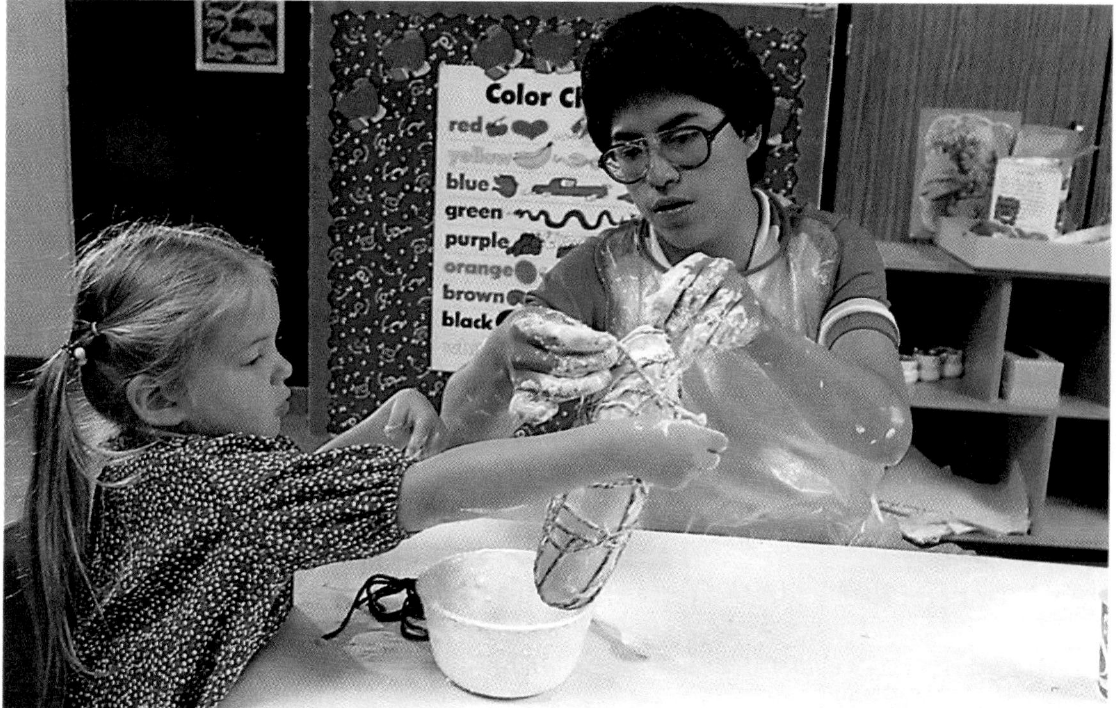

Working with children gives teenagers the opportunity to interact with children and learn how to guide their behavior.

portunity, or don't take the opportunity, to study parenting. Even if they did, of course, they would not be guaranteed a future of trouble-free parenthood. There is probably no such thing. Many parents recognize today that parenthood can be more challenging than any job they've ever had, and they seek assistance from all kinds of sources. In addition to community resources, there are magazine articles, books, and television programs dealing with the full range of potential parenting problems. While these are often helpful, they do not satisfy the needs of many parents. Other kinds of help are needed. Some parents are finding the help they need in programs called parent training.

Parent Training

It is important for people to recognize that seeking parent education or training does not indicate that they are bad parents, but rather that they wish to be good parents. The parent training programs now in existence are very different from each other. All the programs are alike in their goal to help parents maintain self-control. All programs hold that an angry parent is likely to give children harsh physical or psychological treatment. Parents who have lost self-control develop frightened, resentful children with low self-esteem. Some of these children become withdrawn and some even run away. Others become compliant, dependent people who cannot make even a simple decision for themselves.

All parent education and training programs maintain that children treat others as they have been treated.

Parents' Creed

If a child lives with criticism,
He learns to condemn.

If a child lives with hostility,
He learns to fight.

If a child lives with ridicule,
He learns to be shy.

If a child lives with shame,
He learns to feel guilty.

If a child lives with tolerance,
He learns to be patient.

If a child lives with encouragement,
He learns confidence.

If a child lives with praise,
He learns to appreciate.

If a child lives with fairness,
He learns justice.

If a child lives with security,
He learns to have faith.

If a child lives with approval,
He learns to like himself.

If a child lives with acceptance and friendship,
He learns to find love in the world.

Dorothy Law Nolte
"Parents' Creed."

Four of the major parenting programs are these:

1. Parent Effectiveness Training
2. Parent Involvement Program
3. Responsive Parent Training
4. The Alfred Adler Institute

All four courses provide stimulating group experiences for the participants. Parents find it helpful to talk about their problems to empathic listeners. Parents also hear about similar problems and find that other people may have even greater problems. This sharing helps parents put their concerns in proper perspective.

These four programs stress the following points:

1. conflict management.
2. behavior management.
3. responsible behavior.
4. discipline.

Each of these areas may be approached from different points of view, but the main objective is to make parents feel comfortable in their parenting role. Each tries to help parents understand conflicts that may occur between parent and child and suggests techniques for solving them.

Parent Effectiveness Training (P.E.T.)

Thomas Gordon is considered the innovator of Parent Effectiveness Training. He believes that parents can and should give up the use of power. He grants that physical power may have to be used in an emergency. For example, if a toddler is running into the street, a parent must use physical power to stop the child. But Gordon firmly opposes the use of psychological power, not only by the parents but by teachers, bosses, and everyone. Psychological power controls by making the person feel guilty or lose self-esteem. Gordon rejects power because he feels it is damaging to people and relationships. Furthermore, he would like to see the word "misbehavior" dropped from our language. Children and other people simply behave. Their behavior, like everyone else's, is aimed at getting their needs met. When it interferes with the parents' efforts to get their needs met, the parents call it misbehavior. Many parents label any behavior that is unacceptable to them as misbehavior.

The P.E.T. approach is very simple. It teaches three basic techniques. They are called

- active listening.
- I-messages.
- the no-lose method.

(Each of these will be described later.) Before using any of the methods, the parent must identify who owns the problem at hand. The owner is the person whose needs are frustrated. How the problem is treated depends on who owns the problem. If the child owns the problem, the parent uses the technique of active listening. If the child's behavior is unacceptable to the parent, then the parent owns the problem. In that case, I-messages or, if necessary, the no-lose method of problem solving is used. The P.E.T. course also suggests ways parents can reduce the number of problems before it becomes necessary to apply any of the techniques. For example, P.E.T. suggests that caregivers put breakables out of a small child's reach. Then things will not be broken and the parents won't have to take further action.

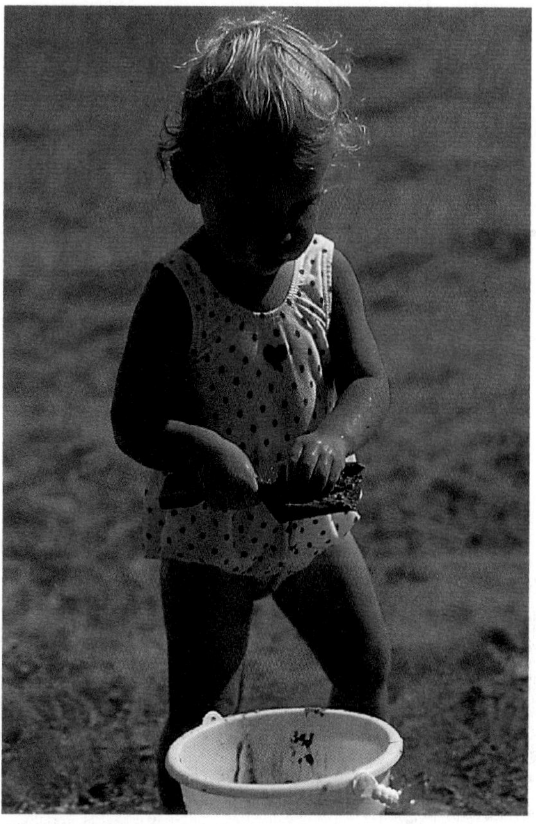

Some people would view this child's behavior as making a mess while others see it as learning a skill.

Active Listening

When something bothers the child but not the parent, the technique to use is active listening. With this technique, parents help children to understand, accept, and deal with their own feelings by themselves. For example, a boy comes home from school angry and crying. He announces that his teacher is awful. His parents could reassure him, analyze the situation, press for details, ignore the problem, get mad at the child, leap to his defense, or present their own views. However, P.E.T. suggests that parents adopt a receptive, in-

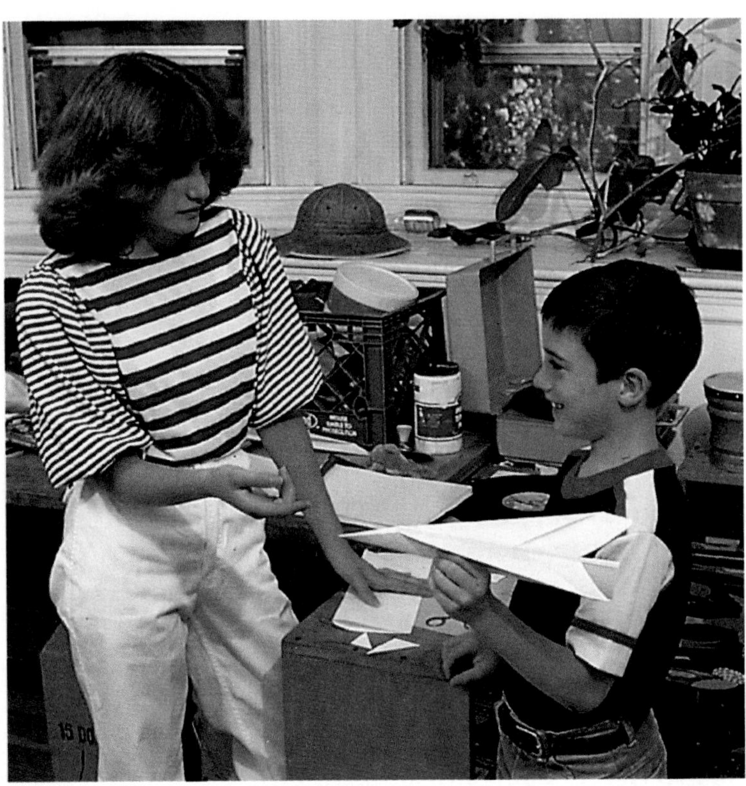

Can siblings benefit from learning how to use I-messages with each other?

terested manner. They can say such things as, "You seem upset." "You're really mad at Mrs. Jones today." "That must have been embarrassing." "I see." "Tell me more." "Hmmmm." If the technique works, the child soon calms down and makes the very statement the parent had to keep from saying, such as "I guess I don't have to like Mrs. Jones to learn arithmetic from her."

I-Messages

When the child's behavior bothers the parent, the parent should deliver an I-message. An I-message does not criticize. It simply informs children that their behavior is interfering with the parent's needs. For example, "I can't hear the TV when there is so much noise." The statement also may express the way the behavior makes the parent feel. For instance, "When I see toys on the stairs, I get worried because someone might trip and fall."

I-Messages Compared With You-Messages

For a full appreciation of this method, contrast I-messages with you-messages. You-messages are the kind many parents have spent years delivering. "You're acting like a baby." "Get out there and mow the lawn, you lazy bum." "Your sister is here to stay, so you might as well get used to it." These statements are not only demeaning to children and damaging to their self-esteem, but, in Gordon's view, they are also inaccurate. When a tired parent sits down to rest and a child keeps pestering, the problem is not that the child is a pest, but that the parent is tired. That is just what the parent should say.

I-Message Delivery

Learning to deliver I-messages is not easy. It requires people to identify their feelings precisely and to expose them assertively. Being assertive is not the same as being aggressive. For example, suppose you are babysitting for 3-year-old Tina and 6-year-old Sam. You are giving Tina her dinner when Sam says, "Play with me! Play with me!" An aggressive response would be "Shut up, Sam. You're a pain in the neck." The assertive answer would be, "Sam, I'm feeding Tina now. You sit here and play quietly. We'll play together when Tina is finished."

Most people first starting to practice this technique rely too heavily on vague words like "angry" and "upset." They need to learn to replace these words with more specific ones like "surprised," "taken advantage of," "ignored," "embarrassed," and "scared."

The great thing about I-messages is that they inform children without directing them. They leave the responsibility for behavior change with the child, where it belongs. Children often respond to I-messages with such remarks as "Gee, Mom, I didn't know it bothered you so much. I'll try to do better."

Use of I-Messages

Active listening and I-messages are recommended for use with positive as well as negative feelings. For example, you can say to a child who brings home a good report card, "You have good reason to be proud of your achievement, and I'm very happy for you." To children during a car ride, you might say, "I'm really enjoying the scenery. It's fun to have you kids sitting still and watching it with me."

Working together can help parents and children learn how to communicate better.

The No-Lose Method

The third basic technique for P.E.T. is the no-lose method. This method has six basic steps for problem solving.

1. Define the conflict ("Our problem seems to be that you want to go to the movies and I want the lawn mowed.")

2. Generate as many possible solutions as you can with the child. The alternatives could include:

a) go to an afternoon movie and

mow the lawn this evening.

b) mow the lawn this afternoon and go to the movie this evening.

c) don't mow the lawn.

d) don't go to the movie.

e) go to the movie tomorrow.

f) mow the lawn tomorrow.

3. Evaluate the alternatives. Look over the previous suggestions. What are the pluses and minuses of each one?

4. See if there is one solution that fully satisfies both parties. The parent and child may decide that mowing the lawn in the afternoon and going to the movie that evening is a good solution.

5. If so, decide how to implement the solution. The parent and child agree on times. The parent offers to give the child a ride to the theater so there is enough time for both activities.

6. Evaluate the solution later to see if it worked. The mown lawn looks good and the movie was great! Everyone is happy. What would the outcome be if the child fell asleep during the movie from being too tired? What if only half the lawn was cut by the time the movie was going to start?

The no-lose method can be discussed or it can be written down. In either case, step 4 is the most important. If parent and child cannot find a solution that satisfies them both, it is forbidden for either party to back down or impose his or her solution on the other. Instead they must try again—right away, tomorrow, or next week. Step 1 is also significant for the parent and child. Often misunderstandings arise from poor communication. If the conflict is not clearly defined, both parties may harbor resentment and frustration.

Parent Involvement Program (P.I.P.)

William Glasser designed this program. He holds that no helping relationship, whether between teacher and pupil or parent and child, can produce a change in behavior unless there is a warm, honest, affectionate relationship between the people. The belief is that people who engage in "irresponsible" behavior see themselves as failures. Unless they can be convinced that someone cares about them, it is hard for them to improve either their behavior or their self-concept.

Many parents develop a pattern of ignoring a child when the child is upset and punishing a child when they are upset. Thus, a good portion of the Parent Involvement Program is devoted to teaching parents how to remain involved. Some techniques are just common sense. When a child comes home in tears, parents are told to stop what they are doing and sit down with the child, just as a parent would do if a best friend arrived upset. Parents are encouraged to spend time with their children and to develop warm and honest relationships. To do this, a meaningful dialogue must be established.

Parent Involvement Program instructors treat the parents the way the parents are to treat the children. They take care to maintain involvement, and they do not ask for perfection. Instead, they show pleasure at a parent's attempts.

The Basics of P.I.P.

In this program there are seven steps.

1. Establish and maintain involve-

ment. In any helping relationship, the first step toward behavior change is to make friends. The parent-child relationship should be warm, personal, and honest. The approach is through conversation—by talking about topics of mutual interest in a friendly way.

2. Help children to see what their current behavior is and understand that it is something they have chosen. Ask, "What are you doing now?" "What did you do yesterday?" "What about last week?" (Don't go farther back than that.) Ask what, not why. Asking why invites the child to blame others, offer excuses and rationalizations, and dwell on feelings. Feelings are important, but behavior is the real issue.

3. Suggest to the children in a friendly, nonjudgmental way that they evaluate their own behavior. Encourage self-judgment by asking them whether their present behavior is beneficial to them.

4. Help the children plan more responsible behavior. Without help, children's plans will be too ambitious. They need small, realistic goals so that progress can be made and success experienced.

5. Ask for a commitment to the plan—a handshake, verbal statement, or written contract. Commitment strengthens the child's motivation and increases involvement with the parent.

6. Accept no excuses. If, as often happens, the child does not meet a commitment, go back to step 3. The child may decide to change the evaluation, revise the plan, or make a renewed commitment to it. Do not ask why the original plan failed. If excuses are offered, say, "Please, you don't have to make excuses." Stay involved, be patient, and never give up.

Guiding children through new skills helps their self-confidence.

7. Don't use punishment. Praise for success is good because it shows involvement. When children fail, causing them physical or mental pain strains involvement with the parent. It also encourages self-involvement, loneliness, isolation, and hostility. Reasonable consequences that are agreed to by the child are not punishment. Examples are having a child pick up all the toys after scattering them all around the home or not getting the car keys until the car is washed.

Responsive Parent Training Program

If your way works, use it. But if you are having problems, you need to change what you are doing. The Responsive Parent Training Program asks parents to learn the principles of human behavior. The parents are then asked to apply those principles to behaviors that occur in their own homes.

	PERFORMANCE						
TASKS	SUN	MON	TUE	WED	THU	FRI	SAT
UP ON TIME							
WALK DOG							
GARBAGE							
MOW LAWN							
HOME ON TIME							
HOME WORK							

Using special graph paper, the parent records the child's behavior. The behavior is noted and plotted without any comment. After studying the graph, the parent is helped to see if the experimental procedure changed the original behavior. For example, John won't get up after being called many times. The number of times he is called and his appearance at the breakfast table are recorded. The parents may then give John an alarm clock, tell him once that breakfast is ready, and allow him to face the consequences of his actions. The parents then find out how their new response to John's behavior affects his behavior. If their plan for helping him develop more responsible behavior does not succeed, they must then modify it or institute a new procedure.

Many parents find that as the behavior being worked on improves, so do a lot of other behaviors, possibly including those of other children in the family. Punishment is always paired with positive reinforcement. For example, Juanita is kept inside one afternoon for running in the street. The next day when she goes outside she stops to look for traffic. Her father praises her for her responsible action.

Positive reinforcement is necessary because it rewards the children for their behavior or changes they make in their behavior. It also supplies them with information about what is considered responsible, intelligent behavior.

Alfred Adler Institute

Rudolf Dreikurs is a psychiatrist and founder of the Alfred Adler Institute of Chicago. Alfred Adler was an Austrian psychiatrist who felt that personality development progressed along a road paved with evidence of either personal superiority or inferiority.

Dreikurs says, "A misbehaving child is a discouraged child." Children need encouragement. Encouragement means avoiding overprotection and giving children plenty of responsibility. It also means adopting realistic standards so that effort as well as achievement can be appreciated. According to Dreikurs, a misbehaving child is expressing a sense of inadequacy or seek-

Overview of Parenting Programs

Parenting Program	Founder	Philosophy
Parent Effectiveness Training (P.E.T.)	Thomas Gordon	Teaches three basic techniques • active listening • I-messages • no-lose method Believes parents should give up use of power.
Parent Involvement Program (P.I.P.)	William Glasser	Seven-step program designed to keep parent involved and based on an affectionate relationship between parent and child.
Responsive Parent Training Program	M.C. Hall	Parents apply principles of human behavior to behaviors that occur in their homes. Special graph paper records child's behavior.
Alfred Adler Institute	Rudolf Dreikurs	Misbehaving children are discouraged children and need encouragement. Program helps parents recognize and understand children's misbehavior and encourage constructive ones.

ing attention, power, or revenge. By misbehaving, the child hopes to lock his or her parents into certain responses or attitudes. Dreikurs' approach helps parents recognize and understand a child's misbehavior. He maintains that a parent's job is to discourage children's misguided efforts and encourage more constructive ones, such as, cooperation and respect for order. Dreikurs also opposes power struggles between parent and child, yet he considers them to be a fact of life and suggests ways parents can avoid them. The chart on the following page outlines Dreikurs' concept.

Theory of Child Development

One of the most useful tools a parent can have in trying to build meaningful relationships with children is the knowledge of child development. Expert researchers have evolved various theories to explain children's behavior. There are many theories on how

The Doctrine According to Dreikurs:
The Four Goals of Misbehavior and How to Tell Which Your Child Is After

Goal	Child's Behavior	Parent's Reaction to Behavior	Child's Response to Correction
Attention	Noisy, restless, shows off	Annoyance; child seems pest or nuisance	Behavior stops, briefly
Power	Aggressive, defiant, insolent, bossy; pouts and cries	Frustration, anger, parent feels leader-ship threatened	Behavior continues, may get worse
Revenge	Violent, brutal, sullen, hurtful of others	Hurt; child may seem mean or nasty	More violent attack
Inadequacy	Won't try, gives up, withdraws	Helplessness, desperation; child may seem stupid or dreamy	No response

Adapted from *Winning Children Over* by Francis X. Walton and Robert L. Powers. Chicago: Practical Psychology Associates, 1974. Distributed ($2.00) by Alfred Adler Institute of Chicago, 600 North McClurg Court, Chicago, Illinois 60611. Reprinted by permission of Practical Psychology Associates.

children's early experiences influence their adult lives. Each theory emphasizes different factors and considers certain life experiences to be more important than others. Nevertheless, each theory contributes to our understanding of the influences of childhood and adulthood, and each one gives us added insight. Whether or not we personally agree with a particular theory is a different matter.

The following theories illustrate the ways three psychologists have thought about behavioral development. The three psychologists we will focus on are Erik Erikson, Jean Piaget, and Arnold Gesell. These individuals have proposed theories that have become highly influential. However, there are other theorists who have also organized facts into equally interesting principles and theories. It is important to keep in mind that all of these theories have their shortcomings. The ones we present are included for their historical and contemporary significance.

Psychosocial Theory

The psychosocial theory of Erik Erikson divides the life cycle into eight stages. Erikson feels that the per-

Children misbehave for a variety of reasons. What do you think has caused this boy to take out his anger like this?

sonality develops continuously throughout the life cycle. As the individual grows, he or she becomes more and more aware of his or her environment. The stages according to Erik Erikson's theory are these:

1. Infancy—Trust vs. Mistrust
2. Early Childhood—Autonomy vs. Shame and Doubt
3. Play Age—Initiative vs. Guilt
4. School Age—Industry vs. Inferiority
5. Adolescence—Identity vs. Role Confusion
6. Young Adulthood—Intimacy vs. Isolation
7. Adulthood—Generativity vs. Self-Absorption
8. Old Age—Integrity vs. Disgust

Each of these stages plays an equally important part in development. In the study of child development, an understanding of the total span of development is essential, particularly since the caring adult is dealing with his or her own developmental tasks while influencing the child's development. The common thread in all eight stages, which Erikson defines, is that a new level of social awareness and interaction becomes possible for the individual.

Erikson intentionally prefaces his descriptions of each stage with the phrase "sense of" because it is the feeling of having achieved or failed to achieve a sense of trust, autonomy, or any of the other stages that is the deter-

A Matter of Fact

In thousands of communities, a form of help for parents is now available. Parents are banding together to provide support for each other. In Ohio, alone, over 300 support groups have been identified. One type of support group was originated and developed in Long Island. Called the Mothers' Center, it was designed to let mothers share their feelings about caring for children. The concept has been copied in 23 other Mothers' Centers in 11 states. In all of them, the primary emphasis is self-confidence and self-worth among parents. Weekly group discussions are held, and shared experiences help the parents to overcome self-doubt and loneliness.

Support groups take many other forms, as well. In your community, they may be sponsored by local churches, community centers, settlement houses, or by agencies dealing in youth services, family services, health services, or mental health services. They are sponsored, also, by some hospitals, universities, and technical schools. For still another form of guidance, parents may join organizations that provide conferences, workshops, and regular newsletters and/or journals to keep up-to-date with the views of experts on parenting and children.

mining factor for development in the next stages. Each stage has the possibility of a positive or negative outcome. Failures, however, at one stage may be rectified by successes at later stages.

Infancy—Trust vs. Mistrust

The infant's first task is to develop a sense of trust. This occurs if the environment provides the basic physical and psychological needs. The child who is warm, fed, cuddled, and who can count on his or her needs being met by parents or caregivers develops a sense of trust. The child whose needs are neglected or not regularly met develops a sense of mistrust. The degree to which a child comes to trust or mistrust others depends to a great extent on the quality of care he or she receives.

In a course on child development, Sharon was intrigued with Erikson's theory of personality. She recalled the different experiences her two children, Mike and Alice, had as babies and preschoolers. She began with experiences that affected the sense of trust. She put a plus sign before a positive experience and a minus sign before a negative one.

Mike

– Mike was born in a busy hospital and fed on a rigid four-hour schedule. He cried a great deal. I decided it was from hunger.

+ After leaving the hospital, I fed Mike more often and he seemed more content.

+ My husband was especially happy that the baby was a boy. He gave him a lot of attention and helped him avoid painful experiences, such as falling when he first began to walk.

– A neighborhood boy bullied Mike and the mother of the "bully" did not try to help the situation.

– A big, aggressive dog in the neighborhood got loose frequently and scared Mike badly a few times.

Alice

+ Alice was born in a hospital providing "rooming-in" facilities. Her needs were met immediately.

– A bad ear infection at three months made Alice fearful. She needed extra attention. (Receiving extra attention was positive in this negative experience.)

– I had to have an operation when Alice was 10 months old. (This is a period when babies are distinguishing between the mothering figure and others.)

+ Alice had unusually good preschool experiences with both children and adults. I stayed with Alice at the preschool until one day she felt safe and happy enough to tell me, "Go home, Mommie."

+ For Alice, the big dog had not been a problem because the family had moved.

Early Childhood—Autonomy vs. Shame and Doubt

In the second stage, from two to three years, children discover new motor and mental abilities. If the parents recognize that children need to develop at their own pace, they will develop a sense of **autonomy** or self-reliance. If parents ignore or discourage this stage, children will begin to doubt themselves and feel shame.

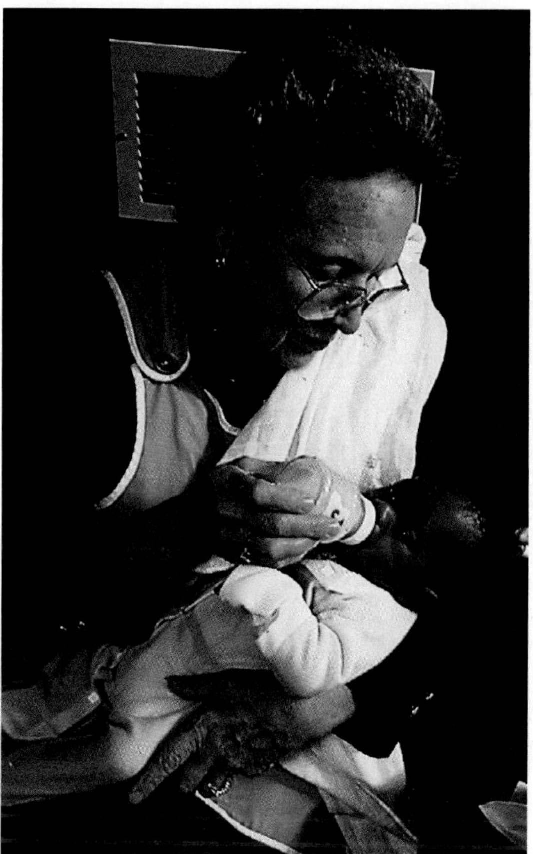

Infants develop a sense of trust when their needs are met by caregivers.

Sharon then listed the following experiences that affected her children's sense of autonomy.

Mike

+ Mike could get his father's attention easily. This gave Mike a feeling that he was a worthwhile person.

+ My husband and I let Mike

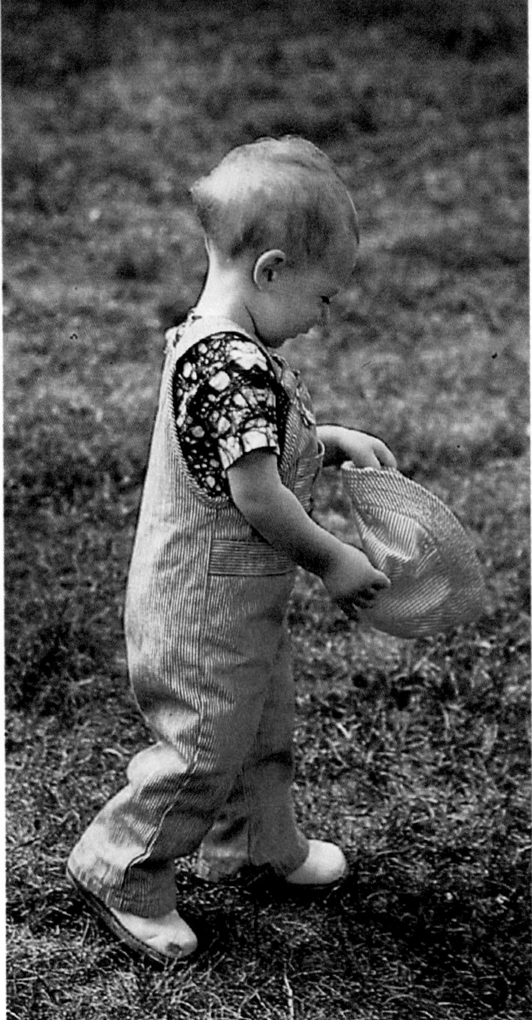

With increased motor skills, children also develop autonomy.

choose what he would wear each day. This made Mike feel that he had some power to make decisions.

– Mike was big for his age and above average in intelligence. My husband and I both felt a need to push toilet training. Mike was considerably annoyed about it. It became a minor battle in the family.

– My husband and I fell into a habit of saying "no" a great deal to Mike because he was so active, strong, and adventuresome. Not until my mother called attention to it did we realize how negative we had been. We could have used distraction some of the time.

Alice

– When Alice's appetite was fairly well-satisfied, she wanted to try to feed herself. Connie, the woman taking care of her while I was in the hospital, couldn't stand the mess. Alice couldn't assert herself so that she could try out her ability to feed herself.

\+ Alice learned to talk early and Connie helped her name countless things.

\+ Alice was toilet trained early and easily. However, at 3 years of age she had numerous wetting accidents. I talked about it with the preschool teacher who understood Alice. The teacher suggested that I tell Alice that it was Alice's responsibility and that I was not going to say anything about it. Alice gloried in being able to stay dry on her own. I had to comfort her one day when she failed herself.

Play Age—Initiative vs. Guilt

In this stage, from ages four to five, the child's imagination is greatly expanded because of the increased ability to move around freely and to communicate. The child initiates fantasy, as well as motor and language activities. This is also the stage when feelings of guilt and anxiety arise. If parents ridicule the child's activities, the child will develop a sense of guilt.

Sharon found it a little harder to

recall experiences which affected her children's sense of initiative and imagination.

Mike

+ My husband praised Mike's block building. When Mike seemed to want the help, my husband would add an idea or help him balance blocks about ready to tumble.
+ At preschool the teacher helped Mike play at being a filling station attendant. She gave him a rag and said that the filling station man put it in his back pocket and used it to wipe off oil. The next day Mike told the teacher that he had been at a filling station. The man there had a rag in each of his back pockets, so now Mike wanted another rag. He also asked to have water in the oilcan so he could pretend that it was oil. More items and ideas were added later.
– The bully in the neighborhood made Mike play the way he wanted to play. Mike never had a chance to use his ideas.

Alice

+ When Alice showed me her crayon scribblings, I would remark about how pretty the red (or another color) was. I didn't expect Alice, at her age, to produce anything.
+ Alice spent a lot of time putting her dolls in chairs at the table and pretending to serve them sandwiches and milk. I usually tried to leave this arrangement alone and not put things away.

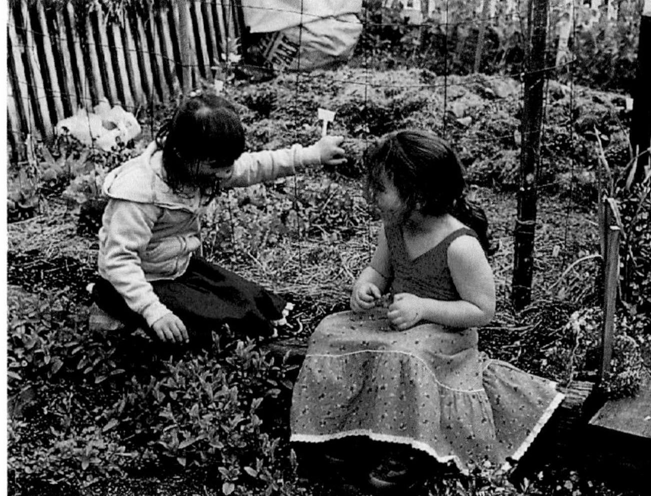

When children are in the play age, parents need to encourage their sense of initiative and avoid feelings of guilt.

+ Alice became interested in letters of the alphabet and asked me what certain ones were. I wasn't sure whether or not I should encourage this. I had heard some teachers say that reading should be left to the schools, but I helped Alice and didn't push her.

School Age—Industry vs. Inferiority

Children between the ages of six and 11 want to learn how to do and make things with others (industry). Wanting to accept instruction but getting no recognition for their efforts, children may develop a sense of inadequacy or inferiority. For example, parents who regularly see their child's efforts as simply "making a mess" may cause the child to develop a sense of inferiority. When parents frequently praise children for their efforts and show interest in their projects and school work, they encourage in the children a

In the school age, children want to learn how to do and make things.

sense of industry. Children's balance between industry and inferiority is affected by the school experience, as well as the home experience. Children who succeed in their academic efforts generally have their sense of industry reinforced.

Adolescence—Identity vs. Role Confusion

During the ages of 12 to 18, the adolescent years, the child's body grows rapidly. Sexual maturity at this stage forces the young person to question old roles and seek new identities. The major task at this stage is to integrate childhood identifications and new biological drives into new social roles. The training of childhood needs to be translated into the behavior of adulthood. The danger at this stage is that identity of the new adult role may become confused, keeping the young person from attaining the level of maturity needed for competent adulthood. It is very important for adolescents to have respected adults at home or elsewhere to use as **role models,** that is, patterns for their own lives.

Young Adulthood—Intimacy vs. Isolation

Only as young people begin to feel secure with their identities are they able to establish true emotional intimacy with others. The intimacy is in friendship and eventually in a love-based, mutually satisfying sexual relationship. A person who cannot enter into an intimate relationship because of fear of losing his or her identity may develop a sense of isolation.

Adulthood—Generativity vs. Self-Absorption

Generativity has been defined as concern for people beyond the immediate family group. Lack of this concern may result in self-absorption, or making personal needs one's primary concern. The adult may be interested in establishing and guiding policies to make life better for future generations or he or she may be lost in self-absorption, with a sense of stagnation.

A sense of generativity is not restricted just to parents. Any individual who is interested in the welfare of young people and is active in making the world a better place to live demonstrates generativity.

Old Age—Integrity vs. Disgust

Persons who have adapted to the triumphs and disappointments of their generative activities reach the end of life with a certain ego integrity. **Ego integrity** results from an individual's ability to look back on life with a sense of satisfaction. Without this sense of ego integrity, people look back on life with a feeling of despair, usually marked by displeasure and disgust. For example, people who look back upon their lives as a series of missed opportunities may feel a sense of despair. They realize that there is no time to start again. People who feel content and satisfied with their lives, on the other hand, feel a sense of integrity.

Developmental Psychology Theory

Another influential theory is the one developed by Jean Piaget. In this theory, Piaget describes the changes in an individual's thinking from infancy to early adolescence. Adolescence is the time when most individuals are capable of logical thought. The development of thought is discussed in four stages. The first two stages describe the development of thinking of children who are under seven years old.

The Sensorimotor Period (18-24 months)

The sensorimotor period covers the first 18 to 24 months of life. It is the period of practical intelligence. Changes in an infant's thinking take place through seeing, hearing, touching, smelling, and tasting. The relationship between biological maturation and development of thinking is clearly evident at this time. When infants can focus their eyes on an object and grasp it, their opportunities for learning increase. They learn about the world by grasping, tasting, and manipulating objects within their reach. There are two important accomplishments during this period. They are:

1. the ability to recognize the permanence of objects and persons.
2. the ability to form **hypotheses** or unproved guesses about the solution of a problem.

Object- and Person-Permanence

Object-permanence refers to the understanding that an object exists even though you do not see it. You can determine whether babies have developed object-permanence by noticing whether or not they look down for objects they have dropped. Similarly, **person-permanence** is the awareness that people exist even though they are out of sight. This idea is important in the development of an infant's relationships with parents and caregivers. You can determine whether babies have developed person-permanence by observing whether or not they smile or wiggle when they hear a parent's voice in another part of the house.

Ability to Form Hypotheses

The ability to form hypotheses is the ability to think of solutions to a problem instead of arbitrarily trying one solution and then another until the problem is solved. You can observe this ability in infants when they want an object resting on a blanket nearby them, and they pull the blanket toward them to get that object.

Preoperational Period (2 to 7 years)

The preoperational period extends from around two to seven years of age.

Look, Listen, and Learn

If you want to learn about children, you can't go wrong by spending time playing with them. But you can also learn a great deal about children by watching them play by themselves or with each other.

This is called child observation. You may be required to observe children involved in play or a learning activity and then to document your observations in a research project. How do you observe children? Here are a few tips:

- Locate a place to sit where the child or children won't pay attention to you. Make yourself "invisible."
- Have a notebook and pen handy for notetaking. You will want to record the date, time, and location of the observation session. Here are some other questions you will want to answer: What is the age and sex of each child? What kind of activity are you observing? Is the activity a learning experience, such as learning the alphabet or names of colors? Is the child involved in play, such as making mud pies? What are the responses of each child? Does the child seem to be interested in what's going on around him or her? Does the child seem bored with it all?
- Remain as quiet as possible. Do not draw attention to yourself.
- Stay unbiased in your judgments. You simply want to record the behavior as it happens. Don't color your observations with your opinions.
- When you have completed your observations, go back over your notes as soon as possible. This will help keep your written comments fresh in your mind. You might want to include other information at this time, such as references from books, or how your classroom learning applies to your observations.
- If possible, follow up your initial observation with a second or even a third session under the same conditions. Note any differences you observe.

The primary achievements of this period are imitation, play, and language development. Children become so skillful in communicating with adults that one might assume, incorrectly, that they think as adults do. Children, however, do not understand the basic relationships between objects or events. Piaget attributes these errors to two deficiencies in children's thinking. One is the inability to comprehend reversibility. The other is a child's inability to see a situation from any point of view except his or her own. This type of thinking is called **egocentrism.**

Reversibility

Reversibility is the ability to understand that a completed process also can be performed in the reverse order,

If this child mirrors the place setting on the other side of the table, what type of thinking is he exhibiting?

so that the materials used are returned to their initial state. Children in the preoperational stage are not yet able to understand that materials can change shape without changing volume or mass. Moreover, they do not understand that a material that has lost its original shape can be made to regain that shape. The following experiment is an interesting way to test a child's capacity for reversibility. Give a child some clay. Ask the child to make two balls of the same size. Then, as the child watches you, flatten one ball to make it look like a pancake. Ask the child if the amount of clay in the ball and in the pancake are the same. Most preschool children will say "no" and indicate that the pancake is larger.

When children say "yes" and can explain that nothing was added or taken away even though the shape of the ball was changed, they have the ability to understand conservation. They recognize that a thing is basically the same even if its shape is changed. When they understand that the pancake can be rolled back into a ball of clay, they understand reversibility. Until they are able to do this, telling them that the ball and the pancake have the same amount of clay will not influence their thinking.

Egocentrism

You can demonstrate the deficiency of egocentrism by the following experiment. Put two placemats on opposite sides of a narrow table. After setting a fork on the left side of one placemat, have a child stand facing it. Now ask the child to reach across the table and set a fork on the correct side of the other placemat. In this situation, the child will place the fork on the wrong side of the mat directly across the table from the first fork. This is because children are capable of thinking only from their own point of view.

Egocentrism often frustrates adults who work with children. In a story group, children will sit right in front of each other to see the pictures. They don't mean to block other children's views. They just want to see and don't realize that they are in front of others. Children also will interrupt a story with a completely unrelated comment, like "I was sick last night." The child just thought about last night. He or she simply wants to share the thought. Children during this period consider only themselves.

Concrete Operational Period (7 to 12 years)

When children have mastered the concept of reversibility and when their thinking is less egocentric, they have moved into the next period, concrete operational. This period is from the ages of seven through 12 years. Children become capable of approaching several types of mathematical operations. They understand numbers and quantity, but only when demonstrated with concrete materials. For example, consider students learning the relationship between addition and multiplication. If the teacher puts 12 objects in three rows, four objects to a row, the students will understand why 4 + 4 + 4 and 3 x 4 are equivalent. At this point, children still do not reason about concepts and ideas.

Formal Operational Period (12 years)

Formal thinking, the final stage in development of thought, is reached around age 12. Reasoning about ideas and events that are in the past, present, or the future is now within the child's scope. Children at this age are capable of abstract thought and are able to deal with a widening variety of problems. Thought has now achieved the stage of being mobile and flexible.

Assimilation and Accommodation

According to Piaget, two processes are essential for development: assimilation and accommodation. In **assimilation** the child incorporates new elements into the existing structure. In **accommodation** the child adjusts his or her thinking to external reality.

A Closer Look

Lisa, an 18 month-old girl, often throws her plastic tumbler from her high chair after she has finished drinking her milk. At her grandparent's house she has a glass tumbler. She throws it, and it makes a loud noise as it breaks into pieces. She frowns, looks puzzled, then cries. Lisa has made a new observation and acquired a new piece of information. She assimilates that information. Now that she knows some tumblers are breakable, she might alter her behavior. Such a change would be accommodation. Through the complementary processes of assimilation and accommodation, she can expand her understanding of her environment.

PEANUTS® By Schulz

Each time children assimilate and then accommodate a new experience, they move a step closer to the next stage in the development of logical thought. This, of course, is not only true during childhood, but is also true throughout life. Each new experience is measured against past experiences.

Our behavior is based on our assimilated knowledge. When we accommodate a new experience, we demonstrate that we understand it as it relates to our earlier experiences. Piaget stresses that experiences and thoughts do not exist alone, but only as they relate to other experiences and thoughts.

Developmental Maturational Theory

Psychologist Arnold Gesell emphasized the important influence of heredity on the way that each particular child matures. Because Prof. Gesell believed that behavior is tied to a child's overall development and maturation, he contended that a given child's behavior will follow a pattern that is somewhat predictable. For example, most two-year-olds experiment with techniques that allow them to demonstrate their independence and to control the situation in which they find themselves. Because language skills are not very advanced at this stage, children must rely on crying, stomping their feet, repeated use of the word "no," or other expressions of resistance. As children mature in language ability, they learn new methods of interacting with people, and we observe changes in behavior. Prof. Gesell admitted that culture, family, and other environmental factors could influence a child's behavior, but he suggested that these would not be as important as the internal control based on heredity.

Individuality is also an important aspect of Gesell's theory. In other words, children reach certain stages of development in their own time. The determining factor is the rate at which each child is maturing. One can describe different stages of behavioral development, but it is impossible to assign specific ages when children reach these levels. We must remember that each child is an individual for whom certain types of behavior will occur regardless of his/her environment.

Because of the individuality of children, a child's developmental progress should be judged according to individual standards. For instance, let us consider two nine-year-olds, Trevor and Ravi. Trevor reads at a third-grade level, while Ravi reads at a fourth-grade level. It would be unjustified to conclude that Ravi is making satisfactory progress in reading, and Trevor is not. In fact, the proper evaluation can be made only by comparing each boy's present performance to his own past performance. Trevor was not physically ready to read when he entered first grade. His eyesight had not matured beyond the farsightedness typical of younger children. Considering his slower start, we must conclude that Trevor is doing very well. Probably, he will soon catch up to Ravi whose reading skills have shown no improvement for the last six months.

In summary, Gesell's Developmental Maturational Theory says that the processes of growth and development are controlled from within. The environment can modify, but not determine, behavior. This concept is expressed by the cartoon in which children become adults with no external influence except the passing of time. Acceptance of this theory leads to the conclusion that each child should be allowed to develop at his or her own pace at home and at school. A child's development is limited if adults fail to challenge or fail to give the child freedom to expand his or her horizons. On the other hand, pushing children to achieve beyond their individual levels of maturity can be discouraging and frustrating to children, parents, and teachers alike. When children cannot live up to unrealistic expectations, their self-image is damaged. Thus, pushing children is counterproductive.

Reprinted by permission of Cary Grossman. From *Saturday Review*, © 1979.

Life's Work

Kimberly Moore

- ➤Educational Program Specialist at Children's World Learning Centers
- ➤B.S. in Home Economics Education/Child Development
- ➤M.Ed. in Home Economics Education/Early Childhood Concentration

Kimberly describes her typical day as being full of variety. She works on curriculum development and provides support and resources for teachers and directors in the child-care centers. Kimberly writes and edits a monthly staff newsletter and creates training workshops and conference presentations. Creating ways to evaluate training needs and then developing interesting and new ways to train individuals fill Kimberly's days, too. Kimberly also travels to different districts to visit the child-care centers. At the centers she suggests changes and new methods of working with children from infancy to school age.

When in the office, Kimberly's day is from 8 to 5. When traveling, she does training during the day as well as evening sessions. Some Saturday workshops and weekend attendance of professional conferences also occur.

Kimberly says the skills necessary for success in her profession include, "an ability to work with a variety of people as well as work independently." She also feels one needs, "a thorough knowledge of child development, early childhood education, and training methods as well as an appreciation for individuals and a variety of teaching styles." In addition, a person must be able "to assess training needs and plan and conduct training seminars for all levels of classroom teachers and center managers."

For a student considering going into Kimberly's profession, she recommends, "Learn to appreciate the process of learning and respect creativity and enthusiasm in the classroom. One must enjoy all types of people and all ages of children. Learn your subject matter well and develop the skill of dealing tactfully, honestly, and positively with everyone."

When asked how her profession will change within the next 10 years, Kimberly says, "As child care becomes more and more necessary in our society, there will be an increasing number of jobs available at all levels. Specific child development training will be valuable for the professions of teaching, management, support, and resource services." Child-care organizations will need more people like Kimberly as companies grow. The future looks promising for child-care.

In Review

Vocabulary

hypotheses
role models
autonomy
generativity
ego integrity
object-permanence
person-permanence
reversibility
egocentrism
assimilation
accommodation

Summary

- ✓ By studying the various theories of child development and the parent training programs based on those theories, you can better understand yourself, your parents, and the responsibilities of parenthood.
- ✓ Parent training programs help to identify values and different parenting styles. Through such programs one can learn techniques for improving parent-child relationships.
- ✓ Parent training programs stress responsible behavior, discipline, and the management of conflict.
- ✓ The Psychosocial Theory of child development from Erik Erikson divides the life cycle into eight stages.
- ✓ In Piaget's Theory of Developmental Psychology, he describes the development of thought in four stages. Throughout all stages children learn by a combination of assimilation and accommodation.
- ✓ The Developmental Maturational Theory proposed by Gesell emphasizes the importance of heredity to the initiation of development in each stage of a child's life. He concludes that children should be allowed to develop at their own pace.

Questions

1. Find out about the kinds of parenthood programs available for adults in your community. Check with the local library, churches, and continuing education programs.

2. Why does Gordon want the term "misbehavior" dropped from the language describing parent-child relationships?

3. Raul wants to wear his tennis shoes to church so that he can play tag with the children in the parking lot after the service. Raul's mother wants him to wear his new leather shoes to church. According to the P.E.T. approach, who owns the problem? Give some possible resolutions of the problem.

4. Make a list of messages that you hear between parents and children. Indicate on your list those that are I-messages and those that are you-messages.

5. The development of children is influenced by both heredity and environment. Which of the theories described in this chapter do you think places the greatest emphasis on heredity? Which places the greatest emphasis on environment? Write a paragraph to explain your answer.

6. What is meant by assimilation and accommodation?

7. What is egocentrism? Give some examples.

8. To which theories do you think your parents either consciously or subconsciously subscribed? Explain your answers.

9. Using Erikson's and Piaget's theories, explain why the first seven years of life are so important.

Activities

1. Think of a conflict you have had. Use the no-lose method of problem solving to define the conflict and suggest several alternative solutions. Is there one that would have satisfied both parties?

2. For two Tuesdays in a row, 12-year-old Becky has "conveniently forgotten" to go to Mrs. Rothman's house on the way home from school to take her piano lesson. Describe how you would deal with Becky's behavior and choose a specific course of action that would be appropriate for someone in a Responsive Parent Training Program. Now, assume that Becky neglects her piano lesson again. What is your next course of action or your modification of the original plan?

3. What were some of the most important influences on your life? Make a list for yourself similar to the one made for Mike and Alice.

4. Find a picture or a cartoon that shows some aspect of a child development theory. Mount the picture or cartoon on a sheet of paper and discuss in class that part of the theory that is illustrated.

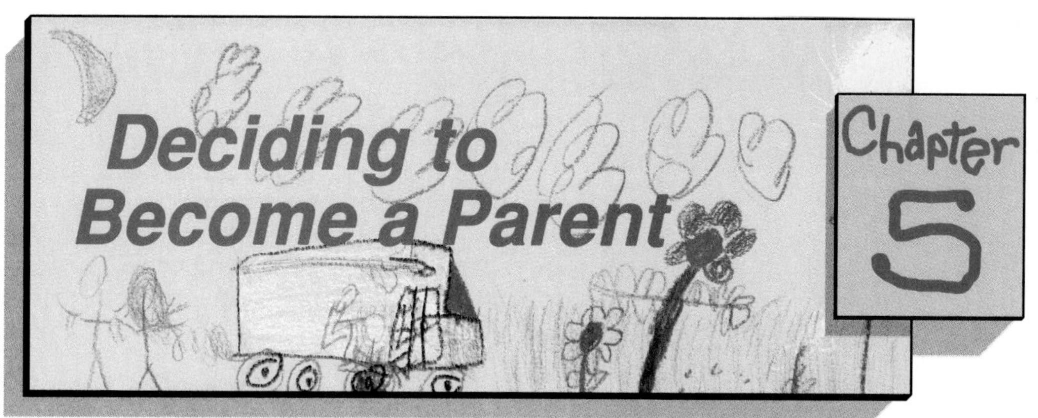

This chapter will help you:

- list the common misconceptions about parenthood and explain why each one is a "myth"
- describe social and emotional pressures placed on people to have children
- list factors for consideration before becoming parents
- describe the effects a baby may have on a couple's relationship
- recognize the "right" reasons for deciding to become a parent
- recognize the roles of non-biological parents

To Be a Parent?

Whether to become a parent or not is one of the most important decisions of anyone's life. There are many good reasons to choose parenthood and also many bad reasons. There are numerous factors to consider seriously before making up your mind.

Myths about Parenthood

Parenthood Is Fun

Because the word "fun" often implies a lack of serious purpose, it is wrong to describe parenthood as fun. The truth is that parenthood can be interesting, enjoyable, and exciting, but it is also a serious responsibility. We can take or leave our activities that are just *fun*. Parenthood is different. Once we have taken on the responsibilities of parents, we don't quit whenever we feel the urge.

Parenting Is Like Playing with Dolls

Dolls are picked up, changed, fed, burped, cuddled, and put back down at the "parent's" convenience. That is not the case with babies. Babies cry when they need food, a clean diaper, or hugging, and this can happen at any hour of the day or night. None can be postponed until the parent feels like "playing." In addition, babies often "spit up," and they often have diarrhea. They can be very cranky when they cut teeth.

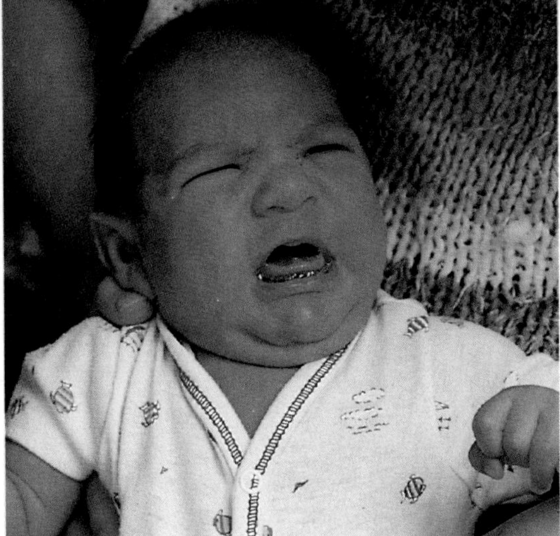

Having a baby is not like having a doll. When babies cry, they need attention.

They catch colds, and they can have runny noses. Sometimes they run high fevers, and parents stay up all night to watch over them.

Children Are Cute, Innocent, and Sweet

This is often true, but not always. Children can be very challenging to their parents. Love for children and acceptance of their behavior has to be guided by knowledge and insight. The cute behavior of a three-year-old may be obnoxious in the six-year-old. Thus, parental response needs to be tempered with insight and self-control.

Having a Baby Can Save a Troubled Marriage

On the contrary, the addition of a child to a family places stress even on the happiest marriage. If two people are not well-adjusted to their life together, the responsibility of parenthood is very apt to drive a wedge into the existing rift. It is not at all uncommon for persons to be jealous of the time their spouse spends with their children. "Three's a crowd" is an apt description of such family situations.

Good Parenting Is Instinctive

People learn both good and bad practices from their own parents. A chain of bad practices can be broken by parents who are willing to learn the principles of child development and good parenting.

Having a Baby Will Fill a Void

Some people, including some unmarried persons, decide to have children as a means of escaping an unhappy life. They may feel insecure about their womanhood or manhood, or they may believe one or more of the other myths just listed. The truth is that mature, happy, emotionally stable people make the best parents. Before considering becoming parents, people should be secure and confident of their ability to nurture a child for a period of 18 or more years. Expecting a child to bring happiness to an otherwise unhappy person is too heavy a burden for a baby to bear.

Factors for Consideration

Being prepared for parenthood and wanting children are two important responsibilities. To give children the best start on life, there are also other factors to consider.

Social and Emotional Pressures

Social and emotional pressures to have children come in many forms. A young married couple who are studying in college preparing for professional careers may experience subtle, or not so subtle, pressure from their parents who are eager to become grandparents. An adolescent may feel peer pressure to prove maturity by becoming a mother (or father). An adolescent girl may feel her only way out of a horrendous home situation is to become pregnant with the hope that her boyfriend will marry her. A married adult who has no desire to be a parent may be pressured by his or her spouse who feels that time is running out on the possibility to have children. A somewhat similar situation can arise for a single adult approaching the end of the childbearing years. Some adults may feel they have the "right" to have a child even though they do not want to marry. However, those people need to consider the rights of a baby to know and love both parents.

There are many other examples, but, like the ones just described, none is a good reason to become parents. Children born as a result of social and emotional pressures on the parents do not have the advantage of being wanted **unequivocally.** Unequivocally means leaving no doubt, being very clear.

Economics

The cost of having a child begins shortly after the woman becomes pregnant. For the health of the mother and **fetus** (unborn baby), an **obstetrician** (doctor who specializes in birth) should monitor their progress at regular intervals throughout the pregnancy. That results in a medical expense. In addition, the doctor bills and hospital bills for the birth of a child can be very large. Even maternity health insurance usually does not cover those bills completely. If the prospective parents' budget is already stretched to its limit, parenthood should be postponed. It is important for new parents to not have the added worry of meeting all their expenses.

Some married couples postpone having children in order to finish their education.

The initial medical expenses are almost insignificant when compared with the total cost of rearing a child. First, there are additional food, clothing, medical, and housing expenses. At school age, the child requires books, fees, lunch money, spending money, etc. College students need tuition, books, room, board, fraternity or sorority fees, and spending money.

The United States Department of Agriculture has estimated that the total cost of raising a child from birth to age 18 is $134,414. This is assuming an inflation rate of 8%. Tuition for private elementary and high schools would make the figure even higher. Private universities today can cost roughly $60,000 or more for four years of tuition, room, and board. State universities cost less, but in many of them, four years will cost $25,000 or more.

Another very important impact on

Having a baby is not inexpensive, and the costs continue to rise as children enter school.

the family finances is felt if one parent leaves a job (and a paycheck) in order to stay home with the children. If both parents continue to work, the cost of daycare needs to be added to the family budget. It is easy to see that having a child is accepting a substantial, long-term economic commitment.

Youth or Age of the Prospective Parents

There are numerous problems for those who have children too early in their lives. A large majority of pregnant adolescents do not finish high school, and almost none ever finishes college. The younger a teenager is when she gives birth to her first child, the more likely she and her child are to live in poverty. A teenaged father who tries to accept the responsibility for a child is no more prepared than a teenaged mother to meet the financial, emotional, and social challenges of parenthood. In many instances, teenaged fathers lend no support—financial or otherwise. In those cases, it is a matter of beget and begone.

Teenaged parents give up the potentially joyous time that could lead them into independence when they suddenly take on the dual roles of adulthood and parenthood. Many, of course, do not gain independence, at all. Instead, they are often forced to be dependent on their parents or government agencies.

Another factor not often considered by adolescent girls is that complications can arise during pregnancy. Health problems related to the pregnancy are more common for teenaged mothers and their babies than for women in the midrange of the childbearing years. The incidence of birth defects is also much higher for babies born to adolescent mothers than to mothers in their 20s. In a study conducted by the Office of Technology

Assessment on behalf of the U.S. Congress, it was found that teenagers and women age 35 and above have a higher risk than other women of having babies that die within the first four weeks of life and that weigh 5 lbs. 8 oz. or less.

The frequency of birth defects and medical complications during pregnancy and childbirth decreases for women beyond the teen years and then increases for women approaching the end of the childbearing years. Older prospective parents should become aware of the potential problems by consulting with their doctors before becoming parents. Other factors the prospective parents need to consider include how a child will influence their own relationship, and how a child will influence their careers. Equally important is their realization that people who have children toward the end of the childbearing years are approaching retirement before those children "leave the nest." Such considerations are not being overly cautious. They are the concerns of responsible parents.

Right Reasons for Deciding to Become Parents

Caring for children is probably the most important job in the world. Rearing all children so as to maximize their opportunity for physical, intellectual, emotional, social, and moral development would result in generations of peace and good will. For this to happen, however, we must have and be parents who have that as their goal. The first step to that kind of parenthood is want-

Teen mothers face a multitude of problems .

ing a child for the right reasons.

One right reason for having children is that you have concepts you would like to share with children of your own. People who express that reason like themselves—that is, they have self-esteem. They have accomplishments of which they are proud. Sharing concepts and values, of course, requires time. Both partners should be stable enough in their careers that they can devote time to their children. Both should be genuinely excited about bringing a new life into being and about helping a child through all the developmental stages. Both parents should have emotional stability and enough love in their hearts to satisfy the needs of each other *and* the children that they *both want.* "Both want" is the key phrase in a discussion of the right reasons for deciding to become parents. Children who can sense that

A Matter of Fact

Three factors that may contribute to a higher percentage of birth problems are:

1. Immaturity of the mother's body. The female body continues to develop toward full maturity for several years after menstruation begins.

2. Proper medical care and nutrition. Teens are less apt to be able to afford proper medical care. Nutrition may be an area they have learned about in school, but they may not follow sound eating practices. Without a doctor's advice (which they may not be able to afford), about new dietary needs, they may be sadly lacking in good nutrition.

3. Traumatic emotional stresses. Teens are more apt to be experiencing problems that seem overwhelming. During pregnancy, a teenaged girl may be rejected by her boyfriend and she may be disowned by one or both parents. She may feel depressed by the uncertainty of her future, she may feel alienated from her friends, and she may find it extremely difficult to decide whether to keep her baby. The depth of her emotions over these, and other very serious problems, can influence the pregnancy in any number of ways. The prenatal development of a baby is dependent on its environment as well as its heredity, and the baby's environment is the mother.

they were and are wanted by both parents enjoy the greatest opportunity for development in all aspects of their childhood.

Parental Responsibility

The law in most states says that natural and adoptive parents are responsible for their children until the children reach legal adulthood. In other words, parents are responsible for their children for 18 to 21 years. It is not true, of course, that parents can never quit. Some of them do. However, public disapproval of child neglect is strong in our society. The courts symbolize this by their attitude toward parents who do not fulfill their obligations as fathers and mothers.

But it is not a fear of the law that should make parents take care of their children. It is a feeling of love that motivates good parents to provide for their children's needs. Besides the basic needs of food, shelter, and clothing, the family should nurture children with constant love, support, and encouragement. These are best provided by parents who have reached stages of maturity that allow them to give unselfishly of their time and energy.

In some ways, parents need to consider how they will raise their children to be competent adults. They must realize they are responsible for educating their children in those areas most relevant to successful family life.

Parents are asked to produce children who will not only replace them, but who will be better than them. For instance, parents face the problem of giving their children more education than they themselves had. This is a sobering thought. It is not enough for parents to produce carbon copies of themselves. Parents are being asked to do what some of the new copying machines are supposed to do—turn out copies better than the originals. The chance of doing this is greatly enhanced by parents who make sure that their family performs the 11 family responsibilities listed in Chapter 2. Parents need to help their children reach their full potential.

One right reason for people to want children is they have a lot of love to give.

Understanding Children

As pointed out in Chapter 4, one of the responsibilities we should be ready to accept before making the decision to become a parent is to learn the principles of child development. We would not, and could not, accept the job of building a bridge before we completed our education in engineering. Likewise, we should be wise enough to understand that parenting is helping children build bridges to their adulthood. We shouldn't attempt the task without understanding the materials we'll be working with and the tools that are available for our use. This book will help you develop those skills.

Understanding Lifestyle Changes

Marriage and family relationships are never static. They are always in a state of flux. Quite often, just when marriage partners have learned to adjust to each other and put their hopes and dreams together, the family unit undergoes some new change. The couple who has successfully created closeness and direction in their marriage is certainly more prepared to take on the responsibilities of parenthood than the couple who has to solve all the tasks of being a couple along with all the tasks of being parents. Most of us have only a limited number of tasks we can tackle at one time.

Even before the baby arrives, the marital relationship can be strongly influenced. Depending upon the kind of communication the couple has and the attitudes they have toward their pregnancy, they may be excited and elated by their anticipation of parenthood. On the other hand, they may become moody with their anxiety about the unknown problems of parenthood.

One concern parents have is to give their children more education than they had.

As mentioned, the arrival of a baby, even for the happiest of couples, can pose some problems for their marital relationship. The husband may feel the wife spends too much time, energy, and attention on the "third party." The wife may feel the same way about her husband. Or she may feel that the husband does not take his share of responsibility. The husband may feel that his wife assumes responsibilities for the baby's care that he would like to share. Usually, couples have to alter the roles they play when a baby arrives. Will the mother quit her job to look after the baby, or will the father? Will a grandparent or relative be in charge of the baby's care? Will the couple put the baby in a daycare center? Who will be responsible for each of the additional household chores? The couple should think through how they will handle these changes. Such questions are best settled *before* pregnancy. Part of being a responsible parent is being prepared.

Unwanted Children

In all of the preceding discussion, we have assumed that prospective parents are weighing the pros and cons of parenthood in a calm, rational, conversational way. Unfortunately, many children are conceived without any responsible decision-making. When this happens in a very stable family situation, the parents often can adapt their lives to this "surprise" in such a way that the child feels welcomed into the world.

In less stable situations, the child may arrive *unwanted.* Nothing is more damaging to a child's spirit and self-esteem. As was mentioned in Chapter 3, some babies sense their being unwanted so strongly that they fail to thrive. They die. Unwanted children can be subjected to two of the worst parenting practices discussed in Chapter 3, neglect and rejection. Without their basic needs of love, support, and encouragement being met, children simply cannot develop normally. It is difficult even to imagine the degree of unhappiness of anyone who has reached old age having experienced only mistrust, shame, doubt, guilt, inferiority, role confusion, isolation, self-absorption, and disgust.

Parents who like themselves help children learn to like themselves and develop a positive self-concept.

Childlessness

Some couples remain childless because they are physically incapable of reproduction. This may occur for many different reasons. Other couples remain childless because they do not want children, again for a variety of reasons. There should be no stigma attached to childlessness—whatever the reason. If the reason they do not have children is physical, the couple cannot change that anymore than they can change the color of their eyes. If couples do not want children, then they are to be commended for not bowing to any sort of social pressures that may be pressing them toward parenthood. They recognize the importance of wanting to nurture children. Possibly our most important birthright is to be *wanted unequivocally.*

Alternatives to Biological Parenthood

Adoptive Parents

One common way to become nonbiological parents is through adoption. Adoption may occur at any time from a few days after birth through adulthood. Children may become adoptable by the death of their parents, by abandonment, by birth to unmarried mothers who feel that adoptive parents can provide better environments for their babies, or many other circumstances.

Qualified adoption agencies do their best to assure that the adoptive parents and the children are compatible. In addition, the agency wants to be certain that couples can provide emotional and financial stability as

As with all families, parents can build solid relationships with adopted children through cooperation and communication.

well as healthful conditions for the children. Adoption proceedings can take many months, or even years, after prospective parents first apply. Some impatient prospective parents try to arrange illegal adoptions by buying a baby from "babies for profit" operations.

Prospective adoptive parents need to consider their reasons for wanting to be parents. Right and wrong reasons are no different for adoptive parents than for biological parents. It is imperative that *both* parents want to adopt.

Most psychologists agree that adopted children need to be told very early in their lives that they are adopted. It is easier for children to deal with the truth when it is told to them by their trusted and loving adoptive parents than it is for them to deal with untruths that they discover in later stages of their lives.

Stepparents

More than 35 million people in the United States live in stepfamilies. No one should take on the role of stepparent without careful consideration. The potential problems are many. The first months or years of any marriage are periods of adjusting and adapting to each other, but in stepfamilies this new relationship must be developed under the watchful eyes of children

Children in stepfamilies need to be reassured of their parents' love.

who may be very resentful. For example, children may be upset when their mother remarries after the death of their father. After a divorce, the children may compare a stepfather unfavorably with their father, who they love and respect. They may feel they cannot like the stepparent without being disloyal to the parent who is now out of the home. An adolescent daughter who has been living with her father and taking care of the household may resent "another woman" in the house when her father remarries.

These and numerous kinds of problems that arise can make it difficult, but not impossible, to develop warm relationships in stepfamilies. Naturally, it's wise to talk through many of the potential problems with all family members *before* the decision to marry. Even so, it will be necessary for parent, stepparent, and children to be especially considerate of each other. There must be flexibility on the part of everyone and a willingness to adapt to the habits, customs, and idiosyncrasies that each person brings to any relationship. One blended family was able to develop into a more harmonious unit by having Saturday morning talk sessions.

The divorced parent who lives away from the family also plays an important role in a stepfamily. Such parents, who truly love their children, will not do or say anything to hinder their children finding happiness in the stepfamily situation. Children should not be asked to love only one or the other of their parents. Neither should the divorced parent try to stand in the way of a warm relationship between children and their stepparent. Likewise, stepparents should not try to replace their natural counterparts in the lives of the children. Theirs is not a substitute role, but rather a completely new role. It requires a new relationship.

Stepparents often have difficulty in disciplining children if they try to do so before they have developed their relationship and gained the respect of the children. Until that happens, it is probably better for the new marriage partners to reach agreement on rules and limits and let the natural parent enforce them. Openness, honesty, and goodwill are essential. Everyone needs to call forth their best communication skills and use plenty of I-messages (Chapter 4).

Prospective stepparents should be aware of financial obligations, as well. For example, consider a man who is separated from his family, but is paying child support. Can he afford to marry a divorced woman who has children? Are stepparents willing to provide equal educational opportunities for their children by an earlier marriage, their stepchildren, and their children by the second marriage? What about other material things? Will all children have similar clothing and housing? Will one family or the other feel neglected? These may seem like unromantic and embarrassing questions for two people to think about when they are considering marriage. One should recognize, however, that stepfamilies often have enough challenge in adapting to new relationships without trying to meet unexpected financial problems at the same time.

Foster Parents

Children may require foster care for any number of reasons. An abandoned baby may be placed in a foster home until adoption takes place. Abused children may become wards of the court system and assigned to foster care. Financial or medical problems may prohibit parents from temporarily caring for their children, and foster parents provide the essential home. Other parents may be in mental institutions or prisons. There are many other reasons.

Foster-care agencies seek volunteers to give foster care. The agencies provide public funds to compensate those people who take foster children into their homes. Foster parents are encouraged to treat these children as true family members with responsibilities, privileges, and ample love, support, and respect.

Foster parenthood, like adoptive parenthood, gives nonbiological parents an opportunity to share values and richness of life with young people. Unlike adoptive parents, however, foster parents must be psychologically prepared at all times to give up their foster children. For example, Rosa and Alex became foster parents to Tina

Foster parents fulfill a valuable role in the lives of children who are in need of a temporary loving home.

when she was only 10 days old. They took care of her until she was six months. Then another family adopted her. No matter that they had cared for other foster babies, it was still difficult for Rosa and Alex to give up this little girl to her adoptive parents.

There are situations in which the foster parents must give up children they have grown to love, even though they know the children will again be abused and/or neglected when returned to their biological parents. Consider the couple, Michael and Lisa, who are in their late 30s. They have two boys of their own, and they took two foster children, brothers, into their home. Over a period of two years, they nurtured these youngsters and watched them make good adjustments at school and home. Seemingly, the boys had nearly forgotten the neglect, abuse, and eventual abandonment by their natural parents. Then the natural parents suddenly returned to the county and the court allowed them to reclaim custody of their children. Imagine how Michael and Lisa feel. The foster parents can take consolation, however, in knowing that they have shown the brothers a better way of life, and they have shared a system of values that will strongly influence them in all the years ahead.

Life's Work

Alice R. Neve

- ➤**Youth Services Coordinator, Librarian, Saint Paul Library**
- ➤**B.A. and M.A. in Library Sciences**

Alice describes her typical day as, "I spend a major share of each day coordinating and planning all aspects of library services for children in 14 libraries. This includes training other librarians to do storytimes for children of all ages and to assist children with the reference questions they have as a result of school assignments." Alice also plans library programs for children, organizes all aspects of the libraries' Summer Reading Programs, develops booklists, and recommends books in the area of science and technology for other librarians to purchase for their children's book collections.

Alice's day in the office is from 8 to 4:30, Monday through Friday. In addition, periodically she needs to attend evening or early morning meetings with other people in the community who also work with children.

Alice says the skills necessary for success in her profession include, "An ability to manage, organize, and facilitate programs and projects." A knowledge of children's literature for a broad age range is required as well as a knowledge of child development and how this relates to reading and literature for varying ages and stages. She also stresses having, "warmth when relating to children, their parents, and other adults working with youth."

Alice feels her most rewarding job accomplishment is "Introducing the world of books and reading to children who have never known the pleasures of having a library card." She says, "It's exciting to be working in a public library at a time when the needs of children and families are changing so quickly. Creating a reading appetite in very young children starts them on the way to success in school and life. That's what being a children's librarian is all about. It is a profession in which you give a lot, but you receive much more from those you serve."

When asked how her profession will change within the next 10 years, Alice says, "Librarians will have to develop more skills in the areas of technology and telecommunications. Youth and their needs are changing so rapidly that librarians must be carefully attuned to the wealth of what is being published to meet their needs."

In Review

Vocabulary

unequivocally
fetus
obstetrician

Summary

- ✓ Deciding whether to become a parent is one of the most important decisions of anyone's life. Wanting to share treasured values with children is a responsible reason to choose parenthood. Giving in to social or emotional pressures is unwise and unfair to the children.
- ✓ Many of the common beliefs about parenthood are actually myths. They represent irresponsible reasons for becoming parents.
- ✓ Responsible parenthood includes a very large financial commitment.
- ✓ Teenage pregnancy often poses health risks for both mother and infant.
- ✓ People who have the maturity required to give unselfishly of their time and energy are best suited for meeting children's needs.
- ✓ Preparation for parenthood should include the study of child development and parent-child relationships.
- ✓ Every potential parent should understand that having children causes major changes in lifestyles.
- ✓ Unwanted children can be subjected to two of the worst parenting practices: neglect and rejection. When children's basic needs are not met, they cannot develop normally.
- ✓ Adoptive and foster parenthood are two of the more conventional alternatives to biological parenthood.

Questions

1. What does it mean for a child to be *wanted unequivocally?* Why is that important to a child?

2. Discuss how considerations mentioned in this chapter apply to:

a) a couple considering adoption.

b) a single woman trying to decide whether to marry a widower who has two small children.

c) a couple volunteering to be foster parents.

d) a couple deciding whether to have a second child.

3. Try to think of someone you know who may now be suffering the consequences of having believed one of the myths about parenthood. Without

using names, describe that person's situation and how you think it might have been changed for the better.

4. Discuss the problems that could cause a higher percentage of problems for teenage mothers and mothers over 35.

5. What are the areas of education for children that are most relevant to family life? If you are a parent who wants to raise your children so they become competent adults, marriage partners, and parents, what courses, training, and skills would you want them to be taught both in school and at home?

Activities

1. A newspaper reported the fatal scalding of a four-month-old boy in the apartment where he lived with his 20-year-old mother and his three siblings, ages three, two, and one year. The mother left the children alone while she went across the street to visit a friend. One of the children evidently opened the shut-off valve on a steam pipe sticking out of the floor that was not connected to the radiator. The three older children may have been saved by the fact that neighbors called the fire department when they saw steam escaping from a window. For the time being, the children were turned over to an agency for children and family services. How might this scenario have changed if some of the ideas found in this chapter had been implemented?

2. In the preceding news story, who played responsible parenting roles (Chapter 1)? Who, besides the mother, may have been irresponsible?

3. Make a list of the activities and opportunities that you probably would miss if you became a teenaged parent. How would these changes affect the achievement of your goals for the future?

4. Mr. and Mrs. Baker have three children whose ages are 6, 4, and 2. Use the estimate that has been included in the chapter to figure out the cost of raising the Baker children. Assume each child will attend the state university and that tuition at that time will be $10,000 per year.

5. If you worked for a foster care agency, what are three of the questions you would ask persons who volunteer to take foster children into their homes?

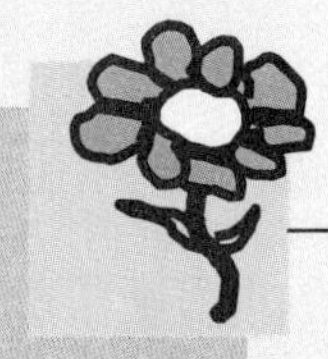

Unit 2
Becoming Parents

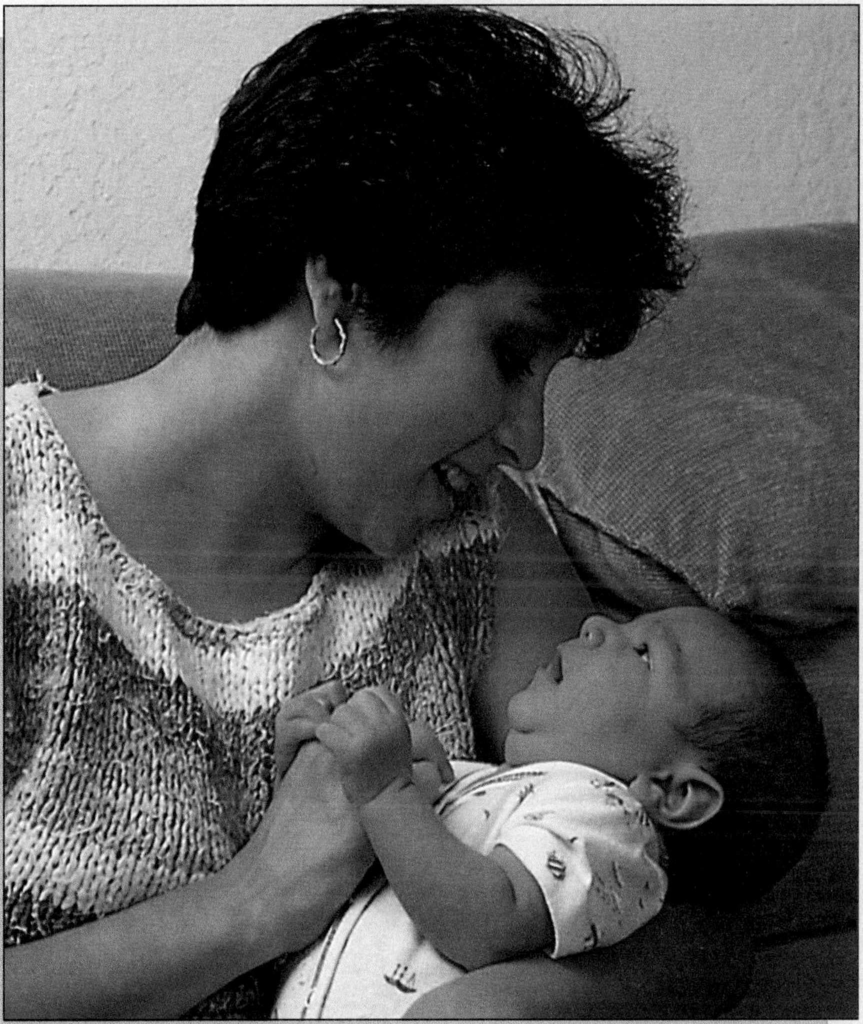

Chapter 6 Prenatal Development

This chapter will help you:

- describe prenatal development during each trimester
- discuss different birth defects and hereditary diseases
- explain how genetic counseling can alert parents to potential problems
- describe the problem of Rh factor incompatibility and how it can be treated
- recognize the role of research in developing alternative birth techniques

World of the Unborn Child

An unborn child is surrounded by its own protective world, a world that meets its basic needs and ultimately produces a unique individual. This new individual will have a particular pattern of growth and development determined jointly by heredity and environment. Many factors will contribute to the uniqueness of the individual. Among these are the traits inherited from the parents, the conditions in the uterus, the kind of home into which the child is born and raised, the manner in which his or her needs are met, and the ideas, ideals, attitudes, and values of the people in the child's life.

We may know more about the moon than we know about the world of the unborn. However, medical science is progressing in its investigation of the world of the unborn where every person has been and where every person was more vulnerable than he or she will ever be again.

Conception

At birth, a female baby's two **ovaries** (reproductive organs) contain approximately a half million potential eggs, or **ova.** Each egg, or ovum, is far smaller than the head of a pin. Less than 500 of these eggs will mature in an average lifetime. During the female's reproductive years, an egg is released

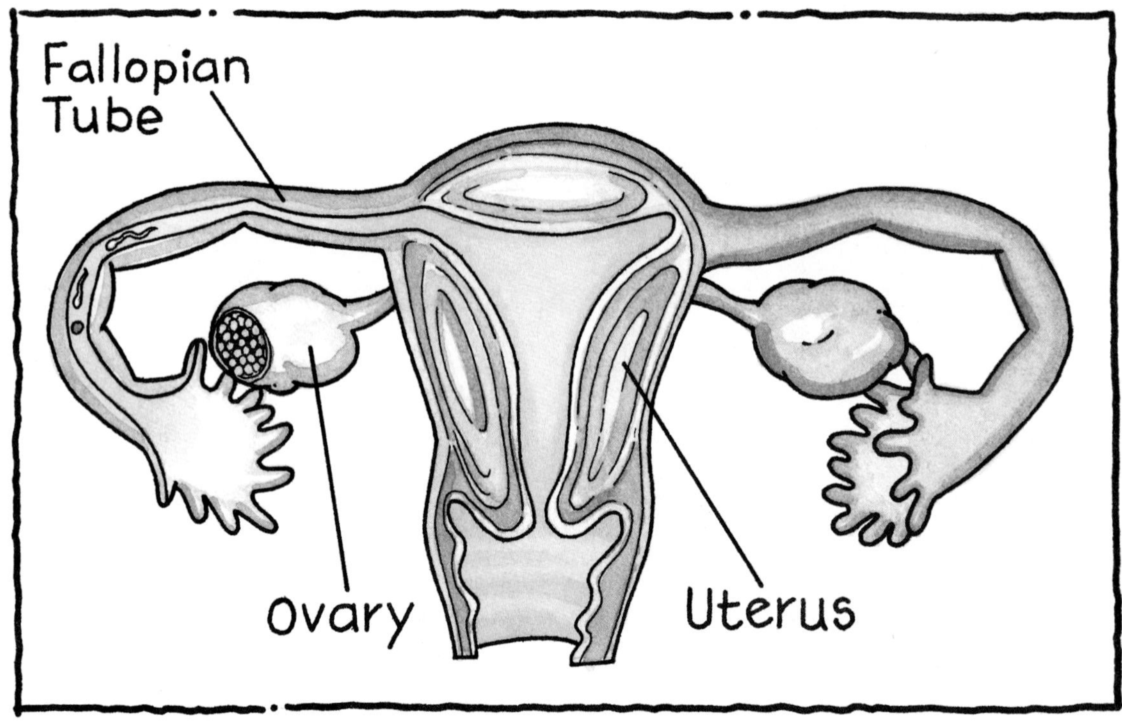

At conception, a sperm cell joins with an egg. The fertilized egg will then travel down the fallopian tube to the uterus where it attaches to the wall.

each month from an ovary and travels down the fallopian tube to the **uterus** (womb). It is believed that the ovaries take turns releasing an egg each month. The process of releasing an egg from an ovary is called **ovulation.** If unfertilized, the egg decomposes in the uterus and washes out with the menstrual flow.

For conception to occur, the egg must be fertilized in the fallopian tube by a single **sperm,** the male parent's reproductive cell. Sperm resemble tadpoles in shape with round heads and long whiplike tails. They are so small that even 100,000 of them together could barely be seen as a dot. When the sperm penetrates the clear outer membrane of the egg, and its nucleus joins the nucleus of the egg, conception is achieved. The newly formed cell is called a **zygote.** It will take about 280 days or 9 1/3 months before the baby is fully developed.

Early Development

During the early phase after conception, the woman herself is unaware of the vital processes occurring within her. Within three or four days, the fertilized egg has divided and redivided into a cluster of 36 to 40 cells that moves down the fallopian tube into the uterus. Within 10 days after conception, the cluster has grown to 150 or more cells and the mass has attached itself to the spongy wall of the uterus. The lining of the uterus nourishes the egg, so the woman does not menstruate. She will not have another menstrual period until after the baby's birth. A pregnancy test performed by a doctor and a medical laboratory will confirm the pregnancy.

The small mass of cells changes into a small hollow organ. From this tiny mass of cells are formed the embryo and some temporary structures that feed and protect the developing organism. The developing baby is called an **embryo** from two weeks after fertilization to the eighth week after conception. Structures that develop include:

- the **placenta,** which will nourish the baby through the **umbilical cord.**
- the balloonlike sac, called the **water sac,** filled with amniotic fluid in which the baby floats.

The development of the embryo is importantly influenced by the prenatal environment, particularly the placenta that determines which materials will pass into the embryo and which will be rejected. Untreated illness or disease, radiation, or the use of alcohol, drugs, or tobacco could harm the baby for life. The mother must provide a safe and healthy environment.

Three weeks after conception, a blood vessel enlarges and becomes the baby's future heart. The nervous system then begins to organize a threadlike spinal cord. As soon as the heart and nervous system have been started, a rudimentary digestive tract begins to develop.

Twenty-five days after the egg has been fertilized by the sperm, the embryo measures about 1/10 inch (2.6 millimeters) in length and is developing at a rapid rate. The embryo does not yet look much like a human being, although it has a rudimentary heart

A Matter of Fact

Do you know anyone who is a twin? Normally, women give birth to one baby. However, about one out of every 88 births results in twins. Twins can form in two different ways. One way is when the fertilized egg splits in half and each half develops into an embryo. Because the twins start from one egg and one sperm, they are *identical twins.* They receive the same chromosomes from their parents. They look alike and are the same sex.

Sometimes the woman's body releases two eggs at the same time. When these are fertilized by two separate sperm, the result is *fraternal twins.* These twins are no more alike than brothers and sisters born at different times. They may not even be the same sex. Even rarer are multiple births of three or more babies. These births may be identical or fraternal. Sometimes they result because the woman was taking fertility drugs in order to conceive. Babies in such large births are usually low in birth weight, premature, and do not have a good chance of surviving.

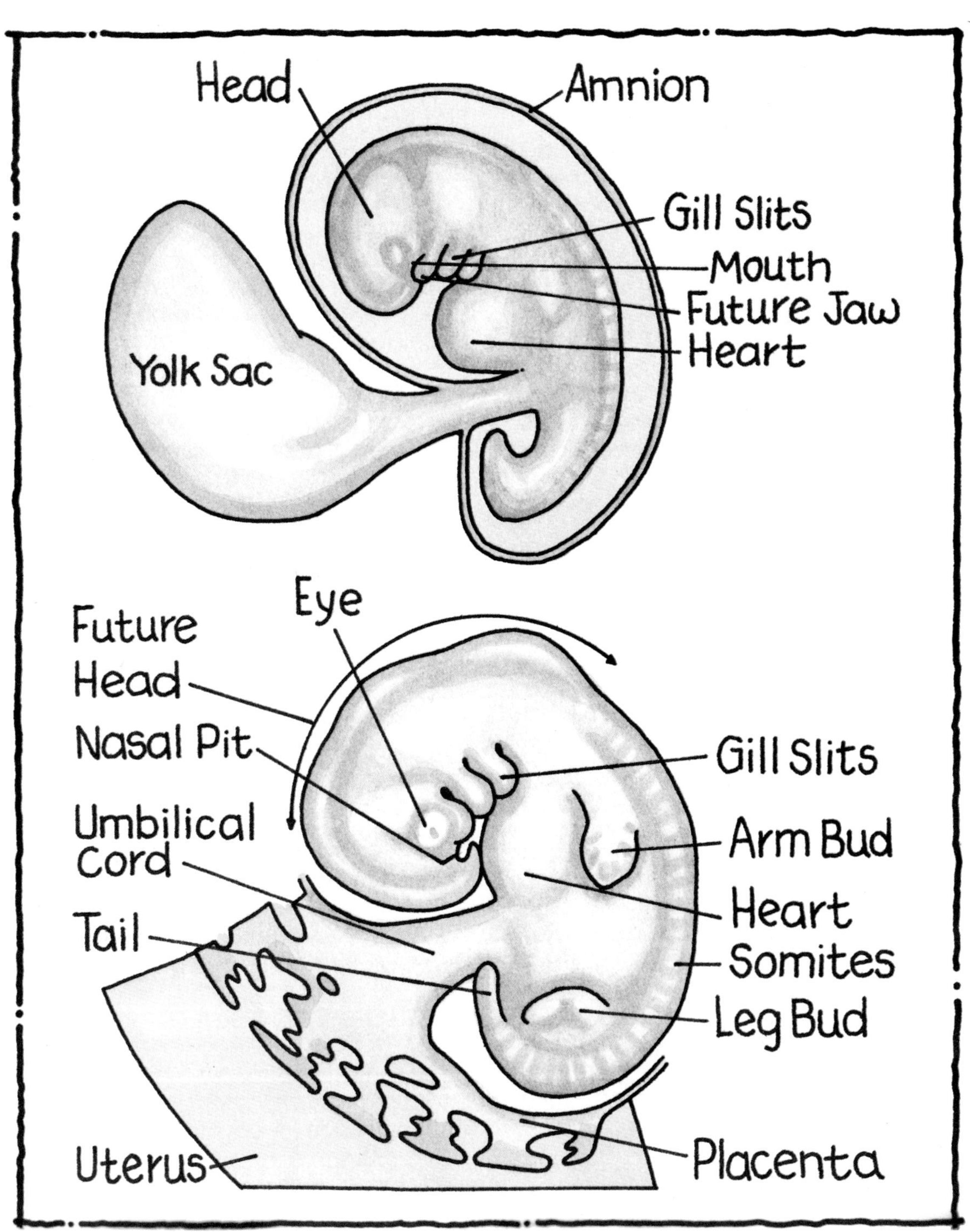
Head
Amnion
Gill Slits
Mouth
Future Jaw
Heart
Yolk Sac
Eye
Future
Head
Nasal Pit
Umbilical
Cord
Tail
Gill Slits
Arm Bud
Heart
Somites
Leg Bud
Uterus
Placenta

beating within it, blood flowing through its vessels, and a brain taking form. It lacks a face and neck so that its heart lies close to its brain. It has no arms and legs. Its belly side, instead of being covered with a body wall, lies flat out over the large yolk sac, which protrudes from the region between the heart and tail. The lungs are beginning to take form. The liver is forming just behind the heart. Almost one-third of the entire embryo is the future head.

In the second month the embryo increases in size to about 1 1/2 inches (3.8 centimeters). Bones and muscles begin to round out contours of the body. A neck develops. Facial features also begin to develop. The forehead becomes prominent, reflecting the precocious development of the brain in comparison to that of the rest of the body. Sex organs begin to form. Limb "buds" elongate. Muscles and cartilage develop. However, the developing face and neck are the main features which give the two-month-old embryo its human appearance.

At the end of the second month, the lower jaw is still small, and the chin is poorly defined. Seen in profile the embryo looks almost chinless. The nose is broad and flat with the nostrils opening forward rather than downward. The eyes are far apart. After the baby is born, it will take several years for the face to overcome the early dominance of the bulging forehead to reach adult facial proportions.

The limbs also pass through a series of changes during the second month. At the beginning of the month, the limb buds are small round stubs that project from the sides of the body. These buds elongate and the free end

Note the growth of this embryo, including the development of the hands.

of the limb becomes flattened into a paddlelike ridge which forms the fingers and toes. Soon five parallel ridges separated by shallow grooves appear within each plate. The grooves gradually deepen giving five distinct fingers or toes in the appropriate limbs. The thumb and big toe become widely separated from the other fingers and toes early in their development. At the same time, constrictions form within each limb to mark off the elbow and wrist or the knee and ankle. At this time, the elbow and knee bend outward away from the sides of the body and the palms and soles are turned inward, facing the body. It is not until the fourth month of development that the arms and legs rotate to their final positions, where elbows bend backward, knees bend forward, and soles face downward away from the body.

It is important for the pregnant woman to follow sound nutrition guidelines.

Fetal Development

The third month marks the beginning of the **fetal period.** The unborn baby is now called a fetus. Sexual differentiation continues with the male sex organs showing more rapid development than the female organs, which remain dormant for a short period. Buds for all 20 temporary teeth are formed. The vocal cords appear. The digestive system begins to show activity with the stomach cells beginning to secrete fluid. The liver begins to pour bile into the intestines. Kidneys begin functioning, with urine gradually seeping into the amniotic fluid. By the end of the third month, spontaneous movements of arms, legs, shoulders, and fingers are possible.

In the fourth month, development of the lower part of the body accelerates so that the proportion of the head size decreases from one-half to one-fourth of the body size. The back straightens and the hands and feet are well-formed. Because the skin is thin, it appears dark red, owing to the flowing of the blood. The skin is wrinkled due to the absence of underlying fat. The fingers can open and close in a grasp. Reflexes become more active as muscles continue to mature. The fetus begins to stir and thrust out its arms and legs. The mother can feel these movements. The fetus is 8 to 10 inches (20.3 to 25.4 centimeters) long.

In the fifth month, structures in the skin begin to attain final form. Sweat and sebaceous glands are formed and begin to function. Hair appears on the skin and nails appear on fingers and toes. The fetus is now lean and wrinkled. It is about 12 inches (30 centimeters) long and weighs approximately 1 pound (0.45 kilogram). The doctor will be able to hear the heartbeat. Fetal movement is clearly felt by the mother.

The eyelids, which have been fused shut since the third month, open in the sixth month. Taste buds appear on the tongue and in the mouth. Taste buds are more abundant at this stage than they are in either the infant or the adult.

From the seventh month on, the fetus is capable of independent life. Generally, the seventh-month fetus is about 16 inches (40 centimeters) long and weighs 3 pounds (1.4 kilograms). If born, it will be able to cry, breathe, and swallow. In order to survive, it will need an **incubator,** a highly sheltered

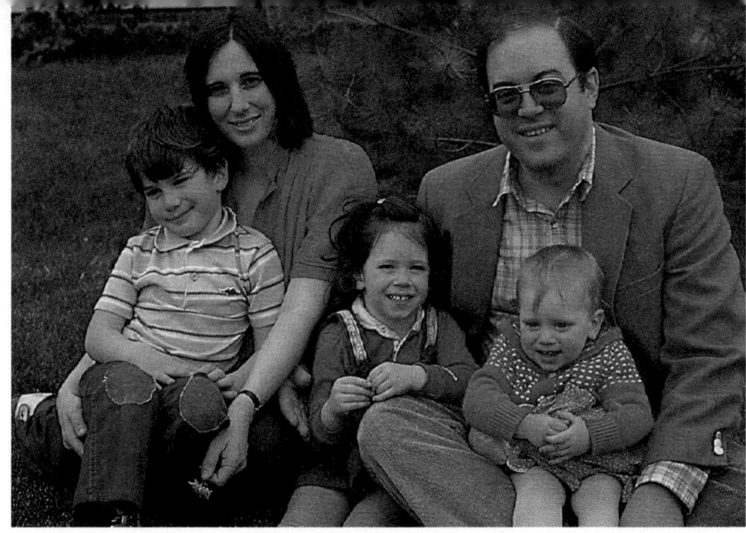

What family similarities can you distinguish?

environment with a controlled temperature, since it is very sensitive to infections.

During the eighth and ninth months, the finishing touches are being put on the various organs and functional capacities. Fat is formed rapidly over the entire body. This smoothes out wrinkled skin and rounds out the body shape. The skin becomes thicker, so at birth the pigmentation is usually slight in all races. Activity can be extensive, so the mother may feel a lot of movement. The fetus can change its position in the now crowded uterus. The fetal organs increase their activity, and the fetal heart rate is quite rapid. The fetus is ready for birth.

Genetic Material

Let's backtrack for a moment and take a closer look at how each person's individual characteristics are determined. The ovum and the sperm each contain the genetic material called **chromosomes.** This is the genetic master plan that determines how each individual looks. The zygote receives 23 chromosomes from each parent. Two of the 46 chromosomes determine whether the baby will be a boy or a girl. Girls have XX pairs of chromosomes, while boys have XY pairs. Each chromosome contains thousands of genes, which determine heredity. For instance, the shape of your face, eye color, and hair color are all determined by genes. This genetic information is stored in the structure of deoxyribonucleic acid (DNA). The atomic arrangements of the helical (spiral) molecules of DNA specify all of our hereditary characteristics. It is the nearly infinite number of possible combinations of genes that makes every person unique, both in body and in mind, even without the important environmental influences that come later.

Sometimes this part of the reproductive process does not work perfectly. Abnormal chromosomal behavior in either the ovum or the sperm can result in a baby being born with fewer or more than 46 chromosomes. One such disorder is Down's syndrome, in which the child has 47 chromosomes. One out of 600 infants is born with this disorder. Certain physical features are characteristic for Down's syndrome children. These include short stature, broad skull, slanting eyes, and stubby fingers. Also typical are motor and

This girl has Down's syndrome, but her family encourages her to reach her full potential..

mental retardation. There are children born with other types of disorders resulting from chromosomal abnormalities. For many of the types of chromosomal disorders that can exist in an embryo, the pregnancy ends in a **miscarriage.** A miscarriage is the end of pregnancy due to natural causes before the fetus is mature enough to survive outside the uterus.

Genetic Counseling

Genetic counseling is scientific advice, based on medical studies and family histories, concerning heredity and in particular, the risks of hereditary abnormalities or **birth defects.** Genetic counselors today often are able to tell prospective parents exactly what the chances are that a certain inherited defect or disorder will appear in their children. Prospective parents who feel their family histories point out a need may seek genetic counseling.

Despite the fact that at least 93 percent of all babies are normal at birth, there are more than a quarter of a million children born in the United States each year with abnormalities due to faulty prenatal development or inherited defects. Some of the inherited diseases that strike many children include the following.

- One of the most common genetic (inherited) diseases is diabetes. Some four million Americans have diabetes. It is believed that one person in four carries the genetic trait.
- Cystic fibrosis is another inherited disease present in the individual from birth. It strikes some 3,500 infants (about 1 in 1000) each year. The disease is often diagnosed at birth, but sometimes it is not detected until later in infancy or childhood. Cystic fibrosis causes a variety of physical abnormalities. Most serious of those is a lung disease

that is usually fatal in early childhood.

- Sickle-cell anemia is a serious blood disorder that causes production of abnormal red blood cells. Infants with sickle-cell anemia are at risk of overwhelming infection and sudden death in the first few years of life. It afflicts some 50,000 infants in the U.S. alone. A treatment that usually leads to a cure has been found.
- Tay-Sachs disease causes a fatty substance to accumulate in the nerve cells of the affected child. The formation of normal cells is impaired, which results in seizures, blindness, loss of coordination, and eventual death.
- Glaucoma, an inherited eye disease which usually does not become apparent until the third decade of life, is a major cause of blindness among people in the United States.
- Phenylketonuria (PKU) affects the body's ability to process and use a specific amino acid. If diagnosed soon enough, it can be treated. If untreated or treated too late, PKU results in severe mental retardation.

One factor in the growth of genetic counseling is the fact that more has been learned about human genetics in recent years than was known previously. Geneticists have estimated that each of us carries an average of five to 10 lethal or seriously abnormal genes among thousands of normal ones. Sometimes abnormal genes are passed to offspring by the mother, sometimes by the father, and sometimes by both. A person may possess such a gene without suffering any ill effects and thus be a carrier. These genes, in certain combinations and under certain conditions, may cause faulty development of the fetus.

A family history is the genetic counselor's basic tool. By investigating as many generations as possible, he or she gains a perspective on the number of normal relatives and ancestors, as well as a perspective on birth defects. If adequate information is not readily available, he or she may search old records—birth, marriage, and death certificates as well as information in the archives of bureaus of vital statistics, church records, and even graveyards. Sometimes a search will provide a hidden clue such as an unsuspected marriage of cousins or other close relatives. Experts estimate the extra risk of defective offspring from cousin marriages to be between one and a half to two times greater than that between nonrelatives. This risk is due to the probability that children will receive a double dose of some detrimental gene each parent carries from a common ancestor.

Some geneticists foresee the day when there may be mandatory premarital tests to determine whether prospective newlyweds are likely to have children with serious defects. Few geneticists believe that unfavorable odds should be reason to forbid marriage, but they do cite advantages in alerting couples to potential problems.

In addition to the family history, physicians may perform tests to determine "carrier status" of the parents, brothers and sisters, and perhaps other relatives. Or, the physician may

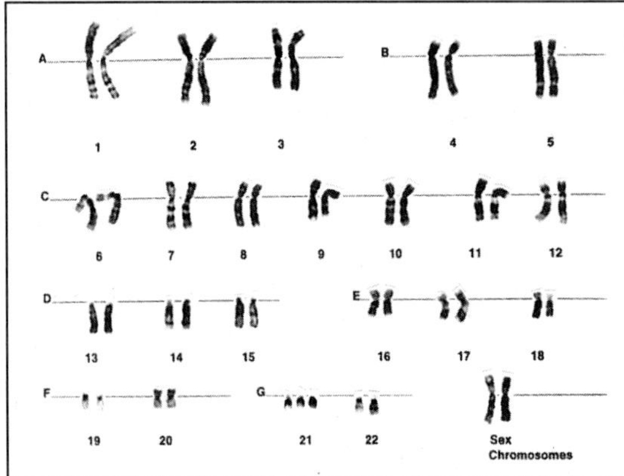

This karyotype shows the chromosomal abnormality of three chromosomes in the 21st set.

do "chromosome analysis" of cells from any or all of them. Chromosome analysis involves isolating and photographing the chromosomes in a single cell. From a picture enlarged thousands of times, each individual chromosome is cut apart, matched in pairs and grouped in a specific order on a numbered chart called a karyotype, as seen in the photo on this page. From this, the geneticist can generally determine whether or not the defect is due to chromosomal abnormality and, in some cases, what caused the aberration. The karyotype shown is that of a girl, because there are two X chromosomes and no Y chromosomes. The girl has Down's syndrome because of the three chromosomes in the 21st set.

Amniocentesis is a test a doctor may perform. It involves placing a needle through the mother's abdomen and withdrawing fluid from the amniotic sac. By checking the fluid, the doctor can identify certain problems that affect the baby's health including Down's syndrome.

Ultrasonography is another test. An instrument is passed over the woman's abdomen. High frequency acoustic pulses are aimed at the fetus. "Backscattering" of the pulses is then detected at the skin surface of the mother. Bones and tissue reflect differently, and depths are indicated by the times required for return of these echoes. The information can, therefore, produce an image. The technique has been extremely useful for the accurate determination of the age of a fetus, for detection of abnormalities, and for research on the stages of normal fetal development.

Rh factor

One out of every 150 to 200 infants suffers from Rh factor incompatibility. The Rh factor is an inherited substance most people have. However, some 15% of the population in the United States has red blood cells that are Rh negative, that is, they do not contain the Rh factor. If a woman is Rh negative and her husband is Rh positive, some of the children may have Rh positive blood. It is the Rh positive baby of the Rh negative mother who is adversely affected. During the woman's first pregnancy, some Rh positive cells may leak into her bloodstream and stimulate production of antibodies against the baby's Rh positive blood. (Antibodies protect the body from germs and disease.) Usually, there is no problem in the first pregnancy. In later pregnancies, though, the mother's antibodies may cause destruction of the fetus' Rh positive red blood cells. Anemia, severe brain damage, or death of the fetus or newborn baby can result.

Today, there are medical procedures

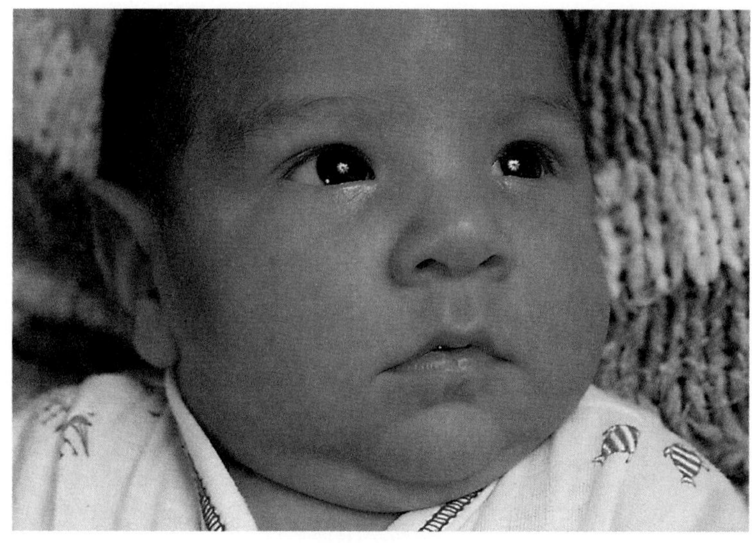

Medical procedures prevent Rh problems and ensure the health of newborns.

that can prevent such problems. An exchange of Rh negative blood for the ravaged Rh positive blood of either the fetus or the newborn infant is possible. Also, there is a vaccine for the mother that prevents her from generating these destructive antibodies. It is important, however, for prospective parents to be aware of this possible complication. It can occur only if the mother is Rh negative, the father is Rh positive, and the fetus is Rh positive. Blood tests of the prospective parents can alert them to this situation.

Achieving Pregnancy by Various Means

Quite often, when a couple has considered all the important questions and decided to become parents, they are frustrated in their attempts to achieve pregnancy. Many years ago, gossips might try to guess whose "fault" it was when a couple remained childless. When **infertility** (the inability to conceive) occurs, it is nobody's "fault," any more than it is your "fault" if you get hives when you eat tomatoes.

The first and second most common causes of infertility in women are ovaries that fail to produce viable ova and fallopian tubes that are blocked. A man may be impotent, he may produce no sperm, or he may produce immature sperm.

Some of these problems can be solved by counseling and/or medical procedures in fertility clinics. Others cannot. In addition to problems such as these, some couples are advised against pregnancy because of genetic abnormalities on the part of one or both partners. All of these barriers to traditional biological parenthood have led researchers to develop alternate reproductive techniques. Some of these are summarized here:

Artificial insemination by donor. A doctor collects sperm from an anonymous donor and artificially inseminates the wife of a man who does not produce viable sperm or who has a transferable genetic defect.

In-vitro fertilization. When the wife's fallopian tubes are blocked, a doctor extracts an ovum from her and impregnates it with a sperm from the husband. The union of ovum and sperm is carried out in a petri dish in the laboratory. The embryo is allowed to grow for two to three days in an incubator. It is then implanted in the wife's uterus.

In-vitro fertilization with one or two donors. The same procedure is used as in in-vitro fertilization. The difference is that the ovum comes from a donor, or the sperm comes from a donor, or both sperm and ovum come from donors.

Embryo transfer. Sperm from the husband is used to artificially inseminate a woman other than his wife. After several days, the embryo is transferred to his wife's uterus.

Surrogate motherhood. If the wife and husband produce viable ova and sperm, but the wife is unable to carry a fetus to term, their embryo can be transferred to the uterus of a volunteer substitute known as a **surrogate mother.** If the wife can neither provide the ovum nor bear the child, the surrogate can be artificially inseminated with the husband's sperm. Finally, if both husband and wife are infertile, one can envision their using a surrogate father as well as a surrogate mother. Thus, they could become parents without providing the ovum, the sperm, or the environment for gestation. In effect, the child would not be different from an adopted child, except that the reproductive process was "engineered" by the adoptive couple.

All of the alternative means of achieving pregnancy have raised serious legal and moral questions. While these have not been resolved, still others loom on the horizon. With the knowledge of genetics and reproduction mushrooming, future generations may need to decide the morality and legality of cloning and the genetic engineering of human babies.

Life's Work

Marjorie Hogan, M.D.

- ➤Staff Pediatrician, Minneapolis Children's Medical Center
- ➤M.D. from Stanford Medical School. Residency in pediatrics at University of Minnesota

Marjorie is involved with the interagency child abuse center at the Minneapolis Children's Medical Center (MCMC). She is part of a multidisciplinary team that evaluates the situation and condition of abused children and recommends what follow-up steps and therapy should be undertaken. Mar jorie also is working on a syndicated television project for parents and caregivers that covers all aspects of child health and well-being.

Marjorie works most of her hours at home with her four young children. She works approximately 10 hours per week at MCMC with the abuse project. The hours required for the video project are variable.

Marjorie says the skills necessary for success in her profession include, "A good medical education background, the ability to work comfortably and sensitively with children and families, a sense of humor, and a strong sense of advocacy for children and the willingness to act on this." She also feels it is important to have "respect for and ability to work with other professionals and people who work with children." Marjorie feels that her most rewarding job-related accomplishment is setting up a system for dealing more effectively with high-risk children and families.

In addition to a strong medical background, Marjorie recommends that students considering going into pediatrics, "Learn about all aspects of children's lives—families, schools, growth and development, nutrition, friendships, etc. Children are complex." In addition, she says. "Have fun. Enjoy."

When asked how her profession will change over the next 10 years, Mar jorie says, "There will be more emphasis on prevention and public health worldwide. This is where most change can be made for the greatest good."

In Review

Vocabulary

ovaries
ova
uterus
ovulation
sperm
zygote
embryo
placenta
umbilical cord
water sac
fetal period
incubator
chromosomes
genetic counseling
birth defects
surrogate mother
artificial insemination
in-vitro fertilization
embryo transfer

Summary

- ✓ Every fetus has a unique set of genes and prenatal environment.
- ✓ Conception occurs when an ovum from one of the female's ovaries combines with a sperm from the male to form a new cell called a zygote.
- ✓ The embryo (and later, the fetus) receives its nourishment through the umbilical cord. The placenta determines which materials are allowed to enter the umbilical cord.
- ✓ Heredity is determined by the thousands of genes contained in each chromosome. Normally, the zygote receives 23 chromosomes from each parent. The genetic information is stored in the structure of DNA molecules.
- ✓ Chromosomal abnormalities often result in miscarriage, but certain disorders in full-term babies can be attributed to extra or missing chromosomes.
- ✓ Genetic counseling provides the type of scientific advice that can help a couple make an informed decision as to the advisability of their becoming biological parents.
- ✓ Infertile couples can now become parents by several different medically assisted procedures, some of which are raising serious legal and moral questions.

Questions

1. What is a trimester? Why is it relevant in a discussion of pregnancy?

2. When should a pregnant woman begin to gain weight? About when will she first feel the fetus move?

3. Roughly how much weight does a fetus gain in the last three months?

4. Why is it important that babies have normal birth weights?

5. How does a woman first recognize her pregnant condition? Why should she see an obstetrician very early in her pregnancy?

6. Some couples seek genetic counseling before pregnancy has been initiated and others seek it after. Do you feel there are reasons to prefer one over the other? What are your reasons?

Activities

1. A husband and his wife contracted with a surrogate mother to be impregnated with the sperm of the husband. In 1983, the surrogate mother bore a child with birth defects. Court suits and countersuits resulted when the prospective parents would not accept the child or pay the surrogate mother the fee she expected. Blood tests showed that the child could not have been related to the husband. How would you rule on the suits if you were the judge? Why? If the blood tests did not rule out a relationship, how would you rule? Why?

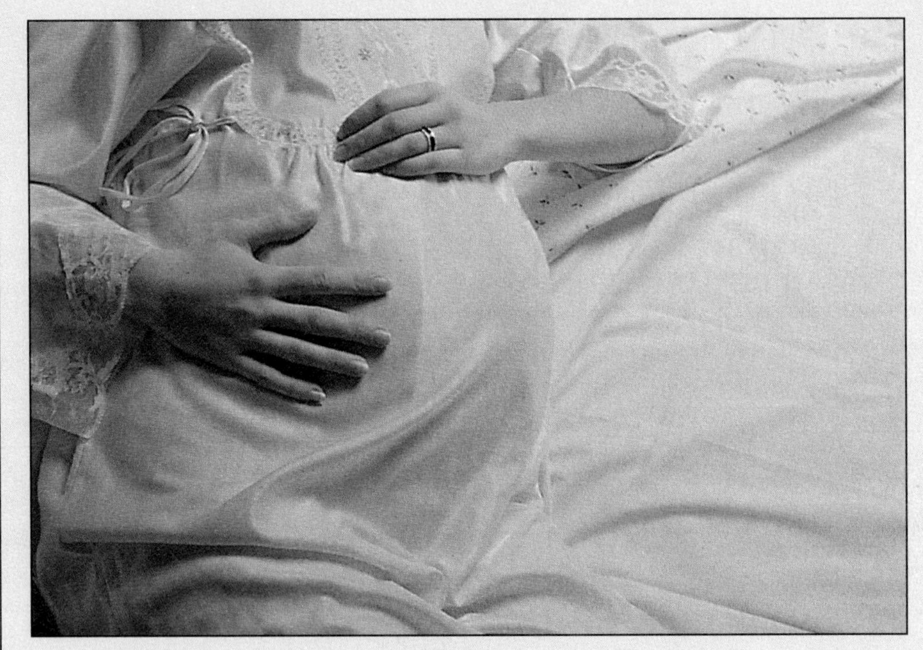

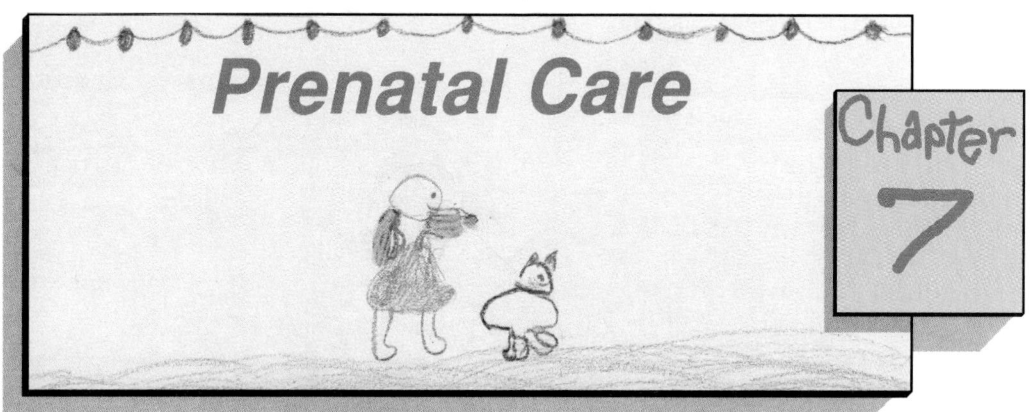

This chapter will help you:

- understand that the unborn baby's health is completely dependent on its mother
- identify eating habits the mother should follow to fulfill her and the baby's nutritional needs
- recognize the danger of drugs on the unborn baby
- explain the effects of alcohol on the fetus
- discuss different illnesses and their effect on pregnancy
- identify discomforts of pregnancy and how they can be relieved
- describe bonding

Fetal-Maternal Body Relationships

The developing fetus lives in the sequestered environment of the uterus. The fetus has exclusive property rights to the womb, except, of course, in the case of a multiple birth. The diagram on the next page shows the relationship of the fetal body to that of the maternal body.

Prenatal Care

Babies are helpless to defend themselves against the heredity offered by chromosomally damaged parents or against the environment created and provided by the prenatal mother. Prospective parents need to be responsible for the welfare of children in these as well as all other matters. Anyone not prepared to give a baby the best possible chance for normal development should make the decision to not have children.

Medical Care

Usually the first indication of pregnancy comes about two weeks after conception when menstruation does not occur. The woman should see a gynecologist/obstetrician at this time. The doctor can confirm the pregnancy and order numerous tests to safeguard the health of the mother and baby.

Also, at this time, the doctor can evaluate the mother's present health status and advise her on nutrition and health practices she should follow. There should be regularly scheduled medical examinations through the pregnancy.

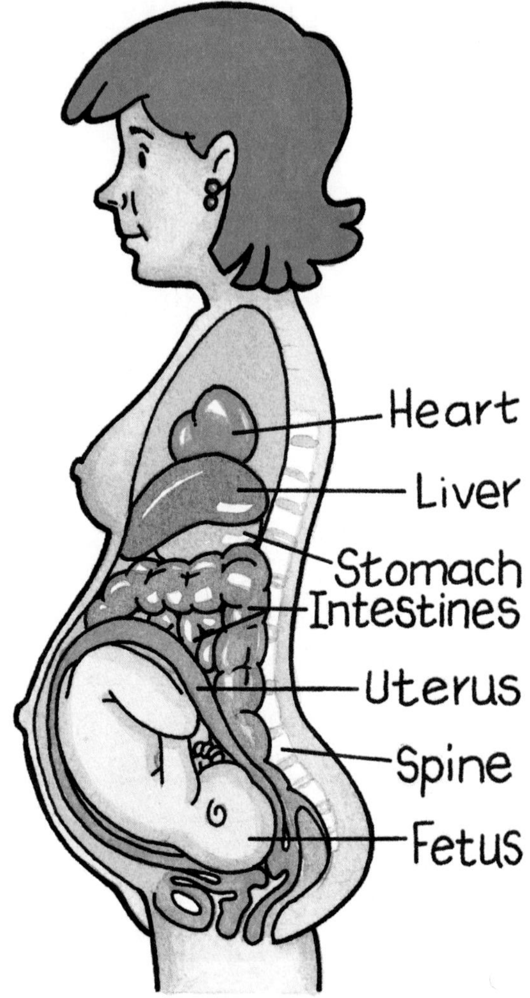

Nutrition

One very important factor that affects the fetal-maternal body relationship is the mother's nutritional habits. A fetus depends totally on the mother for the supply of the nutrients it needs for normal physical and mental development. The mother should know, therefore, what she must eat to satisfy the needs of her own body and those of the developing fetus. Dietary deficiencies can contribute to premature and abnormal births. **Stillbirth,** (the birth of a dead fetus), death within the first few days of life, birth defects, small size, and illness during infancy also may result.

Nutrition, however, needs to be considered long before pregnancy. It is important for girls to acquire proper eating habits early in life for their own good health and that of their future children. The adolescent's diet is perhaps most crucial in this respect. A woman who starts her pregnancy with a good nutritional condition can provide the best environment for her baby. A poor diet may damage either the baby, the mother, or both. For example, if there are dietary shortages of iron, ascorbic acid, and vitamin B_{12}, the baby will take these nutrients at the expense of the mother. If there are shortages of iodine and vitamins A and E, however, the mother will get them before the baby does.

If the mother actually "eats for two," she will gain much more weight than she should. If she eats only what she

Daily Nutrition Guide	
Food Group	**Servings Needed Per Day**
Milk	
1st trimester (adult)	3 or more
1st trimester (teenager)	4 or more
2nd and 3rd trimester (adult)	4 or more
2nd and 3rd trimester (teenager)	5 or more
Meat or Meat Equivalent	3 or more
Breads and Cereals	4 or more
Fruits and Vegetables	4 or more total
Rich in vitamin C	1 to 2
Rich in folic acid	1 to 2
General	1 to 2
Fats and Oils	1 to 2 tablespoons as needed for calories
Sugars and Sweets	As needed for calories

ate before pregnancy, she will not gain enough. Experts agree that only about 300 additional calories per day are required. It is essential that the food constituting those 300 calories and all the other calories in the diet be chosen wisely.

A pregnant woman should increase her consumption of protein to three or more servings of protein foods each day. (Daily needs for adults are two servings.) Protein foods include meat, fish, eggs, poultry, beans, cheese, peanut butter, etc. A pregnant woman following a vegetarian diet needs to consult with her physician in order to get adequate amounts of all essential proteins. She needs to be especially careful to adjust her diet.

The embryo and fetus grow by the division of cells. Essential to that process is a supply of folic acid, which can be found in leafy green vegetables, liver, and legumes such as peas and beans. At least four servings of fruits and vegetables each day will provide the necessary folic acid and the essential vitamin C, as well.

Proper diet can provide virtually all the vitamins a pregnant woman and fetus need. Vitamin A is in milk, butter, and both dark green and yellow vegetables. Vitamin D is in fortified milk, cheese, and yogurt. Three or more servings per day of milk or other dairy products such as yogurt and cottage cheese can supply these needed vitamins. Dairy products also supply calcium, the mineral that is essential for development of bones in the fetus. Teenagers have higher requirements for the nutrients provided by the milk group. See the chart on this page for details.

In addition to protein, fruits-vegetables, and milk, a pregnant woman needs four or more servings per day of grain products, such as *whole-grain* breads, pasta, rice, oatmeal, cornbread, grits, etc. Constipation is

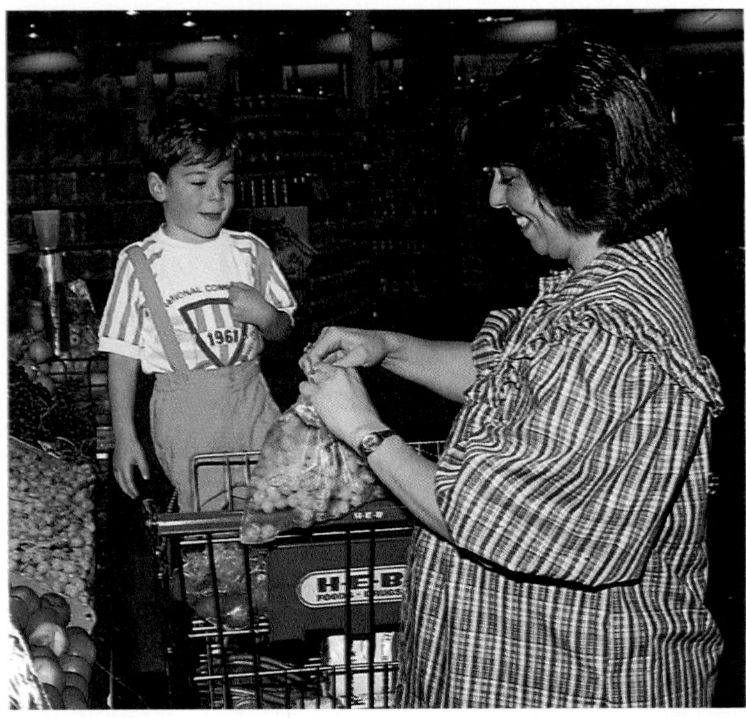

Pregnant women need to eat four servings a day of fruits and vegetables in order to get an adequate supply of folic acid and vitamin C.

common during pregnancy, and the undigested fiber of whole-grain breads and cereals can help alleviate this problem. Whole grains are also a source of vitamin B.

If the pregnant woman follows recommended balanced eating guidelines, she will have all of the essential minerals, with the possible exception of iron. Increased amounts of iron are needed during pregnancy to avoid anemia. Iron supplements are usually recommended in addition to iron-rich foods like leafy vegetables, dried fruits, lean meat, and liver. The fetus will take iron from the mother even if her own needs for iron are not met.

A woman should not take any dietary supplements such as minerals or vitamins unless they are prescribed by her doctor. In addition, women should stay away from the multitude of weight-loss schemes during pregnancy, and a large majority of the diets should be avoided at all times. Most fad diets do not supply the nutrients the human body needs, whether pregnant or not.

Weight Control

Pregnancy for mothers of all ages should result in a weight gain somewhere in the range of 22 to 35 pounds. Of course, if the woman is underweight when pregnancy begins, then she should gain more. On the other hand, if she is overweight initially, it is important that she not try to lose weight during her pregnancy. If the mother deprives herself of nutrients, she deprives the fetus, as well.

In the first trimester, there should be relatively little change in weight. As we have seen, the fetus weighs an ounce or less at this stage. Near the end of this period, however, and throughout the second trimester, there is significant development of the mother's support systems. The uterus grows to make room for the fetus, which becomes many times larger. The placenta grows to keep up with the expanding nutritional and waste disposal needs of the fetus. The mother's volume of blood increases, and she begins to store fat that will be utilized later when she begins to nurse her baby. These essential functions will not be realized until the mother gains the proper weight. In the third trimester, most of the weight gain is that of the fetus.

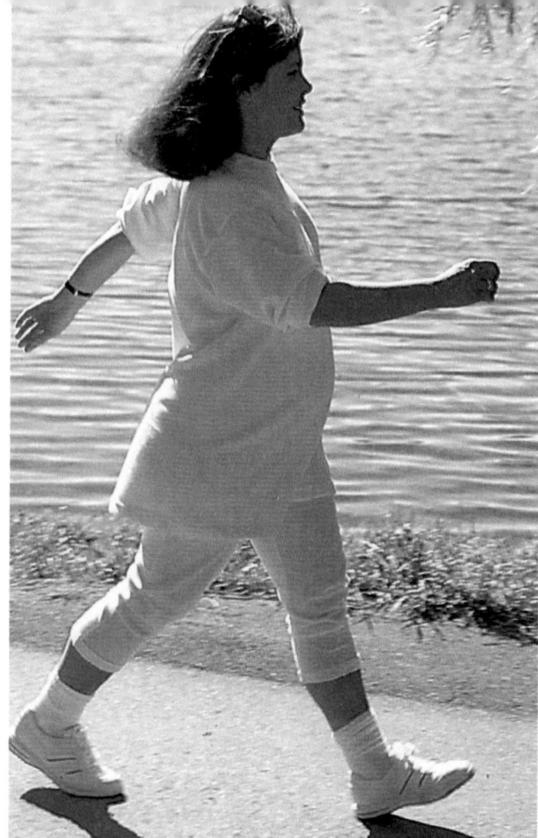

Walking is an excellent exercise for keeping a pregnant woman in shape.

Exercise

Many women today are very conscious of weight and body fitness. Exercise is very important for the pregnant woman and her unborn baby. Staying active will help her feel better. Outdoor exercise has the added benefit of fresh air and sunshine. Walking is an excellent exercise.

Women who have been active in sports can continue. However, they should stop when they feel tired. If a woman wants to start a new sport or exercise, she should discuss it with her doctor.

Pregnant women should not lift heavy objects or move furniture. It could harm the unborn baby.

Dental Care

Good oral hygiene practices, regular checkups, and proper nutrition will help the woman maintain healthy teeth. Proper daily dental care should continue. In addition, a pregnant woman should see her dentist as early in her pregnancy as possible to be checked for tooth decay, gum disease, and other dental problems. The dentist should be informed of the pregnancy to consider the use of local X-rays, anesthetics, and pain relievers.

Drugs

In light of the fact that a fetus is totally dependent on its mother to provide a suitable environment, the mother needs to avoid ingesting anything that might even possibly be harmful to the fetus. Through sad experience, medical science has learned

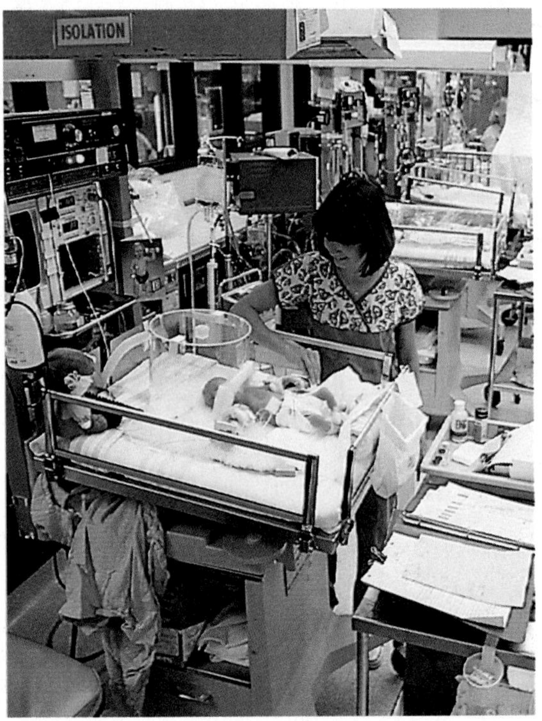

Babies born with fetal alcohol syndrome are usually of low birth weight and may suffer from alcohol-related birth defects.

that certain barbiturates produce asphyxiation and brain damage. The tranquilizer thalidomide caused the birth defects of missing and/or deformed limbs. Researchers reported in 1985 that the acne-fighting drug Accutane may be as dangerous to the fetus as thalidomide. Their results indicate that babies are 26 times more likely to have serious birth defects if their mother took Accutane during the pregnancy or even shortly before conception. Mother and doctor, together, must weigh risks and benefits of any drug prescribed during her pregnancy.

Of course, there are many nonprescription drugs available at the pharmacy for headaches, motion sickness, common colds, etc. Most of these are thought to be safe, but no drug, even a nonprescription one, should be taken without the knowledge of the mother's doctor. The doctor may advise against the use of the drug.

The effects of some street drugs (such as cocaine and marijuana) on a fetus are not yet well defined, but research points to a correlation with premature births. Chromosomal damage of reproductive cells has been linked to the use of marijuana. Obviously, the only safe approach for avoiding the possibility of damaging the fetus is to abstain from their use. The extremely harmful effects of heroin on the fetus are well-documented. Drug addicts' babies are addicted to drugs even before they are born. They go through serious and painful withdrawal from the influence of the drug shortly after birth.

Alcohol

Alcohol is another mind-altering drug. Because alcohol is readily transmitted through the placenta, the fetus is "under the influence" every time the mother is. Researchers have attributed the following birth defects to alcohol: shorter and lighter in weight than normal, abnormally small heads, facial irregularities, limb abnormalities, and heart defects. Most were mentally retarded and suffered from behavioral problems, such as hyperactivity. Such a significant number of babies studied showed these symptoms that researchers named the "fetal alcohol syndrome." For every baby born with fetal alcohol syndrome, several more are born with only some of the features. When only some of the characteristics are present, the problem is called "alcohol related birth defects." Alcohol also causes a greater incidence of miscarriage.

Research with monkeys has shown that the equivalent of three to five drinks, consumed quickly, eliminated circulation to the fetus, temporarily. Thus brain damage could result from oxygen deprivation. More research is required to determine how much alcohol is too much. However, the U.S. Surgeon General has warned that pregnant women should abstain from alcohol completely. Many doctors advise their patients that this is the safest approach. New York City now enforces a health regulation requiring all restaurants, bars, and liquor stores to display signs reading, "Warning. Alcoholic beverages during pregnancy can cause birth defects." One can only hope that every mother will recognize that her unborn baby cannot read warning signs. It is up to her. Consider, too, that a fetus cannot say "no" to a drink when the mother says "yes." It is up to the mother to accept the responsibility of protecting her unborn baby from the known and the unknown harmful effects of alcohol and other drugs.

Tobacco

The U.S. Surgeon General has reported to Congress that when a pregnant mother smokes she introduces numerous risks for her unborn child. The risk of miscarriage is increased by 70 percent. The risk of premature birth is increased by 36 percent. The risk of stillbirth is increased by 25 percent. Newborn babies of smokers are twice as likely to have subnormal weights and heights and, therefore, be at risk in other ways during and after birth.

It has been shown that the babies of smokers suffer long-term effects as well. Smokers' children have more emotional and behavioral problems and are more hyperactive than the children of nonsmoking mothers. Smokers' children have more

A Matter of Fact

A pregnant woman's exposure to chemicals can pose a danger to her unborn child. She should not handle weed killers or pesticides. X-rays and other forms of irradiation should be avoided. In the workplace, a pregnant woman needs to be alert to chemicals or irradiation that may be harmful. Although the negative effects of exposure to low-level radiation from video display terminals (VDTs) have not been entirely documented, it is a good idea for the woman to increase her awareness on how to protect herself.

Even an enjoyable task such as painting a used baby crib poses health risks. Be sure the work area is open and well-ventilated. Paint fumes must not be inhaled. Better yet, see if someone else can do the work. The pregnant woman definitely should avoid paint cleaners. A pregnant woman should tell her doctor if she has been exposed to chemicals or irradiation. Her pregnancy then can be carefully monitored for signs of danger.

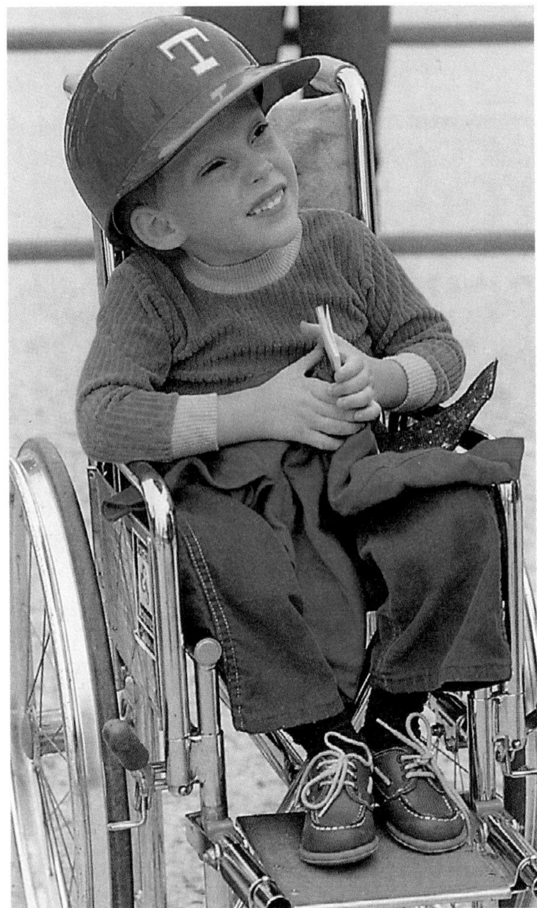

Some illnesses during pregnancy may result in a birth defect.

respiratory illnesses, and their risk of "sudden infant death syndrome" is four times greater. A British research study of 17,000 children has shown that smokers' children lagged behind in both mental and physical growth, even through 11 years of age.

Just as for alcohol, the fetus cannot say "no" to smoking if the mother says "yes." The mother must act responsibly and protect her unborn baby against the numerous risks that result if she smokes during pregnancy.

Caffeine

Opinions vary about the dangers of caffeine during pregnancy. Nevertheless, pregnant women would be wise to watch their intake. Keep in mind that coffee, tea, many soft drinks, and chocolate contain caffeine. Healthier choices would be milk, fruit juices, and fruit and vegetable snacks.

Illnesses

Most pregnancies are uncomplicated and result in a healthy baby. However, the following are some problems that can occur in pregnancy.

Toxemia (Blood Poisoning)

Toxemia is a serious complication. Its cause is unknown, but it can be treated successfully if diagnosed early. A woman should be alert for these symptoms: a sudden weight gain, swelling of feet and hands, severe headaches, dizziness, blurred vision, changes in the urine, and increased blood pressure. Toxemia usually occurs only in the last half of pregnancy.

Untreated toxemia can progress to convulsions that are dangerous to both the woman and fetus. Toxemia usually can be controlled at home by following a doctor's instructions.

Rubella

Rubella is better known as German measles. In children and adults, it is a mild disease. However, if a woman is infected just before or during pregnancy, it can cause heart disease, blindness, hearing loss, or other serious health problems for the baby.

Pregnant women should avoid contact with anyone who has German measles. If she is exposed, she should report it to her doctor. The baby's development will be carefully monitored.

Sexually Transmitted Diseases

Sexually transmitted diseases (STDs) are infections spread through sexual contact. They are also called venereal disease. The most serious are gonorrhea, syphilis, herpes, and AIDS (acquired immune deficiency syndrome). The diseases may be passed on to the unborn baby and cause illness, birth defects, or death. Prompt treatment of gonorrhea and syphilis will prevent complications during pregnancy.

Gonorrhea may spread to a baby's eyes during the birth. Therefore most states require doctors to treat a newborn's eyes with a medicine that kills gonorrhea germs.

Herpes symptoms can be treated and relieved. There is no cure for AIDS.

Discomforts of Pregnancy

Discomforts are not usually serious, although they can make the pregnant woman feel very bad. Fortunately, many of them can be relieved. If they persist, the woman should see her doctor.

- **Morning Sickness**

During the first three months of pregnancy, a woman may feel nauseous. This is caused by hormonal changes. Nausea and vomiting may occur anytime during the day. Eating

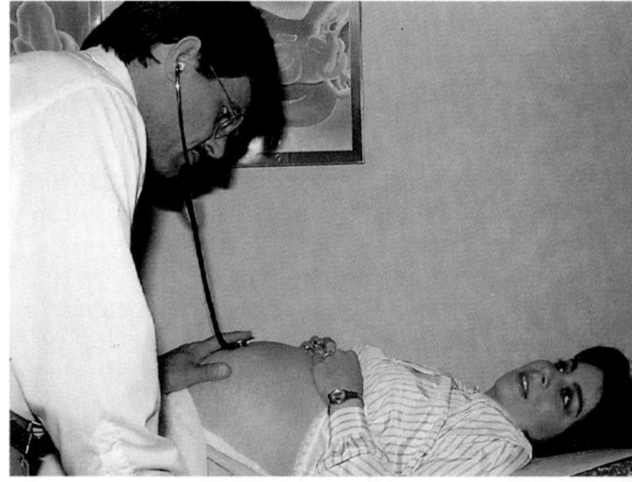

If a woman experiences persistent discomforts during pregnancy, she should consult her doctor.

dry cereal, toast, or crackers in the morning before getting out of bed may help a woman overcome the feeling of sickness. Eating five small meals a day and avoiding greasy foods may help, too.

- **Heartburn**

Heartburn is a burning sensation in the digestive system. It is caused by hormonal changes that slow down digestion and by pressure of the uterus on the stomach. Women suffering from heartburn can follow the same eating suggestions as for nausea. Changing a sleeping position to elevate the head may help, too.

- **Varicose Veins**

Varicose or enlarged veins occur in the lower legs usually. The enlarged uterus pressing on the abdominal veins causes this problem. Varicose veins usually shrink and disappear after the birth.

Women should avoid wearing tight nylons or socks. If possible, they should not stand for long periods of time. Lying down with feet raised for a few minutes several times a day will relieve swelling.

- **Shortness of Breath**

An enlarged uterus can press on a woman's lungs. Moving slowly will help her conserve her breath.

- **Backache**

A woman's posture changes during pregnancy. The growing uterus pulls on back muscles. To prevent strain, pregnant women should wear low-heeled shoes. She should not lift heavy objects. Exercises also may help.

- **Leg Cramps**

During the latter part of pregnancy, women may experience leg cramps. These can be caused by pressure from an enlarged uterus. They can get relief by heat, massage, or exercises that stretch the calf muscle.

Bonding

It is not surprising that most mothers feel totally involved in the prenatal development of the fetus. As mentioned earlier, a woman first experiences a change in her bodily functions only a little more than two weeks after conception. By the end of the first trimester, important developments in her support system begin to increase her own body weight. Twenty weeks into the pregnancy she can feel the fetus move. She makes regular visits to her doctor, and she is conscious of the fact that she must eat properly for the welfare of her baby. She also may have changed her habits regarding rest, smoking, or drinking. With this involvement and caring, she feels an attachment, a **bonding** to her unborn child, though she has never seen it.

Research has now been able to show that the unborn baby is equally bonded to the mother. Specially devised tests show that newborn infants prefer both the sound of their own mothers' heartbeat and their own mothers' voice to the voice of another woman. The same group of tests indicate that newborn babies prefer to hear children's poems that were read aloud by their mothers during the last six weeks of pregnancy, rather than poems that had not been read during that period. Because infants are able to recognize sounds associated with the period of gestation, one might infer that the unborn baby is capable of some degree of learning.

While it is impossible for fathers to be involved in the pregnancy in exactly the same ways, there is no reason the father cannot become strongly bonded to the child, even before the birth. From the first awareness of pregnancy through childbirth and beyond, the mother needs and appreciates support. By being a supportive companion, the father can sense involvement and growing bonds between this new being and himself.

By reading and discussing changes with his wife and the doctor, the father can know what to expect, and he can understand each of the stages of the pregnancy. He can use a stethoscope to hear the baby's heartbeat. With his hands on his wife's abdomen, he can feel the baby kick. He can listen to his wife and empathize with her sensations, feelings, hopes, and fears.

Increased bonding of both mother and father with the unborn baby may come as a "spin-off" from ultrasonog-

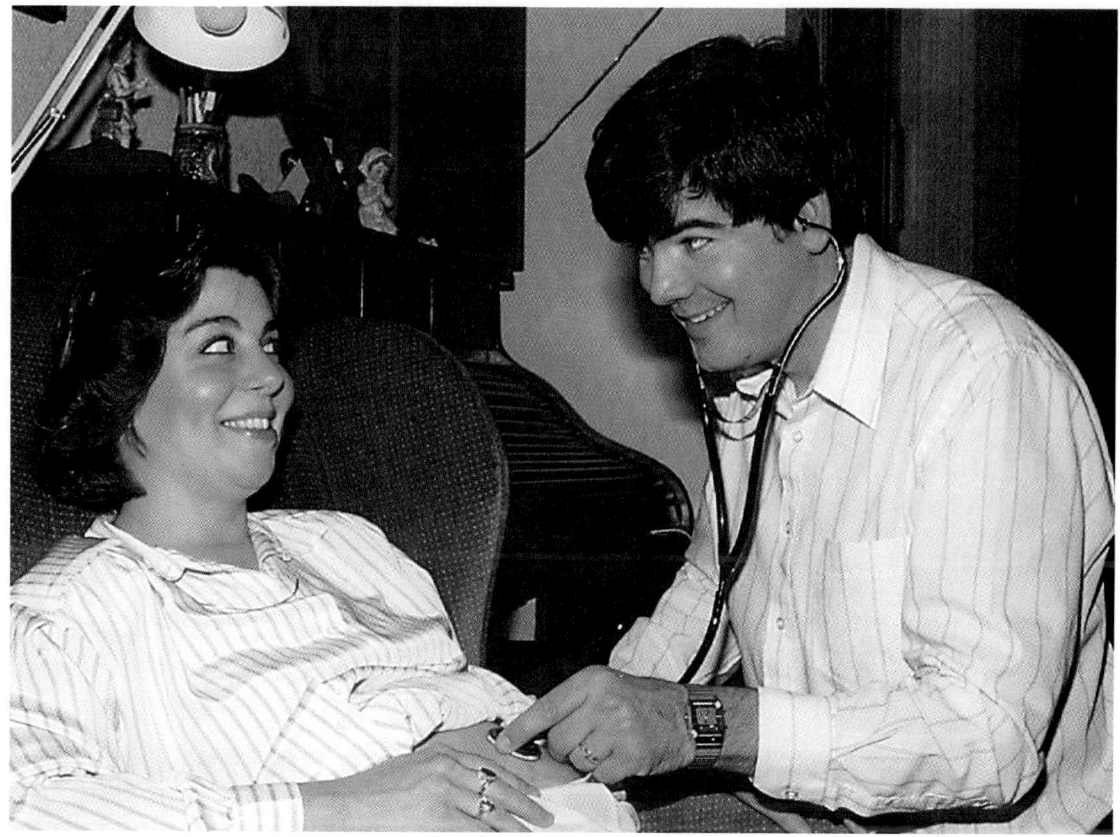

Hearing the baby's heartbeat can help a father join in the bonding process.

raphy. A spin-off of ultrasonography arises because both mother and father can see a moving image of their unborn child. Many parents have expressed excitement and an enhanced sense of bonding resulting from the experience.

Together he and his wife can plan changes that need to be made to provide nursery space in the home. The father may join in shopping for a crib and all the other essentials.

By being supportive and understanding, the father will not only sense a bonding to the unborn baby, but will strengthen his relationship with his wife. A loving marital relationship, as stress-free as possible, is an important ingredient of a healthy environment for the fetus. At birth, the baby should represent a joy to share, rather than a threat to the strength of the bond between the parents.

Life's Work

Dianne R. Meyer

➤**President, Beautiful Bambino, Inc.**

➤**B.A. in Mass Communications**

Dianne's typical day is divided between her family and her career as a clothing designer. For her business, she spends time doing bookkeeping, packaging orders, checking supplies, and other day-to-day business tasks. She also works at designing new children's outfits and then developing catalog sheets to promote her clothing.

Dianne says her days are long. "When you have a business and a family to take care of, the work never ends, so you are constantly busy."

Dianne says the skills necessary for success in her profession include, "creativity, an eye for design, sales ability, the need to succeed, and energy." Her most rewarding job-related accomplishment was selling her line of clothing to a major department store chain after "they called me."

For a student considering going into Dianne's profession, she recommends, "Get experience in all facets of the business— sales, sewing, designing, shipping, bookkeeping, etc." She says it's important to "get experience from wherever and whomever you can. Learn as much as possible from every job you get. I have worked in a wide variety of places. I'm very glad I did because I can now use all that experience to make my own business better."

When asked how her profession will change within the next 10 years, Dianne says, "Cottage industries are becoming more popular in the children's wear business. Many people are discovering they have the skills to design clothing that other people are willing to buy. And you don't have to be in a huge company to make it."

In Review

Vocabulary

stillbirth
bonding

Summary

- ✓ The fetus is totally dependent on the mother for its nourishment and environment. If the fetus is to develop normally, the mother must obtain medical care, must have proper nutrition, and must avoid the use of alcohol, tobacco, or any other drug not prescribed by her physician.
- ✓ A woman may experience certain discomforts during pregnancy. These are not usually serious and many of them can be relieved.
- ✓ A woman experiences bonding with her unborn child. A father also can feel bonding by being supportive during the pregnancy and empathizing with the woman.

Questions

1. Why is it important for a woman to have a nutritious diet before she is pregnant? While she is pregnant? What are the four food groups that can supply the nutrients we all need?
2. When pregnant, a woman should consume about 300 additional calories per day. Can she satisfactorily meet those needs with candy bars, soft drinks, and potato chips? Why?
3. What are some of the effects of tobacco, alcohol, and other drugs on the developing fetus?
4. How might the marital relationship be affected if the mother is strongly bonded to an infant, but the father is not?

Activities

1. Design a menu for one day for a pregnant woman. Explain your choices.
2. Make a poster to warn pregnant women against the use of drugs, alcohol, or tobacco. Make arrangements to display it in your school or community.

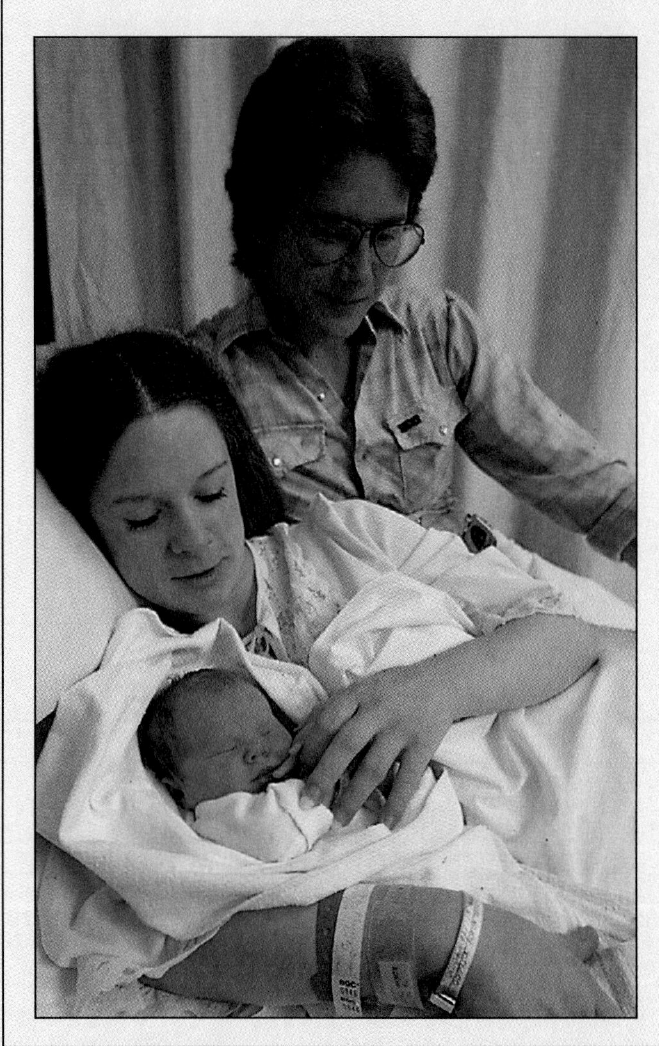

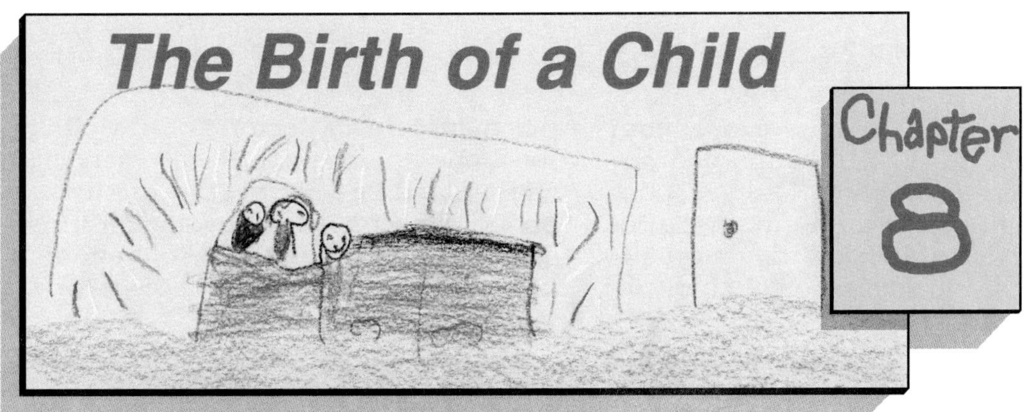

This chapter will help you:

- recognize the importance of choosing an experienced obstetrician
- give examples of how expectant parents can help their other children prepare for the new baby
- describe different birth procedures
- identify the three stages of labor
- discuss complications that could arise during birth

Preparation for Birth

Preparation for birth has many aspects and should begin when the woman first suspects she's pregnant. As mentioned in Chapter 6, it is wise to begin a series of regularly scheduled visits to a doctor from the start.

There are many questions to be asked of a doctor during a pregnancy, so it is important to have a friendly relationship. If the doctor seems abrupt or cold, or makes the mother feel uneasy in any way, she should choose another doctor. Doctors should be willing to discuss their philosophies regarding pregnancy and childbirth and should be patient in explaining why they choose certain procedures.

The mother will wish to know who will deliver her baby if, for some reason, her own doctor cannot be with her during labor. Will she be able to have some visits with this other doctor during her pregnancy? Will her husband be allowed to be with her during the birth? Does the doctor believe in Lamaze childbirth training for husbands and wives? Does the doctor know about the Leboyer deliveries? What does the doctor think of those methods? (These methods will be discussed later in this chapter.) When is Cesarean delivery indicated? **Cesarean birth** is when the baby is delivered through a surgical incision in the mother's abdomen. What percentage of the doctor's deliveries are Cesarean compared with the national average of 17%? What does your doctor think about birthing rooms? Does your hospital have birthing rooms? Thoughtful answers to these questions and others that come to mind can be very effective in helping the parents to prepare physically and emotionally for the birth of their child.

Answers to many worrisome questions will come from reading reliable, up-to-date books and magazines. Expectant parents should read informative literature on pregnancy and childbirth. Many fears of these very natural occurrences arise from ignorance. Reading also will give suggestions of questions the parents may want to discuss with the doctor.

Another part of preparing for the arrival of an infant is providing space in the house or apartment and purchasing the items that will be used in caring for the baby. There may be redecorating and alterations to the living space. Mother and father may need to buy a crib, a buggy, diapers, a layette, and many other items. Many parents prefer to accomplish such preparations before the beginning of the third trimester, when the mother may not be quite as agile as usual.

If the baby is to be born in a hospital, there are other details not to be left to the last minute. These include packing of personal items to take to the hospital and the plans for getting there. Sometime in the third trimester, the doctor or nurse probably will provide the mother with a list of the necessities she should pack. If there is any possibility that the husband will not be available when labor begins, there should be people who are willing and able to help the mother get to the hospital. Telephone numbers for the father, the helpers, the doctor, the hospital, the ambulance service, the taxi service, etc., should be kept next to the home phone. Working women who continue on the job until the baby is born should keep the numbers handy while at work, too.

Siblings

When the expected baby is not the first child, the older siblings also must be prepared for the new arrival. Parents need to recognize their children's continuing needs for love, support, and attention throughout the pregnancy and beyond. With the proper introduction to the impending event, the siblings can become just as delighted as the parents about having a new little one in the family. Of course, this will happen only if the older children feel secure in the knowledge that a baby will not displace them in the hearts of the parents.

Young children usually have questions about where the expected baby is, how it got there, how it can breathe, etc. This is an ideal opportunity for parents to give frank answers in terms that are simple enough for children to understand. In this way children can gain factual information regarding human sexuality and will not be influenced by the myths they may hear from other children later on. This kind of openness in the parent-child relationship will be invaluable when the children are somewhat older and ready to discuss values, sexual love, and sexual morality.

Parents should answer questions regarding reproduction using correct terminology, but should avoid answers

Helping older children adjust to the idea of a new brother or sister is part of preparing for the birth.

that provide more information than the child really wants or is ready for. For instance, if Johnny asks, "Where did I come from?" it may not be time yet to get out the diagrams of the human anatomy. It may be that Johnny's new friend has mentioned that he moved here from Cleveland, and that makes Johnny ask the question. A close relationship with plenty of dialogue will help the parent sense what information the child is seeking and how much the child will understand. Most importantly, the answers should always be honest and correct. If a question is puzzling even to the parent, finding the answer can be a good cooperative activity for parent and child.

Parents need to make arrangements for someone to take care of the children when the new sibling is born. Often, this responsibility falls to a grandparent, but that is not always a possibility. Because the parents do not know precisely when birth will occur, these arrangements should be made well in advance. The children need to be aware of the plans and feel comfortable with them.

"Daydreaming"

While preparing for an addition to their family, parents usually spend a considerable amount of time thinking about their expected child. Is it a boy or girl? What will she or he look like? What will his or her personality be like? It is important during this preparatory stage for parents not to develop fixed expectations that easily can lead to disappointment. For example, some parents have pictures in their minds of how beautiful their children will be. In

What Do Babies Need?

Planning ahead to have everything ready when the baby arrives is an important task for parents. Babies don't need an entire wardrobe, fancy clothes, or costly furniture. However, the following are some basics that parents should have for their baby.

A Place to Sleep

- Ideally, this is a crib, but all that is needed is something with sides to prevent the baby from rolling out. Watch out for sharp protruding edges. Close spacing of crib rails prevents a baby's head from being caught. Newer cribs are made with this safety feature. Older cribs may not be.
- A firm mattress to lie on. The pad or mattress should be waterproof or have a waterproof casing.
- Crib bumpers to keep baby's arms and legs inside the crib.

Bedding

- Flannelette-covered waterproof sheets (2 or 3), large enough to cover the mattress.
- Crib sheets (3 or 4). Fitted sheets are easier to use.
- 18-inch-square waterproof flannelette sheeting (4 to 6). Place under baby to protect sheets from soiling from diapers or spitting up.
- Lightweight blankets (2).
- Heavier blanket.
- A pillow isn't desirable.

Clothing

- Cotton receiving blankets (3 or 4). Used in warm weather or for bundling before and after baths.
- Cotton knit nightgowns (3 or 4). Long ones are better because they don't get kicked off as much. Good for sleeping in most climates.

fact, however, most newborn babies are quite homely, with misshapen heads, beady eyes, wrinkles, and discolored skins. Also, parents should not expect to have children who are extensions of themselves. For example, professional athletes or dancers who want their children to follow in their footsteps might have babies who are the wrong sex or have physical defects that eliminate all possibility of meeting the parents' expectations. For their security and well-being, babies need total acceptance—just as they are.

- A blanket bag, sleeping bag, or coverall. Easier to use than a heavy blanket for cold weather sleeping. Best if machine washable and easy to get on and off.
- Cotton knit shirts (3 or 4). Easiest to use are those that slip over the head and have large arm and head openings. Leaving an inch of bare midriff will save on laundering because if shirt is tucked into diaper, it will get wet.
- Sweaters (2 or 3). Choose washable ones with few buttons.
- A knitted cap for baby going out in the cold weather.
- Cloth diapers (3 to 6 dozen). Disposable diapers may be preferred, but are more expensive.
- Plastic pants for use with cloth diapers (2 to 3).
- Clamps or safety pins (for cloth diapers).

Feeding Equipment

- Nursing bottles with caps (6 to 8 8-oz. bottles). Boilable plastic ones will prevent breakage.
- Nipples (one for each bottle with a few spares).
- A bottle and nipple brush.
- Pan to heat water for warming bottle.

Bathing Equipment

- Small tub or dishpan.
- Mild soap.
- Washcloths.
- Full-size towel or receiving blanket for drying.
- Baby shampoo.
- Baby lotion (if desired).
- Warm room so the baby does not get chilled.
- A table or counter top at a convenient height.
- Nail clipper to keep fingernails short. The nails should be clipped while the baby is resting or relaxed.

Birth Procedures

An important part of preparing for the birth is to choose the birth procedure. Today, parents can choose from a wide variety of programs for the birth of their child. For more than half a century, it was traditional for American babies to be born in hospitals surrounded by doctors and teams of professional aides. Husbands were not allowed to be present at the birth. Have you ever seen the image of the expectant father pacing in the waiting room?

Parents enjoy daydreaming about their unborn child, but their dreams should not overshadow their acceptance of the child for what he or she is.

This traditional mode of childbirth is giving way to various other forms, most of which involve the father. Today it is quite common for fathers to be present at the birth of their child.

Home Delivery and Birthing Centers

Some people are choosing home delivery with the assistance of a certified nurse midwife. In some states, it is permissible to be assisted by a lay midwife. This is an unlicensed person who has learned the midwife practice not through nurses' training, but only through experience.

Other parents are choosing **birthing centers,** which may or may not be affiliated with hospitals. These try to maintain a family atmosphere, and the rules regarding visitors are much more relaxed than in the traditional hospital setting. Labor and delivery occur in the same "birthing room." The parents are given ample time after the delivery to cuddle the infant and to share with each other the joy of their new child.

In these nontraditional births, the use of medication or surgical procedures is minimal. While there may be distinct advantages in these alternative methods, they also have their shortcomings. In cases where there are known complications, choosing to give birth at home instead of where the finest medical facilities are available could be dangerous to the mother and

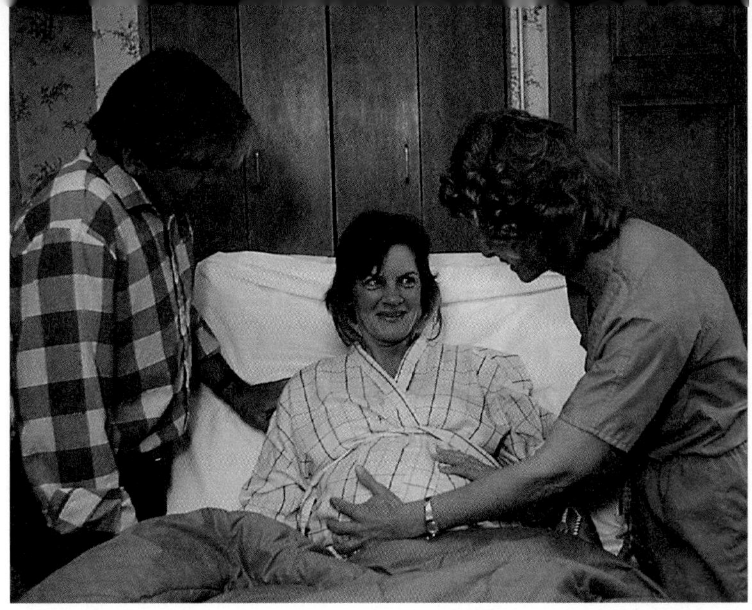

Some expectant parents choose having a midwife help in the delivery. When would this not be a wise decision?

child. For example, if an Rh negative mother has an Rh positive child who needs a blood exchange (Chapter 6), the baby's chances for survival are greatly enhanced when an alert hospital staff can deal with the problem instantly.

Sometimes, of course, *unexpected* complications arise during labor and birth. The attendant, whether a midwife or doctor, should be aware of the symptoms of complications and be prepared to take the necessary actions. Essential medical care for mother and baby is needed as quickly as possible. If the parents have chosen home delivery with a midwife, they can take advantage of the latest medical techniques throughout the pregnancy in order to minimize the probability of there being any surprise complications. One example is ultrasonography discussed in Chapter 6. It shows the position of the baby and, therefore, gives ample warning if the baby will be born feet-first or buttocks-first instead of head-first, which is usual.

Even after the safe delivery of a child, there are some disadvantages to giving birth in the home setting. Several tests designed for evaluation of the infant's condition can be done routinely in the hospital, but they will be omitted after a home delivery.

Hospitals

Many hospitals now recognize the desire that many parents want to share the birthing experience. Some hospitals have birthing rooms, and some programs include the concept of "rooming in." Traditionally, newborn infants spent most of their time at the hospital in a nursery away from the mother. The father saw the baby only through a window. "Rooming in" means the mother and baby share the same room. The father, too, has much more opportunity to hold and become acquainted with his baby.

Even the traditional position of the mother during delivery has come into question. On a delivery table, the woman assumes the lithotomy position, flat on her back with knees raised and apart, feet fixed in stirrups. In the birthing rooms and in the homes, deliveries occur in beds rather than on delivery tables, so the position is somewhat modified.

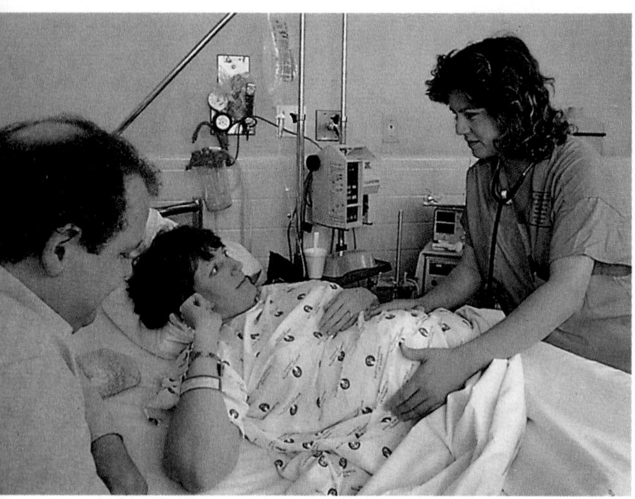

The father-to-be and the medical staff can help an expectant mother cope with the pain of labor.

Very different, alternative positions are now being recommended by a few obstetrical experts. All of these positions are variations of erect positions that were mentioned in ancient writings—sitting, standing, kneeling, or squatting. All have the advantages of using gravity to assist abdominal contractions in expulsion of the baby and of maximizing the elasticity of the tissue surrounding the birth canal. Some hospitals now use a birthing chair for delivery that keeps the woman in a more upright position.

Childbirth Methods

More and more hospitals are now allowing husbands to be present during labor and birth. The husband participates as his wife's "coach" if the couple has taken **Lamaze** training. Lamaze is available in many hospitals, clinics, and community centers. The Lamaze method is an approach toward natural childbirth. During the last two months of pregnancy, the parents attend Lamaze classes in which the mother learns breathing techniques and practices exercises that she will find very useful during each stage of labor. The father learns how he can assist during labor by calming his wife, reminding her of what she has learned, and lending emotional support. Through such instruction, the father can give maximum support to the mother and gain the best possible opportunity for bonding to the infant.

Through proper exercise and psychological preparation for the birth, the mother increases her ability to cope with the pain she encounters in labor. This reduces the amount of medication required to control the pain and is, therefore, a distinct advantage for both mother and infant. The mother is more alert to this wondrous experience, and the baby is not subjected to drugs, which easily pass through the placenta.

Still another mode of childbirth was initiated by Leboyer in France. His thesis is that traditional procedures are too stressful for the neonate (newborn). He champions the idea of "gentle birth." The delivery room is kept quiet and dimly lit. Upon birth, the baby is set upon the mother's abdomen with the umbilical cord intact so that the baby does not need to begin breathing immediately. When the cord ceases to pulse, it is cut, and the breathing baby is placed in a warm bath.

There is not sufficient research to show whether babies born by the Leboyer method become better adjusted people because of this birth experience. Nevertheless, the technique does represent one approach to smoothing the transition from the cozy environment of the womb to that of the outside world.

The Birth

Anytime during the last month of the pregnancy, **lightening** occurs. This represents a transition toward the final stages of pregnancy. It is called lightening because the head of the baby moves down into the pelvic cavity, relieving some of the pressure the mother has felt. Usually the mother finds it easier to breathe after this movement, but she also may experience new pressure on her bladder. With the baby in this new position, both mother and child are ready for the onset of labor.

Labor

Labor begins approximately 38 weeks after conception. It consists of three stages. During the first stage, which lasts an average of 10 to 12 hours, the mother experiences abdominal contractions at regular intervals. As the hours pass, the intervals become shorter. Each contraction pushes the baby's head against the **cervix,** the opening between the uterus and the birth canal. The connective tissue of the cervix softens and allows it to open wider with each contraction. Sometime during this phase of labor, the bag holding the amniotic water will break.

During the last few hours of the first stage of labor, the mother will go to the hospital, birthing center, or wherever the delivery is to occur. Attendants will be monitoring the contractions and the vital signs, such as blood pressure, pulse, and the fetal heartbeat. Also, during this first stage, the mother will need the loving support of her husband or "coach." She may need reminders of proper breathing and muscle relaxation, and she may greatly appreciate some tender massaging. The interval between contractions may become as short as 60 seconds. If the mother needs medication for the control of pain at any time during the labor, that time is apt to be near the end of the first

During the first stage of labor, the cervix begins to dilate (left). When the cervix has opened to 4 inches, the first stage of labor ends.

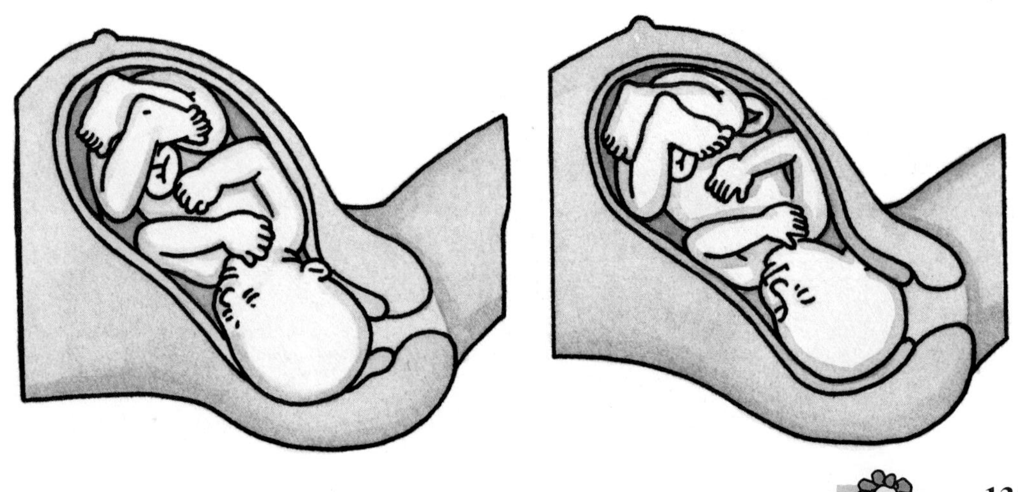

stage. The first stage ends when the cervix has expanded to about 4 inches (10 centimeters) in diameter, allowing the baby's head to enter the vagina.

The second stage of labor is the birth of the child. The time required varies greatly, but 45 minutes is probably average. The doctor will perform an **episiotomy.** This minor surgery is performed to avoid the tearing of the distended tissues at the end of the birth canal. Torn tissues heal with more difficulty than a smooth surgical cut. (The wound is stitched together immediately following labor.)

First, "crowning" occurs, the top of the baby's head becomes visible. After the whole head appears, it is rotated to the side, the shoulders are expelled, and the remainder of the torso follows. The baby is checked to make certain there will be no impediment to breathing, and the umbilical cord is severed and tied. Measuring and weighing are followed by an evaluation of the baby's overall condition.

The third stage of labor requires only about 10 minutes. In this stage of labor, the placenta and the amniotic sac are expelled.

Complications

One complication arises when the fetus is in the **breech position**—buttocks-first or feet-first. As mentioned earlier, ultrasound imaging can alert the doctor to this situation. It is a better tool than X-rays for this purpose because it has no known harmful effect. The breech position often requires a Cesarean delivery. In this type of major surgery, the abdominal wall and the wall of the uterus are cut and the baby removed through the incision. Cesarean delivery is used also when the birth canal is too small, when the cervix doesn't open properly, or when extremely long labor is placing undue stress on the mother and/or baby. Today, over 17% of American births are Cesarean. According to some

During the second stage of labor, contractions push the baby out of the uterus. The baby's head becomes visible (left). Next the whole head appears. It looks misshapen from pushing through the birth canal, but it's only temporary.

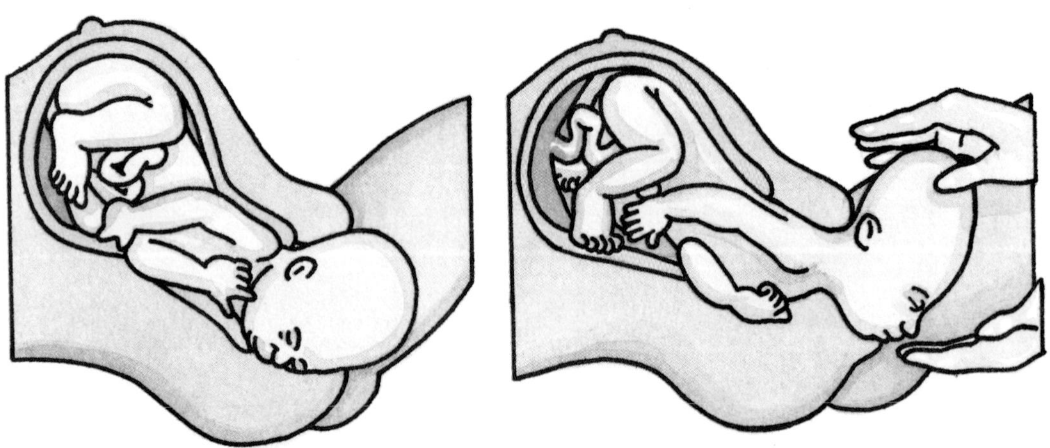

obstetricians, that percentage is much higher than is absolutely essential.

When Cesarean deliveries are performed, anesthesia must be used. Sometimes it is general anesthesia. That means the mother is unconscious. Often, though, regional anesthesia is preferred. A spinal block allows the woman to remain awake, but she has no feeling below her waist.

A very real danger of feet-first and buttocks-first deliveries through the birth canal is **anoxia** resulting from damage to the placenta or umbilical cord. Anoxia is the failure of the fetus to receive enough oxygen. It can destroy brain cells. It also may be fatal. Brain damage may result in cerebral palsy or mental retardation. Other factors that can cause various degrees of anoxia during pregnancy are anemia in the mother and the use of tobacco, alcohol, or other drugs.

In some difficult births, including vaginal delivery of breech babies, the doctor will intervene by using forceps to grasp and reposition the baby and to assist the mother's contractions in the final expulsion process. Babies of forceps deliveries often have temporary marks on their faces and heads. Forceps must be used with extreme care to avoid the very real possibility of causing brain damage to the child.

The Next Step

The birth of the baby marks a major turning point in life—for both the baby and the parents. In Unit 3, you will learn about these new experiences.

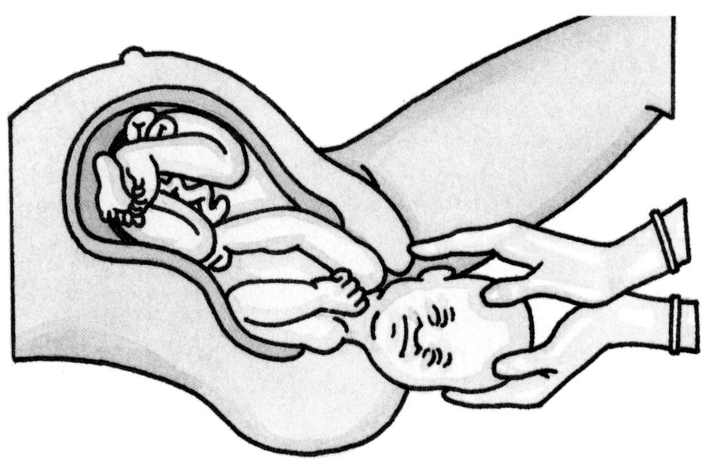

The baby's head is rotated to the side, and the shoulders follow.

In Review

Vocabulary

Cesarean birth	Lamaze	episiotomy
midwife	lightening	breech position
birthing center	cervix	anoxia

Summary

✓ Preparation for the birth should include choosing a doctor, providing space in the home, purchasing the necessary equipment, and deciding on a birthing method.

✓ The first stage of labor lasts about 10 to 12 hours. During this phase, the opening from the uterus to the birth canal enlarges to a diameter of about 4 inches. Also, during this stage, the bag holding the amniotic fluid will break.

✓ In the second stage of labor, the baby is born—usually head first. If the baby is oriented feet-first or buttocks-first, a Cesarean delivery may be necessary.

✓ In difficult birth, damage to the placenta or umbilical cord can cause anoxia. Both anoxia and careless use of forceps can cause brain damage to the child.

Questions

1. How soon after conception should one begin preparation for birth?
2. What are the objectives in Lamaze training?
3. What are the advantages of giving birth to a child in your home while attended by a midwife? What are the disadvantages?
4. Why is it important to minimize the use of tranquilizing or pain-controlling medications during labor?
5. What benefit might a wife realize from having her husband present during delivery? What benefit might the husband realize?

Activities

1. As an expectant mother or father, what considerations would be important to you in the selection of an obstetrician?
2. Discuss the disadvantages of telling a small child that babies are delivered by storks.

Unit 3
Infancy

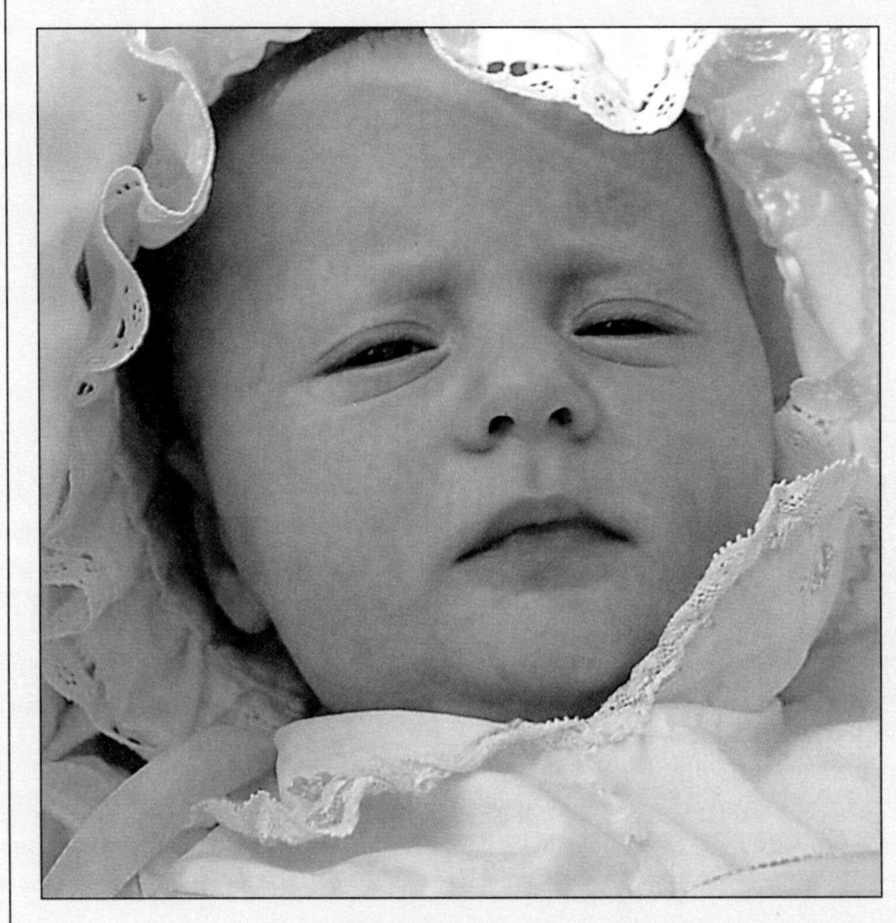

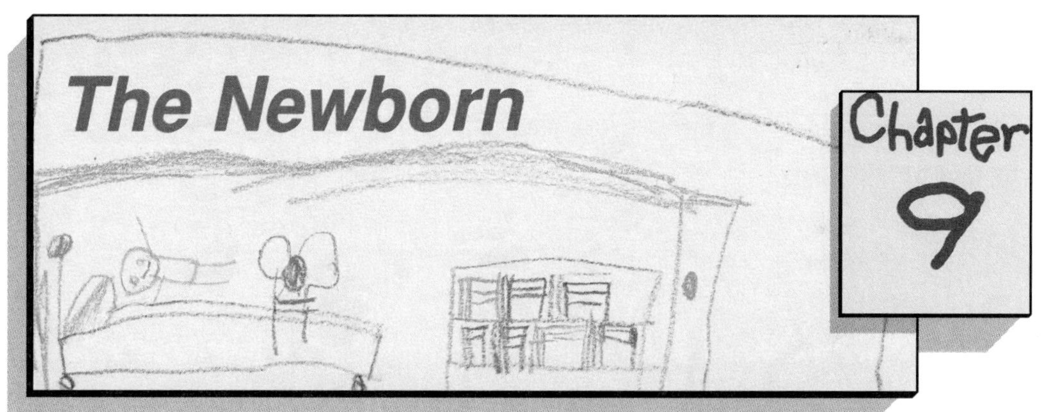

The Newborn

Chapter 9

This chapter will help you:

- learn how physicians evaluate the condition of a newborn baby
- learn what parents should expect regarding physical size, appearance, and abilities of their newborn baby
- recognize that the father's role in nurturing an infant can be as important as the mother's
- identify what newborn babies need in the way of medical care, nutrition, routine care, loving care, and safety
- become aware of the increased stresses on family relationships when a baby arrives in the home

Healthy Arrival

The most crucial time for the newborn is in the first minute after birth, the time when all systems must begin to function on their own. The transition from being a fetus dependent on the mother to being an air-breathing, independent individual is complex, but it is a change the full-term newborn is ready to make.

For fetuses, the oxygen, nutrients, and waste products all pass through the placenta. At birth, babies suddenly must breathe, eat, and eliminate for themselves. Fortunately, they are well equipped to cope with the stresses of their new environment.

The **Apgar score**, based on a quick series of tests given to newborns one minute after birth, assesses the baby's physical health. Dr. Virginia Apgar, born in 1909, was the first woman physician ever appointed a full professor at Columbia College of Physicians and Surgeons and head of obstetric anesthesiology at the hospital. Dr. Apgar devised a scoring system in 1952 for the tests observed during the more than 17,000 births she attended. Apgar scores run from zero to 10. A cumulative score of 10 means the baby is in the best possible condition one minute after birth. Scores of seven, eight, or nine indicate good condition. Four, five, or six shows fair condition.

Apgar Scale			
	Score		
Sign	0	1	2
Heart Rate	Not detectable	Below 100	Above 100
Respiration	Absent	Slow, irregular	Good, crying
Muscle Tone	Limp	Some flexing of hands, feet, limbs	Active motion
Reflexes*	No response	Grimace	Cough, sneeze
Color**	Blue, pale	Arms and legs blue, body pink	Completely pink

* When stimulated by suction in nose.

** If the natural skin color of the child is dark, other tests for color are applied.

Zero, one, two, or three indicates poor condition. As for survival, infants who score zero have an 85 percent chance of living four weeks. A score of 10 indicates a 99.9 percent chance of surviving the same period.

The value of this relatively quick and simple evaluation is twofold. First, it demands that the baby's response to the birth process is immediately assessed. Second, it identifies infants in need of special postnatal care. If necessary, the infant then can receive needed medical attention without delay.

Current research shows that at one year of age, 3.6 percent of all babies who had Apgar scores of zero to three were neurologically abnormal. These infants were mentally retarded or had suffered other brain damage. Those with scores of four to six were in better shape with only 2.8 percent showing abnormality. Only 1.6 percent of those with scores of seven to 10 were abnormal. The Apgar score is determined as shown above.

Physical Appearance

Any parent can experience a sense of shock at the first sight of their tiny, wrinkled, blotchy offspring. Newborns look strange to many people who have in mind a two- to three-month-old baby when they think of a baby. These two stages look quite different. Most newborns have elongated heads and puffy eyes. The eyes are usually the most prominent feature.

The amount of hair varies with each baby. It may be abundant or scanty, covering the head and parts of the body, especially the back. This hair is usually only temporary. It disappears when the permanent hair begins to grow. Permanent hair is often a different color from that which first appears on the baby.

The size of babies at birth varies, often in accordance with the age, health, and habits of the mother. At birth, the average newborn weighs between 7 and 8 pounds (3 to 3.6 kilograms) and measures approximately 20 inches (50 centimeters) long. The range, however, is from 3 to 16 pounds (1.4 to 7.3 kilograms) and from 17 to 22 inches (42 to 55 centimeters). Boys are generally slightly larger and heavier than girls. Premature or low birth weight babies usually require special care of an incubator in order to survive. The incidence of small babies is greater for teenage mothers.

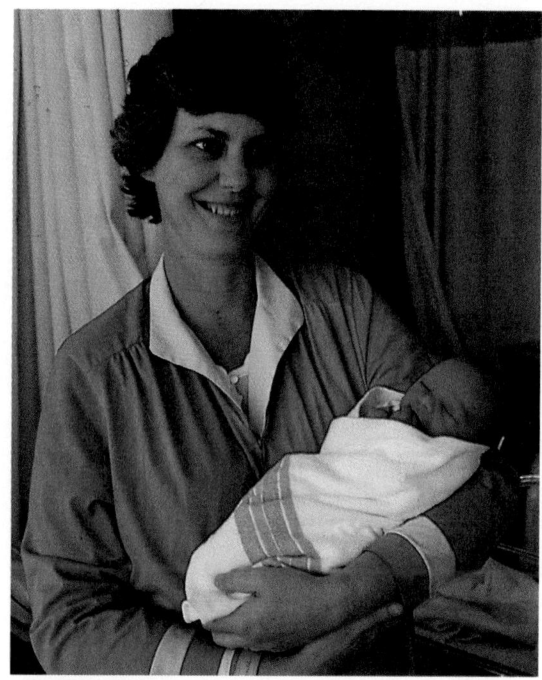

Newborns seem so small and helpless, but they are well equipped to cope with their new environment.

Medical Care

One of the most important concerns for parents of a newborn baby is whether the child is normal in all respects. As discussed in this chapter, the Apgar test should be used immediately after birth. About 93 percent of the babies born in the United States are normal so, obviously, a vast majority of couples are delighted by the news that their new babies appear to be whole and healthy. In addition newborn screening helps to evaluate the newborn's condition.

Newborn Screening

Before the baby is released from the hospital, a newborn screening process is performed to detect health problems. In most states, newborn screening is required by law unless the parents refuse because of religious beliefs. Nine congenital disorders are detectable by the screening. These include PKU, sickle cell anemia, and cystic fibrosis (discussed in Chapter 6).

The screening process involves collecting a few drops of blood from the infant's heel onto a special filter paper. The dried blood spots are analyzed by a medical laboratory. If the screening test results reveal an abnormality, the lab notifies the family's doctor or refers the family to a qualified specialist.

By discovering in the first week of life that an infant has PKU, treatment can be started. This will avoid the mental retardation that results from untreated PKU. Not all of the diseases uncovered by the testing are as treatable as PKU. However, the test can help reduce the

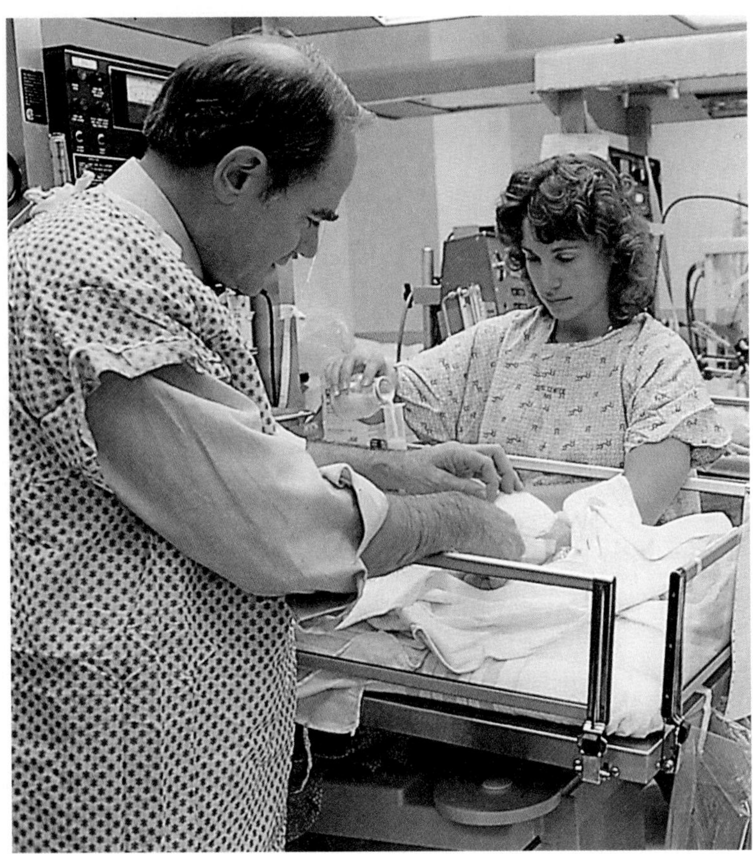

Before newborns leave the hospital, the hospital staff screens them for medical disorders.

risk of death from some of these diseases during infancy and indicate treatment that may improve growth and development in childhood.

Continued Care

Parents are concerned about continued normal development of healthy babies. It is wise for couples to choose a **pediatrician** (a medical doctor who specializes in children's health) even before the birth. Parents need to choose a pediatrician with as much care as they did their obstetrician. No doubt they will have many questions, especially first-time parents, and they need to feel the doctor is willing to take the time to help them. Pediatricians like to evaluate the baby's health at regular intervals in the weeks, months, and years ahead. They can determine whether development is occurring within normal ranges. For example, they will advise parents what height and weight changes to expect of their baby. Because of their expertise, they can often detect abnormal behavior long before it would be obvious to the parent. On the other hand, they can often allay fears by reminding the parents that babies are all *individuals*. They develop at various rates through all their stages. In other words, a baby may learn to walk at nine months, while another may take 14 months. Both are in the normal range, and they may prove to have equal physical and mental growth.

During some of the early visits to the doctor's office, the infant will begin **immunization** (protection against disease). This consists of a DTP injection for diptheria, tetanus, and pertussis (whooping cough) and an oral dose of polio vaccine. These treatments usually occur three times—at roughly two, four, and six months of age.

There will be other times, too, when the baby will require medical attention. Parents should be alert to changes in their baby's behavior that could indicate an illness. For example, the baby may vomit, lose appetite, cry excessively, sweat unduly, be listless, have a runny nose, have diarrhea, or have a rash. Running a fever is a pretty sure sign that the baby is ill, and high fevers can cause brain damage and other serious problems. Before calling the doctor, therefore, it is important for parents to take the baby's temperature and make a list of observations. If the doctor thinks the caregiver can handle the problem without an office visit, the doctor's instructions need to be written down and followed exactly.

Getting to Know the Newborn

Physical Abilities

Newborns can see and smell. They are sensitive to pain and touch. They are able to hear through most of the last trimester of gestation. The same research that established bonding of unborn babies to their mothers by the sound of their voices (Chapter 7) has shown that two-day-old babies can distinguish their father's voices. The only sense that may not function well at birth is taste.

What newborns can do or feel depends on the development and efficient functioning of their central nervous systems. When only two hours old, they will follow a rapidly moving light with their eyes. Their pupils will dilate in darkness and constrict in light. They will suck a finger or nipple inserted into their mouths. They will turn in the direction in which their cheeks or corners of their mouths are touched. This behavior is sometimes called the **rooting reflex.** It enables babies to find and secure food. Newborns are likely to show this response after several touches rather than the first touch. This reflex helps newborns find the nipple when feeding. They can cry, cough, turn away, vomit, and lift their chins from a prone position. They can grasp an object placed in the palms of their hands. They can hiccup, sneeze, blink, yawn, and stretch. Their bodies will react to a loud sound. They can flex and extend their limbs, and smack their lips.

At least three reflex patterns which disappear later are present in most babies at birth.

1. One of these is the **grasp reflex.** In this reflex, the hand closes strongly when the palm is touched. This reflex is much weaker at the end of the first month. In most children it is gone by the fourth month, the time when voluntary actions of the hands are possible.

2. The **Moro** or **startle reflex** is set

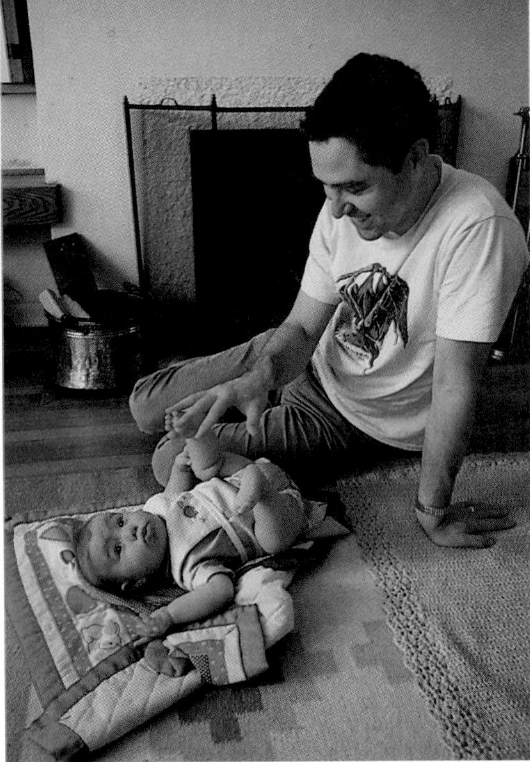

When a newborn's foot is stroked, the toes fan up. Older babies curl their toes down when the foot is stroked.

off by any sudden, intense stimulation, such as a loud noise or tapping on the abdomen. In this reflex, infants spread their arms apart and then bring them together as if they were hugging someone. Their legs move in the same way. This reflex disappears around three months of age.

3. A third reflex is the **Babinski reflex** which causes the fanning up of the toes when the sole of the foot is stroked. This gives way to the plantar reflex (curling down of the toes when the sole of the foot is stroked) which appears as the nerve centers mature.

Much of the behavior of newborns is in response to inner needs. Activity in some infants is greatest just before nursing. For others it is greater after being fed. In addition to general body movement, newborns are also active in an "attentive" way. They take in their environment. They react to sounds. In general, an infant's bodily activity varies with visual and auditory stimulation. For example, bodily activity usually decreases as the intensity of visual stimuli increases. A decrease in activity also follows initial responses when sounds persist.

Coping Techniques of the Newborn

It is fortunate that infants are so competent at birth because their new environment subjects them suddenly to many unfamiliar stresses, such as hunger, heat, cold, and pain. During the first weeks of life, most of their behavior is in direct response to these stresses. If they are hungry, excited, cold, tired, or in pain, they cry and thrash their arms and legs. The infant takes an active role in finding and securing food, first by crying, then by turning toward the source of stimulation. These reactions alter their environment significantly by bringing a person to tend to them. During the early weeks, their crying changes into various sounds. Parents quickly learn to recognize which sounds mean hunger, pain, fatigue, or the need for cuddling, loving, and holding. Henceforth, according to the behavior of those who serve them, certain aspects of the infants' behaviors will be reinforced, while others will be discouraged.

Thus, infants do a great deal to adapt themselves to the world and cause the world to adapt to them. Crying and food-seeking behavior are the principal methods of affecting their

Infants quickly learn that crying brings help.

environment. These two activities also foster the relationship between parent and child.

A father can participate in the feeding of the baby. A father can bring his baby to the mother for breast-feeding. He can remain with them during feeding and share in the closeness of family. He can talk with his wife and to his baby. Babies appreciate the cooing and singing of fathers, as well as mothers. Remember, babies as young as two days can distinguish their fathers' voices from those of other men. During bottle feeding, fathers can supply as much warmth as mothers can. By participating in the feeding, changing, bathing, cuddling, talking, and singing, fathers can develop bonds with their children that will influence their relationship throughout their lives.

A good feeling comes from meeting babies' needs. In addition, when two people touch, both people receive sensory and emotional satisfaction. It is in this situation that babies begin to build relationships with their fathers, grandparents, sisters, and brothers, and other caregivers. Much of an infant's behavior is based on a need to maintain a secure and stable physical and psychological environment. Balance is restored by food seeking, sucking, and swallowing, through breathing and moving, and by having baths and dry diapers. Babies may feel hungry, cold, tired, and wet all at the same time. One of these feelings—hunger—is more pressing than the rest and must be cared for first.

Caring for the Needs of a Newborn Child

Newborns feel that the world is a pretty good place when people feed them, keep them at a comfortable temperature, and help them develop and use their skills in different situations. When they feel this way they will naturally develop feelings of trust. Trust is essential to lasting relationships.

Feeding and Nutrition

The pediatrician will give parents advice regarding the baby's nutrition. That counseling will continue with each regular visit and any other time the parents request it.

The only food newborns need is breast milk or infant formula. There are definite advantages to both mother and child when newborn babies are breast-fed. At first, the breast secretes a substance called **colostrum.** By breast-feeding from the first day, the baby can be automatically immune to many forms of infections because colostrum contains antibodies from the mother. Milk is produced in the breast starting about three days after birth. Breast milk contains all the nutrients the baby needs, and it contains no bacteria and no substances that could cause allergic reactions.

For the mother, there are many advantages of breast-feeding. During pregnancy, a small amount of fat was stored in her body in preparation for breast-feeding. Breast-feeding will help her to lose that fat in the natural way. In addition, breast-feeding assists the hormonal changes that are essential to the return of the uterus to its normal size. Possibly most importantly, however, is the fact that breast-feeding is unique in its potential for bonding between mother and child.

For the baby, the feel of the breast and bottle are different. The breast is warm, flexible, and more responsive to the sucking movement than the hard bottle. Taste is different, too. Human milk has a small amount of fat at the beginning and a large amount at the end of nursing. Also the feel and smell of the mother's body are likely to be more intense in breast-feeding since baby is held close to the mothers body.

Some mothers choose not to breast-feed. She may find nursing painful or may be unable to produce all the milk the baby needs. She may need to return to work and find that breast-feeding does not fit into her schedule.

If, for whatever reason, the mother is unable or does not wish to breast-feed the baby, the best alternative is infant formula, which contains virtually all the same nutrients as mother's milk. Cow's milk is not advised. It contains too much protein and too little of several vitamins and minerals. Skim milk and lowfat milk do not contain the fats and carbohydrates infants need for normal development.

Whichever method is chosen, of greatest importance in the feeding situation is the relationship between the two people. At one time, it was believed that babies should be put on

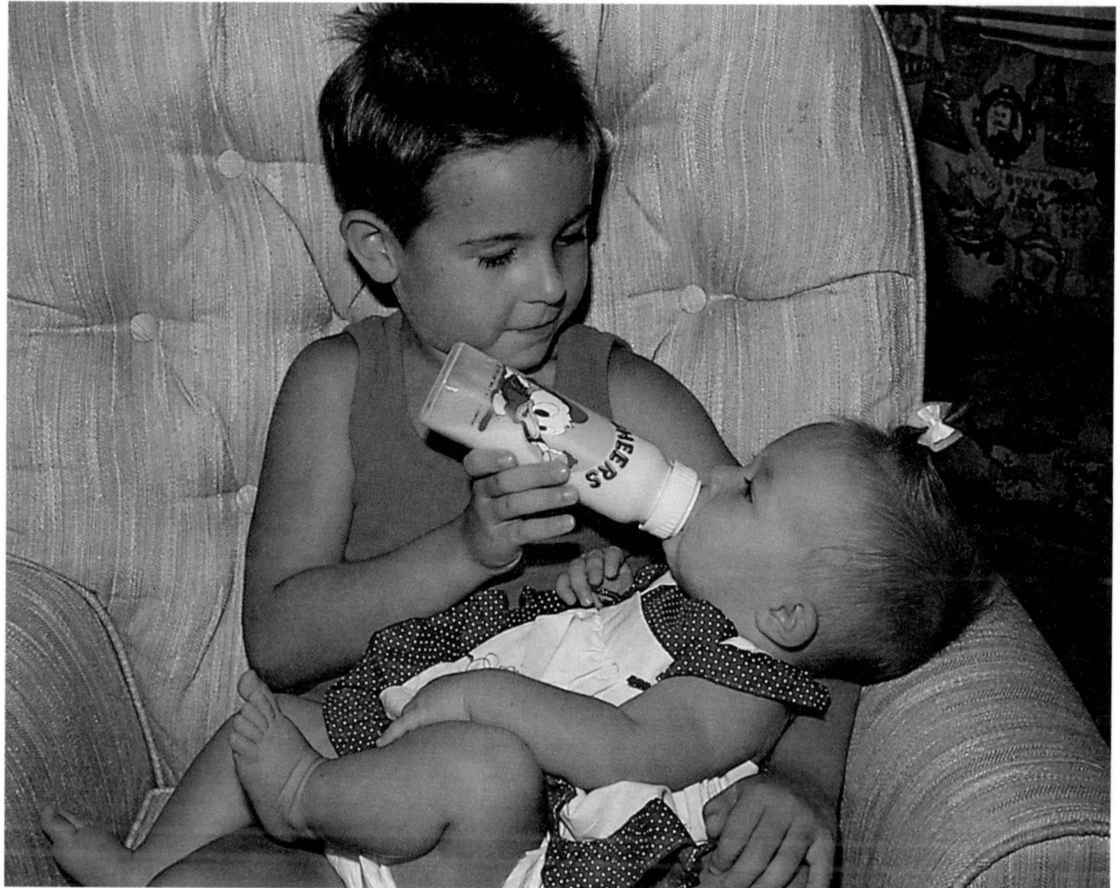

Other family members can feed the baby. Remember cuddling is an important part of a baby's mealtime.

a feeding schedule and that it be strictly followed. Now, experts realize that babies need to be fed when they are hungry. They need to eat as much as they want and when they want. Their stomach can only hold a small amount at one time, so they will need to eat often. Usually, this is six or seven times a day, about three to five hours apart.

During feeding two people contact each other and cooperate. The feelings that go along with this act promote personality development in both people. Babies' feelings of confidence and trust are enhanced by successful use of their skills for getting food. The sensory stimulation promotes growth and a feeling of well-being. In substituting bottles for breast-feeding, it is important to imitate the psychological situation as well as the nutritional one. In other words, holding and cuddling during feeding may be as important as getting the formula right. Although breast-feeding is confined to mothers, anybody can hold and cuddle babies.

Daily Food Guide	
Daily Food Guide During Breast-Feeding	**Suggested Number of Servings**
Fruits and vegetables	5 or more servings
Milk and milk products	4 servings
Meat, fish, poultry, dried beans, peas, nuts	3 servings
Whole-wheat or enriched breads and cereals	4 to 6 servings
Fats and sweets	vary according to calories needed

Nutrition

Nothing parents do in the care of their baby will be any more important than assuring proper nutrition. For a mother who is breast-feeding her baby, this means she must eat properly herself. She needs adequate supplies of protein, fats, carbohydrates, vitamins, and minerals, all of which she can obtain from a balanced diet including all four food groups. See the chart above. For bottle-fed babies, proper nutrition means being fed the prescribed formula, and only that, until their development indicates to the pediatrician that other foods are appropriate.

Why is proper nutrition so important to infants? Research is now showing that even brief periods of poor nourishment in infants can cause irreversible brain damage. Brain cells are increasing rapidly, both in number and size. Two-thirds of the brain development is completed in the first year of a child's life. By age three, that stage of brain development is finished. Thus, if proper nourishment is not provided during the early stages of brain development, no amount of good nutrition after three years of age can correct the damage. Infants who are poorly nourished will have fewer brain cells. As a result, they will have short attention spans and poor memories.

There are also severe physical problems associated with poor nutrition in children. Chronic malnutrition causes lower body resistance. Thus, malnourished infants are subject to greatly increased risks of infectious diseases, diarrhea which can lead to dehydration and death, pneumonia, debilitating meningitis, etc.

In the 1980s, a study of nutrition was conducted by the Center for Disease Control based in Atlanta. They reported that, in the United States, there are a half million malnourished children under the age of six. That does not mean, necessarily, that they do not have *enough* to eat. It means they are not eating balanced diets that provide all the nutrients children need to maintain health and normal development. Malnutrition is not restricted to children of poverty-stricken parents. It can occur when the parents neglect the parental responsibility of good nutrition, or when the parents do not know what constitutes proper diet.

Love

The most important ingredient any caregiver can bring to his or her relationship with a baby is love. Babies need to sense love if they are to develop emotionally, intellectually, and even physically. As we have noted before, when babies are deprived of love, they do not thrive. Sensing love, babies develop trust and feel comfortable about themselves and their relationships with others. Lacking this trust, they will be unable to experience love for others. Parents can shower their babies with expressions of love as a part of routine care.

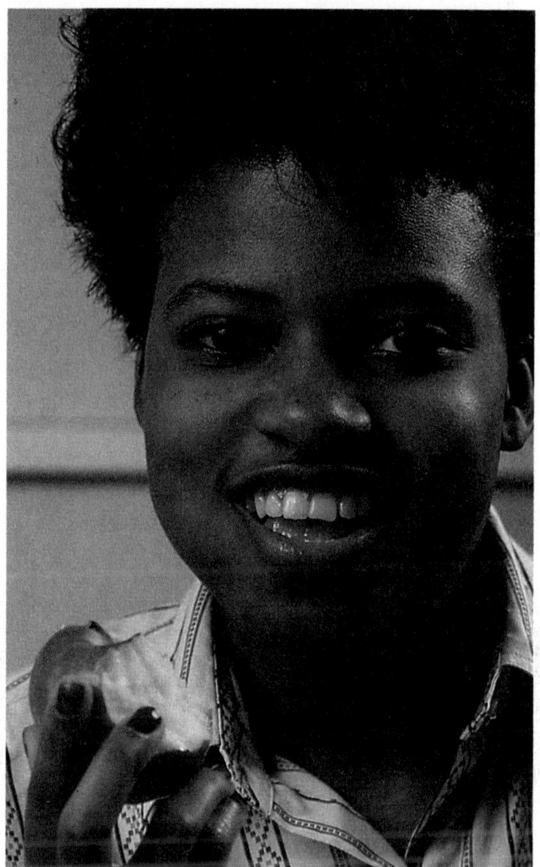

Breast-feeding women must be sure to follow proper nutritional guidelines.

Routine Care

Babies need to be fed, burped after each feeding, changed, bathed, and cuddled. They enjoy and learn from caregivers singing and talking to them, and caregivers enjoy watching and listening to the babies' responses. Verbalizing will help them to gain verbal skills. All these activities involve touching and/or interacting that can provide tender moments and ideal opportunities for building and strengthening the bonds between parents and child.

To maximize the enjoyment of routine care and minimize the possibility that it will become drudgery, parents must recognize the importance of each of these interactions to the lifelong relationship that has been established. With the proper attitude toward child care, each interaction becomes an opportunity rather than a chore.

Parents can help themselves to generate appropriate attitudes toward child care by setting **flexible schedules.** A schedule gives a sense of

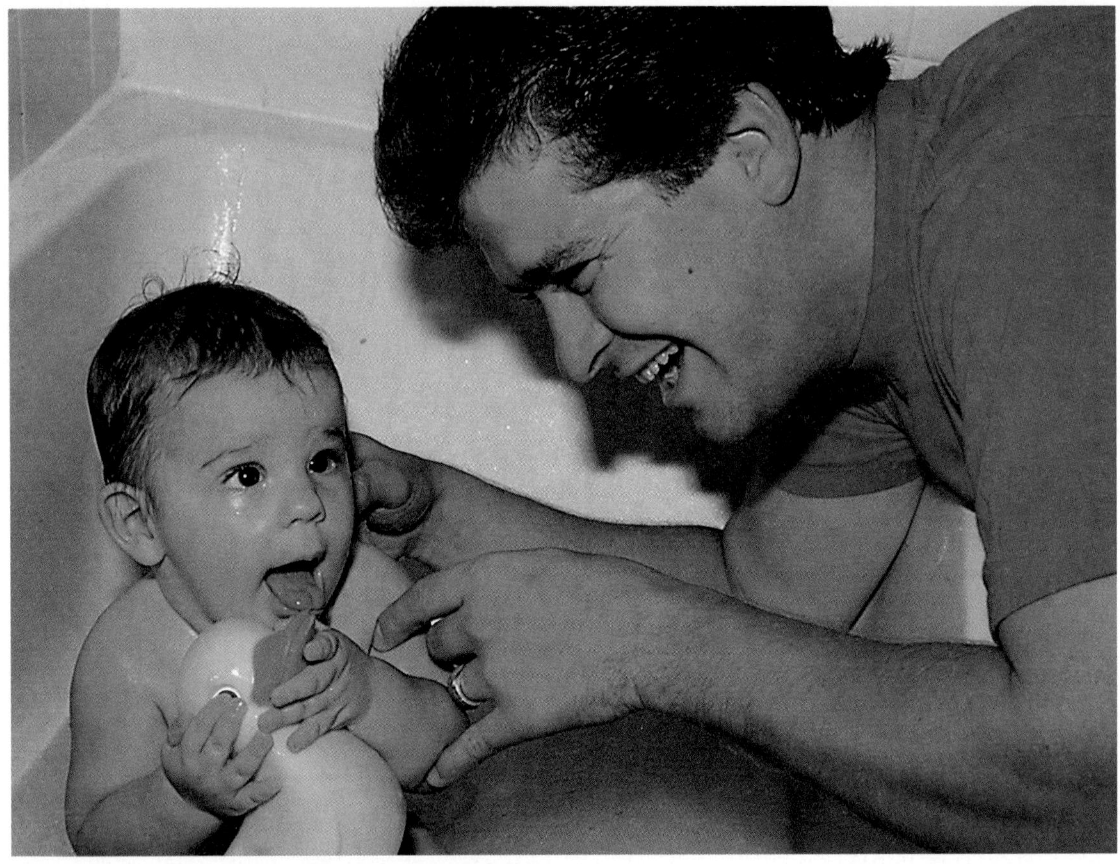

Both parents can enjoy sharing in meeting the routine care needs of their baby.

order to life and is a comfort in the face of numerous tasks that need to be accomplished each day. At the same time, trying to stick to a *rigid* schedule with a baby in the house can cause considerable frustration. As mentioned in Chapter 5, babies cannot be picked up and put down as if they were dolls. Babies have great influences on parents' activities. A flexible schedule is best, therefore. Caregivers should choose periods of time, rather than specific times, in each day when they would like to accomplish tasks.

Keeping to the flexible schedule may require a great deal of cooperation on the part of all family members. Fathers, mothers, and other family members may have certain roles they normally play, but they need to take over other people's roles from time to time. Mothers and fathers may be able to postpone other household duties or reassign them to other family members. Wives may discover that their husbands have hidden talents. Children may be thrilled to assume responsibilities they've never been given before, if parents let them know their contribution to the family effort is meaningful and very much appreciated. This period in family life is a time for everyone to get in tune with each other as well as with the new baby's schedule.

Warming the formula and sanitizing bottles are activities that we often associate with infants, but breast-feeding eliminates those tasks from a parent's busy schedule. (Of course, the dishwasher has eased the time problems, too.) There are other nonessentials caregivers can eliminate. For example, it is not necessary to bathe a baby *every* day. Cleanliness is very important after every diaper change, but a full bath every day can lead to skin rashes because of the removal of natural oils. When bathing a baby, use the following procedure.

A baby can be bathed as soon as the umbilical cord has dried up and fallen off. This is usually about one week. Some babies love a bath from the start. Others object the first few times it is tried. They will learn to tolerate it—and maybe even enjoy it. To bathe a baby, use a large dishpan for a tub, and fill it with water warm to the touch. Test the water temperature with your wrist or elbow. To keep the baby from slipping, it is a good idea to place a towel on the bottom of the tub.

• Before you start, make sure you have all the bath supplies within your reach. This includes soap, shampoo, washcloth, and towel. The most important rule in bathing a baby is *never, never* leave the baby alone, not even for an instant.

• Remove the clothes and diaper. Place the baby into the tub. Slip your right hand under the baby's shoulders with your thumb over the baby's right shoulder and your finger under the baby's armpit. Support the baby's rear with your left hand, hold the baby's right thigh with your thumb and fingers. Carefully lower the baby into the tub feet first. Keep the baby's head out of the water.

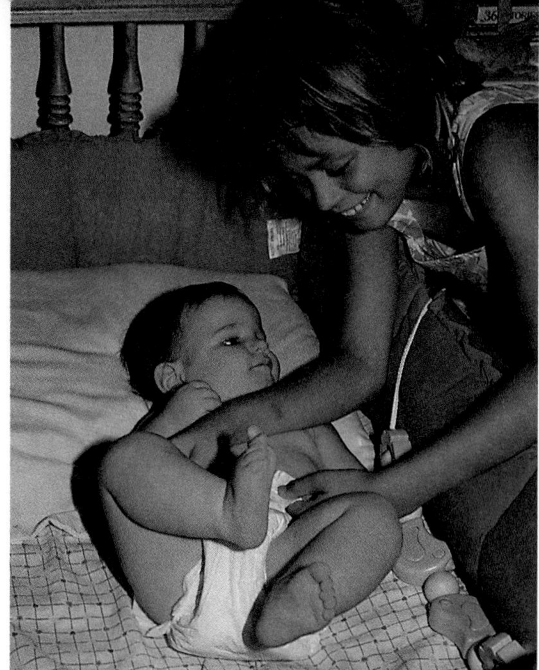

Assuming some caregiving tasks for a younger sibling may become a responsibility for older children.

• Soap the front of the baby's body. Wash inside the baby's skin creases. You don't need to turn the baby over to wash the back, simply reverse your hold by putting the baby's chest on your left hand.

• Some babies develop a condition known as cradle cap. This is a yellowish crust which forms on the scalp. Cradle cap can be controlled by washing the baby's hair every day. Rubbing a little baby oil onto the scalp will loosen the crust so that it can be removed easily with a washcloth. Never rub the baby's scalp vigorously. If

A Matter of Fact

Diapering the baby gives one the chance to show that the baby's comfort is important. A smiling parent who talks sweetly while diapering gives the baby a chance for a deepened sense of trust and love.

Babies need to be kept very clean, so they need frequent changes of wet and soiled diapers. The baby's bottom needs to be carefully washed after the soiled diaper is removed.

Here's how to diaper a baby:

1. Take off soiled diaper. If the baby's diaper was wet, clean the baby with a warm, clean washcloth and apply a small amount of baby oil. Use toilet paper or tissue to remove soil from a bowel movement. Then wash the baby with a warm, clean washcloth. Baby powder and oils are not essentials. Cornstarch is cheaper and is perfectly safe to use if the baby seems to have a rash. If talcum powder is used, it should be placed in the hand and carefully patted onto the baby's bottom. Shaking the talcum powder carelessly could cause the infant to inhale the powder.

2. Put on a clean diaper. The choice of diapers depends on considerations of time and money, as well as convenience. Professional diaper service or disposable diapers will cost at least six times as much in the first year as purchasing cloth diapers and laundering them at home. Hold the baby's ankles and lift the body slightly. Slide the clean diaper underneath the baby. If you are using cloth diapers, place extra thickness of the diaper in the back for girls and in the front for boys. Bring the diaper up between the baby's legs and pin with safety pins. Keep your finger between the diaper and the baby's skin as you pin. If you like, you can cover the diapers with plastic baby pants.

   If you choose disposable diapers, look for male and female versions. Disposable diapers for boys will contain extra protection in the front. Those for girls will have extra protection in the middle. Disposable diapers stay fastened with adhesive tabs, so safety pins are not needed.

3. Take care of used diapers. Throw away used tissue, toilet paper, and other soiled supplies. Put disposable diapers in a covered trash container. Do not flush disposable diapers down the toilet. This will clog the plumbing. Wet cloth diapers should be placed in a diaper container filled with a water and borax or vinegar mixture. Rinse soiled diapers first by holding the diaper firmly in a clean, flushing toilet. Then place the soiled diaper in the diaper container.

treating cradle cap with baby oil does not work, consult your pediatrician.

• Lift the baby out of the tub using the same safety hold. Then place the baby onto a dry, warm surface, and gently pat dry with a large towel. Be sure you dry the baby's skin creases. To keep the baby's diaper area dry and comfortable, use baby cornstarch. This prevents redness and chafing.

Caregivers should use bathtime as an opportunity for closeness and fun. Babies enjoy warm water, and bathtime commotion can help to build motor skills.

Crying

Everyone in the family should be aware of the fact that babies cry. Because they are individuals, some babies cry more than others. Sometimes they cry for no apparent reason. Crying can be frustrating and even irritating, especially to those who do not understand that it is normal for babies to cry. Some terrible child abuse has resulted when a baby would not stop crying on command. Thus, all family members should be willing to calmly sing or talk to a crying baby, walk with a crying baby, sit in a rocking chair with a crying baby, and have unfailing patience with a crying baby. Babies sense nervousness and tension in those around them. Their resulting insecurity will only make them cry more.

Caring for Family Relationships

It would be unfortunate to neglect old family bonds while forming bonds with the new baby. A husband may need to be especially attentive to family needs when a new baby enters the household. His wife inadvertently may pay less attention to older children and to him, as well. Both parents should recognize that this can happen and work at their own relationship to assure that no rift develops. They also must make sure that no older child feels displaced because of all the attention to the new family member.

The mother may not necessarily be feeling her best. If she had an episiotomy during the birth, there is some soreness. The shrinking of the uterus requires about four to six weeks, and she may experience some cramping from this, especially in the early stages, during breast-feeding. The hormonal changes involved in this recovery process may contribute to depressed feelings. She may not regain her shape as quickly as she thought she would, and this could be distressing. Adding to all of these things is the physical strain of being up every few hours of the night to feed the baby. A mature, caring husband can do much to help her through this passing phase, which has come to be known as postpartum blues.

Some parents experience an even greater challenge. They have no spouse to help with the work schedule or baby care. If possible, they should ask other family members to help them out. Perhaps they can find a neighbor who could lend a hand if they in turn can do a favor for the neighbor.

Safety

Babies are helpless creatures. They are totally dependent on us to keep them safe. It is our responsibility as adults, therefore, to be ever alert to all the possible hazards in a baby's life. The following is by no means a complete list, but it will serve to show examples of how caregivers must think when caring for a baby.

A. The slats in a baby's crib should be close enough together so that the baby's head could not *even come close* to fitting between them. Numerous cases of strangulation have resulted from babies getting caught.

B. Don't leave a baby unattended on the changing table, *even for a second.* The same goes for *any place* from which the baby could fall.

C. Don't leave a baby unattended in the bath, *even for a second.*

D. Don't prop a bottle for a baby and then leave. The baby could *choke and die.*

E. Protect your baby's tender skin from overexposure to direct sunlight.

F. Use caps or bonnets to protect babies' ears on windy days, even when it is warm.

G. Use approved safety measures to protect your baby when riding in an auto.

The Safe Nursery

Safety is the most important consideration to keep in mind when selecting furnishings for a baby. These tips will help you evaluate the safety of new or secondhand nursery equipment.

Cribs

More infants die every year in crib-related accidents than with any other product related to children. Thousands of infants are injured seriously enough to require emergency-room care.

If you're buying a new crib:

- Remove and dispose of all plastic wrapping materials. Never use thin plastic cleaning or trash bags as mattress covers. The plastic may cling to a child's face and cause suffocation.
- If you buy bumper pads for the crib, make sure they fit around the entire crib, tie or snap in place, and have at least six straps.
- Buy cribs with corner posts that are less than 5/8 of an inch taller than the rails. These corner post extensions can catch a child's

clothing or any strings that may be around the child's neck and cause strangulation.

If you buy a crib secondhand:

- Never use a crib with missing slats. The slats should be securely in place and no more than 2 3/8 inches apart.
- Use a snug-fitting mattress. The mattress is too small if you can fit two fingers between the edge of the mattress and crib side.
- Older crib designs may allow an infant's head to become caught in the openings between the corner post and the horizontal piece that runs along the top of the crib. Select a crib design either without the curved openings or corner posts, or one where the opening is too large for the head to become trapped. Unscrew high corner posts or saw them flush with the headboard or footboard.
- If you paint or refinish the crib, use high-quality household enamel paint and let it dry thoroughly. Old paints you may have around the house are unacceptable. They may contain a higher percentage of lead if manufactured before February 1978. Check the label on the paint can to make sure the manufacturer does not caution against using the product on items such as cribs.

Crib Safety

- Cribs are useful for a limited amount of time. Once the child reaches 35 inches in height, he or she has outgrown the crib and is ready to sleep in a bed.
- If you place a crib next to a window, don't let drapery cords get near a child's reach. They could strangle a child.
- Don't hang a toy on a string, laundry bag, or any stringed object on the corner post where a child could become caught in it and strangle.
- Lock the side rail in its raised position as soon as the child can stand up. Lower the mattress to its lowest position and take out the bumper pads or large toys. Active toddlers have been known to use these items to climb out of the crib.

High Chairs

- If you're buying a new high chair, look for one with a wide base. A wide base will make the chair stable.
- Look at different models and compare the sturdiness of straps and belts. Look for straps that are easy to operate, and use them every time. Babies are surprisingly strong.

High Chair Safety

- Don't let a child stand up in a high chair.
- Keep the high chair far enough away from a table, counter, or wall so that the child can't push off from it.
- Each time you set the chair up, be sure the locking device on a folding high chair is locked.
- Don't stray too far from the high chair, especially if the child has

Playpens

- The mesh netting on a playpen should be a very small weave—smaller than the buttons on a baby's clothing. Don't use a playpen with holes in the mesh sides. They can entrap a child's head and cause strangulation.
- The slats on a wooden playpen should be no more than 2 3/8 inches apart.
- Check for holes or tears in the vinyl or fabric-covered top rail of playpens. A teething baby may chew off vinyl pieces and choke.
- If staples are used to attach the mesh netting to the floor of the playpen, make sure they are not loose or missing.

shown an ability to unfasten the safety straps.

Safety for Hook-on Chairs

- Used as substitutes for high chairs, hook-on chairs are attached to the table edge. Don't place the chair where the child's feet can reach table supports to push off from and dislodge the chair from the table.
- Use the restraining straps, and don't leave the child unattended.
- A hook-on chair with a clamp to lock it onto the table offers additional security.

Playpen Safety

- Large toys and bumper pads can be used for climbing out. Remove these items from inside a playpen.
- Don't tie items across the top of the playpen. They can strangle a baby.
- Don't leave an infant in a mesh playpen or crib with the drop-side down. Infants can roll into the space between the mattress and loose mesh side and suffocate.

Back Carriers

- Back carriers make it easier to go shopping, hiking, or walking with a baby because both arms are free. Don't carry a newborn or young infant in a back carrier. A baby's neck is not able to withstand jolts and avoid neck injury until four or five months of age.
- Buy a back carrier suitable for the child's size and weight. Try it on with the baby in it. The back carrier should be deep enough to support the baby's back. The leg openings need to be big enough to avoid chafing the baby's legs yet small enough to prevent the baby from slipping out.
- Choose a back carrier that is sturdily made with strong stitching or heavy-duty snaps. Look for a padded covering over the metal frame near the baby's face to protect the baby from bumps.

Back Carrier Safety

- Always use the restraining straps to hold the baby in the carrier.
- Be sure the child's fingers are out of the way of the frame joints when folding the joints.
- Promptly repair ripped seams, missing or loose snaps, and frayed seats or straps—or discard the carrier.
- When you lean over, bend from the knees to prevent the child from falling out of the back carrier.

Safety for Diaper Pails

- Keep the diaper pail closed tightly, and out of a child's reach.

Children have fallen head first into them and drowned. The U.S. Consumer Product Safety Commission reports that children have also been known to reach into diaper pails and eat the cake deodorizers.

Pacifier Safety

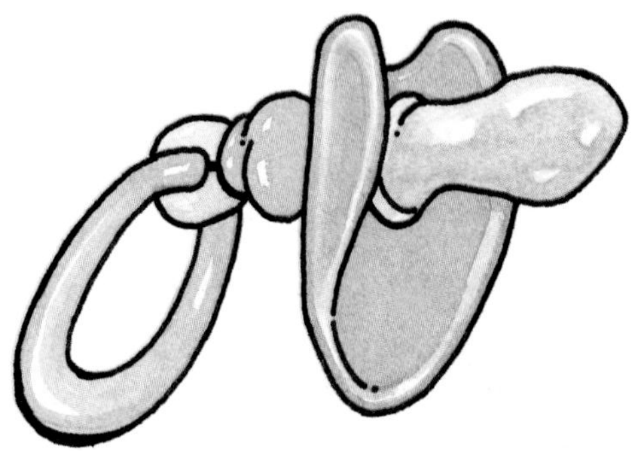

- Buy pacifiers strong enough so that they will not come apart. A baby could choke or suffocate on small pieces.
- Pacifier guards or shields must be large enough and firm enough to prevent the pacifier from being sucked entirely into the baby's mouth.
- Pacifier guards or shields must have ventilation holes. They make it possible for the baby to breathe if he or she gets the pacifier stuck in the mouth.
- Pacifiers cannot be sold with a ribbon, string, or cord attached.
- Check for deterioration periodically due to age, exposure to food, and sunlight. Throw the pacifier away immediately if you notice a change in texture, tears, holes, or weakening.

While many parents give their babies pacifiers, the fact is that pacifiers are in no way essential for a baby's welfare. Pacifiers serve only to keep babies quiet which, of course, slows their attempts to attain verbal skills.

Life's Work

M. David Ricks and Gail B. Ricks

- **President and Vice President of Cultural Designs Shadow**
- **David Ricks, B.S. in Industrial Arts Education and post graduate management and supervision courses**
- **Gail Ricks, B.S. in Business Administration**

The Ricks design and manufacture baby products, including the BA-BA Baby Bottle Identification Collar. Their day begins with telephone calls to prospective customers and their sales representatives across the country. They oversee the manufacturing and distribution of their product. Throughout the course of the day, time is allowed to meet with customers, vendors, and associates who handle other functions such as advertising and marketing.

The Ricks say, "Being self-employed, they must be committed to the company and be prepared to spend as much time as necessary to accomplish their goals." That means not following regular office hours. They both average 11 to 16 hours a day, six days a week at their work.

The Ricks say, "Good communication skills are needed in every phase of this type of career. Time management and financial management are needed as well as professionalism in your business behavior." The Ricks feel that receiving a U.S. Utility Patent on a product that they invented and then selling the product to a national retail chain store is their most rewarding job-related accomplishment.

For a student considering going into the Ricks' profession, they recommend, "Be prepared to encounter an uphill climb for many days and nights. And do not become discouraged when you hear the word 'no.' You may hear it 25 times before you hear one 'yes.' But remember that the yes answers are the ones that you are developing your skills and talents for."

In Review

Vocabulary

Apgar score
rooting reflex
grasp reflex
Moro reflex
Babinski reflex
pediatrician
immunization
colostrum
flexible schedule

Summary

- ✓ A newborn baby's physical health can be evaluated within the first minute after birth. One such evaluation is a series of tests resulting in an Apgar score.
- ✓ Babies vary greatly in their appearance at birth, but some things they have in common include: they are tiny, they are wrinkled and blotchy, and they have puffy eyes.
- ✓ Newborns can see, hear, smell, cry, cough, vomit, hiccup, sneeze, blink, yawn, and stretch. They can flex their limbs, lift their chins, and root for the nipple to obtain food.
- ✓ Despite all the abilities of newborn babies, they are totally dependent on their parents or other caregivers to satisfy their needs for food, shelter, cleanliness, medical care, and attention that includes holding, cuddling, loving, and intellectual stimulation.
- ✓ Babies develop certain coping techniques by which they gain a degree of control over their environments. Babies' actions and parents' reactions form the basis of ongoing interpersonal relationships.
- ✓ The importance of proper nutrition for infants cannot be stressed enough. Malnutrition in very young children has devastating, permanent effects—both physical and psychological.
- ✓ Cooperation between mother, father, and other children in the family can spread the responsibilities and the joys of having an infant in the home. This is a time when each family member should be especially sensitive to the needs of all other members.
- ✓ Proper care of an infant requires parents and other caregivers to be aware of certain common-sense safety rules.

Questions

1. Why is the Apgar score so significant? How does it serve the newborn?
2. What would be your expectations from a baby who had an Apgar score of nine? of two?
3. Define the following mechanisms of the newborn: startle reflex, grasp reflex, and Babinski reflex.
4. How do the reflexes listed in #3 serve as defense mechanisms?
5. "Newborn" is the term used for an infant during the first 10 to 14 days of life. What are the newborn's coping techniques?
6. Describe the physical appearance of a newborn baby.
7. What are the physical abilities of a newborn?
8. What can fathers do with newborn babies to build the foundation of a lasting relationship?
9. If you think your baby is sick, and you call your pediatrician, what question can you expect the doctor to ask first?
10. What reasons are there for parents to learn about nutrition and to provide a balanced diet for their baby?
11. A new baby in the home could possibly be disruptive to family routine and to personal relationships. Discuss ways that a family might use the experience, instead, to reinforce relationships.

Activities

1. Do you think you can spoil newborns by responding to their crying? Explain your answer.
2. Babies start to develop a feeling of trust soon after they are born. Give examples of what parents can do to help babies develop this trust.
3. Research statistics show that most fathers who are child abusers had little to do with the abused child as a newborn infant. Suggest a possible explanation for this observation.
4. As a library exercise, find books and articles on nutrition. Write down the typical number of servings from each of the basic food groups that an adolescent needs each day.

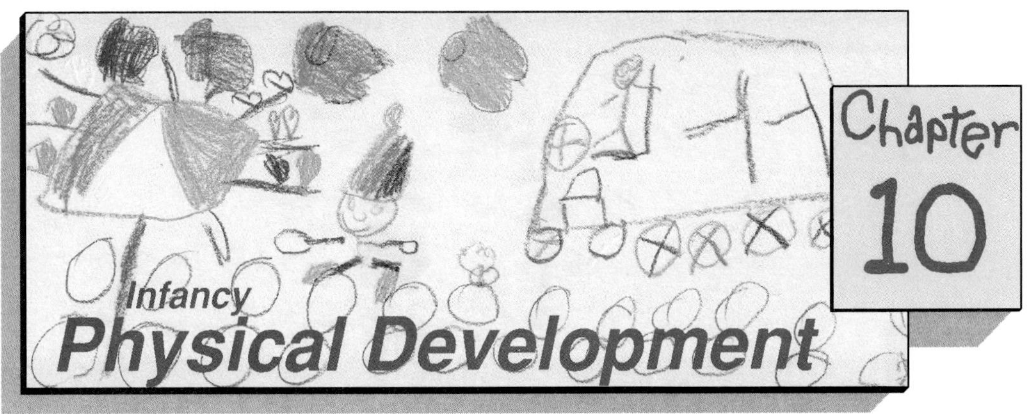

Infancy Physical Development

This chapter will help you:

- identify the stages of physical growth in infants
- identify the sequence in motor development leading to locomotion
- identify the sequence in motor development leading to manipulative skills
- recognize the importance of trust to normal motor development
- understand the parent's role in encouraging sensorimotor development
- understand the parent's role in providing a safe environment for a developing baby

The Maturing Infant

Maturation is the process of coming to full development. Maturation involves emotional, social, intellectual, and physical growth. It is the emergence of personal characteristics and behavior through the growth process. It is becoming more and more evident today that children mature at an earlier age than in the past. This accelerated growth rate may be due to several factors: scientific and medical advances, increased knowledge of psychological needs, and better nutrition.

Infancy is the period of life when development is most rapid. The intensity and range of learning during this time exceeds that of any other period. Maturation is clearly evident during this period by skills the infant develops. It is dramatically shown by physical growth.

As mentioned in Chapter 9, on the average, newborns weigh 7 or 8 pounds (3 or 3.6 kilograms) and are about 20 inches (50 centimeters) long. After the first month or so, infants begin to look like the babies seen in advertisements and photo albums—chubby and smooth skinned with button noses. New, coarser hair comes in during infancy replacing the fine hair of the newborn. Compared with older children, babies have large foreheads, large eyes,

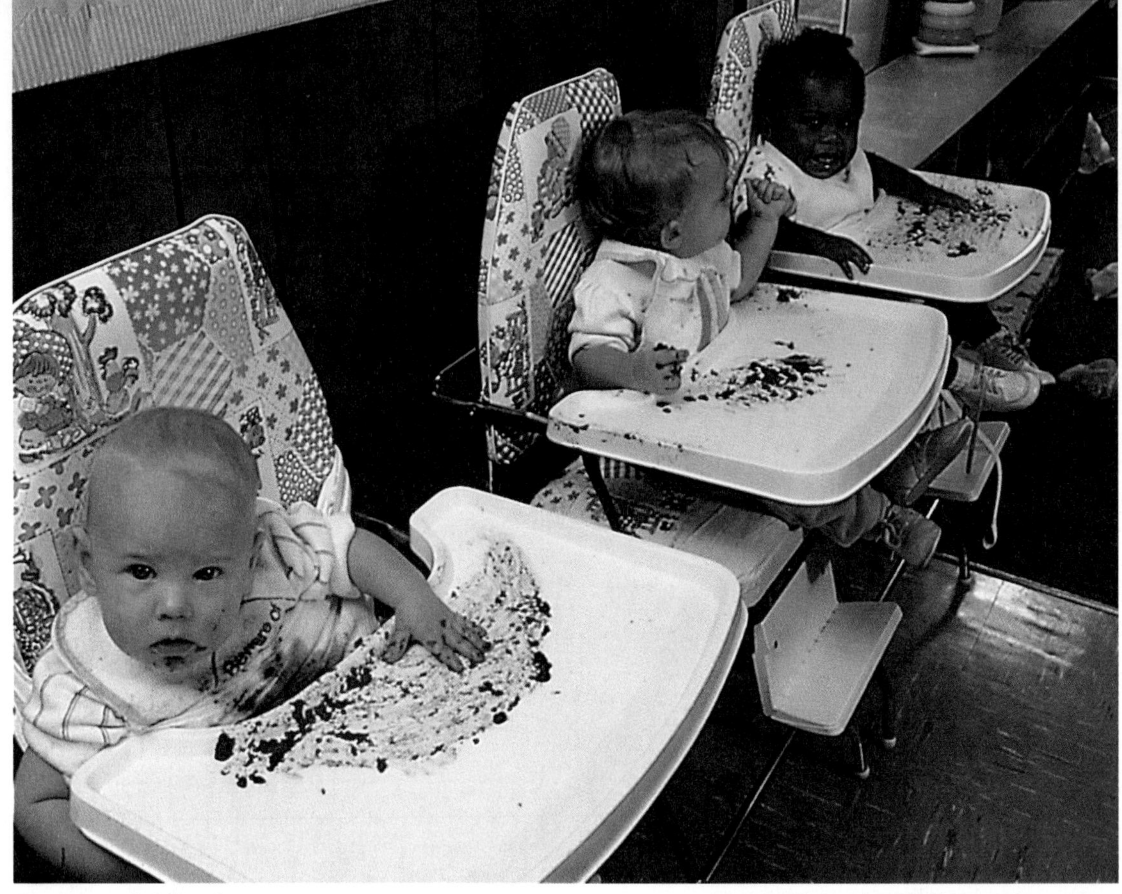

Eating solid foods is an experience in tastes, textures, and small-motor skill coordination.

small noses, small chins, and plump cheeks. Their hands and feet are chubby and their abdomens are round. Their skin is soft and delicate. In four or five months, their birth weight is doubled. It is tripled in a year. Their height is nearly doubled at about two years of age.

Teeth

Infants' first teeth start appearing around six months of age. However, they may begin as early as three months or as late as 12 months. The average one-year-old has about six teeth.

When a tooth is coming through the gum, the gum may be sore. This can make a baby irritable. Baby nonaspirin pain relievers or sucking on something cold may help relieve the pain. Teething lotions should not be used.

Nutrition

As discussed in Chapter 9, at first infants need only breast milk or formula. They will stay on this at least through the first year.

At about four to six months, babies can start eating solid foods. Start slowly at first to give babies a chance to get used to different tastes, textures, and temperatures. Begin with simple foods such as rice cereal or applesauce.

Introduce only one new food at a time and feed it for several days. Watch for allergic reactions. By introducing only one food, parents will know which food is the culprit if the baby has a reaction. Vomiting, diarrhea, a skin rash, or signs of fussiness are indications of an allergy. Stop feeding that food. If babies don't react to a food, it can be fed to them any time in the future without worry.

Sleep

Young infants sleep a lot. Many spend most of the day sleeping. They wake up when they are hungry or need changing. At the end of the first year, babies still need a lot of sleep, but less than newborns. Most one-year-olds sleep through the night. They may wake up briefly and softly talk or play in their cribs. Parents should let them go back to sleep by themselves unless they are obviously hungry or in trouble or pain.

Sleep needs for individual children vary. Some 18-month-olds need only eight hours. Others may need as much as 17 hours. Parents should not try to force a set number of hours of sleep. Imagine trying to keep an active infant quiet and in bed.

Parents should establish a regular bedtime from the start and then notice what time the child prefers to get up. If it's too early in the morning for the parents' comfort, they can move the bedtime to a later hour at night.

Parents can tell if children are getting enough sleep by watching how they act in the daytime. Alert and active children probably are getting enough sleep. On the other hand, lack of sleep may cause children to be cranky and underactive.

A bedtime routine should be estab-

A Matter of Fact

Many caregivers today are preparing homemade baby food. It's not too difficult, and it's less expensive than commercial baby food. Nutritious foods should be chosen, such as fruits, vegetables, meat, and poultry. In addition, the amount of sugar and salt can be controlled.

To make baby food, follow these steps:

- Small amounts of the family's food can be adapted for a baby. Set aside the baby's portion.
- Cook foods until tender. Do not add spices, sugar, or salt. Remove skin, seeds, extra fat, gristle, or bones from foods before or after they are cooked.
- Cut the cooked food into small cubes. Foods then can be mashed, strained through a sieve, or pureed in a blender. A baby-food mill will grind cooked fruits and vegetables to a smooth texture. Meats and poultry will be coarser, but edible by a baby.
- Before feeding the baby, test the consistency. Rub a small amount between your fingers. If the particles feel too large, process the food again. If the food is too thick, thin with milk, fruit or vegetable juice, or cooking water. If it's too thin, add infant cereal.

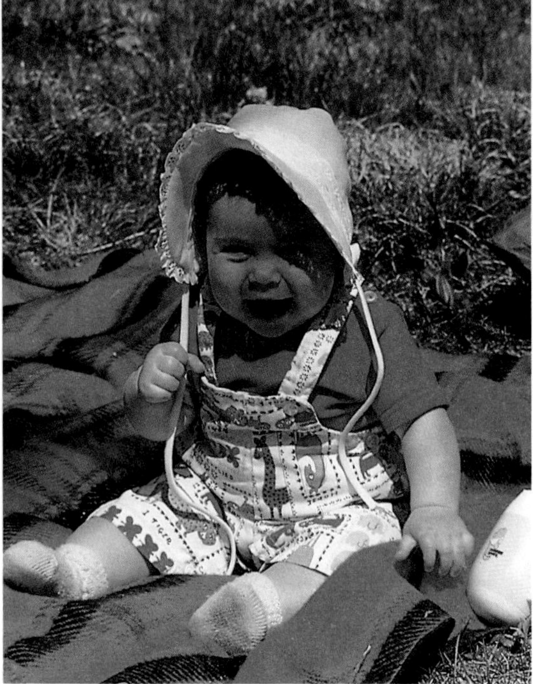

A new skill, sitting alone, is achieved before infants progress to crawling.

lished for children. Parents need to create a ritual that's pleasant, relaxing, and quieting. Singing songs while cuddling relaxes both parent and child. Parents should avoid scary or action-packed TV shows and loud music.

Most children also nap twice a day. Just as with nighttime sleep, children should nap in their own room and bed.

Locomotion

As you read in Chapter 9, the newborn has no effective means of movement from place to place. From a supine (face up) or prone (face down) position, the infant may shift about a little. This movement, however, can hardly be called **locomotion** (the power of moving from place to place). In order for newborns to change position, they must rely on someone else.

As infants grow and develop, they progress through the developmental stages of locomotion. The five developmental stages of locomotion occur as follows:

1. sitting with support
2. sitting alone
3. active efforts toward locomotion
4. creeping and walking (with support)
5. walking alone

The last stage occurs around 13 months, although some children walk alone as early as nine months or as late as 17 months. Keep in mind that each child is as unique in development as in personality. Ages given throughout this book are the average. Children learn in stages. Each stage is a prerequisite for the next one.

Each infant develops a unique pattern of growth. Some children move from one stage to another very rapidly, but then remain longer in the next stage. Their progress is determined by the maturing of the brain as well as the satisfaction they get from any one stage. For example, babies who are very proficient in crawling may be satisfied. They do not try very hard to proceed to the next step. Then, when they do try to walk if they meet with accidents or overprotection by adults, they may continue to crawl for a longer period. Ultimately, however, they will become as proficient at walking as they are at crawling. Babies' worlds expand and stimulation increases greatly when they learn to move from one place to another.

The parts of the brain concerned with locomotion grow as the baby passes through the locomotor sequence. The motor region of the cortex matures faster than the other regions. The cerebellum, the part of the brain concerned with balance and posture, grows slowly during the first few months, but then grows rapidly between six and 18 months.

The following sequences describe in detail the progression of locomotor development during the first and second year. Note that because these groupings cover a range of ages, such as one to three months, within the grouping a particular skill may progress through various stages. For example, one-month-old infants lift their chin up slightly when lying face down. Three-month-old babies are capable of lifting their head up high when lying prone. Therefore you see both skills listed for that age group.

First Year

1-3 MONTHS

- Holds head up for a few moments when lying on stomach
- Pushes with both feet against a person's hand
- Kicks feet vigorously when lying down
- Moves about in bath, kicks feet, etc.
- Lifts head up slightly when lying on back
- Rolls from side to back
- Lifts head high when lying prone

4-6 MONTHS

- Holds back firmly when held in sitting position
- Lifts up head and chest when lying prone
- Holds head erect when body held in sitting position
- Lifts head and shoulders when lying on back
- Rolls from front to back or from back to front
- Plays with his or her toes
- Demonstrates first stages of crawling: pushes on hands, draws up knees, etc.

7-9 MONTHS

- Sits without support
- Demonstrates first stages of walking: moves feet alternately when held up
- Tries vigorously to crawl, using both hands and feet
- Makes some progress crawling forward or backward

10-12 MONTHS

- Stands when held up
- Sits well in a chair
- Pulls up from crawling or sitting positions by grasping the furniture
- Stands holding onto furniture
- Crawls well or gets about freely by some other method—for example, bear walk
- Sidesteps around the inside of crib or playpen holding onto railings
- Walks when led by adult holding one or both hands

Second Year

13-15 MONTHS

- Stands alone
- Walks alone, at first unsteadily
- Kneels on floor or chair, balances in this position
- Crawls up the stairs, but not yet down
- Likes to walk pushing a toy or cart

16-18 MONTHS

- Walks well
- Stoops to pick up a toy without losing balance
- Climbs into a low chair
- Walks backward
- Likes to walk pulling a toy on a string

19-21 MONTHS

- Crawls up and down stairs
- Jumps with both feet off the floor at the same time
- Runs
- Walks up stairs, holding adult's hand
- Climbs and stands up on a chair

22-23 MONTHS

- Jumps off a step, both feet off the ground at the same time
- Seats self at a table, placing chair first
- Walks up and down stairs holding adult's hand or banister
- Kicks a ball
- Climbs stairs confidently

Adapted from Ruth Griffiths, *The Abilities of Babies*. University of London Press, Hodder and Stoughton, England.

Manipulation Skills

Babies use their hands to find out about the world and change it. They cannot do much with their hands until they can sit up, although they try in the early weeks. The grasp reflex, present at birth, is still strong during the first three months. This reflex consists of grasping anything that is placed against the palm such as a rattle or another person's finger. The grasp reflex disappears before the first half year.

Studies of how babies learn to use their hands have shown that there are

A Matter of Fact

What toys are right for infants up to six months old? A toy made for watching is a good choice for this age group. "Watching" toys include hanging objects or mobiles that move by the wind or wind-up action.

As the infant gains control of his or her hands, squeeze toys (make sure any noise they make is not too loud or sudden), rattles, disks, interlocking keys on a ring, and toys on suction cups are good toy choices for infants four months and beyond.

Infants are aware of newness in objects, people, and events—and they begin to develop definite preferences! To promote make-believe play for infants, select soft toys a baby can grab, stuffed animals, or soft handpuppets held by an adult.

Babies love to look at themselves in mirrors. This fascination with mirrors peaks at four to six months. One idea is to attach a large, unbreakable mirror to the crib, playpen, or wall within the baby's line of vision.

What's right for infants 7 to 12 months old? Now infants are to the point where toy exploration is a serious business. They like to open and close, empty and fill, push and pull, bang, poke, twist, squeeze, drop, and shake.

For manipulative play, choose roly-poly toys, activity boxes and cubes, and containers with objects to empty and fill. Construction toys such as rubber blocks are appropriate. After about 10 months of age, two- to three-piece puzzles, brightly colored and lightweight for a crib, are fun.

Infants in this age group like splishing and splashing in the tub. Look for activity boxes for the bath or simple floating toys. Some infants will enjoy books. Cloth, plastic, and small cardboard books are appropriate for this age. They like to look at pictures in books while an adult reads.

four steps involved in the process. These steps are:

1. making eye contact with the object
2. approaching the object with the hand
3. grasping the object
4. disposing of the object. At first babies do this with little skill or accuracy. As they mature, though, their actions become more refined, fluid, and directed.

Using our hands actually takes great skill. We take for granted the coordination that is required to tie a shoelace, peel an orange, or wind a watch. **Fine prehension,** that is, the ability to pick up and hold small objects, requires coordination of the fingers, hands, and arms. It also requires good visual attention. This coordination does not come readily to babies. It takes several weeks and months for their nerves and muscles to mature. It also takes time for children to learn about their environment.

During the first three months, babies contact objects with their eyes

Look, Listen, and Learn

The child's ability to grasp small objects can be observed by placing cereals such as Cheerios on the high chair tray or table. Infants at this age love to eat the small circles because it allows them to perfect their thumb and forefinger coordination as well as their hand-to-mouth coordination.

Small cubes of toast and quartered banana slices can also be given. Care needs to be taken so that the infant doesn't choke. Anything that is available will be grasped and put in the mouth, so the infant needs to be guarded and guided away from buttons, coins, marbles, pills, and small pieces of hard candy.

Here are some other ways to observe an infant's reflex actions:

- Hang a colorful mobile above a baby's crib, and watch the eyes of the baby as you move the mobile slowly to the right, then slowly to the left. Does the baby follow the movement of the mobile with the eyes?
- Place a squeeze toy within the baby's reach, and make a sound with the toy that the baby can hear. What was the baby's reaction?
- Hand a baby a toy. How does the baby reach for the toy? Are both arms raised? Does the baby reach too high? Are the movements fluid? Based on your observations, what level of manipulation has the baby attained?

You may want to create observation exercises of your own. Can you come up with others?

more than with their hands. At first they only look at objects in their line of vision and just for a few seconds. In a short time, they are following moving objects in many directions and regarding them for a longer period of time.

As the grasp reflex weakens in infants, they begin to initiate the touching of objects by reaching. They make their first attempts at reaching when they are around four months old. Before grasping an object, they make visual contact with it and approach it with their hands. Their first reaching movements are awkward. Both of their arms are active and their whole body strains as they reach. They exhibit crude shoulder and elbow movements. By six months of age, they are likely to be successful in reaching an object on the first try.

From four to six months, a baby's reaching movement seems to consist of three separate acts, raising a hand, thrusting it forward, and lowering it. Up to seven months old, babies raise their hands rather high when reaching for an object. From seven months to

Note how children progress from a pawlike grasp to precise dexterity.

one year, they lower the height of their approach. By 10 months, their reaching movement is fluid and better directed. There is no trace of the three separate acts. Their reach is now graceful and accurate. Infants' first attempts at grasping an object are just as awkward as their first attempts at reaching one. Six-month-old infants lack the fine dexterity needed to pick up an object gracefully and accurately by using a thumb and forefinger grasp. The baby's first grips involve the palm. When reaching for an object, a six-month-old baby positions his or her forearms directly above an object and uses a palm grasp to secure it. The thumb generally points down from the extended hand giving a pawlike grasp. At this time, a baby might use both hands to grasp the object.

By seven months of age, infants begin to lose their clumsy pawlike grip. They have better control of their fingers. At 10 months old, infants can grasp small objects with their thumb and forefinger. As infants mature, their grasp becomes more refined and precise. Around 15 months of age, their grasp is much like that of an adult. One hand can now do one thing while the other does something else. The two hands also work smoothly toward one goal. Gradually through this sequence of development, one hand becomes the preferred hand. The infant uses that

A Matter of Fact

What toys are right for the one-year-old? Toddlers are very curious. They are constantly experimenting with toys containing hidden objects or combining objects with other objects. Toddlers can put simple puzzles together, scribble spontaneously, and imitate adult caregiving and housekeeping tasks.

If you'd like to choose a manipulative toy, choose a simple pop-up toy that is operated by pushing a button or knob, round nesting cups consisting of few pieces, or easy-to-stack toys where order is not necessary. A pattern-making toy, such as a peg board with a few large pegs, would make a nice gift for a one-year-old toddler.

The active toddler enjoys moving toys. Look for ride-on toys that a toddler propels with the feet. No pedals or steering mechanism for this age group! Animal ride-ons or ride-ons with bins for storage are appropriate.

A push-and-pull toy with special noise and action effects are enjoyed by one-year-olds. Keep it simple, sturdy, and with large wheels.

Toddlers will enjoy balls that are soft and lightweight, especially those that have appealing noises and visual effects. Large balls are easy for this age group to maneuver.

Certain types of outdoor and gym equipment promote active play in the older toddler. Remember that all gym equipment requires adult supervision. Consider tunnels for crawlers, swings with seats that are curved or body-shaped, simple climbing structures, and low slides with handrails.

Later, children enjoy toys that imitate adult caretaking tasks. These include simple housekeeping equipment such as a play kitchen, a toy doll with accessories, and a toy telephone.

hand more often so it becomes more skillful. Whether a child is right-handed or left-handed doesn't matter. People who use both hands equally well are called **ambidextrous.** When children begin to toss toys off a high-chair tray or out of a playpen, their development is progressing normally. Most parents do not appreciate this stage. You may hear them complain, "I'm always picking up the toys. It's like a game. Throw the toy down then watch me pick it up and give it back. It goes on and on." Annoyed parents may threaten to take the toys away. By showing annoyance with children's accomplishments rather than pride in their normally healthy growth, the parent may retard future development. A parent's attitude, whether it is encouraging or discouraging, does not go unnoticed by children.

Sense of Self and Growth

In infancy, locomotor growth is closely linked with the sense of self. The first development in the sense of self is the sense of trust. This sense of trust lays the groundwork for a feeling of security throughout life.

The sense of trust is well established if the infants' basic physical needs are met. Beginning with the first experience of securing food and receiving care, the growth of trust continues through experiences with people and things. If babies continue to receive care, they become confident that they will be fed when hungry, changed when wet, rocked when restless, and stimulated when bored. They also grow confident that they can cause these satisfying experiences to happen.

The person who creates these good feelings comes to stand for trust and security. Thus, a four-month-old baby girl crying from hunger will stop crying and even smile when she sees her mother or hears her father's footsteps. She trusts that she will be fed.

Building trust also involves learning that people or objects of trust exist even when they cannot be seen. The game of peekaboo dramatizes the appearance and disappearance of trusted people and objects. When playing peekaboo, infants live and relive the frightening situations that have happy endings.

As infants learn that their mothers exist apart from them, they also learn that they exist apart from their mothers. Their sense of self begins from this knowledge and grows as they explore their own bodies. Fingering a toy or blanket gives a certain sensation. Fingering their own hands gives another. Reaching, grasping, securing, releasing, and touching all tell them about themselves and other things. They learn what they can do or what they can trust their bodies to do. If they feel good about other people, their environment, and themselves, the sense of trust grows. If they experience discomfort, disappointment, and anxiety, the feeling of mistrust develops. This feeling may lead to an attitude of fear and suspicion toward the world. It may even persist into the adult years.

Parents' Role in Sensorimotor Development

Mothers, fathers, other family members, and caregivers help babies know the world and deal with it. When they cuddle, kiss, stroke, sing, or talk to babies they are really teaching. Picking up babies gives many different experiences. They touch something different. A person holding them close and talking or whispering gives them a different hearing sensation. They even experience a completely different visual world. For example, where before they were lying in a crib, now they're raised up and looking at a room from the vantage point of an adult. Infants' knowledge of the world is acquired through sensory experiences. Picking up an infant is only one small act among many educational experiences. Propping children up, talking or singing to them, giving them toys, and frequently changing their position to prevent fatigue and boredom enrich their sensory experience.

Too many people who care for infants do not realize the real importance of their jobs. Infant care is often viewed with boredom and may be carried out with little or no enthusiasm. This may be due, in part, to the fact that

There's a whole world waiting to be explored.

caretakers do not understand what they should be doing or expecting of infants. Such boredom also may stem from the fact that our society does not recognize child care as a valuable career. It is romanticized in literature, poems, and songs, but not given a place of prestige on the career ladder in our culture. Parents often take it for granted. While raising children has sentimental value and is important to the family, it does not provide many parents with the gratification of a career. Actually, rearing children can be parents' most significant contribution to society and can give them their most enduring satisfaction. However, for child care to be a challenging and purposeful job, the concepts of child development need to be understood and appreciated. Parents also need to understand themselves as much as possible. Some of parents' concerns are due to their own personality problems.

Safety for Infants

As an infant develops the locomotion and manipulation skills, the mischief begins. More importantly, however, the serious safety risks increase in number. Parents should take certain steps to eliminate potential hazards, and they need to carefully watch their tots' activities. The following is only a partial list of precautions:

Babies can choke easily on chunks of food. Before being placed in a baby's dish, all foods should be cut into small pieces that are easy to chew and swallow without choking. Even relatively soft foods like hot dogs or grapes can be hazardous because of their round shapes. Cut them in half so they are no longer round. Cut foods into 1/2-inch pieces. Never leave nuts or hard candies in the reach of children under four years old. Popcorn, berries, and fish with bones can be dangerous, too.

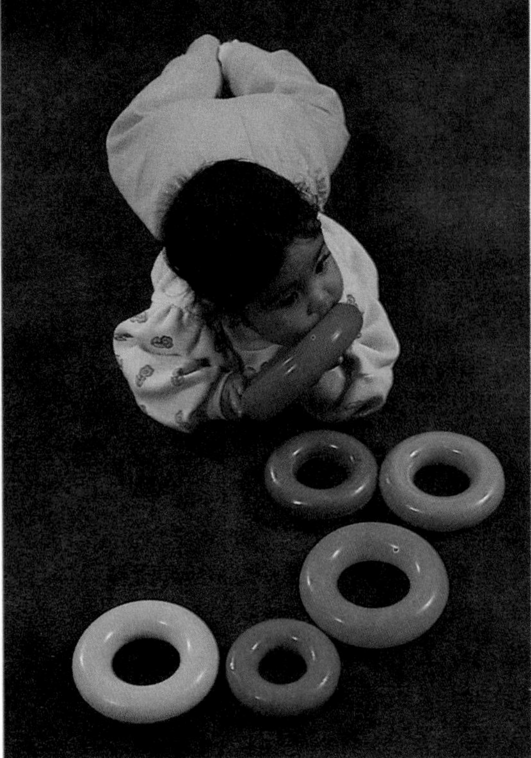

Because babies put everything in their mouths, toys must be large enough to not be swallowed.

Babies like to put everything in their mouths. Keep small toys and all objects they can swallow out of reach—marbles, dice, jacks, etc. The alkaline contents of little disk batteries, which we use in electronic devices such as watches and cameras, can cause severe burns if those batteries get stuck in children's throats.

Never let a child chew on an electrical cord. Unplug cords when they are not in use and put them away. Babies receive severe burns when they place the live ends of cords in their mouths. Put covers over unused wall outlets so children cannot stick objects into them and get electrical shocks and burns. Such covers are available in hardware and variety stores.

Make sure medicines or drugs of any kind are stored well out of the reach of babies. Also, many of the materials usually stored under the sink should be kept in safer places. Babies enjoy playing with anything they find in kitchen drawers and cabinets. Make sure all insecticides, disinfectants, detergents, drain cleaners, dry-cleaning agents, etc., are well out of the reach of children.

Toddlers love to play in the bath tub, but never leave them alone or with another child, *even for a second.* Many unattended babies have drowned in bath tubs. They can stand up, slip, and fall causing serious damage to their heads. They also can turn on the hot water and scald themselves. Setting the thermostat on the hot water heater below 130°F (54°C) prevents this problem for all family members.

When babies can crawl up on chairs, they can crawl up on window sills, as well. Window guards are available to prevent children from falling out. Windows also may be kept locked at all times or carefully fixed so they cannot be opened far enough to allow a child to go through.

Keep all sharp objects out of reach and avoid giving babies any toys that have sharp or rough edges. Also, avoid buying toys that young children could take apart and toys that could break. Also avoid buying toys with sharp edges, sharp points, and small parts. Babies could swallow part of a toy or cut themselves on a sharp edge. Although the Consumer Product Safety Commission has issued regulations relating to toys, it still doesn't mean all toys on the market are safe for small children.

Infants should never be left alone in the home with other children who are

A Matter of Fact

Infants may choke on food or a small object. The object may become lodged in the throat. The danger is that the object may cut off the air supply. Just a few minutes without air can cause brain damage—or death. As a caregiver, you should know what to do in case an infant chokes.

You must act quickly. Look in the infant's throat. Can you see anything caught? If you can, do not reach in and try to grab the object. You may lodge it further in the throat. Can the infant cough up the object? Can the infant breathe? If not, the Heimlich Maneuver can be used.

First, turn the infant face down over your arm with the infant's head lower than the rest of the body. Use your hand to support the infant's neck, jaw, and chest. Give four quick blows on the baby's back between the shoulder blades using the heel of your hand. If the food does not come out, turn the infant over. Again keep the head lower than the rest of the body and support the head, neck, and back. Placing two fingers below the infant's rib cage and above the navel, give four quick chest thrusts. Then use artificial respiration—try to breathe for the child. If the infant does not start breathing, repeat the Heimlich Maneuver.

If this doesn't work, call for emergency medical help. Continue the Heimlich Maneuver and artificial respiration until medical help arrives.

The thing to remember in performing the Heimlich Maneuver on an infant is that too much pressure can harm the infant. Certain techniques are specific to infants. There is no substitute for the proper training in performing the Heimlich Maneuver correctly *before* you need to use it.

The American Red Cross offers courses in first-aid and cardio-pulmonary resuscitation (CPR). Contact your local chapter of the American Red Cross for more information.

not old enough to be aware of dangers to themselves, as well as dangers to infants. As one example, consider the case of children 5, 4, and 2 years old, who were left without parental attention for 15 minutes. While the two-year-old napped, the older two children played with matches and set the house on fire. The older children escaped, but the two-year-old didn't. As another example, see activity 1 in Chapter 5.

Matches, lighters, smoking materials, ashtrays, and flammable liquids must be kept out of the reach of children. Care must be taken, also, to assure that they cannot turn on stoves or ovens. Because so many youngsters have set their clothing on fire, federal law requires that all children's sleepwear be made of flame-retardant fabric.

Just as newborn infants are required to be in approved child restraint devices when traveling by car, older children also should be strapped into their own car seats. All 50 states now have laws requiring the use of approved

Once babies become mobile, parents must follow additional safety precautions.

child restraint devices in cars. Even though they enjoy their new-found locomotion skills, they will accept being strapped in when they have never known anything different. Remember to set a good example and wear your seat belts. Traffic experts have estimated that auto deaths and injuries of children would be reduced by 60 percent if all parents used child safety restraints.

Life's Work

Clayton R. Davis, D.M.D.

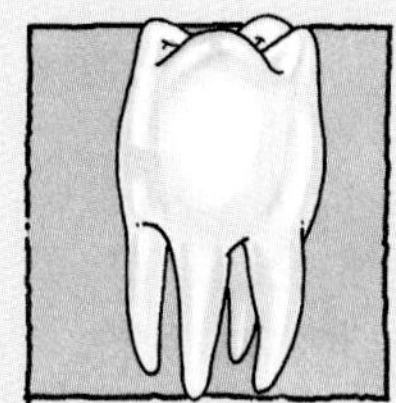

➤General Dentist
➤B.A. from University of North Carolina
➤D.M.D. from Medical College of Georgia School of Dentistry

Clayton says, "As with many other professions, a typical day for me consists of a lot of problem-solving and trouble-shooting. And one must enjoy the challenge of analyzing, solving, and handling the situations as they arise. The two main areas of focus in a solo private practice are treating the patients and running the business. It is not unusual to have these two separate aspects of the dental practice overlap and intertwine throughout the day."

Clayton sees patients approximately 34 hours a week. Then he spends an additional 8 or so hours on lab work, treatment planning, dental meetings, and keeping up to date on dental literature.

Clayton says the skills necessary for success in his profession include four main areas:

1) "Patience. Good dentistry is not easy and must be accomplished under the confines of time, difficult access to the work area, and the anxieties of the person attached to the tooth you're working on.
2) "Human compassion and a deep, honest caring for the people you treat.
3) "A passion for technical excellence. This means keeping abreast of the latest advances in dental procedures and materials. And it means constantly looking for ways to improve your clinical skills.
4) "Communication skills. Explaining things to patients reduces fear, gains trust, and raises their appreciation for dentistry. This helps young children have an early positive experience.
5) "Teaching skills. Giving talks on dental issues to children helps them understand the need for proper care of their teeth."

For a student considering going into dentistry, Clayton says, "The dental profession needs good, talented young people. There is currently a nationwide shortage of dental assistants and dental hygienists, and some predict a possible shortage of dentists by the year 2000. But don't enter the profession because you think it will make you rich. It won't. Enter it because it excites you and you think you have what it takes to be good at it."

In Review

Vocabulary

maturation
locomotion
fine prehension
ambidextrous

Summary

- ✓ The rate of development during infancy is greater than during any other stage of life. Included in this process of maturation are emotional, social, and intellectual development and physical growth.
- ✓ Infant locomotion progresses through five stages from sitting with support to walking alone. Each child has a unique pattern of progression through the stages. During the second year, children refine their locomotor skills, acquiring the ability to jump and climb stairs confidently.
- ✓ The manipulative skills of reaching and grasping develop in predictable patterns. Parents who understand these patterns can share children's joy in their accomplishments, thereby encouraging continued growth.
- ✓ Parents who create a loving atmosphere in which children's needs are met and growth is encouraged help their children develop a sense of trust.
- ✓ Parents who understand the concepts of child development appreciate that child care is challenging and purposeful. They recognize that every contact with the child is an opportunity to teach, to share a new experience, and to build a lasting relationship.
- ✓ Responsible parents are aware of potential dangers to children who have acquired locomotor and manipulative skills, and they take action to protect their children.

Questions

1. What would be the usual sequence in which a baby would develop the following skills?
   a. reaching and grasping
   b. holding head up without support
   c. using finger and thumb in opposition
   d. sitting alone on the floor

2. Discuss why you think babies in high chairs seem to enjoy throwing a spoon on the floor, over and over again. How would you relate that enjoyment to your own enjoyment of bowling, golf, tennis, or some other sport?

3. Babies have to explore themselves, as well as their surroundings. They discover their fingers and toes, they discover that they are able to grasp, they discover that they are able to roll over, etc. How can parents help babies feel good about the self they are discovering?

4. If you had a 14-month-old baby boy who crawled everywhere and stood up to the coffee table, but would not take one step without holding on to something or someone, would you:

a. scold him for having no courage
b. spank him for refusing to try
c. do nothing
d. coax him with candy
e. call the pediatrician

Why would you choose your course of action?

5. Compare the reaching movements of a five-month-old baby with the operation of a crane at a construction site.

Activities

1. Make three additions to the list of safety precautions at the end of this chapter.

2. Which of your safety precautions and those listed at the end of this chapter are made necessary by babies' locomotion skills, which by manipulation skills, and which by a combination of both types of skills? Make a list of the safety precautions and note your decisions.

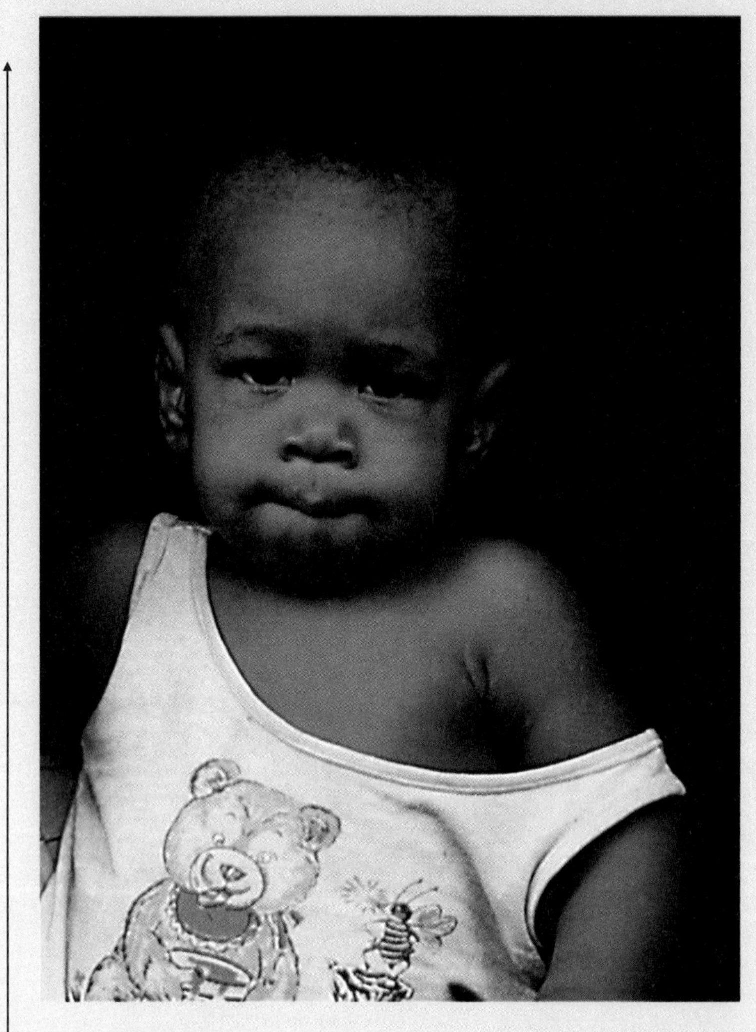

Chapter 11: Intellectual - Emotional Development

This chapter will help you:

- recognize the individuality of intellectual and emotional growth in very young children
- appreciate the importance of early stimulation in developing intellectual and emotional potential
- understand how babies emerge from an emotional state of oneness with their principal caregivers to an acceptance of their separateness
- recognize the "no" stage of toddlers as an essential step in their emotional development
- identify the stages in the development of intellectual functions

Personality

A person's personality is always developing. There is no time between birth and death when the personality is not growing. Every experience a person has helps to shape his or her personality. For example, two-year-old Susan likes to play catch. Her parents encourage her interest and play with her. Susan's family lets her know they are proud of her ability. Susan not only develops athletic skill, but a good self-concept. This will encourage her to try new activities. This willingness to try becomes part of her personality. Contrast this situation with one in which the parents make fun of a child's attempt to learn something new.

All persons are individuals with their own emotional and intellectual needs. Everybody has their own ideas, interests, and skills. Infants, just as older children and adults, must be recognized as unique individuals who are growing both intellectually and emotionally.

Throughout the first few years of life, children engage in learning activities with natural enthusiasm and delight. Infancy, in particular, is a time of extremely rapid intellectual and emotional growth (just as it is with physical growth). It is a period when primary emotional relationships are formed. It

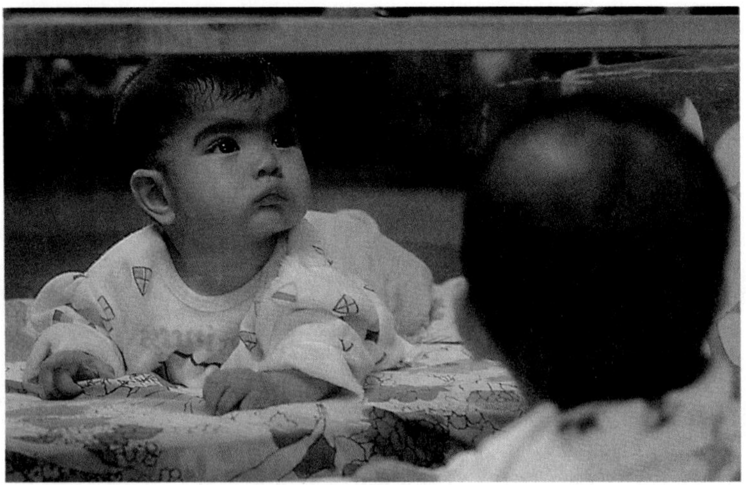

Mirrors are wonderful self-discovery toys for infants.

is also the time when children begin to explore, manipulate, and master their environment.

Studies of how people learn have indicated that the period from birth to about six years of age is important for the individual's cognitive development. **Cognitive development** refers to the ability to think. Psychologists estimate that 50 percent of mature intelligence is developed by the age of four. Another 30 percent is developed by the age of eight. Research also has indicated the advantages of stimulating an infant's emotional and intellectual development. Some psychologists, in fact, believe that if children do not receive proper stimulation when they are very young, they will never reach their full intellectual and emotional potential.

Emotional Growth

There are two major stages of emotional growth. The first is the **symbiotic period.** During this stage, babies experience oneness with their primary caregivers. (Traditionally this was their mother.) In other words, babies cannot distinguish that their primary caregivers are separate from themselves. The next stage is **individuation.** In this stage, babies learn that they are people separate from their caregivers and that their caregivers are persons separate from them. Individuation occurs between five months and three years. It progresses in the following steps.

Emerging from Oneness (5 to 10 months)

This first phase of individualism is marked by experiments in separation. Infants begin to explore their caregivers' faces and hair. They learn that their caregivers have mouths. They learn that their caregivers have eyes and that they themselves have eyes. Their fumbling attempts at feeding themselves and then trying to feed their caregivers are also experiments in separation.

Another experiment in separation that begins at this time is the game of peekaboo. This game is an index of the child's emotional and intellectual growth. Dawn's mother gently tosses a light blanket over Dawn's head. Dawn, five and one-half months old, kicks her feet and giggles. When her mother pulls off the blanket and exclaims, "Peekaboo," Dawn is delighted. Several days later, Dawn covers her own face with the blanket. As her mother approaches, Dawn kicks and laughs. When her mother remains quiet, Dawn, in turn, lies quietly, waiting for a response. With her face still covered, she kicks and giggles again. Seconds pass. She remains still. Then, as if the silence is too much, she pulls the blanket away. She looks a little startled, but then her face lights up with a big smile.

Dawn's behavior indicates that even small babies are ready and willing to try brief separation. They can carry in their minds a memory of people they love and anticipate the joy of seeing them. Her behavior also may be viewed as an early form of teasing or joking.

In a more general sense, Dawn's initiation of the peekaboo game relates to a growing capacity to:

1. Make a decision.
2. Put the decision into effect.
3. Recognize desirable and undesirable results.
4. Respond to the situation brought about by her own efforts. In fact, "intelligence" is neither too general nor too exaggerated a term to describe what Dawn is developing. From the moment of birth, infants are trying to come to grips with their environment and establish mastery over it.

What part do parents play in this step of emerging from oneness? Perhaps the best way to measure their influence is to examine what would happen if they did not respond to the child's playful behavior. Suppose that Dawn's mother did not react to the situation. She was too busy. She would change Dawn's diapers, then go about her own work. If Dawn's playful attempts were regularly met with little interest, Dawn probably would not continue to make such efforts. It would prevent her from making progress.

The emotional deprivation that babies suffer when an adult fails to establish a close relationship with them through play and affectionate care is difficult to replace later on. Parents should talk to babies and encourage a give-and-take response to their sounds. For example, if the baby makes a cooing sound, the parent might respond, "Cooo, Cooo. Are you a mourning dove, or are you my little turtle dove?" This response followed by a hug and a kiss will be interpreted by the baby as an encouragement to make more sounds. Progress toward language is nurtured by the parents' talking and responding to the baby. In addition, body movements and gestures affect how infants' language skills develop, how they form abstract concepts, and how they develop confidence.

The peekaboo game actually helps to show the whole process of early learning and the part parents play in it. It indicates, for example, that the games babies play are often in earnest. Toddlers who reach their arms high above when parents say "so-o-o big!" are learning about spatial relationships.

Children enjoy discovering the world around them.

The infant who drops a ball into a box is wanting to learn about the container and the ball. The nine-month-old who goes to a radiator and pokes an exploring finger at it will probably learn about the concepts of hot, cold, and burn.

From six to 10 months, the physical skills of creeping and standing turn infants into active individuals. They are mobile and capable of experiencing new things. They begin to look around more and scan the faces of strangers. There are also indications that the infant can find comfort and pleasure, not only in the primary caregiver, but also in other people and objects. This is a strong sign of emerging from oneness. Soft blankets and nighttime bottles may become precious objects that children have difficulty giving up.

Emerging from oneness does not mean there is any breakdown in the bond between parents and child. Babies in this age group become strongly attached to warm and loving parents and other caregivers. The quality of the attachment depends on the number of caregiving interactions, but more importantly on the quality of those interactions. Often a child of six to nine months has a more special relationship with one parent than the other. It is a passing phase, however, and the attachment may be roughly the same for both parents by the time the child is a toddler.

Junior Toddlers (10 to 18 months)

As you learned in Chapter 10, from 10 to 18 months, babies learn new motor skills. As they start to walk and their hand movements become more coordinated, they enjoy exploring. At the time babies start to walk, they are called **toddlers.** Toddlers venture farther and farther from their parent. Often they become so absorbed in their own activities that for short periods of time they are oblivious to their parent's presence or absence. They want to spend much less time sitting on laps and cuddling. Unless the parents recognize this as a normal stage of development toward independence, they may feel a sense of rejection.

In this phase, the child's response to brief separations from the parent is particularly interesting. For example, consider a 14-month-old boy who has a normal, strong attachment to his mother. She leaves the kitchen after calmly saying to him, "You play with your pots and pans. I have to go to the laundry room, but I'll be right back." For the first minute, he may withdraw

A Matter of Fact

It's too much to expect a toddler to eat meals with the manners of a crown prince. But it's helpful for a child to interact with family members during a meal. Children learn by imitating others, so they should be allowed to eat with other family members. In addition to the opportunity of introducing table manners, sometimes children behave better and enjoy mealtimes more when they sit down at a table to a family meal. Here are some tips that help make mealtime less stressful and more enjoyable for all members of the family.

- Cover the floor directly under a toddler's seat with a plastic shower curtain, or a large sheet of vinyl or paper. This will help when it's time to clean up.
- Purchase a child-sized spoon or fork with a short, straight, broad, solid handle. The spoon should have a wide mouth. The fork should have blunt tines. Children will feed themselves with a spoon first. They learn to use a fork later.
- Unbreakable bowl-shaped dishes are recommended when children first start feeding themselves.
- Caregivers needn't become discouraged when children alternate between the use of tableware and their fingers. Children will gradually decrease the use of their fingers as they become more proficient with tableware.
- It's hard to get an excited child to settle down to eat. Caregivers can suggest quiet activities before mealtime.
- If guests are expected, a toddler can be fed beforehand. Very young children require a lot of attention during meals, and it may be difficult to give it to them while entertaining guests. On the other hand, three-year-olds are not too young to begin learning the social graces, and they can learn best by participation.
- Children should be given the same freedom of choice at mealtimes as the others. Serve small portions and give children enough time to eat. They don't need to be the center of attention at meals.

into himself and focus attention on the memory of his mother. But then, having no concept of time and lacking the maturity to understand when he can expect to see his mother again, he may become upset and start to cry. The same response may occur when the child is left with a new babysitter. This problem can be avoided by the sitter playing with the boy a few times when the mother is home.

During the period from 10 to 18 months, the child's experiments in separation pose a serious challenge to some parents. They must encourage the child's independence and still be available when needed. It can be a trying time for parents. At one time,

Toddlers go through a "no" stage when they begin to assert their independence.

they did everything for their child. Now they must change their behavior. It can be difficult for a parent to sit back and watch a child try to master a new skill. The parent has to overcome the urge to help out all the time. Parents also must deal with the stubborn, negative behavior that is part of a child's learning how to say "no." The parent, out of love, may try to help only to be told "No! Me do it" by the child. It is often difficult to reach a balance between offering support and fostering independence. At 14 months, for example, the baby may want no help in drinking from a cup, eating pizza, turning pages, climbing stairs, etc. Spilled milk and torn pages require parental patience.

Some parents are unsure of themselves. They may feel insecure in their jobs, their relationships, or other areas of their lives. They may lack the self-confidence they need to cope with the trials of parenthood. For them, the "no" stage of toddlers can be frustrating. If parents do not understand that toddlers must begin to assert their independence, then the parents may feel they are losing control over their child. It is often a parent's attempt to reassert control that leads to child abuse.

A Closer Look

When 14-month-old Bobby decided to feed himself his cereal,

he had trouble holding the spoon, so his mother used a large bib with a pocket to catch what didn't reach its proper destination. She put plastic on his table so she could gather more of what missed Bobby's mouth. When Bobby got tired of trying, she fed him. This went on for a short time and then she announced to his father, "Just when he seems to get the hang of it, he doesn't want to do it any more."

If Bobby put his feelings into words, he might say, "I proved I could do it. I am capable. I am not interested in doing it any more." On the other hand, he might wish to say, "Learning a new skill requires a lot of concentration, and I need a rest," or "I'm hungry and I'm too slow at this. Please help!"

A Closer Look

While walking one day a grandmother, mother, and 18-month-old girl approached a low curb on the sidewalk. Suddenly the little girl announced vigorously, "Me do, me do." A very understanding mother and grandmother said, "OK." They stood on each side of the child, not helping but ready to catch an unsteady yet determined little girl. She barely managed to step down without falling, but her smile revealed her sense of achievement. Nevertheless, she grasped her mother's skirt the moment she had accomplished her task.

Toddlers very often have a favorite blanket or stuffed toy that provides them with a great deal of security. Some parents seem embarrassed by this, but they shouldn't be. Children associate the softness of a teddy bear or the smoothness of the satin edging on a blanket with the secure feelings that cuddling gave them when they were "lap babies." There is no need to encourage children to give up "security blankets." They rely on them less when they discover other ways to handle stressful situations. It is probably not surprising that many of the same stuffed animals appear years later on the beds in college dormitories.

Senior Toddler (18 to 24 months)

Junior toddlers become senior toddlers when their walking improves and their self-awareness increases. In an effort to share their lives, senior toddlers keep bringing objects to their parents and demonstrating new skills. At this time, their behavior is marked by extremes. One day they may want everything done for them. The next day they may refuse all help. Sometimes these toddlers cling to their parents to the point that they are always underfoot. At other times they dart about hoping to be chased or scooped up in their parent's arms. The elated mood, characteristic of earlier months when they behaved as if they owned the world, vanishes.

As new skills let them move away from the parent, a child can feel much more helpless and lonesome. Feelings of separateness and aloneness may eventually lessen self-esteem. Parents

A Matter of Fact

The following are some guidelines that can make taking a toddler to a restaurant easier and more enjoyable.

- Children have special needs. They may become impatient if there is a wait before being seated. Children can be taken for a walk outside the restaurant to prevent this. Caregivers may be able to read quietly to children, too, if the restaurant has seating available.
- If not watched, children will snack on appetizers and bread, and leave no room for their meal. Most restaurants have children's portions. Caregivers may wish to inquire about this.
- Children may be more comfortable eating in a restaurant if they bring along their own cup and tableware.
- Nowadays restaurants often have quiet activities to keep hands and minds occupied while waiting for dinner. The activities may include paper placemats to color or placemat puzzles and trivia games to work on. Some restaurants have miniature wishing wells where children fish out small toys.

need to recognize that this is a vulnerable period for the child and act accordingly. They need to understand how the child feels about separateness in order to pace their separateness from the child. That is, some children try a new skill, but then need the security of the parent. By giving support and acceptance, the parent can help the child weather this normal crisis. For example, Jack and Joan Kincaid constructed a fence around their backyard so that two-year-old Vanessa could play there safely while Joan was busy working in the garden. From her sandbox, Vanessa could always see her mother, so she was content playing alone. One day, however, she was frightened by a squirrel jumping through the tree branches above her head. Joan calmed her by talking to her about little animals and birds, but Vanessa would not return to her sandbox. That night, Jack read Vanessa a story about a squirrel family. The next day, Joan played with Vanessa in the sandbox, and the following day she sat in a chair nearby while Vanessa played alone. Finally, Vanessa felt secure, and Joan returned to her gardening.

Falling asleep represents a new dual separation—from the parents and from light. It is not surprising that sleeping problems, especially difficulties in going to sleep, are common between the ages of 18 and 24 months. In fact, some type of sleep disturbance, including waking during the night, is almost universal. A nightlight or the mother's or father's presence with the child for a short time after the light is turned out is often helpful. These actions encourage the child to master the feeling of separation. Some parents give in to their child's worries and let the child sleep with them. This does not encourage growth. It retards it.

Intellectual Functions

We use the term cognitive development to refer to the ability to think. As you read in Chapter 4, Piaget states that cognitive development takes place in stages. The first major stage goes from birth to about 18 months. It is called the period of sensorimotor intelligence. At the end of this stage, the infant has established a basic knowledge of the world. Piaget describes the six substages of this period as follows.

Simple Reflex Actions

Infants first learn about the world through their reflexes. For example, by sucking and grasping, they experience their environment.

Primary Circular Reactions

Infants learn to touch their fingers together and then to their mouths. They repeat simple acts like thumbsucking or fingering a blanket.

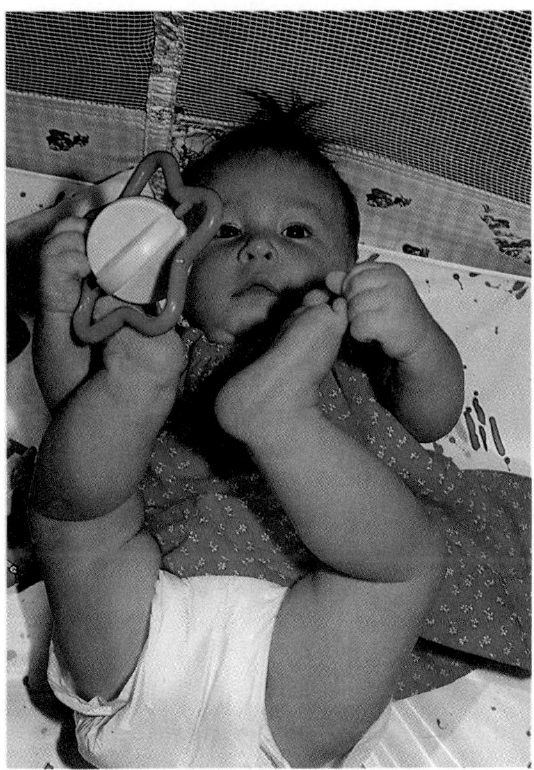

What reaction is this girl learning about by playing with her mobile?

Secondary Circular Reactions

Infants now learn to manipulate events or objects in their environment. When a change in the environment results from their actions, they are likely to repeat those actions. For example, infants who learn they can move a mobile above their beds by kicking or wiggling tend to repeat their actions.

Coordination of Secondary Schemas

In this substage, infants put more than one plan into action. Their behavior is truly intentional. For example, they hit toys with hopes of grasping them.

At this time, object-permanence begins to develop. That is, a child learns that an object (mother, bottle, etc.) exists even though it is moved, hidden, or placed in a new relationship with other objects.

Tertiary Circular Reactions

Instead of merely repeating events, babies try to produce new events. At first, they look for the vanished object in the place where they found it initially. Later, they look for the vanished object in the place where it disappeared instead of the place where they found it the very first time.

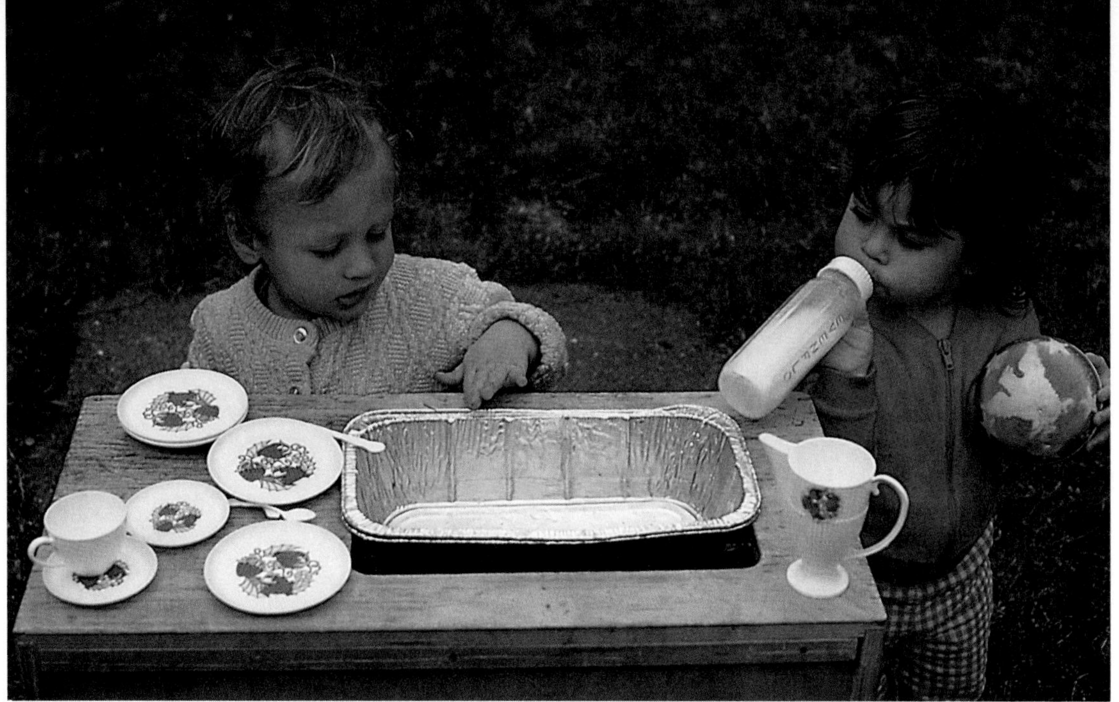

Children love to imitate their parents' actions, even something as simple as washing the dishes. Through imitation, they demonstrate they have a mental image of the activity.

Throwing and dropping toys are common kinds of play at this age. Through this type of play, infants examine how things move, as well as the disappearance and reappearance of objects. Thus, this type of play helps infants build their understanding of the permanence of objects.

Invention of New Means Through Combinations

Instead of having to go through a series of physical actions, toddlers mentally find solutions. That is, they think through a problem. They show these new powers by imitation, pretending, and insightful problem-solving. For example, by washing the face of a favorite teddy bear, the toddler is using a mental image of his or her parents' behavior. Thus, when infants imitate a past event, they show that they have a mental image of it. When they pretend, they use a mental image of a behavior pattern to act out that pattern in a new situation.

The achievement of imitation, pretending, and insightful problem-solving marks the end of the sensorimotor stage. Remember the average age for beginning and ending a stage is always approximate.

Parental Influence on Intellectual Development

Psychologists agree that emotional, social, and intellectual development depend on both heredity and environment. They do not agree, however, on their relative importance. Some feel heredity is more important. Others place more emphasis on environment.

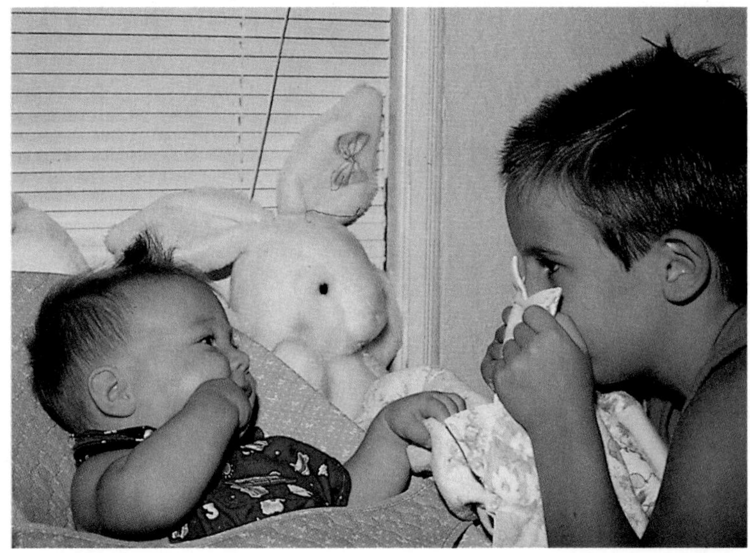

In what way can a game of peekaboo with an older sibling be a learning experience for an infant?

Nutrition is part of the environmental influence and, in Chapter 9, we discussed the necessity of a balanced diet for normal intellectual development. Another potentially important environmental influence on intellectual development of very young children is parental stimulation.

You can get a feeling for the extreme positions regarding the importance of parent-child interactions by studying the work of Glenn Doman, founder of the Institute for the Achievement of Human Potential, and the work of Jerome Kagan, a professor of psychology at Harvard University. In the Better Baby Program, developed by Doman, babies as young as eight months are exposed to flash cards to stimulate reading and mathematical skills. While Doman points to prize students who can play the violin or translate foreign languages by the ages of three and four years, many other child psychologists are skeptical of the program's usefulness. Some are critical of it, raising questions about potential harmful effects on emotional and social development.

On the other hand, Kagan's theme is that most psychologists place far too much emphasis on the importance of early environment on emotional, social, and intellectual development. Nevertheless, he does state that children cannot develop to their full potential without stimulation, regardless of their genetic mental capacity.

Psychologists whose views lie more toward the center of the controversy agree that parents should be encouraged to provide plenty of intellectual stimulation by talking, reading, singing, and playing games. Of course, parents also are encouraged to provide a secure atmosphere that allows children to try, fail, and try again.

For stimulating babies' verbal skills, talking *at* them is not as important as talking *with* them. Toddlers need to be given the opportunity and the encouragement to talk. Children love to play games of identifying the parts of the face, articles of clothing, cats, dogs, and everything that they see in picture books. Another good technique is for parents to say the words that describe what the child is already doing. "Oh, are you playing with your blocks?" "Do you like your cookie?"

Restating in different words what the child says provides caregivers opportunity and encouragement for conversations. For example, suppose a little boy says "Dinka wawa." His mother might say, "Sure, you may have a drink of water. Would you like a big cup or a little cup?" After drinking the water, he may knock the cup to the floor and say, "Faw down." His father might say, "Yes, your cup did fall down. Do you want to get down from your high chair?" Restating in a different way and opening the door for more conversation is more effective than repeating exactly what the child has said. Repetition may reinforce, but it is not particularly stimulating.

Fathers as Primary Caregivers

Traditionally, mothers have been the primary caregivers for infants. Today, with increasing numbers of mothers working outside the home, more fathers are sharing the caregiving responsibilities during the hours that both parents are home. Other parents have arranged their work schedules so that they are home during different times of the day. For example, the father may work days while the mother stays home. Then when the father comes home in the evening, the mother goes to work. In other situations, the father stays home with the children because he does not have a job, or because it is a mutually agreeable arrangement. In some cases, the father or mother's career permits working at home.

Seventeen infants have been tested by Dr. Kyle Pruett, a child psychologist at Yale University, to find the effects of having fathers as the primary caregivers. The fathers' occupational levels ranged from professional to blue collar. For babies between two and 12 months old, their problem-solving abilities were six to 12 months ahead of average. Their social skills were also ahead of schedule by two to 12 months. Babies between the ages of 12 and 22 months were equally advanced in their development.

Dr. Pruett did not attribute the observed behavior to better quality care by fathers than mothers. Instead, he noted that the average working mother formed a stronger bond with her baby than the average working father did. Thus, when the father was the primary caregiver, the infant experienced the parenting of *two* strongly bonded parents rather than one strongly bonded parent and one weakly bonded parent. It seems safe to infer the following from these results: No matter which parent takes the role of primary caregiver, if the other parent also forms a strong bond with the baby, social and intellectual development will be enhanced greatly.

There are other very good reasons for fathers to take active roles in the care of their very young children. The basis of any relationship is trust, and babies learn to trust those who regularly and

Fathers can build strong bonds with their children by participating in their activities.

dependably respond to their needs. Thus, both parents can lay the foundations for their life-long relationships with their children from the very beginning. Boys who have always known their fathers to be tender, loving, caring people can become the same kind of persons because they desire to identify with respected models. The behavior of the father will strongly affect their sex-role images in the minds of both sons and daughters.

Life's Work

Jeanne Vergeront

- ➤ **Director of Exhibits and Education, The Children's Museum**
- ➤ **B.S. in Preschool and Kindergarten**
- ➤ **M.S. in Environmental Design**

Jeanne's typical day allows her time for individual work as well as time for meeting and working with others. Her work involves handling concrete details and long-range visioning. During the day, she has contact with the museum staff, visitors, and people from the community. She researches exhibit topics, plans timetables, organizes materials, and plans work assignments.

Jeanne's office hours are from 9 to 5, Monday through Friday. At times, she attends evening meetings and weekend programs at the museum.

Jeanne says that the skills necessary for success in her profession include organization, research, planning, and evaluation. In addition, one must have a knowledge of child development, exhibit design, and analysis and synthesis (breaking things down into smaller parts and connecting smaller components with one another). Other important skills she says are, "dreaming, imagining, and then being realistic."

For a student considering going into Jeanne's profession, her advice is, "Learn about and be committed to the human basis of design. Study developmental characteristics of groups, how people perceive, what their expectations of settings are, etc. For the designer this means hands-on work, observation, reflection, reading, respecting other professionals, and, of course, respecting the user."

When asked how her profession will change within the next 10 years, Jeanne says, "Children's museums are a relatively new phenomenon. Within the next 10 years, there will be more information about how children use exhibits, what exhibit features are attractive to children, and what influences their interactions with their family and others."

In Review

Vocabulary

cognitive development
symbiotic period
individuation
toddler

Summary

- ✓ Fifty percent of our mature intelligence is achieved by the age of four, and 80% by the age of eight. Early stimulation is critical for full development of intellectual and emotional potential.
- ✓ From birth to about five months, babies are in their symbiotic stage of emotional growth characterized by a sense of oneness with their primary caregivers. From five months to about three years, they progress through stages of individuation, that is, they emerge from oneness and experiment with their separateness.
- ✓ The stage in which a toddler says "no" repeatedly is a normal phase of emotional development. By testing separateness, children are taking their first steps toward independence. This phase is much less frustrating to those parents who understand its importance to the child's growth.
- ✓ According to Piaget, during the first 18 months, babies' cognitive development occurs in six stages—beginning with learning gained by reflexive action, and ending with imitation, pretending, and insightful problem-solving.
- ✓ No matter which parent takes the role of primary caregiver, if the other parent also forms a strong bond with the baby, social and intellectual development will be enhanced greatly.

Questions

1. What is the symbiotic period?
2. What is the individuation period?
3. What do you think is going on in children's minds when they play peekaboo? Why is this an important game?
4. How can understanding the importance of the early activities of infants influence your responses to them?
5. Pair each of the following stages with the appropriate stage of intellectual development as defined by Piaget:

a. sucking the thumb
b. feeding a doll at a small table
c. looking for a toy where it was found once before.

6. Why can we not give exact ages for each of Piaget's stages of intellectual and emotional development?

7. Why do toddlers go through a "no" stage? Under what circumstances can this stage lead to child abuse?

8. When should parents insist that their child stop carrying a security blanket or sleeping with a stuffed animal?

9. When should one begin talking to an infant?

10. What role can a father play in the emotional and intellectual development of his child if he is not the primary caregiver? When should he begin to play that role?

Activities

1. Discuss your own observations of an infant in a new learning experience. How old was the baby? Describe the child's behavior.

2. Watch a group of toddlers playing. Which actions are helping them learn about spatial relationships? How are they learning about the permanence of objects?

3. Interview the parents of a toddler. Find out how they deal with the child frequently saying "no." How do they overcome the urge to help when the child is struggling with a new skill?

Unit 4 The Preschool Child

This chapter will help you:

- ✎ identify typical growth patterns for preschool children
- ✎ appreciate the importance of good health to normal physical development
- ✎ recognize how family moods and attitudes can affect a child's eating and sleeping
- ✎ learn when children develop control over their organs of elimination and how this determines when toilet training should begin
- ✎ understand how children's early experiences regarding nutrition and toilet training can influence adult behavior

On the Go

Preschool children seem to have boundless energy. From the moment they wake up, they bounce to their feet and expect everyone to rise with them. For the rest of the day, they seem to be in constant motion.

Children differ in the rates at which they progress through a sequence of behavior patterns. They differ also in speed, strength, and accuracy of their muscular coordination and in their balance and grace. The chart on page 204 is an overview of a group of children and does not describe any particular child perfectly. It does help us, however, to have a feeling for the average development for various ages. An activity is listed in the chart only if 50% or more of the group could perform that activity at the designated ages.

Growth from Two to Five

Preschoolers do not grow as rapidly in height as they did during infancy. For instance, Andrew was 20" long at birth. When he was three months old, he measured 24". That's an increase of 4" in 3 months, or a 20% increase. On his first birthday, he measured 30". That was a growth of 10" or a 50% increase. When he was two years old, he was 35" tall. That was 5" in one year,

Motor Development

Age Three	Age Four	Age Five
	Eye-Hand	
Puts on shoes, unbuttons clothing	Can use scissors to cut on a line	Throws well
Catches a ball with arms straight	Dresses self	Catches small ball with elbows at sides
Copies circles and draws a straight line	Catches ball with elbows in front of body	Fastens buttons he or she can see
Builds towers of blocks		Copies designs, letters, numbers
	Locomotion	
Walks on tiptoe	Descends steps—alternate feet	Has narrow stance
Stands on one foot	Does stunts on tricycle	Skips
Jumps from bottom stair	Gallops	Hops on one foot, 10 or more steps
Hops on both feet		Walks straight line
Rides tricycle		Descends large ladder, alternating feet easily
Propels wagon, one foot		Establishes hand preference

or a 75% increase from birth length. At four years of age, Andrew is 40" tall. He has doubled his length at birth. However, his growth has slowed to 5" in the last two years. Compare that to the 4" he grew in his first three months. Andrew's growth is an example of average children. Also, during the preschool years, boys and girls are similar in height and weight.

Body proportions change because various parts of the body grow at different rates. In infants, the head and upper body are more advanced in their development than the legs and lower body. At age two, the head is still large

This represents the average growth rate of children from ages 6 months to 3 years. As children mature, their body proportions change so they are no longer so top heavy.

in relation to the trunk and legs. The abdomen sticks out because some of the internal organs are closer to adult size than the trunk is. The toddler is top-heavy. The head itself grows according to the same principle. That is, at this age, the top of the head is better developed than the lower part. A large cranium and a small lower jaw give the characteristic baby look to a two-year-old. Between the ages of two and five, the legs, trunk, and jaw grow more rapidly than the head, and the body loses its diminutive or "cute" look. By the time preschoolers start kindergarten, their proportions more nearly resemble those of school-age children than those of toddlers.

Much of the growth in the size of the brain occurred prenatally. After birth, the brain continues to grow rapidly. The following table shows typical brain weights and body weights for the children at various ages. They are expressed as percentages of brain weights and body weights for adults.

Brain Size Chart

Age	Body Weight	Brain Weight
0 months	6%	25%
6 months	12%	50%
3 years	28%	80%
10 years	60%	95%
15 years	83%	100%

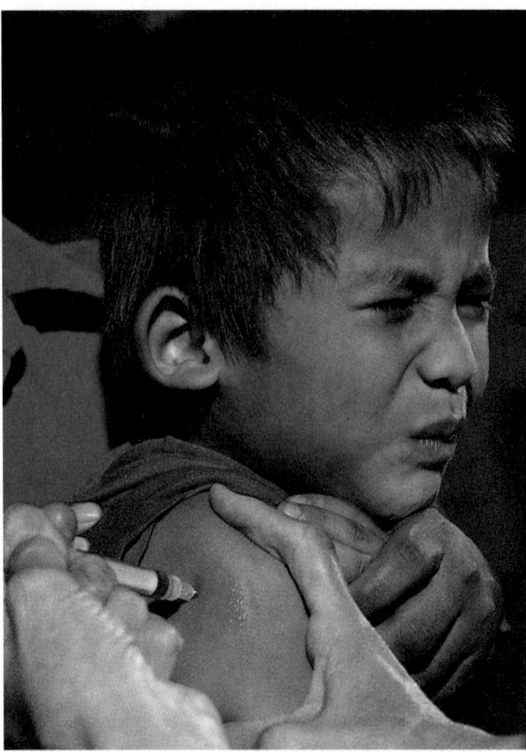

As painful as they may seem, vaccines are necessary to help resist diseases.

We can see that, throughout childhood, the brain is well ahead of the body in approaching its adult size. We can also appreciate the importance of proper nutrition and mental stimulation before children reach school age.

Health Care

Good health is extremely important to normal physical development and growth. Fortunately, medical advances have provided ready availability of **vaccines** that can almost totally eliminate the hazards of many of the worst diseases. A vaccine contains small amounts of the disease germs. By their body systems fighting the germs in the vaccine, children develop a resistance to the disease. Then if they are exposed to the disease later they will not get sick.

The World Health Organization has declared that the smallpox vaccine has wiped out the disease in all nations, but many other diseases are still with us. Parents can help to protect their children from these other diseases if they comply with the laws of all 50 states that require proof of immunization before enrollment in school. Of course, parents can help more if the vaccines are given to their children earlier, as soon as the vaccines can be administered safely.

Immunization for diptheria, tetanus, pertussis, and polio should have been completed by the time the baby is about six months old (Chapter 9). At about 15 months, the toddler is ready for an MMR shot for measles, mumps, and rubella (German measles). Some doctors are predicting that there may be a vaccine to protect infants from meningitis (inflammation of the brain or spinal cord). Presently, various types of meningitis afflict 20,000 children per year.

Bones of preschool children have more cartilage and are less dense. Their joints are more flexible. Their ligaments and muscles are attached less firmly than older children's. Thus, it is easier to damage preschool children's bones, joints, and muscles by pressure and pulling. At this age, malnutrition, fatigue, and infections can have harmful effects on the skeletal system.

Dental Care

Poor nutrition and infections are also detrimental to children's teeth. Throughout childhood, the normal development of both primary and permanent teeth cannot occur without sufficient calcium and the other nutrients found in a balanced diet. Proper diet, of course, is a parental responsibility. Parents also must see that children's infections are properly treated so that fevers do not interfere with healthy development of the teeth. In addition, by ensuring that children are immunized against diseases, parents can minimize the number of illnesses.

By the time children reach the age of 24 to 32 months, they have 20 primary teeth. Although these teeth are temporary, they are extremely important. Having healthy teeth allows young children to eat the variety of foods essential to their general health. When permanent teeth begin to appear, healthy primary teeth provide the guides that ensure proper positioning. If the primary teeth are carrying dental disease (caries), the permanent teeth can become infected also.

Proper care of primary teeth should be recognized by parents as a part of routine care. As soon as teeth begin to appear in a baby's mouth (about six months), parents can clean them daily by carefully wiping each tooth with sterile gauze.

We all know it is important for us to brush our teeth after eating sweets. It is just as important that older toddlers and preschoolers not be put to bed with bottles of milk or juice as pacifiers. Cavities are almost certain to result

Proper dental care will keep her smiling.

from this practice. There is nothing wrong, however, with a bottle of water. It makes a good mouthwash.

The muscles developed by babies when they suck help the primary teeth to become properly positioned. However, when they have reached the age of about 2 1/2 years and have all of their primary teeth, it is advisable that they be weaned. In addition, there should be regular brushing with a very soft toothbrush at least twice a day—after breakfast and before bed.

Naturally, at this age, they need some help from their caregivers. Regular visits to the dentist are important. Of course, fluoride has been

Daily Caloric Requirements

Age	Average Number of Calories
Children	
1-3	1300
4-6	1700
7-10	2400
Males	
11-14	2700
15-18	2800
19-22	2900
23-50	2700
51-75	2400
76 and up	2050
Females	
11-14	2200
15-22	2100
23-50	2000
51-75	1800
76 and up	1600
During pregnancy	Add 300
During lactation	Add 500

These are large calories, which are also called kilocalories. Adapted from Food and Nutrition Board, National Research Council Recommended Dietary Allowances (Ninth Edition). Washington, DC: National Academy of Sciences.

proven beneficial in avoiding cavities at all ages. Your dentist can tell you whether there are fluorides in your local drinking water and whether supplemental fluorides are recommended.

Food and Rest

Preschool children cannot afford to fill up on **junk foods.** These are foods high in calories, but lacking in valuable nutrients such as proteins, minerals, and vitamins. Their need for growth-promoting and healthful foods is great, yet they cannot eat much at one time. Their stomachs can hold only half the capacity of the average adult stomach. Added to that is the fact that because they are so active, their food energy (caloric) requirement is more than half as great as that of adults. Therefore, children may need to eat more than three meals a day. They may need snacks between meals. Be sure those snacks are healthful.

Keep in mind that the values shown in the table on this page are average values. Energy intake requirements are based on several factors including size, health, and activity level, as well as age. Carbohydrates and fats are sources of energy, and a well-balanced diet includes both in proper proportions.

Diet Principles

The Food and Nutrition Board of the National Research Council has published recommended daily dietary allowances for people in the U.S. Their tables include the amounts of protein, vitamins, minerals, trace elements, and electrolytes that people require in their diets to maintain health at various ages. The tables also include the maximum amounts of trace elements, such as copper and manganese, that are safe. You can find two tables in the Appendix. Healthy children between the ages of one and six years can obtain all the nutrients they need (except iron) from the diet recommended by the Iowa Dietetic Association in its *Simplified Diet Manual with Meal Patterns*, pages 210-212. The sizes of servings for children of different ages have been recommended by the U.S. Department of Health and Human Services.

1. The diet should provide adequate nourishment, variety, and color, and be pleasing in texture and flavor.

2. A sick child may regress in performance, and the regression may become worse throughout a long illness. For instance, a five-year-old child may regress to the performance of a four- or three-year-old so far as eating is concerned.

3. Children should not be allowed to drink so much milk that they are too full to have other foods. If children drink too much milk, change their habit by serving it at the end of the meal or between meals.

4. For younger children, it is important that meat be tender, moist, and cut into strips or bite-size pieces.

5. Young children like crisp finger foods. Serve them regularly.

6. Excess fat can dull the appetite. Avoid fatty gravies, pastries, or repeated use of fried foods.

7. Highly seasoned foods are often not well accepted. Use seasonings in moderate amounts.

8. To meet energy needs of the individual child, serve larger portions or add different foods.

9. Vitamin and mineral supplements may be prescribed by a physician.

Following these guidelines will help children have a balanced and healthful diet. The key to it all is variety. For example, Angela eats two oranges every day for her fruit serving. For a vegetable she only wants corn. Angela is not getting all the nutrients she needs because there is not just one food that is nutritionally complete. Her parents need to encourage her to try different foods. If she doesn't like cooked carrots, her parents should then try them raw. By slowly introducing her to new foods, Angela's parents can help her develop more choices.

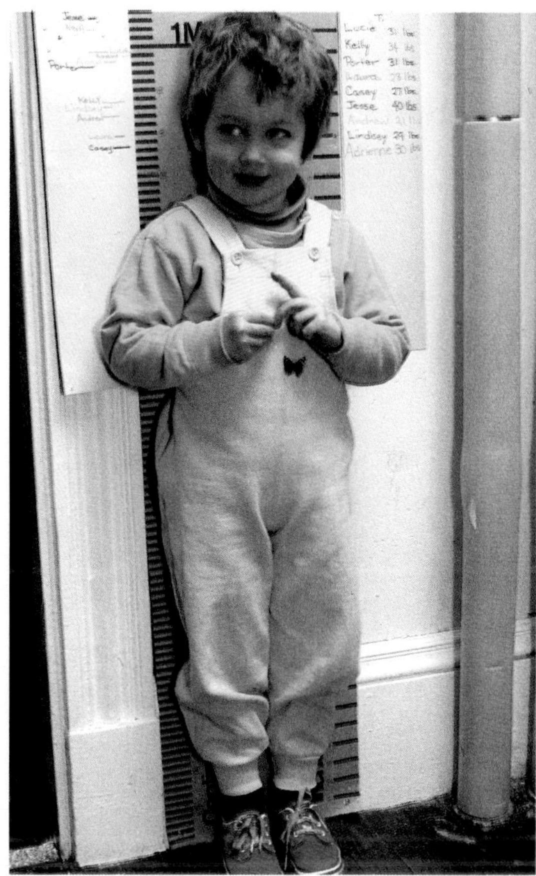

Children need proper nutrition to keep them healthy and growing.

Making Mealtime Enjoyable

You probably don't like all the same foods as your friends. Your tastes vary. This is the same for preschoolers, too. Children this age often prefer a vegetable raw rather than cooked. They

Food Choices

Food for the Day	Description
Milk	
2-3 cups	Milk may be fresh, dried, or evaporated; skim, lowfat, or whole; use as a beverage and in cooking; yogurt.
Meat and meat substitutes	
2 servings (total 1-2 oz.)	Meat, fish, fowl, eggs, cheese, dried beans or peas, or peanut butter.
Fruits	
2 or more servings	Fruits may be fresh, frozen, or canned; served whole, diced, or as juice. Look for canned fruits packed in natural juices.
Vegetables	
2 or more servings (including potato)	Vegetables may be fresh, frozen, or canned. Serve plain, in mixed dishes, or as juice.
	Choices of fruits and vegetables should include one good source (or two fair sources) of vitamin C daily and a good source of vitamin A at least every other day.
Breads, cereals, and grains	
2-4 servings	Use whole-grain or enriched breads, cereals, and grains; whole-grain or enriched macaroni, spaghetti, noodles, and rice.
Fats	
in moderate amounts	Salad oils, fortified margarine, butter, cream, mayonnaise, salad dressings, bacon.
Liquids	
6-8 cups	Water and other liquids such as fruit or vegetable juice, lemonade, broth, or soup.

may like the crunchy texture of raw celery just as much as its fresh flavor. The texture of food seems to be as much a part of eating as taste for the preschooler. In general, meals can be made more enjoyable for preschoolers if foods consist of different textures—crisp, chewy, and soft. Children will enjoy feeling the slipperiness of gelatin and spaghetti, the crinkliness of lettuce, and the soft, airy feeling of something whipped.

The appearance of the food can enhance or depress a preschooler's appetite just as it can an adult's. Crisp stir-fried or steamed vegetables look and taste better than overcooked ones. Yogurt with fresh fruit has more appeal than plain yogurt. A meal consisting of bright colors and contrasts is more

Size of Servings for Children

Food	Children's Age		
	1 Year	2–3 Years	4–5 Years
Milk and yogurt	1/2–1 cup	1/2–1 cup	1 cup
Meat, fish, poultry, cottage cheese, or mild processed cheese	1/2 oz.	1 1/2 oz.	2 oz.
Eggs	1 whole	1 whole	1 whole
Potatoes or vegetables, cooked	2 Tbsp.	3 Tbsp.	4 Tbsp.
Vegetables, raw	1 or 2 small pieces	2 or 3 small pieces	3 or 4 small pieces
Fruits, fresh, canned, or frozen, dessert	1/4 cup	1/3 cup	1/2 cup
Citrus fruit and juice	1/3–1/2 cup	1/3–1/2 cup	1/3–2/3 cup
Bread	1/2–1 slice	1 slice	1–1 1/2 slices
Cereal/Grain	1/4 cup	1/3 cup	1/2 cup

Note: Some children have difficulty digesting milk. Try substituting yogurt, which most people can digest.

attractive to children than a meal in which the same color is repeated in every food.

A peaceful and pleasant atmosphere at mealtime is also necessary for a good appetite. The mood of the family affects children's social and psychological development, as well as their eating habits. It may, for example, lead to a feeling of autonomy, to use Erikson's terms, if they are encouraged to feed themselves. "You're really doing well." It may lead to a feeling of shame, if they are frequently criticized for their eating habits. "You're a slob. I can't believe you can't even eat right."

The mood of the family at mealtime may make the child feel agitated and anxious or happy and secure. Children have a better chance of eating an adequate meal in an atmosphere that is calm and pleasant rather than one that is tense and unhappy. Mealtime is not a good time for arguments or very serious discussion. It should be a time the family enjoys spending together.

Atmosphere and attitudes toward food are especially important when children are between the ages of two and three years old. This is the time

Mealtimes need to be happy and pleasant times.

when the growth rate begins to slow. The appetite decreases. In addition, children at this age are striving to assert their own independence. They want to feed themselves, although at times they toy with their food. They may fuss over what they will and will not eat. They also want to select the amount they eat, and then feel that their behavior and decisions should be acceptable to those around them. Forcing children to eat may interfere with their developing sense of autonomy. Food may also seem like a form of punishment. "You can't leave the table until you eat everything on your plate." Appropriate limits and restrictions, however, will not interfere with their progress. Children who are not disciplined at all, who are allowed to throw food or grab food from another person's plate are certainly not being helped in their development. In such situations, both the child and the family suffer. As with all forms of discipline, however, it is important to enforce mealtime rules calmly, patiently, and with love. Children often learn by watching others. By practicing good table manners, the family shows children what behavior is appropriate.

Conscientious parents provide good meals for their children and, naturally, want their children to eat the nutritious food that will keep them healthy. Those parents need to recognize, however, that the probability of children becoming malnourished is very slight when they have balanced diets set before them. If children choose not to eat carrots one time, they

Suggested Menu Plan for Children

(Select from foods described)

Breakfast
- Fruit or juice
- Cereal with milk and/or egg
- Whole-grain toast with margarine or butter
- Milk

Lunch or Supper
- Soup or juice, as desired
- Meat or meat substitute
- Vegetable
- Whole-grain bread with margarine or butter
- Fruit
- Milk

Dinner
- Meat or meat substitute
- Potato, pasta, or grain
- Vegetable, cooked
- Vegetable or fruit as salad
- Whole-grain bread with margarine or butter
- Fruit
- Milk

A Matter of Fact

If you are in charge of designing meals for children, here are some creative tips:

- Sandwiches cut out with cookie cutters offer visual appeal. There are many shapes available. Try dinosaurs or other animals, hearts, diamonds, spades, clubs, music notes. You can find many interesting cookie cutters at stores that sell cooking tools.
- Spell the child's name in green beans, corn, carrots, or peas. This may be a great way to get children to eat veggies. You can use many foods to spell the child's name—even raisins.
- Make a catsup or mustard "smiley face" on a hamburger bun. Condiments in plastic squeeze bottles will give the perfect grin. Jellies also are available in squeeze bottles. Squeeze a jelly smile on the morning's whole-wheat toast.
- "S'mores" have been around for years. They're graham cracker sandwiches filled with a square of chocolate and toasted marshmallow. For a variation, try chocolate-covered grahams with toasted marshmallow, mint-favored chocolate chips instead of milk chocolate, or spread peanut butter on the graham crackers before adding the toasted marshmallow.
- Remember ants on a log? Fill the trough of a piece of celery with peanut butter and top with raisin "ants."
- Look for place settings made for children. Bowls and plates can be made of china and illustrated with the Beatrix Potter characters, or they may be dishwasher-safe and illustrated with Disney or Sesame Street characters. Colorful, inexpensive placemats, in plastic or fabric, can help you teach color and texture concepts. Child-size forks and spoons may have colorful handles, and the child's name or initials. It's time to put the old food-on-a-spoon-mimicking-an-airplane tactic to bed. It usually doesn't work anyway!

probably will eat them next time. On the other hand, if their refusal of carrots causes a confrontation with parents that results in a test of wills, then eating becomes an emotional activity. Parents need to realize that arguing over carrots may not be that important. A variety of foods throughout the day following the guidelines for a balanced diet is what parents should strive for.

Parents also should avoid praising children as "good" because they eat their food or condemning them as "bad" because they do not eat their food. Children should eat because they are hungry—not because they seek to gain praise or to avoid criticism.

Parents who compare one of their children with another are bound to

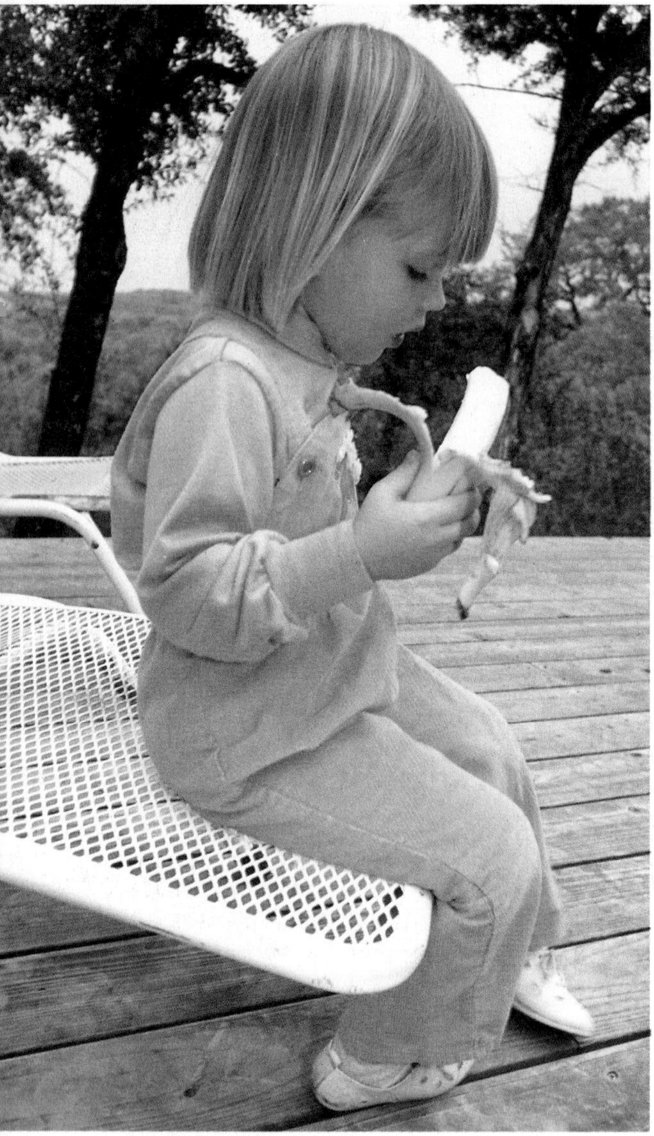

When children want snacks, choose healthful ones.

create **sibling rivalry.** Sibling rivalry is competition between children in a family for their parent's approval and love. This is a common trap that parents fall into at mealtime. "Billy, eat your green beans! Look how nicely Carl has eaten his." Carl may become overweight as he continues to demonstrate what a "good" boy he is. At the same time, Billy may not get proper nutrition as he continues to gain attention by resisting his parents efforts to force him to eat.

We cannot overemphasize the importance of good eating habits for very young children. As pointed out in Chapter 9, proper nutrition is absolutely essential to normal growth, psychological development, and emotional health. Moreover, your lifetime eating habits strongly reflect the habits developed in early childhood. Thus, parents must recognize the vital role they play in helping children achieve long-term healthy attitudes toward food.

Rest

Children have the best chance of eating well if they are well rested. Being tired from lack of sleep can depress the appetite. Limits also must be established in regard to preschoolers' sleeping patterns. When motor activities are thrilling and the sense of autonomy is at a crucial stage of growth, children may find it very hard to go to bed and sleep. For these reasons, it is important to minimize excitement prior to bedtime. Don't turn on suspenseful TV programs at this time of the evening. Establish a set, unhurried routine before bed. This reassures and soothes most children. An affectionate but *firm* goodnight from parents helps induce sleep in the resistant child.

The amount of sleep children need varies and it's difficult to judge how much a particular child needs.

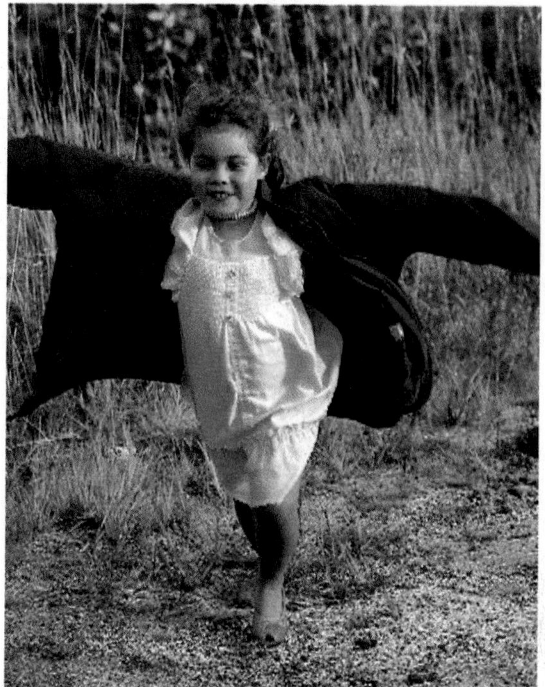

This much activity means a good night's sleep is needed.

However, the behavior of the children tells whether or not they are getting enough sleep. Signs such as good appetite, agreeable nature, cheerful attitude, bright eyes, good posture, curiosity, and waking cheerfully indicate that the child's sleeping pattern is suitable.

Look, Listen, and Learn

The preschool years are filled with action. During these years preschoolers become good runners, and for variety's sake, they will add a swerve. Their eye-hand coordination is improving, too. You can observe the development of these skills in preschoolers by using the following:

- Toss a ball to a child. How is it caught? Does the child hold her or his arms straight, with the elbows in front of the body, or with elbows at the sides?
- Draw a circle on a piece of paper and ask the child to copy it. Can he or she do it? Next draw a flower. Can that be copied?
- Play follow the leader. Ask the child to hop, walk on tiptoe, and skip. Can he or she perform all tasks? Does the child hop on both feet or one foot?

What other types of observation examples can you suggest? How will they help in the evaluation of the physical development of preschoolers?

Toilet Training

There are marked individual differences in the ages at which children develop control over their organs of elimination. It has been found that bowel control develops first. In order for children to control elimination, their muscles must be sufficiently strong and coordinated. Furthermore, children must be aware of the feelings that precede elimination. Only then are children ready for toilet training. This can vary from 18 to 36 months. Temporary lapses, however, may occur when children are tired, ill, or emotionally excited.

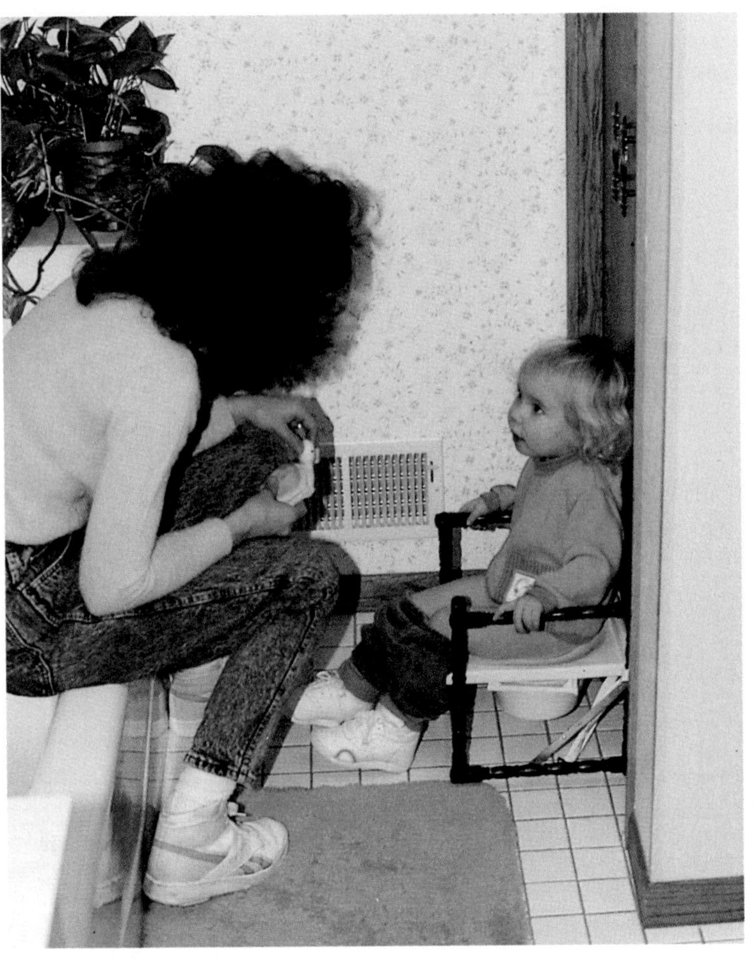

Toilet training should not be forced on a child. The child needs to have reached a point of physical maturity. Also, a child's potty chair will make the child feel more secure.

Most children remain "dry" during the day between the ages of two and two and one-half years, though they have frequent lapses when they are tired or excited. It is another year before they stay dry at night. This, too, is subject to many lapses. By the time children are ready to enter school, bladder control should be so complete that fatigue and emotional tension will not interfere with it to any degree.

Before inviting a toddler to begin toilet training, parents must have purchased a comfortable child's toilet seat. This may be a potty chair or a plastic insert for the adult toilet seat. The child needs to feel safe and secure while on the toilet. Any fear of falling can divert the child's attention from the goal of toilet training. For times when the family is away from home, the portable plastic insert is quite handy.

Use the following procedure. Start the training only when the child indicates that he/she is aware of the elimination process. For example, some children say "wet," or they place their hand on their diaper, or they stop their play to urinate or have a bowel movement. Parents should help the child connect this recognition with the opportunity to use the toilet. The caregiver must be alert to these indications if the child is going to be placed on the toilet in time.

Place the child on the toilet and stay there so you can talk with him/her. Your calm, patient, and pleasant attitude will do much to help the child develop a healthy attitude toward these natural body functions. Healthy attitudes developed at this early age are apt to persist through adulthood. If the child urinates or has a bowel movement, he/she should be showered with praise. The caregiver should show genuine appreciation of the accomplishment. If nothing occurs, and the child asks to leave the toilet, allow him/her to do so with acceptance and good humor.

Toddlers learn by their own observation that parents and older children use the toilet. Their natural tendency to be "copycats" is an important motivation for them to become toilet trained. Give the child several chances each day to use the toilet. As soon as the child has been successful several times and received the hugs and warm praise, the toilet training is accomplished. Positive parental reaction to success is much more effective in toilet training than negative reaction to failure.

The later toilet training is begun, the less time it will take. Children who begin training after 20 months tend to learn quickly and have little upset. Parents, however, must keep in mind that children frequently will have temporary lapses in control over their bowels and bladders. To regard children under the age of two as "problems" if they wet or soil themselves when they are still too immature to have the control would be much the same as viewing children in the crawling stage as "problems" because they are still too immature to walk. When parents regard their children in this way and try to "train" them out of this behavior, unhappy confrontations can occur. Both children and parents experience undue stress. Such confrontations can make toddlers feel that their parents disapprove of them. Eventually, they may feel that they have failed and will disapprove of themselves. Parents pushing children to learn before they are ready only frustrate their progress.

Influences on Adult Character

According to psychoanalytic theory, a child's early environment paves the way for later adjustments or maladjustments. With so many changes early in life, there are many opportunities for problems. Infants are predominantly passive, inducing adults to do things for them. During the ages of one to three years, they become gradually less dependent on others. Thus, children's first three years take them from complete dependency to the beginning of independent thought, action, and attitudes. They begin to manipulate their environment. They master walking and talking, and they begin to learn about cleanliness. Experiences they have with these various developmental tasks and activities in early childhood

One theory holds that adults who bite their fingernails did not have their oral drives satisfied as babies.

may influence their personality traits in the years to come. For example, if a child's hunger is not satisfied adequately on a regular basis, he or she may become a dependent and pessimistic adult. These feelings will be stronger when the person is anxious or insecure. Sometimes the frustrated individual may develop ambivalent attitudes. He or she may be described as friendly-hostile. Such a person may make a biting remark, and later try to make amends by being friendly.

A Closer Look

Jerry had been a vigorous eater as a small baby and had hung onto his bottle as soon as he was able to do it. When he started crawling, he took his bottle with him. His mother became disgusted with his attachment to the bottle and deprived him of it abruptly—in other words, she weaned him forcibly. Jerry resorted to sucking his thumb. He grabbed at everything he could reach. Sometimes he even attacked those who frustrated him. He ground his teeth. In time he became an avid nailbiter.

As an adolescent, when Jerry was frustrated, he indulged in food, particularly sweets and bottled drinks. If he had extra money he would buy himself presents to ease his sense of frustration.

The theory also holds there can be lasting effects for individuals who do not have the oral drives satisfied when they are young. For example, many babies who are forced to drink from a cup before they are ready to be weaned from bottle- or breast-feeding become adults who are preoccupied with eating, drinking, and/or smoking. When emotionally upset, they may eat, bite their nails, drink, or engage in some other form of oral gratification.

If a child's oral drives have been overindulged, other personality problems may arise. Optimism and self-assurance may develop to a point beyond which these traits are desirable. Individuals who have received such treatment may be so sure that everything will turn out all right that they feel no need to work toward their goals.

During the child's second year toilet training receives a great deal of attention. Children's attitudes, which are forming at this time, are influenced by their parents' particular attitudes. If parents give the impression by words, intonations, facial expression, or body language that changing diapers and elimination is dirty and disgusting, they may make their children feel that they have done something wrong or shameful. Children are sometimes made to feel that there is something dirty about the parts of their bodies that are covered by the diapers. Such attitudes can lead to unhealthy attitudes about normal body functions in adulthood.

In varying degrees, all parents in our culture emphasize cleanliness. Attitudes toward cleanliness vary to be sure, but inevitably there are conflicts between the child's wishes and the parental standards. In some homes, cleanliness has a moral aspect so that the dirty child becomes the bad child.

In Review

Vocabulary

vaccine
immunization
sibling rivalry

Summary

- ✓ The patterns of growth and development of muscular coordination are unique for each child.
- ✓ Normal growth and physical development depend on environmental, as well as hereditary factors. Bones, teeth, muscles, vital organs, and the central nervous system require proper nutrition and health care for normal development.
- ✓ Family attitudes and the general atmosphere of the home can strongly influence a child's appetite and pattern of rest.
- ✓ The later toilet training is begun, the less time it will take. The age when children are ready for the beginning of toilet training may vary from 18 to 36 months. Starting training before the child has gained muscular control of the bladder and bowels is counterproductive.

Questions

1. Briefly describe the physical growth of a child from two to five years old.

2. How do the bones of a preschool child differ from those of an adult? How do these differences affect the way that you handle the child?

3. What is the correlation between food and rest?

4. What besides nutrients must be considered when planning food for children?

5. Why does it usually take less time to toilet train a child who begins training after 20 months?

6. In Chapter 3, you will find the statement, "There is no better time

than dinner to share the joys and problems of the day." In light of the discussion in Chapter 12, give some examples of subjects that it would be better not to pursue at mealtime.

7. List some kinds of behavior that could indicate a preschooler is not getting enough rest.

8. List some steps that parents can take to help a preschooler get more rest.

Activities

1. Observe a group of preschoolers who are all approximately the same age. What differences do you note in their sizes and physical development?

2. Plan three days' menus for a three-year-old child. Show the amounts as well as the kinds of food you would serve. Follow the diet principles recommended by the Iowa Dietetic Association.

This chapter will help you:

- recognize the fact that thinking processes are different for preschoolers and adults
- identify the stages of development in a preschooler's concepts of space and time
- recognize the importance of early experiences on later attitudes toward intellectual activities
- appreciate the importance of play to the intellectual development of preschoolers
- learn how parents and other caregivers can influence the intellectual development of preschoolers

Preschool Thinking

During the preschool years, children progress toward more complex thinking. They leave the period of sensorimotor intelligence, the intellectual landmark of infancy, and enter the preoperational stage of thinking as described by Piaget. Their capacity for thought increases and becomes more controlled than in the sensorimotor stage. They are now able to **internalize,** to some extent, external events and actions. Internalize means to incorporate values or patterns within the self.

There are several distinctive characteristics of preschool thinking. Thinking at this stage is relatively unsocialized. That is, to children the world revolves around them. Very young children do not feel a need to justify their statements or explain how they came to their conclusions. They often ignore what other people say and take little note of how other people think. They begin to adjust their thinking to that of other people only as they become aware of themselves as thinkers and as they are able to consider several aspects of a situation at one time.

Another characteristic is that very young children's thinking focuses on physical objects and is based on perception rather than reason. They are greatly influenced by what they see, hear, or experience at any given moment. They do not understand transformations or the concepts of space and time. For example, Dawn at age three was taken on vacation in January. She left snow-packed Chicago to fly to Jamaica where the temperatures were in the upper 80s. While there, she decided it must be summer in Chicago. She was disturbed to see snow when she returned home.

One of Piaget's famous experiments illustrates preschool thinking. The experiment involves pouring water from one glass container to another glass that is taller and thinner than the first. When asked whether there is more, less, or the same amount of water in the second glass, the child answers either that there is more because the container is taller, or less because the container is thinner. The child centers on either the height or width of the glass. The child is unable to take both into consideration at the same time. In contrast, a child who has reached the next stage of thought, the period called concrete operations by Piaget, would consider both dimensions and would deduce that the amount of water is the same. Next time you're at the grocery store, look at this "deception" in packaging used to make the consumer think that one package holds more than another because of a different-size box or container. In reality, if the weights of the packages are identical, the consumer gets the same from either one. The advertiser is really appealing to a very elementary stage of thinking and reasoning. Wise consumers look at the weight of the contents to find the better buy.

A third characteristic of children at this age is that reasoning is from the particular to the particular rather than from the general to the particular or the particular to the general. As an example of the latter, suppose that a little boy eats two pieces of chocolate covered candy. The round piece is a cream filled and the square piece is a caramel. As a preschooler, he might not generalize the information available and guess that he should choose a square piece if he prefers caramels. Thus the very young child's understanding of the world lacks generality.

The fourth and final characteristic of the thinking of preschoolers is that thought is centered on one perspective, their own. They are egocentric and do not understand situations from any point of view except their own. Further, they do not realize that they are limited in this fashion.

An example of egocentricity has been shown in an experiment conducted by Piaget on children. He presented each child with a model of a mountain scene and then determined whether the children could perceive that views other than the one they were looking at did exist, even though they could not see them. Piaget was trying to discover whether the children had developed a mind's eye, a mental as well as a physiological capacity to "see." He found that although there was a distinct lessening of egocentricity (that is, older children began to perceive the possibility of the existence of a thing even though they were not seeing it), it did not entirely disappear. This should not surprise us since egocentrism is present in most adults to some degree or another.

For Better or For Worse

By Lynn Johnston

ARE THERE EIGHT ZILLION, KAFILLION, KADILLION, KAJILLION LEAVES IN THE WHOLE WORLD, MOM?

SURE, LIZZIE - WHY NOT?

THE LEAVES SURE ARE PRETTY NOW, HUH, MOM.

I KNOW WHY. DO YOU?

SURE! ALL SPRING AND SUMMER, THE LEAVES MAKE FOOD FOR THE TREE...

UNTIL IT GETS TOO COLD. THEN THE TREE GOES TO SLEEP AND DOESN'T NEED THIS FOOD... SO IT CUTS OFF NOURISHMENT TO THE LEAVES....

AS THE LEAVES DIE, A CHEMICAL CHANGE IN THEM PRODUCES THE COLORS - AND THE COLOR VARIES ACCORDING TO THE SPECIES OF THE TREE!

GRANDMA SAYS GOD PAINTS THEM.... ONE BY ONE.
10-21
LYNN

Young children have an egocentric viewpoint of the world.

Time Concepts

A part of egocentrism is the failure to understand the concept of time. A baby who is completely egocentric is concerned only with the present: *At this moment,* I am hungry, I am too warm, I am wet, or I am content, etc. The lessening of egocentrism is clearly illustrated in a child's gradual understanding of the concept of time. This understanding derives from the child's own bodily needs and actions. The following list describes the extent of a child's concept of time at various ages between 18 months and four years. This list is adapted from work by L. B. Ames, "The Development of the Sense of Time in the Young Child," *Journal of Genetic Psychology.*

18 Months—has a sense of time related to being hungry, tired, etc.

21 Months—uses the word *now;* waits when told to *wait a minute;* will sit and wait in a chair.

2 Years—Uses words *today, now,* and *afterwards;* understands that he

or she can play *after lunch;* begins to use the past tense of verbs.

30 Months—uses words that imply parts of the day such as *morning* and *afternoon,* and parts of a week such as *tomorrow* and *yesterday;* begins to understand past, present, and future concepts, although he or she uses future words more than past words.

3 Years—talks about the past and future as well as about the present; likes play wristwatches.

42 Months—uses past and future tenses accurately; more refined use of time words, such as *on Sunday, last Saturday;* still some confusion, such as "I'm going to take a nap yesterday."

4 Years—has a clear understanding of the sequence of daily events and may know days of the week; broader concepts expressed by referring to the seasons of the year, or the name of the month.

A Closer Look

A preschool teacher, trying to use three-year-olds' concepts of time, pointed to a large wall clock and said, "See where the big hand is on the clock? It is up at the top now. When it gets down to the bottom (pointing), it will be time to go home."

For the benefit of the children who would keep asking to go to preschool during Christmas vacation, the teacher said that they had to get their Christmas presents first and then Mommy or Daddy would put a circle around the day they were to come back. (The teacher pointed to it on the calendar). At home the children could cross out each day before they went to bed at night. Finally they would reach the day with a circle and they would come back to preschool.

Space Concepts

The young child's increasing perception of space, as with time, indicates a lessening of egocentrism. Spatial concepts also are derived from bodily needs and actions, although they are perceived later in life than the time concepts. These observations are from L. B. Ames and J. Learned, "The Development of Verbalized Space in the Young Child," *Journal of Genetic Psychology.*

1 Year—makes gestures indicating up and down.

18 Months—uses the words go, *come up, down, on,* and *off.*

2 Years—uses the words *big, all gone, here;* increased interest in coming and going.

30 Months—spatial words are often rigid and exacting: *right, right here, right there;* word combinations are used for emphasis and precision; the most frequently used words at this stage are *in, up, on, at.*

3 Years—choice of words shows refinement of space perception: *back, corner, over, from, by, up on top, on top of;* interest in detail and direction develops; uses names of cities.

42 Months—uses words *near, under, between;* interest in comparative sizes: *littlest, bigger, largest;* increased interest in location: *way down, way off, far away;* can place a ball on, in, under, and in back of something when told to do so.

> ### Look, Listen, and Learn
>
> **Preschool children enjoy playing "Simon Says." You may need to modify the game for younger children. They have enough to do just following verbal directions or imitating the actions without keeping a second fact in mind—did the leader say "Simon says"? Finding elbows, wrists, and putting hands "on," "under," or "on top of" are fun and help children understand space concepts.**

4 Years—uses even more expansive words: *on top of, far away, out, in, down to, way up, way up there, way far out, way off, behind;* can give home address; words used most are *in, on, up in, at,* and *down.*

Intellectual Development

Children's experiences in the years before they are six may influence not only their attitudes toward intellectual ideas, but also their actual ability for grasping them. Play is a way for children to learn.

It is important to understand the nature and function of play for children. There are two forms of play that are important for the intellectual development of young children. The first form of play is activity that is self-initiated by the child. It is lacking in structure, other than that given it by the child's own interests and imagination. The second form is adult-prescribed activity, initiated and directed by the toys given to the child or by the adult. If preschool toys are made so that it takes at least two children to handle them, children can learn to work together.

Play helps children advance to new skills. Through play, children learn how to relate to others and how to use toys and equipment. Both give children the chance to learn to deal with reality.

At first, young children treat other children as things. Gradually, they learn what kinds of fantasy play can be experienced only by themselves and what kinds can be shared with others. This is an essential step toward the intelligent grasp of the ideas of others. For example, when Anita plays "store" with Andrew she learns that he invents a deli where customers come and order food. By herself, Anita has always played "grocery store" where her stuffed animals "shop." Andrew's idea is completely new to Anita. She has reached a stage of development in which she learns other people have their own ideas.

Children also make intellectual progress as they use toys and equipment. If the first use of the "thing" world is successful and guided properly, the pleasure of mastering toys becomes associated with that of mastering conflicts. If activities provide enough challenge to be interesting but not frustrating, the average child will meet them with enthusiasm and develop self-confidence.

The goal, of course, is not merely knowing about toys but gaining the understanding of the larger physical and

Children's play often imitates the real world around them.

social environment and one's place in it. To help three- or four-year-olds develop into normal five- and six-year-olds through their play is not done by pushing or pressuring them. Rather caregivers need to encourage children's basic abilities as they are developing. This is not simple because children, of course, do not all progress in the same fashion or at the same rate. What is an intriguing challenge to one child may be either too difficult or too boring to others.

As children grow and their experiences increase, they acquire more and more information and learn more effective ways of recalling and applying it. In infancy, information is stored in patterns-of-action. These are what Piaget calls **schemas.** For example, babies learn quickly that their crying brings an attentive caregiver to their crib. They also learn that a smile causes the caregiver to laugh and talk in a very pleasant voice. They recognize these patterns-of-action as causes and effects. Thus children become acquainted with their environment through what they can do with it. By the time they are in elementary school, they have an array of concepts with which to understand their world. Such stability comes only as children's perceptions and actions are adapted to the

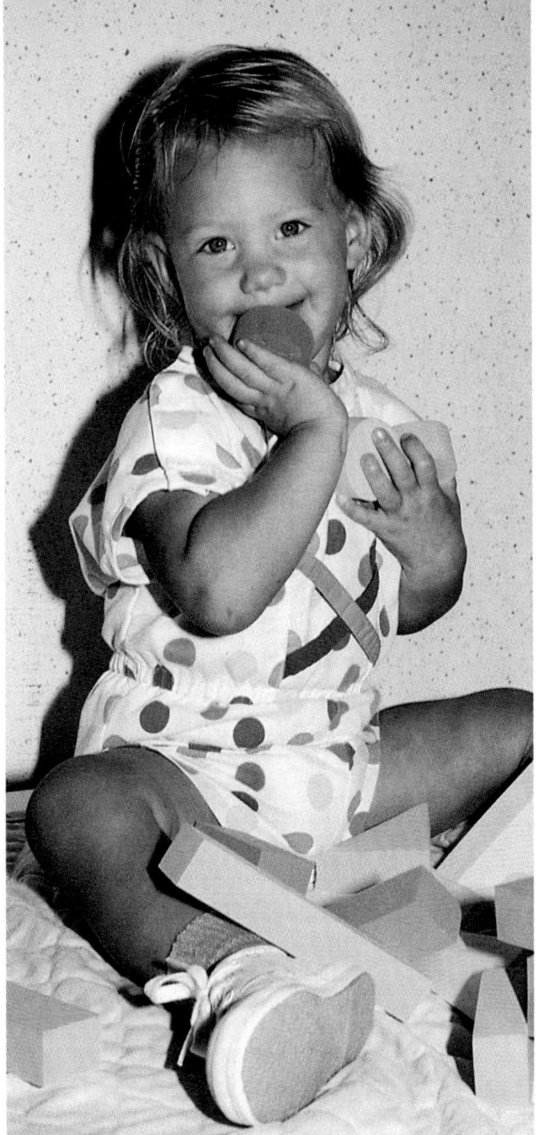

What concept can a child begin to understand by playing with building blocks?

ways others act. Thinking becomes less egocentric and more socialized.

According to Piaget, the adaptive processes involve assimilation and accommodation (Chapter 4). As children observe and interact with the world around them, they continually acquire new information. As you recall, assimilation is the incorporation of the new knowledge into existing systems of thought. Incorporating pieces of new information may very well require that children adjust their thinking and behavior patterns. That process of adjustment is called accommodation. The two processes are reciprocal and interwoven. Thus, assimilation leads to accommodation and vice versa. For instance, Clay sees it raining. Later he notices it has stopped. The same thing happens again. Now Clay knows the rain will stop because it has before.

A Closer Look

Jean, age five, saw the lake in the area where her family was moving and was excited. Her enthusiasm made her mother try to caution her because Jean had never been in a lake before. Her mother said, "Lakes are fun, but you must be with a grown-up when you go near them. This lake is deep and over your head." Jean's immediate reply was, "But I'll stay on top." Clearly, she needed more assimilation and accommodation. It is not always easy, however, for adults to help small children in the process of assimilation and accommodation. For example, see the next case study.

A preschool teacher was visiting a park that had a very clear lake. She marveled at a duck paddling about. Because the lake was so clear, she could see parts of its body and feet under the water. The duck would give a little push with one foot or the other and glide forward. There's nothing unusual about that, but the teacher couldn't swim. A three-year-old boy standing near asked, "How can he do that?" The teacher thought, "How do you explain the displacement of water to a three-year-old?" She couldn't think of an answer so she said, "That is just what I was wondering."

The content of play and extent of its egocentricity reveal something of children's progress toward socialized thought. An older child, possibly a six-year-old, can think about the relationship between two or more variables. A younger child, possibly a three-year-old, tends to focus first on one variable and then another.

Most preschool children cannot concentrate their efforts on any one project for long. Young preschoolers tend to have shorter attention spans than older ones. For example, young preschoolers, around three years old, turn pages of a picture book very quickly. In contrast, older preschoolers, around five years old, weave simple acts together into more complicated activities that take more time. To stack blocks and knock them down takes only a minutes. To make a town out of blocks with apartments, fences, and street patterns, can take half the afternoon.

The growing awareness that objects have many properties, that they can be viewed along different dimensions, and that they can be classified in a variety of ways is a result of children's play. They are learning as they play. Through manipulation—touching, lifting, holding, arranging, sorting, and so on—children begin to note similarities among objects. In this way, also, they notice differences in objects. Eventually, just as they can sort objects into similar groupings such as size, color, and shape, they can order them on the basis of their differences, arranging them from smallest to largest or darkest to lightest. The origins of conceptual thinking are in these activities.

Many researchers in recent years have concluded from their studies that babies are born with an inclination to search for cause-and-effect relationships. Even two-year-old children answer "why" questions by using the words "because" and "so." Three- and four-year-old children can repeat

Look, Listen, and Learn

One of the easiest ways to illustrate differences and likenesses is with a collection of bottles. Caution: Do not use fragile glass ones that could break and hurt a child. Ask the question, "How are these bottles different?" This helps the child point out differences in height, weight, material, color, use, shape, and the way the tops are put on the bottles. Next ask, "How are the bottles alike?" The child can point out similarities in function, size, height, etc. Even such a common item as a shoe can call for discussing what it is, its color, its use, its parts (such as the sole), the material it is made of, and so on.

A Matter of Fact

A regularly scheduled storytime is the perfect time for a caregiver to encourage a child's interest in reading. Reading to children enhances their language development and furthers their reading skills. Reading to children gives caregivers the opportunity to expand children's curiosity and awareness. This wonderful, cuddly sharing time also gives children a greater incentive to want to learn to read by themselves.

Caregivers should review the stories and poems they intend to read to their preschoolers—and then read only quality stories and poems daily. Singing and reciting childhood rhymes and telling stories also helps children. Dramatic play is another help. Children need the opportunity to observe the written word around them and to try their hand at writing. Caregivers can do this by supplying large crayons and newsprint for scribbling.

Here are other ideas that will help get children interested in words:

- Turn off the TV before the show ends. Have the child describe and then act out the ending.
- Create your own word games. Hang a list of rhyming words in the child's room.
- Listen to the radio and tapes. Expose the child to music. Have the child talk about what he or she hears in the music.
- Have the child make up stories in which the child is the main character.
- Introduce the child to your local library. Children's librarians are knowledgeable about the books appropriate for different age groups.

stories such as fairy tales if the events follow in a logical order according to the principle of cause and effect.

The Role of Parents in Intellectual Development

Today, we are faced with a rapidly changing world. There are increasing demands on people to develop highly trained mental skills and expertise. One approach to achieving excellence in education in order to meet these demands is to begin the formal education of children at an earlier age. As mentioned in Chapter 11, there is even an institute dedicated to developing "super babies." Most psychologists agree, however, that the appropriate time for children to learn to read and do arithmetic problems is probably close to the traditional age range of five to seven years. Nevertheless, parents can stimulate the intellectual development of preschoolers without pushing them beyond their readiness.

Parents can teach children to be good listeners by being good examples as listeners. By listening and interact-

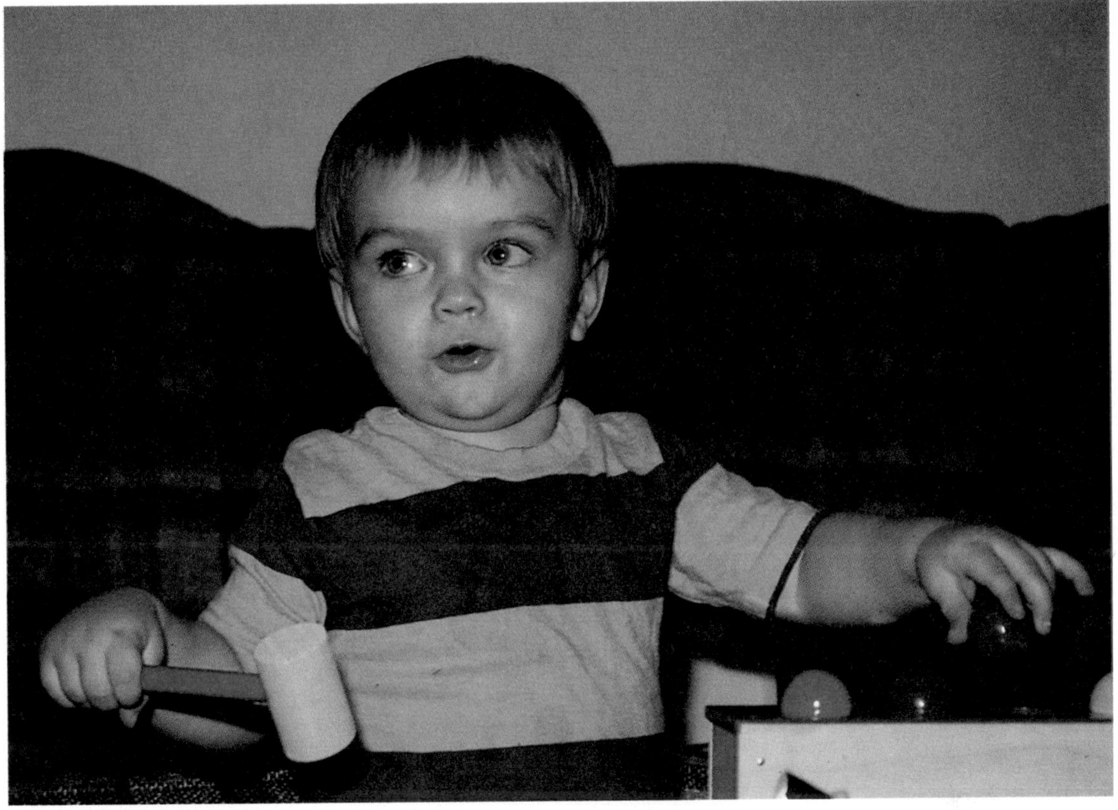

Thoughtfully chosen toys can provide a learning experience for children.

ing, parents can encourage children to develop their verbal skills. By reading to children as they snuggle up close, parents demonstrate the enjoyment books can bring, and they stir the imagination of the listener. Playing games is a vital source of intellectual stimulation for children. Even more important than the acquisition of knowledge from the games is the *attitude toward knowledge* that comes from the challenge of learning while having a lot of fun with a loved one. For that reason, parents should take every opportunity to play games with their preschoolers.

There is no need to push, but when children show number readiness, parents can help their children learn to count. Using objects for counting helps children visualize numbers. Counting to 10 on fingers is one way. Ed's father helps him while putting on his shirt. "Let's count how many buttons you have, Ed. One. Two. What comes after two? That's right, three!" Cindy's pet cat had kittens. Her parents helped her count six in the litter. Understanding numbers opens up the possibility for lots of games. How many blocks can we pile up before they crash down? What shapes can we form on the table when we play dominoes? How high can you count while standing on one foot before you lose your balance? The number of games is limited only by the creativity and imagination of the parents.

By watching "Sesame Street" on television, children gain an awareness of letters, as well as numbers. Whether their awareness comes from television or from other experiences in their homes, when children are ready, they can recognize letters, words, and even understand how spelling is related to rhyming. This, too, opens many doors for games with parents. Again, there is no need to push children. They should be allowed to learn at their own rates. Parents should be alert to the possibility that pressure can make children resistant. A humorous example is given in the following case study.

A Closer Look

When Dawn was five years old, she learned the sounds of the letters and enjoyed playing phonetic games with her father. At the dinner table one evening, he explained to her that if she thought about the sounds of letters, she could spell many words. He used bat, hat, and cat as examples. With just that much information, she was able to spell fat, mat, pat, rat, and sat. She was not able, however, to spell flat. Her father ignored the obvious signs of her frustrations, and he persisted in trying to get her to understand the sounds of two consonants together. Suddenly, she dropped her head on the table and moaned, "Dying, dying! Can anyone spell dying?" Thus, the game ended in good fun, and Dawn had taught her father a lesson more valuable than the one he taught her.

Preschools

Children's intellectual development depends not only on their activity with material things and isolated concepts, but also on their social interaction with other children. Characteristically, preschool children have difficulty in conceiving a point of view different from their own. But interacting with other children confronts them with the necessity of accommodating themselves to others' ideas. When doing things together, children must communicate with each other. Such communication is an essential factor in intellectual development.

Traditionally, children interacted with their siblings and with other children in the immediate neighborhood. Mothers took responsibility for the safety of their own and other children by supervising their play. That scenario, however, is no longer typical.

As discussed earlier, there are increasing numbers of small children living with single parents or with parents who both work outside the home. Thus, there is a growing demand for quality daycare centers and preschools. Some authorities say that preschool education for two- to five-year-olds is more important than a college education. A good preschool experience should enhance children's intellectual development. The question of what comprises a good preschool

How does playing together contribute to children' s intellectual development?

program is, then, just as complex as the question of what comprises a good college education.

Teaching Approaches

As we already have discussed, preschool children are still in the early stages of intellectual development. Thus, their ability to solve problems is just beginning. Their attention spans are still quite short, and new information should be presented to them in small bits that relate directly to knowledge they already have acquired. Because children in one age group vary so much in their stages of intellectual development, a good preschool curriculum is individualized.

One approach in preschools has been to have teachers prepare the necessary materials so there can be various activities for each of the children. The youngsters are not thought of as a group, and they interact with one another only if they happen to be interested in the same activity. The teacher does not instruct a class but, instead, guides and counsels individuals in their activities.

Preschools need to give children time to have fun.

On the other hand, if the approach is so individualized that it becomes a tutorial relationship between teacher and child, the children lose the motivation that comes from belonging to and interacting with a peer group. In addition, they are deprived of the opportunity to develop their social skills. There are benefits to be gained from teacher-directed activities, as well as from child-directed activities. A balance of the two is desirable.

One attempt to achieve that balance is with teacher-guided, small-group learning situations. That approach was the one utilized in the highly successful Perry Preschool project in Ypsilanti, Michigan. With only about six children per teacher, each child could be motivated individually. The teacher could adapt the program for the maximum intellectual and social benefit of each child. The project was based on a "plan-do-review" cycle. Children develop plans for an hour of activity, carry out the plans, and evaluate their tasks at the conclusion of the hour. The cycle is designed to develop initiative,

When children are able to put together a puzzle, what level of intellectual development have they achieved?

responsibility, competence, problem-solving ability, and social cooperation.

A more structured approach is utilized in Montessori preschools, which are patterned after the principles first formulated by the Italian educator, Maria Montessori, in 1912. The Montessori schools in the United States differ considerably from one to another, depending on the administration and personnel. However, they tend to adhere, in varying degrees, to the original philosophy. All of the children learn to accomplish certain sensorimotor tasks in particular, orderly sequences, rather than in individual ways. Children are given choices of activities and schedules, but there are fairly rigid rules set on techniques, clean-up, and behavior. Some people believe that the structured approach limits children in their language learning, their social interactions, their creativity, and their cognitive learning.

The Question of What to Teach

A controversy exists today as to how we can best serve the interests of children in preschools. Throughout the world, many schools for children of all ages have stressed the learning of facts and skills rather than the development of thought processes. Most modern educators, however, believe that children should be taught fundamentals, and then challenged to develop problem-solving abilities through processes of logical thinking.

At first, children can learn simple tasks of sorting objects or pictures according to directions. This is a beginning step for learning the **concept of analysis** in which we separate a whole unit into its parts so we understand its workings. Later activities allow children to see the relationships between objects, and this is a step toward the **concept of synthesis** in which we put together individual objects or facts to create a functional entity. Disassembling wooden toys and separating the parts according to sizes, shapes, or colors and assembling picture puzzles are examples of these kinds of activities. As intellectual development progresses, children are able to recognize more than one relationship be-

Good preschools offer individualized instruction, yet also give children the chance to interact.

tween objects. They also can understand situations in which two or more variables change simultaneously.

The activities in preschools should challenge children to develop small-muscle skills, large-muscle skills, and verbal skills at the same time they are acquiring the concepts that will prepare them for reading and doing mathematical problems when they are of school age.

In addition to the teacher-directed activities, there should be child-directed activities that involve interactions with other children. Through "pretend" games, children can express their views of reality as they see it. Pretending also allows them excellent opportunities to be creative. Creativity can be encouraged through art activities that are suitable for young children, such as finger painting, coloring, and working with clay.

Intellectual activities in preschools should be exciting and challenging. By the time children have finished preschool, they should have good self-concepts. They should have confidence in their ability to solve problems and should enjoy creating with both their minds and their hands. They should have acquired general concepts of numbers, verbal skills, and social skills that allow them to interact intellectually with their peers, as well as their teachers. With all of this, however, it is imperative to remember that the basic purpose of daycare centers and preschools should be to provide a home atmosphere, not a school atmosphere.

There should be plenty of warm and loving interactions with adults who enjoy the profession of helping children develop into humane, bright, healthy, active, enthusiastic, and creative school children.

The Effects of Preschool

For a number of reasons, researchers find it difficult to evaluate the effects of preschool care compared with home care. First, one cannot generalize on the quality of care received in either preschools or homes. There are good and bad preschools, and there are good and bad homes. Second, there are statistical differences (cultural, economic, and genetic) between those parents who send their children to preschools and those who don't. Thus, if researchers find statistical differences between those children who attended preschool and those who didn't, it is difficult to determine whether those differences are due to preschool experiences or to any parental differences. Third, there are no tests available to give reliable measurements of overall psychological development. Despite these problems, researchers continue to evaluate the effects of preschools because daycare has become such an important part of modern life.

Possibly the conclusion that can be stated with the most certainty is that preschool children catch colds, flu, and other minor ailments more often than home-care children. However, their physical growth and development do not suffer. Socially, preschool children show greater maturity both with their peers and with adults. They are also more outgoing and cooperative with children they never met before. On the negative side, preschool children are somewhat noisier, rowdier, and more aggressive.

Traditionally, mothers were the primary caregivers. Thus, researchers have tried to determine whether children form their strongest bonds with their caregivers in preschools rather than with their mothers. The conclusion is that the mother-child bond is not weakened by the preschool experience so long as the mother regularly spends quality time with the child during the hours that she has available.

So far as intelligence is concerned, it can be said that preschool is not detrimental to children's IQ scores. In fact, the preschool children show more rapid cognitive development than home-care children. That is, they have more knowledge at a given age. Soon after they enter school, however, the home-care children catch up.

The effects of preschool were easier to determine in the Perry Preschool Project, mentioned earlier in this chapter, because it was a controlled experiment. All of the 123 children were economically disadvantaged. The children were *randomly* assigned either to the preschool program or to a no-preschool group. The preschool program focused on developmental principles, not on academic skills that are traditionally learned when children reach school age. The unequivocal success of this high-quality program can best be understood by studying the following table, which compares some of the achievements and experiences of the two groups when they reached 19 years of age.

Perry Preschool Project

Comparison of achievements and experiences of 19-year-old youths who had been in either the preschool group or the no-preschool group.

	Preschool %	No Preschool %
Completed high school	67	49
Attended college or job-training programs	38	21
Classified as mentally retarded	15	35
Hold jobs	50	32
Support themselves by their own or their spouse's earnings	45	25
Satisfied with work	42	26
Arrested for criminal acts	31	51
On public assistance	18	32

Finally, it is important to remember that all of the research on the effects of preschools is, by necessity, statistical. Thus, we can study averages and trends, but we cannot use these to make predictions for individuals. It is impossible to say how any one child will respond to the daycare experience. After all, the one fact we do know is that each child is an individual.

Life's Work

Anastasia Mitchell

➤**Freelance Illustrator**
➤**Bachelor of Fine Arts**

There really isn't a typical day in this profession. Anastasia says, "I may be at the drawing board for 16 hours straight, working on an illustration with a tight deadline. Or I may actually only draw for a couple of hours and spend the rest of the day making appointments to show my portfolio, calling on clients, or preparing for a new job by finding reference material or brainstorming for ideas."

Anastasia says she must be very flexible with her time. More often than not a job will last well past 5:00 and sometimes into the next day. There isn't any "overtime" compensation, however.

Anastasia says that, of course, good drawing skill is necessary for success in her profession. She adds, "I think being conceptually creative is equally important. The idea sells as well as the visualization. A professional attitude and dedication are also necessary. You must think of illustrating as not just drawing or fun, but as a business."

Anastasia says her most rewarding job-related accomplishment was "being able to donate my services to illustrate a brochure for Camp Courage, a camp for special needs children. I hope that my illustrations will help persuade people to give time or money to the organization."

For a student considering freelance illustrating, Anastasia's advice is, "be persistent. It takes time for the public to realize that you're serious and professional. Also, you must do your absolute best on every job, no matter how big or small. You never know who might see it."

When asked how her profession will change within the next 10 years, Anastasia says, "The illustration field, like fashion, is always changing. Styles of art come and go. Also, with the advance of computer graphics and photography, needs vary. You just have to try to be the best at what you do."

In Review

Vocabulary

internalize
time concepts
space concepts
schemas
concept of analysis
concept of synthesis

Summary

- ✓ Preschoolers have different thought processes than adults. From the children's perspective, the world revolves around them.
- ✓ Children develop intellectually through their play. Their play may be self-initiated or adult-prescribed.
- ✓ During the preschool years, children grow from egocentric thought toward more socialized thought.
- ✓ By being good role models, parents and other caregivers can help children learn the joy of learning, the art of good listening, and the path to imaginative thinking.
- ✓ Activities in preschools and daycare centers should be exciting and challenging. Most importantly, preschools and daycare centers must provide home-like atmospheres in which children and professional adults share warm and loving interactions.

Questions

1. What are the four main characteristics of preschool thinking?

2. A little boy says, "Mommy, when I grow up, I'm going to marry you." Obviously, he is not yet aware of two concepts that he will take for granted when he is older. What are they?

3. Why should parents take the time to play games with preschool children?

4. A concept is a mental picture or image brought to mind by some word or phrase, some event, some object, or anything that carries meaning for an individual. Imagine that you are a preschooler. Describe your concept of one of the following words: dinner, mother, father, home, playground.

5. If parents try to restrict their child's handling of objects, the child will be deprived of developing meaning in which way(s)?

A. motor manipulation

B. sight exploration
C. reasoning
D. questioning

6. Toys such as nests of cubes, puzzles, and tricycles promote the child's perceptual development in which area(s)?
A. space
B. weight
C. number
D. time

7. It has been said that play is a child's work. Explain this statement.

8. If you were leaving a three-year-old child with a sitter at 9 a.m. and intended to return at 1 p.m., how would you explain your plans so the child could understand?

9. Imagine that your neighbor has just asked you, "Why did you decide to enroll your child in preschool?" What list of considerations would you include in your explanation?

10. As a parent, what could you do to help your preschool children to prepare for happy and productive school years?

Activities

1. Design an experiment you could use with preschool children to illustrate egocentric behavior.

2. Suppose that you and your spouse are parents of a preschool child, and you both work outside the home. You would like to find a person to take care of your child at home. Write a want ad listing all the qualities and attributes you would want this caregiver to have, including her or his education, philosophy of preschool education, and the facilities available in the home.

3. Preschool children maintain stronger bonds with their parents than with the adults who provide daycare if the parents regularly spend quality time with their children. Describe an evening of "quality time" for parents and a preschool child, beginning with the late-afternoon pickup at the preschool and ending with the last "Goodnight."

4. Think of how teenagers and adults sometimes need a "retreat." Business men and women may come home and unwind by telling their spouses the troubling events of the day. Teenagers may require some time alone in their rooms to think through bothersome social interactions. Imagine that you are the operator of a preschool. What steps would you take to satisfy the needs of little children when they want to retreat?

This chapter will help you to:

- ✎ recognize the interdependence of emotional and social growth
- ✎ identify the physiological and behavioral events associated with emotion
- ✎ understand the relationship between emotional development and parental nurturing
- ✎ learn some of the sources of fear and anxiety in children and some of their responses to their fears
- ✎ accept the universality of jealousy and learn how parents can help children to manage their jealous feelings

The Importance of Love

The gifts of love that children receive from their parents are returned in kind. Children can love others only when they feel secure and loved.

Emotional and social development are quite dependent upon one another. It is not a question of "either...or." You can find examples of this mutual interdependence in your own life. Think about people you know. You are easily drawn to people who are emotionally giving and loving. You want to be with them. On the other hand, when you meet people who are withdrawn or grudging, you tend to refrain from being with them.

Sympathy causes a positive social response as does a warm smile. An angry frown discourages social interaction and may stimulate aggression. Hostility provokes hostility, kindness stimulates kindness, withdrawal causes withdrawal, and friendliness leads to friendliness.

How can you tell what message people are sending if they don't say anything? A smile or frown has meaning. Folded arms or an outstretched hand say something, too. They are forms of communication—facial expressions and **body language.** How do children learn what facial expressions and gestures mean? When children see a parent smile and hear words of praise

What are these three expressing by their body language? Which one seems unhappy with the way the game is going?

at the same time, they know their behavior is pleasing. Seeking to cause repetitions of these warm feelings, children repeat the behavior that brought about the favorable response. Likewise children learn to associate a frown with those times that parents have verbally disapproved of their behavior. Thus, sensitive children often can be disciplined by an expression or a gesture. By observing and analyzing body language and expressions children can recognize and respond to people's emotions.

Behavioral Events

Behavioral events of emotion may be best understood in contrast to physiological events of emotion. **Physiological events of emotion** are reflected in changes in ones' physical state, such as changes in pulse, blood pressure, and muscle tension. **Behavioral events of emotion** are reflected in changes in one's feelings and emotional reactions. The behavioral events are further divided into two classes. One concerns feelings, or affective behavior. It is, for all practical purposes, unobservable behavior. For example, a child who has had a frightening experience with an angry dog may *feel* frightened even by playful dogs. The child may show the fear with body language, but otherwise does not act on the fear. The other class of behavior is called effective. This observable behavior has an effect on the individual's actions. The frightened child may run away from the dog or hit the dog with a stick. Either one is an example of effective behavior.

The preschool child shows a variety of behavioral events of emotion. Some of the most common are love, anger, fear, jealousy, rivalry, and aggression. This chapter will focus on some of the emotions which are most significant in the child's development.

Love

The preschool child has a variety of love relationships with different family members. The home atmosphere in which the parents have a mutual love, trust, and respect for each other creates the best surroundings for the emotional development of the child. **Nurturing** is the main component of love relationships, and it is found in this environment. Nurturing is defined as a willingness to promote well-being and development of the loved one. Parents ordinarily have strong nurturing feelings for their children. However, there must be an acceptance of nurturing by the child. Thus, the love a child feels for a parent has a significant measure of this acceptance in it. The child counts on the parents' nurturing, expecting it and accepting it as a part of life. Children need reassurance, from time to time, that their trust is well founded.

For children to grow up feeling secure, they need to know that their parents continue to find pleasure in their company. When children are being affectionate, sweet, cute, amusing, and endearing, part of their motivation is to gain the acceptance of their parents. Another part of their motivation is to promote their own happiness and well-being.

As children mature, they become nurturing. Although still dependent on others for company and nurturing, they can now give as they accept. The objects of dependency also change. Dependent in the beginning on their parents or other primary caregivers, children come to depend upon other family members, then upon peers, teachers, and other adults.

A Closer Look

Susie, age four years, brought in a pretty dandelion and said, "Here, Daddy, you can have it." The father remarked about how yellow it was and played the childhood game of having her see if he liked "butter" by rubbing the dandelion under his chin.

Susie also brought special paintings from school for her father and for her mother saying, "I made them for you." Her parents always showed interest in the things she brought them and in the thoughtful things she did for them because they understood that these were expressions of love.

Grandparents and Love

One aspect of emotional development for children is experiencing love from people other than parents and siblings. Such relationships establish new role identities for children and allow children to sense different types of love feelings toward others.

The love children experience with grandparents depends upon the role the grandparents play—informal, formal, or distant figures. The informal grandparent tends to be playful, joining the child for the purpose of having fun. Children usually establish a mutually joyous relationship with this grandparent.

Formal grandparents give the child gifts and occasionally help parents, but see their roles in strict terms. These grandparents do not offer advice, and they leave parenting strictly to the parents. From this the child derives a degree of satisfaction, knowing that some nurturing and some response are forthcoming.

Distant-figure grandparents feel remote from the child and acknowledge little effect of the child upon their own lives. Although these grandparents give gifts on special occasions and go through certain motions, there is little feeling or response. Naturally, children will not feel strong ties to distant-figure grandparents. The youngsters may be respectful, but they are apt to reflect the aloofness of the grandparents.

A humorous, playful grandparent adds an element of fun to a child's life.

Attitudes Toward Others

In the development of attitudes toward others, the infant or the child changes through processes of assimilation and accommodation. Remember that assimilation is defined as the way in which children understand their environment and interpret it. For example, if a child is disciplined, one interpretation may be, "You punished me because you are angry." On the other hand, parents should try to help the child understand that she or he is being disciplined because the parents care about the child and the child's behavior. Whichever interpretation the child assimilates will determine his or her attitudes.

To define accommodation, think in terms of adjusting to differences, that is, bringing differences into agreement or harmony. The social behavior of children becomes more complex as they grow older and have particular experiences. As they mature, they become less self-centered. Their awareness, orientation, and attitudes change. This tends to be so whether the behavior considered is self-centeredness, attention to others, exchange of ideas, friendship, quarrels, sympathy, nurturance, aggression, dependence, masculine or feminine roles, intergroup attitudes, or withdrawal from the group. For example, let's consider aggression. A child who lives in a household where aggression and abuse are common is apt to exhibit similar behavior on the playground. The child may discover, however, that aggression makes him or her unpopular and causes confrontations with playmates. He or she may then adopt the more sociable and mature behavior of a respected playmate.

Attitudes toward others have three kinds of components. The first has

Differences of opinions—or having to share a favorite toy—sometimes leads to quarrels.

been termed affective components such as liking and disliking. The second group is cognitive components such as knowing what people do and how they influence others. The third group has been termed behavioral components. These components are rooted in the personality of the individual.

The affective components of our attitude toward another person have to do with our senses. Do you like his or her looks, voice, composure, etc.? The cognitive components involve more depth of observation and thought. How does this person interact with other people? How does that interaction affect my mental picture of this person? The behavioral components are those aspects of our observations that cause us to behave in certain ways toward this particular person. Do I avoid this person because he or she is mean-tempered? Do I want to be near this person because he or she is amusing?

Attitudes Toward Self

Children's views of themselves are created by how they are treated by others and by how they interpret the emotions, actions, and statements of others. Adults should realize that young children see everything as either black or white, with no shades of gray. They consider themselves either naughty or nice, good or bad, lovable or awful. Adults also need to remember that to be human is to have all kinds of feelings—love and hate, courage and cowardice, tenderness and detachment. Children, like adults, are wrestling with conflicting feelings. Recognizing these facts, we need to respond to children in ways that will help them learn to like, accept, trust, and respect themselves. In communicating with a child, statements of understanding and encouragement should precede statements of advice or instruction. Moreover, all communication should preserve the self-respect of both the child and the adult. These goals can be achieved when there is empathy in the parent-child relationship, as discussed in Chapter 3.

Parents need to communicate with their children in such a way as to help children develop positive attitudes toward themselves. For example, if a three-year-old is scared of getting into a swimming pool, a parent may say, "You chicken. There's nothing to be scared about. Don't be a baby." That would not help self-esteem. On the other hand, if the parent says, "You can play on the side here. Maybe later you'll want to get in the water with me. You let me know when you're ready." That response lets the child know that the feeling is natural and the parent understands. The child is not being forced into an action he or she is uncomfortable with and cannot handle. That response also does not hurt the child's self-image.

Erikson's View

Erik Erikson has based his theory of development on what he has observed of children in their homes and in the presence of their families. Author David Elkind discussed Erikson's theory in a *New York Times Magazine* article entitled "Erik Erikson's Eight Stages of Man," copyright 1970 by The New York Times Company. In his work, Erikson maintains that people are constantly establishing new orientations to themselves and to their social world. As you read in Chapter 4, Erikson believes that personality develops continuously throughout the entire life cycle, and that each stage of development has a positive and a negative component. A new dimension of social interaction becomes possible in each stage of the life cycle.

The first stage, trust versus mistrust, mentioned briefly in connection with infants' needs is by no means resolved in the first years of life. Rather, it recurs at each successive stage of development. For example, young children who go to school with a sense of mistrust may later trust a particular teacher. Thus, trust is an attitude that can be developed with time.

During the ages of two and three years, a sense of autonomy versus a sense of shame and doubt emerges. (See Chapter 4.) At this age, children are developing more sophisticated motor and mental abilities. They take great pride in their new achievements and want to be left alone to do them.

The development of a sense of autonomy means that children acquire a clearer concept of themselves. They learn that they are distinct in body and action. The two-year-old's frequent use of *me do, my,* and *mine* typifies this sense of self.

Use of the term "terrible-two's" is unfortunate. Two-year-olds can be as charming as children at any other age if parents recognize the reasons for the apparent negativism. In this stage, children say "no" in order to affirm their separateness. It is the first sign of their natural desire and need for independence. Even though they will not be ready for total independence for possibly another 20 years, the process begins at age two. Independence does not just happen—it evolves. It is a slow process, requiring parental understanding, patience, and considerable compromise.

When parents recognize that preschoolers need to perform at their own rates, the children gradually develop a sense of having some control over themselves and their environment. In other words, their sense of autonomy emerges. However, if their parents or siblings insist on doing everything for them, even those things the children are perfectly capable of doing themselves, they may develop a sense of shame and doubt. When parents are overprotective and criticism is not constructive, children may develop an extreme sense of shame and doubt concerning their ability to control themselves and their environment.

If children emerge from this stage with a sense of shame and doubt overshadowing their sense of autonomy, they will be at a disadvantage in attempting to achieve autonomy in adolescence and adulthood. They may find it difficult to make new friends when they transfer from one school to another. They may be overly susceptible to peer pressure if they are afraid to express their independence by saying "No!" They may doubt that their talents will let them succeed in college or trade school. They may be shy about applying for a job because they fear failure. On the other hand, small children whose sense of autonomy outweighs their feeling of shame and doubt will be well prepared for the successive stages in their approach toward independence. The balance of autonomy to shame and doubt established at two or three years of age, however, is delicate and subject to change.

Children in the autonomous stage enjoy showing off their new talents.

Erikson says the components of the next stage are those of initiative versus guilt. Four- or five-year-olds have considerable control over their bodies. They initiate activities on their own rather than merely responding to or imitating the actions of others. As children initiate activities, they will feel

Some children feel a sense of doubt. They may be shy and feel uncomfortable around others.

either a sense of pride or a sense of guilt. Children who are allowed to initiate physical activities such as running or bicycle riding will develop a secure and well-defined sense of initiative. When parents answer their children's questions instead of putting them off or ridiculing them, their sense of initiative is further strengthened. But if parents treat children's activities or questions as bothersome, worthless, or naughty, the children may develop a sense of shame, doubt, and guilt so severe that it persists throughout their lives.

Sexual Curiosity and Sexual Identity

Children of preschool age have a natural curiosity about their bodies and other people's bodies. Depending on adult responses to their questions, children can feel comfortable with this normal curiosity or they can be made to feel naughty, dirty, or guilty. When caregivers recognize this curiosity as a normal stage of a child's development, they can answer the questions openly, honestly, and calmly, using correct terminology for the body parts. Early recognition and acceptance of the facts of sexuality help children to have positive self-concepts.

Our sexuality is mental, of course, as well as physical. The attitudes we have toward the roles of males and females in our society depend on our experiences early in life. For example, a father who "roughhouses" with his son but plays quietly with his daughter is demonstrating how he expects them to behave. Parents who would not think of giving toy trucks to little girls or baby dolls to little boys teach their children sexist attitudes whether they intend to or not. Such attitudes may be so deeply ingrained in various aspects of people's lives that they have to make a concerted effort to avoid perpetuating them.

Small children should be encouraged when they show talent or interest in intellectual or athletic activities, regardless of the traditional sex roles identified with those activities. Discouraging children affects them emotionally by telling them, in effect, that there is something wrong with their natural interests.

Children learn from example. If a mother is a certified public accountant, her children will not accept the traditional belief that girls are not supposed to be good in math. If a father is loving and sensitive, his children will know that tenderness is not necessarily a

At one time, boys were supposed to act like boys and this type of behavior was "inappropriate."

female trait. If parents do not exhibit sexist attitudes, their children will tend to be free of the restrictions that have kept many people from achieving their potential in the past.

Fears

If you sneak up behind a friend and shout "Boo!" your friend is likely to jump. You may get the response, "You scared me!" Such a fright is an emotional outburst of short duration. There are other fears, however, that are not so short-lived.

An emotional outburst is just one of many possible variations in the expression of fear. In order to understand children's fears and the different ways they can be expressed, we have to study personality traits and the basic needs of human beings. Trust and autonomy are just two of the many components of an individual's personality that determine the nature of his or her fears, the mode of expressing those fears, and the manner of dealing with them.

Fears in response to noises, strange objects, situations, and persons are among those that decrease with age. Fears of preschool children, who have established trust in material things, are based primarily on imagination. Fears of the dark, of being left alone, and of imaginary creatures are among those that increase during the preschool years. As children's imaginations increase so do their imaginary fears. Most children fear wild beasts,

In the minds of children, all kinds of monsters are hiding under the bed. As children's imaginations increase so do their imaginary fears.

ogres, and monsters. That may not be surprising if we think of the fairy tales that preschoolers hear.

A Closer Look

Alan, who was not quite three years old, had wanted to stay at the university preschool his older brother attended. Since there was plenty of student help for adequate supervision, Alan was allowed to stay. All went well for a few days until some male college students looked in the window of the door. Alan saw them and became frightened. He ran to the teacher and crawled up into her arms. The teacher said in a calm voice, "Are you afraid, Alan?" Alan nodded his head vigorously. The teacher said, "When you are afraid, you come to me and I'll hold you."

After several similar incidents, the teacher could tell that Alan was not fearful because he stayed on the teacher's lap for a shorter period each time. Alan then went to hanging onto the teacher's skirt and finally to looking for her when he was afraid, feeling reassured just to see her from a distance.

The teacher concentrated on helping Alan to overcome his fear. After Alan saw the male students several times and nothing happened to increase his fear, he overcame it. It took time. The process couldn't be rushed. The teacher comforting him and not making him feel silly for being afraid gave Alan the reassurance he needed.

A Closer Look

Katie, age five, was left in the care of a high school girl while her parents attended a lecture. The sitter used fear to control Katie at bedtime. She said, "Go to bed right now or I'll call my mother and have her pick me up and I'll leave you here all alone." At this, Katie went to bed. The next morning she told her parents what the sitter had said and then Katie said, "I was kind of afraid, but then I thought of the telephone number you left on the kitchen table to call if we needed you. I thought if she leaves, I'll just go downstairs, dial the number, and tell you to come home. But then I began to wonder, Dad, if I did, would you answer the phone?" "No, Katie, I wouldn't," her father answered. "You would have had to ask for us." Katie answered, "Oh, that's OK." Katie's ability to use the phone and her trust that her parents would come home if she called, enabled her not to panic at the sitter's threat.

The correlation between children's fears and violence on television has not yet been adequately evaluated. *CO-ED Magazine* has estimated, however, that the average child will have seen 11,000 TV "murders" by the age of 14 years. Some programs are especially violent. Even cartoons can be violent. "The Bugs Bunny/Road Runner Hour" was rated at 48 violent acts per hour. Of course, violence is not necessarily restricted to TV. Observing violence between family members causes children great anxiety and fear.

Parents can control what is *shown* on television only *indirectly*—by writing to the networks, the producers, and the sponsors to express their views on the programming. Parents should have *direct* control, however, over which programs are *watched* in their own homes. Moreover, parents also have sole responsibility to ensure that children neither observe nor experience real-life violence between family members.

In general, as with all human learning, fears proceed from the concrete to the abstract. For example, preschool children are afraid of wild beasts. (They are concrete, though improbable.) Older children have abstract concerns such as fears of not being liked. Most fears are learned, so there is a high correlation between children's fears and their parents' fears.

Anxiety

Anxiety is a worry or deep concern about possibly impending danger or misfortune. Children cannot very well experience normal emotional development if their environment causes them

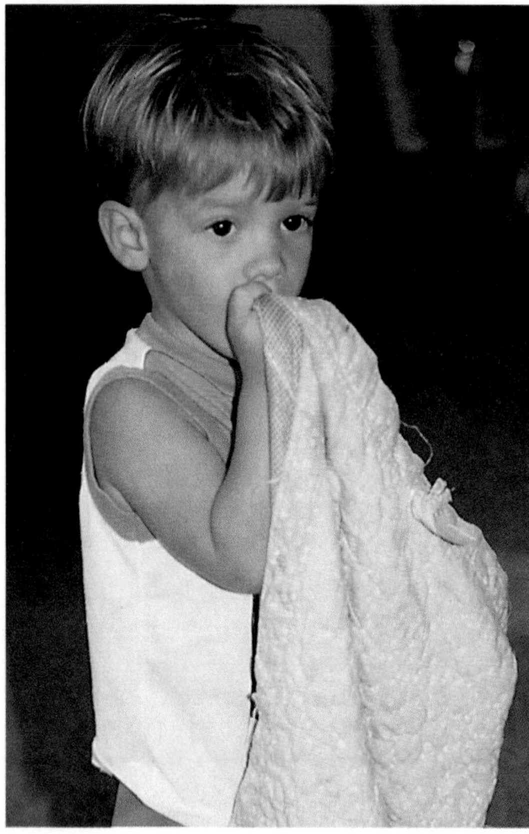

A feeling of anxiety can cause a child to turn to a familiar object for support.

constant or chronic anxiety. There are numerous circumstances that can cause chronic anxiety in children, so we shall discuss only a few as examples.

1. Parents need to take precautions so that preschool-aged children do not fear they will lose their parents' love when a new baby is expected. With proper explanations and reassurances, parents can make this a gratifying, emotionally developmental experience for the child, rather than one that brings on a sense of insecurity. The child can participate in the family plans and preparations.

2. Parents who constantly compare a "bad" child with a "good" sibling create an atmosphere in which neither the parent-child relationships nor the sibling relationship can develop normally.

3. Children who don't have the chance to develop any lasting relationships outside the home can become anxious about the continuous challenge of the new and unknown. This can come about, for example, with frequent moving or frequent changes in daycare.

4. Children of a divorced couple are prime candidates for anxiety if bitterness between the parents continues. In such cases, one parent often expects the children to reject the other parent. This puts the children in a situation in which they may feel guilty if they don't. They feel they are disappointing that parent. On the other hand, they don't want to reject a parent they love. If the divorce is amicable, children suffer less anxiety than they experience living with both parents in a home that is filled with confrontation and tension.

5. Remarriage of a single parent can lead to chronic anxiety for the children if anyone involved is not willing to adapt to the new arrangement and work at strengthening the new bonds that are formed (Chapter 2).

6. In Chapter 7, we discussed the harmful effects of alcohol on the fetus. Unfortunately, a child's problems with alcohol do not necessarily cease when the umbilical cord is cut. Alcoholism is devastating to the alcoholic and to the family of the alcoholic. Because all relationships are apt to be strained, the

Look, Listen, and Learn

Children, like everyone else, have both positive and negative emotions. Sometimes the expression of an emotion is easy to observe. For example, two three-year-olds playing together may start to fight over a toy. This is an expression of aggression. Other times, the emotion expressed may not be so obvious. As you interact with children, be aware of several ways children express emotions:

- Art—drawing, finger painting, clay modeling, reciting poems, storytelling, dancing, and dramatic play.
- Nature and outdoor activities—children express feelings through their bodies when they participate in outdoor and nature-related activities.
- Communication—communicating with others gives children the opportunity to talk about their fears, worries, and joys.

Observe a group of children and look for the following:

- A positive emotion. What happens? Can you determine why the child felt that emotion?
- A negative emotion. What happens? Why did the child feel that way?
- How are the children expressing their emotions? How does play help them express their emotions?

After your observation, think about the ways children express their emotions that differ from adults' expressions? Which are easier to "read"?

air is charged with tension. Children in such situations often suffer anxiety.

Jealousy

Jealousy is an emotion that all young children feel. How this natural emotion is handled during childhood will determine how people will cope with it as adults. **Jealousy** is the angry feeling that results when individuals are frustrated in their desire to be loved most. A French proverb states it this way, "Where there is no jealousy, there is no love." **Rivalry** is the angry feeling that results when individuals are frustrated in their desire to do their best, to win, or to place first. Very often an individual feels jealousy and rivalry toward the same person, although these emotions can be separated.

It is important for adults to accept that jealousy exists in everyone. Children are likely to feel jealous of the baby who displaces them as youngest in the family and to feel rivalry with the older children who are stronger and more able than they are.

A brother who teases his sister at home may come to her defense when someone else treats her that way.

Children's displays of jealousy range from bodily attacks on siblings, to ignoring the presence or denying the existence of the younger sibling. Some children even undergo a personality change at the time of a sibling's birth.

If children were loved for themselves as unique individuals with special skills and interests, they would have less reason to be jealous of their siblings. In spite of how jealous siblings may be of each other, they also love each other. Ambivalence is the key to understanding many incidents in behavior of siblings toward each other. For example, brothers may fight and quarrel at home, but will protect each other when a neighbor picks on them.

Parents and children also feel jealousy and rivalry toward one another. Themes of jealousy and rivalry are present in some of the most disturbing situations existing in family life. Wanting to be first in the affections of the opposite-sexed parent has as its corollary jealousy of the same-sexed parent. "I'm going to marry Daddy when I grow up," or "Daddy likes me better than he likes you," are some of the statements that illustrate this emotion. Thus, the same-sexed parent represents what the child hopes to become, indeed the person who attracts and holds the other parent.

A Closer Look

Sumiko and Sigrid were five-year-old kindergarten friends who walked to school together. After school, Sumiko's father drove them home from school and they would tell him about the exciting events of their day. During a particularly cold week, another friend, Nancy, also rode with them. When Sigrid got into the car on the third day, she announced, "There are too many people in this car!" Then, when Nancy began to tell what happened to her that day, Sigrid spoke at the same time and in a louder voice.

Jealousy and rivalry are inevitable. However, to help children minimize these feelings, parents should:

- accept and appreciate each child as an individual.
- avoid using competition to motivate siblings.
- avoid making comparisons between children.
- understand and accept the child's feelings of jealousy.
- accept the faults of each child.
- appreciate the talents of each child.
- spend time alone with each child.

Anger and Aggression

Anger is the feeling that accompanies being restrained or blocked in progress toward some sort of fulfillment. Anger involves lashing out rather than withdrawing as is often the case with fear. Unproductive expressions of anger, such as kicking, screaming, and throwing things, occur in late infancy and in the early preschool years, when children experience many frustrations and new challenges.

One form of reaction to frustration is called a "temper tantrum." The child may lie on the floor kicking feet, flailing arms, and screaming. Some children hold their breath and may bump their heads on the floor. Naturally, this can be very upsetting to a caring parent who does not want the child to be hurt in any way. Usually, a temper tantrum is the result of a confrontation. The child wants to do something, and the parent says "No." In a sense, the child uses the tantrum as a "tool" to "terrorize" the parent. The child is holding himself or herself "hostage" and creating anxiety for the parent. The youngster is hoping that the parent will give in and say "yes" to the original demands.

Unless a parent enjoys such experiences (which is highly unlikely), he or she must never allow children to get their way by having a temper tantrum. Giving in one time assures that there will be a second time. Giving in the second and the third time establishes a pattern of behavior that will be extremely difficult to break. The behavior may persist throughout childhood, adolescence, and adulthood.

When children try a temper tantrum, they are testing their ability to exert power in the parent-child relationship. If children gain attention by the technique, even though the parents do not give in to the original demands, children have still learned

Children will test their power in their relationships with adults. The adults need to learn when to draw the line without damaging children's quest for independence.

that tantrums gain attention. Thus, if children feel the need for attention at some future time, they are likely to have another tantrum.

Tantrums are unpleasant for both parent and child. If children learn from the start that tantrums gain neither attention nor parental agreement to demands, then they are unlikely to continue such unpleasant experiences.

The parent should make certain that a child having a tantrum is safe from physical harm. For example, the child might be moved away from the sharp edge of a coffee table, or picked up off a tile floor and placed on a rug or carpet. Beyond that the parent should state *just one time,* "I'm not going to pay any attention to you until you stop behaving this way." The parent must then stand by that statement, even if the child holds his or her breath. Remember, we humans breathe when we need to.

Aggression is the actual attack which accompanies anger. Aggression can be a hostile attack against another person. It also can be a controlled and productive attack on problems. This

Outbursts of anger may result in tears.

can be constructive, resulting in increased knowledge, power, and status. Then the anger that accompanies aggression is an energized feeling that aids in problem solving and contributes to the sense of initiative.

Competition between people can involve either hostile aggression or controlled and productive aggression. Many difficulties arise from the dual nature of anger and aggression. While a hostile attack is dangerous, there is a great advantage in being able to fend off an attack and take the initiative.

A Closer Look

Three-year-old Ben had just moved into the neighborhood, and the new playmate he liked best was Ron, a four-year-old. Ron seemed to be liked by all the other children. Ron's mother had helped him to learn that he should take turns. He should lead at times, but he should follow others when their ideas were good. He related to other children well.

Ben, on the other hand, exhibited a demanding personality as a response to coping with his very aggressive younger brother. He always insisted on having his own way and refused to take turns.

Ben's behavior was frustrating to Ron, who complained of this to his mother. One day, she decided to sit near them as they played so she could see what happened.

After a few exasperating experiences, Ron was nearly in tears and shouted at Ben, "You always have to have your way. You won't take turns." Ron's mother added in a quiet, matter-of-fact way, "Yes, Ben has to learn to take his turn and share, doesn't he?" Of course Ron agreed and said, "It isn't any fun playing with him when he always grabs things and wants his way." Ron's mother said, "I think he can learn to take turns. It may take a little time." Ben's eyes were big, and he was thoughtful while Ron and his mother were talking. He liked Ron so much and wanted to play with him. Ben said, "OK, you can have the police car first, this time."

Some parent-child interactions influence children to use hostile, aggressive behavior. When parents use physical punishment on the children, or when they show hostile and aggressive behavior, children are more likely to be hostile and aggressive themselves. Children also learn to behave aggressively when parents permit it, approve of it, or even instigate it.

To encourage the development of self-control in children, parents should:

- clearly express what behavior is allowed and what is not.
- disapprove of hostile aggression and stop this behavior.
- avoid physical punishment.
- provide for children's physical needs.
- answer children's call for help promptly.
- provide children with opportunities for achievement.
- create an atmosphere of emotional warmth in the home.

Life's Work

David Fenley

➤**Actor with the Children's Theatre Company**
➤**B.A. in Russian Area Studies**

David is involved in four or five productions during the year. He is one of nine members of a full-time acting company. David says, "At any given time I may be performing in one show and rehearsing another. Time offstage is usually spent in part preparing to rehearse. I may have to do historical research for a role, learn to speak in a certain dialect, work on a style of movement or dance, work on singing, even learn to walk a tightrope (yes, I did!)."

Acting is not a 9 to 5 profession. Some days begin at 8 a.m. for David and end at midnight. Other days involve only a few hours in the afternoon. The schedule includes morning shows for school audiences and evening and weekend shows for the general public. Monday is traditionally a day off. David says, "Somehow it all evens out. If you are in the theater, you most certainly can have a 'normal' fulfilling life. You just learn to live by a different, more flexible clock."

"The most incredible, heartfelt hug of a three-year-old child," is David's most rewarding job-related accomplishment. "Somehow this man inside a costume had really become Raggedy Andy to her. What she had imagined in stories and in playing with her Andy doll was suddenly alive and real," David says.

The advice David would give to students considering acting is, "Don't become an actor if you can do anything else and be happy. But if this is something you have to do, then train where you can: high school, community theater, college, graduate school, or private classes. Study art, literature, languages, philosophy, history, politics, and psychology. Audition, audition, audition. And be prepared not to act. Learn how to support yourself financially and emotionally when you are not cast."

When asked how his profession will change, David says, "The next 10 years will be a challenge. TV and movies can dazzle with special effects that the theater can't duplicate. It's time to explore what the theater can do that film cannot. I think that lies within that intangible, living thing that happens between a live audience and a live actor. I see regional theaters and smaller local theaters becoming more important and vital."

In Review

Vocabulary

physiological events of emotion
behavioral events of emotion
body language
nurturing
anxiety
jealousy
rivalry
anger
aggression

Summary

- ✓ Emotions produce both physiological and behavioral events. Behavioral events can be either affective or effective.
- ✓ A part of emotional development for children is learning to love people other than parents and siblings.
- ✓ A child's attitudes toward others develop through the processes of assimilation and accommodation.
- ✓ For children, self-image depends on how they interpret the emotions, actions, and statements of other people with whom those children interact.
- ✓ Jealousy and rivalry between siblings is natural. They are minimized when parents appreciate the unique talents and limitations of each child—making no comparisons.
- ✓ Except for guaranteeing the child's safety, parents should ignore temper tantrums. Giving in will only assure a repeat performance.
- ✓ Aggression is an attack. When controlled, aggression can be a positive force in solving problems. Hostile, physical aggression, however, can be dangerous.

Questions

1. How is love associated with nurturing? List five relationships in which nurturing can occur.

2. Describe the relationship you have had or would like to have with a grandparent. Is this an informal, a formal, or a distant-figure grandparent?

3. When do self-concepts begin to develop? What can parents do to help children of preschool age to feel positive about themselves?

4. Recall three incidents you have observed that could tend to induce sexist attitudes in preschool children.

5. What is autonomy? When do children begin to develop it? How can a high school student demonstrate the development of a sense of autonomy?

6. What factors determine what we fear as preschool children? As adults?

7. What can parents do to help children overcome their fears? What role does empathy play?

8. Without using names, describe a real situation that you believe is creating anxiety in a child (any age).

9. How could you help a small child accept a younger brother or sister?

10. How does rivalry differ from jealousy?

11. How can parents discourage aggression in their children?

Activities

1. Observe a preschool child over a period of several days. List four incidents and describe the child's responses to each incident. What do these responses tell you about the child's self-concept?

2. Think of the fairy tales you learned during your preschool years. List the titles of five stories and the fears they might possibly create in children.

3. Observe children on a playground and list the examples of aggression that you see. Discuss their causes.

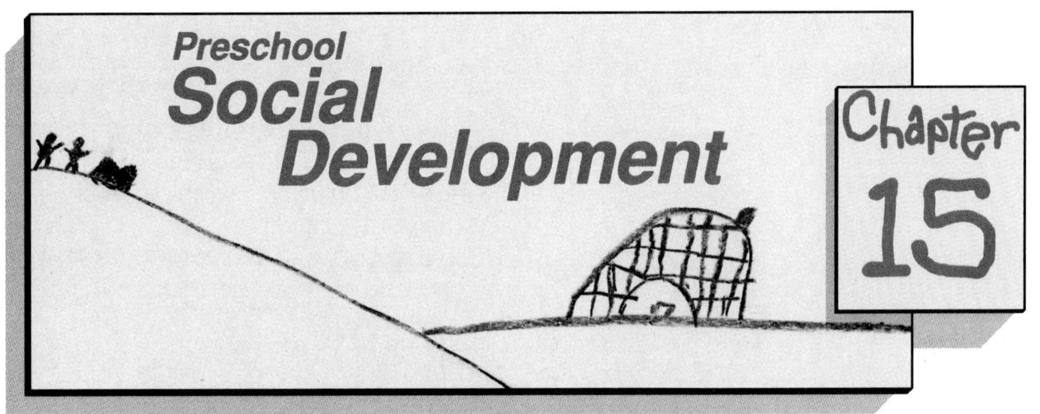

This chapter will help you:

- define socialization as it pertains to child development
- recognize the two basic guidance patterns used by parents to socialize their children
- understand the concepts of positive and negative reinforcement in the socialization process
- understand the two main theories of socialization: the social learning theory and the developmental theory
- recognize that the specialized education and training required for the socialization of special needs children are aimed at satisfying the same basic needs common to all children

Socialization

Socialization may be defined as the process of training individuals for their particular social environment. It is a learning-teaching process that takes the individual from the infant state of helplessness and egocentricity to the adult state of independence and responsibility. Individuals need to adapt to their society's norms of behavior. For example, in our society people shake hands when they meet. In some other countries, friends kiss each other lightly on each cheek. Learning which custom is appropriate is part of socialization. Becoming socialized involves learning the values, attitudes, knowledge, and skills of a society. In short, it involves learning the **culture.** Socialization molds the child's potential into the pattern of functioning that we call **personality.**

Steps in Socialization

Children have begun to be socialized when they first respond to their

Children in other countries, such as this girl from Italy, learn different social customs than those in the United States.

caregivers in a consistent way that indicates recognition. Some people say that the first sign of socialization is the smile. The smile typically appears as a response to the father or mother around the age of six to eight weeks. The following actions are other early signs of socialization in the child:

- stops crying when the parents appear.
- laughs at parents' antics.
- plays peekaboo.
- waves goodbye.
- pulls at parent to indicate a need for help in reaching an object.
- gestures or tries to climb onto the adult's lap to be cuddled.
- cries when parents leave them with another caregiver.
- acts differently with strangers than with parents.

These are some of the early steps in socialization and may be referred to as social responses. Socialization, however, includes not only social responsiveness but also social control. For example, initially children will simply obey when commanded to stop a dangerous activity. Later they may say, "no, no" to themselves as they point at a hot radiator. They have learned self-control.

As they grow older, children show other signs of socialization. For example, they will begin to share, offering portions of their food to others in their families. Eventually, they postpone some of their own immediate gratification to do things that may be rewarding only in the distant future. They may save money from a part-time job and apply it to their future education. At this point, they have come a long way from the first early stage of simple social response.

Variations in Socialization

Children are socialized in different ways depending on the culture and the time in history. In the 1800s, children were to "be seen and not heard." When visitors called on a family, the children were not allowed to participate in the conversation. Nowadays, children may be the center of attention when people visit. Consider a culture in the world in which women are expected to remain at home. Their society frowns upon them having a career. Compare that to our own society. How are young girls in those two situations socialized?

A Matter of Fact

Guess what children look forward to with more anticipation than Christmas? Their birthdays!

Here are some tips for planning a child's birthday party that will make the birthday boy or girl feel special.

- A good rule of thumb is to limit the number of party guests to the child's age. For example, a four-year-old would have four guests.
- A birthday is an event to be celebrated, so let the child express creativity and individuality. Brainstorm the focus of the party with the child. Will the birthday party be centered around a theme? Will there be an event? Find out what the child is interested in, and let this interest guide your planning.
- A birthday party doesn't need to be expensive to be fun. Just being with friends is important. Some party ideas that aren't costly include: neighborhood scavenger hunt, coloring or drawing contest, baking cookies or making pizza, and storytelling.
- If you have enough room, think about letting a much younger or older sibling invite a friend to the party. In this way, the sibling can be included in party activities without the problems of "tagging along" or jealousy.
- Have the birthday boy or girl create the party invitations, and make sure they are delivered in plenty of time before the big date.
- Sometimes it's hard for the birthday boy or girl to calm down after the party. When the guests have gone, provide the child with quiet time to read a book or take a nap.
- If the child is old enough to write, help him or her write "thank you" notes to children who brought gifts. Although this is sometimes hard to do, it is a valuable lesson in good manners.

In the United States today, the way children are socialized has many repercussions, as it undoubtedly had in previous centuries. For example, children who do not learn social control may break the law and be placed in prison. They become a burden on society because the institution is supported by every taxpayer. If adults are unemployable because they lack socialization, they have to receive government support. Because of this increasing concern for proper socialization, specialized professions, institutions, and government agencies, have been formed. Parents who seek help can obtain the advice of specialists. On the basis of tests, they try to help children compensate for deficiencies and maximize their social development toward latent potentials.

This attempt at socialization by individuals or groups outside the family has further repercussions. The general

At one time, child-rearing was mostly the mother's responsibility. Now, fathers have the opportunity to enjoy spending time with their children.

public does not always understand how specialists reach their conclusions. Furthermore, young adults and older people may have different views of how to socialize a child.

There are differences in socialization among social classes and ethnic groups. Prior to the late 1960s, middle-class parents reportedly used socializing practices that psychologists considered effective and desirable. They indicated more concern with their children's development and with understanding their behavior. They used love-oriented discipline. They reasoned with their children. They encouraged independence and achievement. In contrast, working-class parents reported using physical punishment, more rigid and authoritarian discipline, more insistence on obedience, and less inclination to let children express themselves.

As you have learned, there is considerable evidence that children learn to deal with others as they have been dealt with. One might conclude, therefore, that children of middle-class parents should have learned to be more tolerant and understanding than lower-class children. They should have learned to use reasoning rather than force to resolve differences and to base decisions on evidence rather than opinions of authority. However, it is hard to determine these effects. Keep in mind that differences within each group may be as great as (or even greater than) those between groups. Determining factors are parents' personalities, their reaction to their careers, the size of the family, housing, and sexes and ages of their children. However, research studies on problems such as these can show only statistical trends. They do not allow the researchers to state, for example, that *all* children raised with love-oriented discipline are more tolerant and understanding than *all* children raised with authoritarian discipline.

Socialization techniques, like everything else, change with time. Thus, it was traditionally middle-class parents who emphasized self-control, the work ethic, competition, and individual achievement. For the past two decades, many parents in all economic classes have leaned toward the permissive style (Chapter 3). The rapidly changing social patterns, such as higher divorce rates, families moving more often, more working mothers, increased numbers of single-parent families, and increased numbers of blended families, all work to change the socialization techniques practiced in our society.

Theories of Socialization

There are two main theories of socialization. The first is represented by the **social learning theory.** The second is based on the **developmental theory.**

According to the social learning theory, children become social and self-confident to the degree that they learn they must adapt themselves to others in order to have their own needs satisfied. According to the developmental theory, the seeds of socialization are present in all people and will come to

Look, Listen, and Learn

Children want to be accepted by others. Socialization helps them do so. Early signs of socialization are a baby smiling at the parents or waving goodbye. Preschools and daycare centers play an important part in the socialization of older children. Observe a group of children and look for the following:

- If one child starts an activity, what do the others do? Do they watch, imitate, join in?
- If an adult initiates an activity, what do the children do?
- How do the children play with the toys? Do they share or fight over them?
- Are any of the children excessively loud or pushy? Are some of the children very quiet or shy?
- Do you see examples of sharing or helping others?
- How do the children react to positive reinforcement from the caregivers? How do they react to negative reinforcement?

Based on your observations, what conclusions can you draw about the socialization of the children? What similarities do you notice? What differences do you see? Be prepared to discuss your observations.

Children learn self-control through love-oriented guidance.

maturity in an accepting and rather passive environment.

The difference between these two theories may be clearer with this example. The social learning theory might be likened to the principle: as the twig is bent, so shall the tree grow. A good environment of proper soil, light, water, and fertilizer is recommended. In addition, active pruning, shaping, and grafting should be practiced.

The developmental theory also would indicate that a tree thrives in an environment of proper soil, light, water, and perhaps fertilizer. But beyond these elements, the theory would maintain that nature knows best how the tree should grow. Pruning, shaping, and grafting are to be left to the natural course of events and the intrinsic nature of the organism.

Each theory maintains that the mature individual is a product of the teaching forces of the family and the environment. If these forces are kind, the resulting individual is a happy one. If these forces are abusive, the result can be unfortunate. Thus, persons are shaped by their experiences.

Guidance Patterns

There are two ways of giving guidance to a child. One is psychologically, through love or intangible reward methods. The second is physically, through concrete reward or punishment.

Love-oriented guidance tends to guide children by demonstrating to them that intangibles are important, such as attention from other people. Physically oriented guidance ranges from inflicting physical punishment on children when they misbehave to awarding prizes for good grades or good behavior. The former is control through developing self-control. Physically oriented guidance, on the other hand, tends to be control through fear. Children behave because they know they will be punished if they don't behave and are caught. Self-control is the better method of social control because it is effective even in the absence of adults. A child who is controlled by fear will be uncontrolled when there is no chance of being caught.

A Closer Look

Mary, a social worker, wanted to do more to help the mothers she was counseling. All too often they spanked, threatened, and shamed their children to control them. Mary wished they could observe the methods used by her niece, Peggy. Peggy had a son, Tim, who seemed to be developing self-control as a result of Peggy's love-oriented discipline.

Peggy was a well-adjusted and secure person, in contrast with the mothers whom Mary was trying to advise. Most of them had stressful relationships with their husbands and/or were struggling financially. Mary knew her job would be difficult, but she was determined to help these mothers see the psychological harm being imposed on their children.

Mary remembered the time that Tim had found her purse and dumped everything out of it. Peggy had said in a quiet voice, "I'm sorry, Tim, but that purse belongs to Aunt Mary. I'll help you put the things back so you can return it to her."

That was remarkably different from the response of Jean, who was one of the mothers Mary counseled. Jean's son was also too young to resist the temptation of Mary's purse, and he had begun to empty it when his mother caught him in the act. In anger, Jean yelled at him, "You naughty boy!" Then she jerked the purse away and gave him a swat on the head.

Another example came to mind. Peggy had waited until Tim was 25 months old before she began toilet training him. She knew that at his age with normal physical development, he should be able to control the sphincter muscle controlling the flow of urine from the bladder. She began the training by getting him to the toilet before he was wet and praising him for being dry. She said nothing negative when they had a failure. Before long, he was announcing successes with pride and feeling disappointment about "accidents."

Jean told Mary that her three-year-old son was hopeless. She had been trying for 18 months to toilet train him. She had spanked him, she had shamed him, she had ridiculed him in front of her friends, and she had refused to change his wet diapers. Nothing seemed to work. The boy was becoming more obstinate with her and more aggressive with the other children. Mary explained to her that the boy may not have been physically able to control the emptying of his bladder when she first attempted to toilet train him. Since then, the confrontational nature of their relationship was affecting him emotionally. Mary suggested a calmer, more loving approach, with praise of successes and understanding for failures. With patience and encouragement, the toilet training could progress, and the point of contention in their relationship would be gone.

Positive and Negative Reinforcement

It is almost certain that children learn faster if they receive both positive and negative reinforcement. **Positive reinforcement** tells them what they may or should do. **Negative reinforcement** tells them what they may not and should not do. By receiving both types

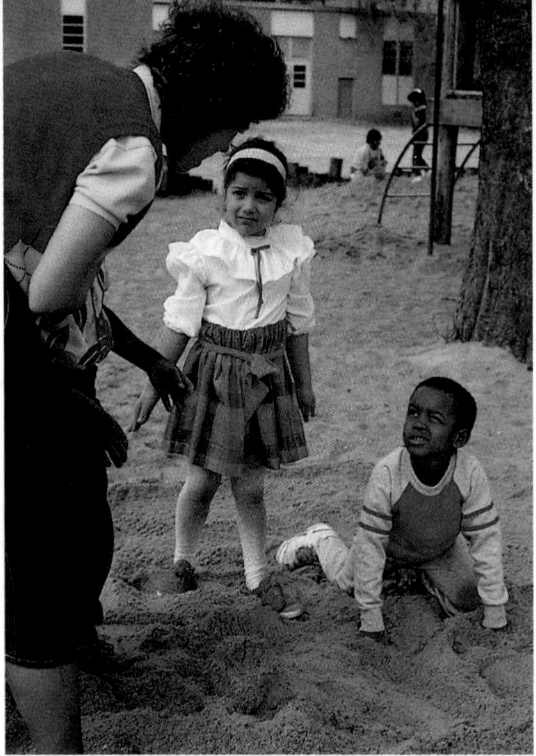

Sometimes children receive negative reinforcement. It needs to be consistent and fair in order for them to learn from it.

of reinforcement, they are more fully informed than if they receive only one type. When reinforcement is administered immediately, consistently, and in appropriate amounts, learning proceeds more rapidly than when reinforcement is delayed, inconsistent, or excessive. In other words, consistency in guidance is important. Children who are controlled in a consistent way learn how to modify their behavior more rapidly than those who are treated inconsistently.

For example, Darrell and his daughter Claudia had a problem. Claudia frequently interrupted Darrell's conversations. When it happened, Darrell would say, "Claudia, I am talking now. It is rude to interrupt. When I am finished, you may ask me your questions. I'll be happy to answer you then. For now, you can sit here by me and play." Every time Claudia broke into a conversation, Darrell responded the same way. Claudia learned that if she was patient, Darrell would then answer her. On the other hand, Bob and his mother, Abby, had the same problem. However, Abby didn't always respond the same way. Sometimes she answered as Darrell did, but other times she spanked Bob and said, "Shut up." Sometimes she just ignored Bob, but on other occasions she would even stop her conversation to say, "What is it, Sweetie?" Bob never knew what to expect because Abby's responses were inconsistent. He continued to interrupt her again and again, hoping to gain her immediate attention.

The reinforcement also needs to fit the child's action. Children need to learn the consequences of their behavior—the effect or result of their actions. For example, if Joanne draws on the walls, she should help her mother wash the walls. If five-year-old Christopher breaks his favorite toy in anger, he should learn from the experience that toys destroyed in anger are not replaced.

All reinforcements are administered from a basis of power. The first type of power perceived by the infant and small child is the physical power of both parents. Generally, fathers are seen as possessing more power than mothers. The father who earns his living by physical labor is more likely to be seen as possessing physical power than the father who works in an office. Later, children learn that physical power is the least esteemed source of power in our society, and that power through social and economic influence

Children see their fathers as very powerful.

or knowledge is more highly esteemed.

The second type of power is sexual. Children come to see their parents as sexually potent figures. The third type of power is wisdom. This source of power is somewhat subtle. In an anti-intellectual society, wisdom and knowledge are not seen as sources of power, although they certainly are to the curious, questioning child.

The fourth type of power is social influence. In any economic class, children in a particular family may see their parents as socially influential. For example, children from a very poor family may be justifiably proud of their parents who speak out at open meetings for educational reform. The couple may be respected throughout the community as leaders and a moving force. On the other hand, there are more parents in the middle to upper economic class who have had opportunities for higher education and leadership experiences. Increased knowledge combines with economic status and leadership skills to provide a greater degree of social influence. Thus, children in middle and upper economic classes are more apt to perceive their parents as deriving power from social status. They recognize that their parents' basis of power is not physical prowess. Their parents' power is based on knowledge, economic status, and social influence. Such

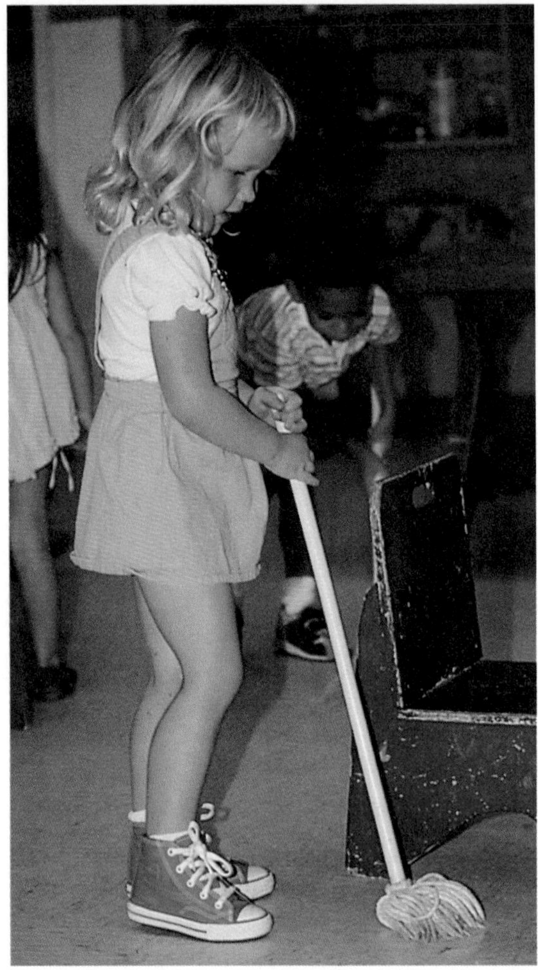

Discipline at this preschool means children are responsible for cleaning up any messes they have made.

children are more apt to submit to the control techniques of their parents, because the parents appear to possess more types of power.

Proper socialization is perhaps an individual's most important accomplishment. Individuals who are successfully socialized enjoy other people and have a generally positive attitude toward the rules of their society. Delinquents, criminals, and people addicted to alcohol or other drugs are extreme examples of those who do not conform to the standard goals of a society. There is little doubt that significant differences exist in the ease with which children are socialized and that children's environments play a major role in their socialization.

Discipline

Sometimes parents think that their children's need for tender loving care means they must not be disciplined or punished and they must be allowed to do as they like. Actually, children who are allowed to do as they like tend to feel insecure, because their parents leave them to act on their own whims and impulses. These children are likely to feel that their parents do not love them enough to give them the direction and guidance they need. Even adolescents who complain about restrictions on their behavior are often unconsciously glad for them, especially if the limits are reasonable and set with a sincere desire for the adolescents' welfare rather than for the parents' convenience. Such restrictions give young people protection and at the same time assure them of their parents' concern and love.

Discipline is basically a form of learning. It needs to be a consequence for an action. If discipline is firm, kind, and consistent, and if the general atmosphere of the home is one of love and concern for the child's welfare, it can contribute to the child's sense of security. The real test of discipline methods is whether they contribute to the child's feeling worthy and loved rather than unworthy and unloved. This must be judged in each individual situation and with each individual child.

Constructive discipline provides children with much of the guidance and encouragement they need in the process of growing up. It can:

1. provide them with opportunities for expressing themselves in acceptable ways.
2. protect them from physical harm.
3. protect them from their own impulses.
4. keep them from infringing on the rights of others.

Both approval and disapproval, if attached to a child's specific behavior rather than to him or her as a person, put the emphasis where it belongs—on behavior. Children need to be sure of their parents' love for them. Guiding behavior rather than criticizing the children's personality does not make the children question the parent's love. "I don't like to see anyone snatch a toy from a playmate" calls attention to the behavior rather than labeling the child, "You are a bad boy" with its unexpressed implication that bad boys are not loved. "That was very nice to share your toy with your playmate" is specific approval of behavior.

Criticism is most helpful if it is constructive. Children need to be encouraged to be their own best, not their parents' best. Pressure for a degree of achievement or performance beyond the child's capacity or stage of development is damaging.

The use of distraction is also a worthwhile idea. Children who are quite young can be distracted easily. Substituting something equally as interesting instead of scolding and calling attention to the undesired behavior helps to change the undesired behavior to a desired one. Children do need to understand what type of behavior is unacceptable. However, not giving attention to some minor incidents while giving adequate attention to desirable behavior reinforces the desirable behavior.

The value of discipline depends on its appropriateness. Good discipline is geared to children's maturity level. It protects them from their own lack of discretion and enables them to direct their energies in areas where they do have experience and choice. Good discipline provides children with a sound foundation for healthy self-discipline.

Cooperation

To have cooperative children, parents have to prepare the way for cooperation. Without realizing it, mothers and fathers often make their demands of a child in a manner that practically invites a refusal or a protest. Most children want to do the right thing, but it is not always clear to them what the right thing is. Grown-ups can help them by making their expectation clear, by expecting it of them, and by giving them a chance to do it. When adults show disapproval in advance, it means they are already convinced children will behave badly.

Thoughtfulness of others is a trait that is instilled in children not by punishment or routine but through genuine display of love and consideration for them and others in the home. Parents who consistently show affection for each other, as well as a warm

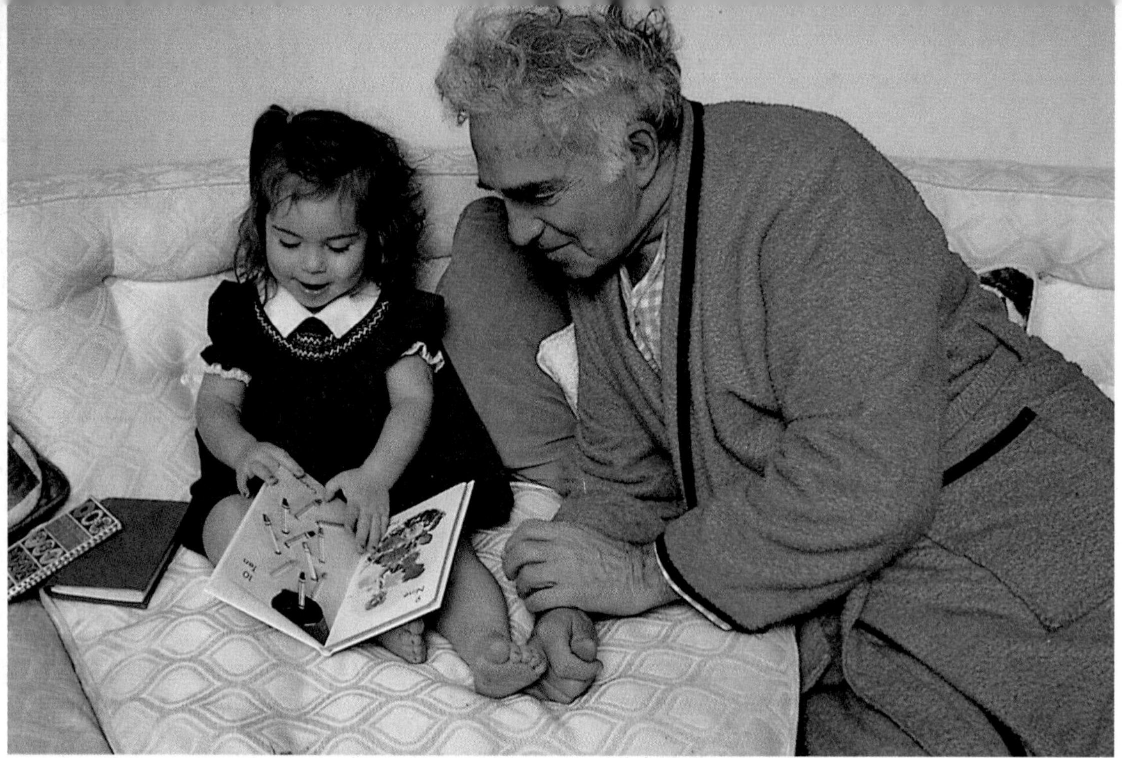

Loving grandparents may become role models for their grandchildren.

regard for their relatives and friends, are training their children to be considerate and well-mannered. Genuine love gives a child inward feelings that are manifested in cooperation, consideration, kindness and all around enjoyable behavior. Children often seem to be able to read a grown-up's mind like a book. They know who means well by them as well as those who are just trying to dominate them. They recognize self-doubt by the uncertainty in voices. They catch what makes people feel uneasy whenever they give way to irritability.

Children need models with whom to identify as they develop. An example to copy is very important for efficient learning. If parents want children to be considerate of others, they must demonstrate that quality themselves. The following approach sets a good example. "I'm sorry, I need to work in this space. Can I help you move your things over to the other table?" An order such as "Get out of my way!" may accomplish the goal of acquiring additional work space, but would be a very poor example of consideration for others.

Skinner's Laws of Learning

B. F. Skinner, a behavioral psychologist, proposed that learning occurs as a result of reinforcement. There is much in his work that applies directly to socialization, guidance, and discipline.

In working with animals, Skinner found that repetition of reinforcement could produce desired responses. Because he found his reinforcement technique to be effective in altering behavior, he called it *operant conditioning*. One example might be the following: A chicken is randomly pecking at various parts of its cage. When it happens to peck at the lever that projects into the cage, it is rewarded with cracked corn. The chicken quickly learns to peck at the lever whenever it wants food. The food has reinforced the accidental pecks at the lever, and a response has been produced by operant conditioning. If the chicken stops receiving food for pecking at the lever, the response is discouraged. The chicken will soon stop pecking at the lever.

On the other hand, if the chicken starts receiving food again before it becomes completely discouraged, then the response is partially reinforced. What the chicken learns from partial reinforcement is that it should just keep pecking at the lever repeatedly until finally the reward is granted.

Skinner's idea was that the very same principles apply to human learning. He did many conditioning experiments with his own small daughters. With the analogy of the chicken, we can understand how parents can sometimes unwittingly use operant conditioning and partial reinforcement in such a way that they encourage undesirable behavior in their children. An example is given in the following case study.

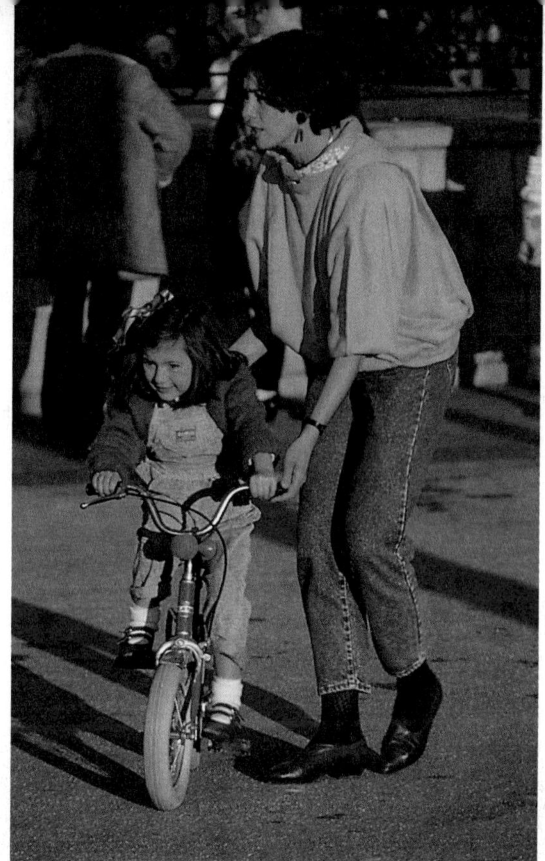

Just as children need help learning how to ride a bicycle, they need help learning what social behaviors are acceptable.

A Closer Look

Four-year-old Valerie was cuddling with her mother in the rocking chair when her eyes fell on the candy dish sitting on the end table. "Mommy, may I please have a piece of candy?" she asked.

"Yes, you may," her mother replied. "I like the way you remembered your manners and used the word 'please.'"

Later that same day, Valerie remembered the candy dish and the reinforcement she had received for the word "please," so she tried it again. It worked. Over the next several days, it worked for her every time. Then, however, she happened to ask her mother for a piece of candy when it was only 30 minutes before dinner, so her mother said, "No, not now."

"Plee—ease, Mommy," Valerie repeated.

"No, honey, it's too close to dinner," was her mother's response as she went about setting the table.

"It won't spoil my dinner, Mommy," Valerie pleaded.

"No, Valerie. I said no!"

"But, Mommy, just one piece?"

"Valerie! Don't beg! Stop your whining. I can't stand begging and whining."

"Mommy, I promise I'll eat everything on my plate, if you let me have some candy. Plee—ease?"

"All right! All right! But just one piece! Now stop your whining. Go play in the family room and leave me alone so I can get dinner on the table."

While Valerie's mother has stated that she hates begging and whining, those are exactly the behavior patterns that she has just reinforced. She can expect more of the same from Valerie until begging and whining are consistently discouraged by not being rewarded.

Special Needs and Socialization

Every child has individual needs. It is essential for parents to recognize that all children are different from one another. For special needs children, those differences are more extreme, and the needs may be extraordinary. Both mental and physical impairments pose special problems in the social development of small children.

Anyone who is familiar with the story of Helen Keller recognizes how difficult it can be to socialize a child who has no functioning means of communication. It took extraordinary patience and creativity to break through to the brilliant mind of that handicapped child and begin the socialization process.

Whether children's handicaps are sight or hearing impairment, mental retardation, or physical problems, they require extra expenditures of money, patience, creativity, and energy by the family. Parents are well advised to work closely with professionals who understand the various problems of special needs children. The earlier the expert help begins, the greater is the advantage to the child and the family. With specialized education and training the children have the best opportunity for reaching their potential.

Special needs children are no different from others in their need to achieve a good self-concept. They need to be included, they need friends, they need time with their family, and they need to be encouraged to participate and perform to their capabilities. Some parents of special needs children make the mistake of being over-protective. Special needs children, like all other children, need to face the real world, adapt, cope, and develop whatever degree of independence is possible. We help special needs children to attain these goals by stressing what they can do, not what they can't do.

Parents and society can promote the process of socializing special needs children by recognizing that an impair-

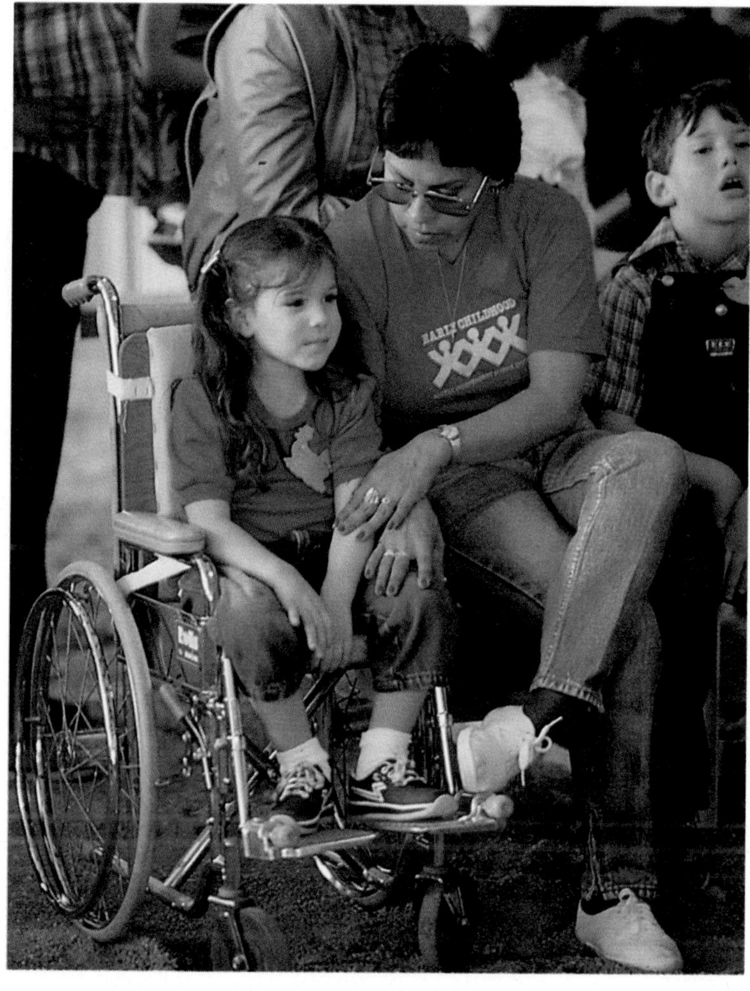

Like all children, special needs children need the chance to participate in activities with others.

ment is just an individual difference and that the special needs person would like to be treated accordingly. The process of socialization is enhanced when we stress likenesses, rather than differences.

In Review

Vocabulary

socialization
culture
personality
positive reinforcement
negative reinforcement
social learning theory
developmental theory

Summary

- ✓ Socialization takes a child from a state of egocentricity to a state of independence and responsibility. It involves learning the values, attitudes, knowledge, and skills of a society.
- ✓ The techniques used to socialize children have changed throughout history. They differ, also, according to ethnic, religious, and economic backgrounds.
- ✓ Both the social learning theory and the developmental theory maintain that the mature individual is the product of family guidance.
- ✓ Love-oriented family guidance helps children acquire self-discipline in accord with conscience. Physically oriented guidance controls children through fear. When conscience is not involved, children do not learn self-control.
- ✓ Socialization of children is accomplished most effectively when they receive both positive and negative types of reinforcement. Each type of reinforcement should be administered in ways that are loving, consistent, and reasonable.
- ✓ Special needs children, like all other children, have the need to adapt to society. Socialization is enhanced when we stress likenesses, rather than differences.

Questions

1. Define the following terms:
A. socialization
B. rivalry
C. aggression
D. reinforcement
2. What are the goals of socialization?
3. Essentially there are two ways of giving guidance to a child. Give an example of each way.
4. In terminology used by B. F. Skinner, explain why parental consistency is essential for effective discipline.
5. How would empathy play a role in a parent's effort to socialize a handicapped child?

Activities

1. Write a paragraph of about 200 words on "The Role of Television in the Socialization of Preschool Children."
2. Observe children on a playground and list examples of aggression that you see. Discuss their causes.
3. Discuss the types of power used in street gangs for positive and negative reinforcement of members' behavior.

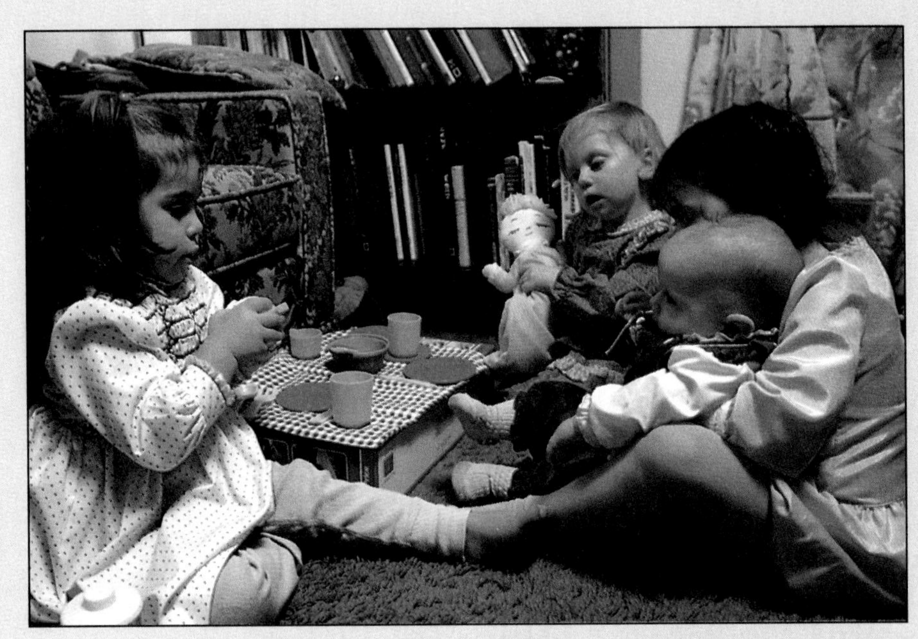

This chapter will help you:

- recognize that play is one of the most vital aspects of normal development for children
- learn how the development of motor skills affects the nature of children's play
- identify ways that play can contribute to the intellectual, emotional, and social development of small children
- understand how interactions with friends while playing influence both emotional and social development
- realize that children can learn ethics, manners, and sportsmanship from play

A Time for Play

Childhood is a time for play. Play is one of the most important aspects of normal development. Play helps children learn about the world around them. The nature of children's play strongly influences their lives and careers as adults. Opportunity for different kinds of play lets children discover their interests and their talents—art, music, math, athletics, storytelling, animals, science, interpersonal relationships, imagination, etc.

Children seem to take special notice of each other even when they are still infants. As they become toddlers, their play is primarily **parallel play.** Parallel play is when toddlers enjoy playing side-by-side, but separately, rather than together. Nevertheless, the play of one is influenced by the play of the other, because each one frequently stops playing long enough to watch the other one. Initial attempts at playing together usually occur when one child imitates another. Playing with other youngsters enhances the intellectual, physical, emotional, and social development of preschool children.

As children move into the preschool stage, they start playing together. This is known as **cooperative play.** They may share toys or join in a game. As children start playing together, their peers become more important to them.

Physical activity helps children develop their large muscles. For this boy, however, fun is probably the most important consideration.

They look to their peers for acceptance as well as friendship.

The nature of the play is strongly influenced by the play children experience with their parents, even if the particular activity has not been taught by the parents. For example, two little boys attend a preschool that has several pets. The boys do not have pets at their homes, so neither has been taught by parents how to play with a live pet. However, they are having fun. Their willingness to take turns holding a rabbit is a reflection of the "giving" attitude of both sets of parents. Their gentleness shows a respect for living creatures that is probably a reflection of their own treatment by their parents.

Development of Motor Skills

Large Muscles

The large muscles are developed in activities such as running, jumping, climbing, riding tricycles, rolling tires, dancing, etc. Children who have only their parents or other adults as playmates are usually at a distinct disadvantage when it comes to the large muscle activities. Adults often don't have the stamina and patience to repeat these activities over and over, and children usually tire of them quickly when playing alone. On the playground with other children, however, they may climb the steps and take their turns on a slide 40 or 50 times without stopping. They may play running games until they appear ready to drop with exhaustion. Their little bodies recover quickly, however, and with a nap or a night's rest they are ready to start their vigorous routine all over again.

Watching the accomplishments of others is a challenge to small children. They are aware of who can run fast, who can jump across the big puddle of water, who can swim the width of the pool, etc. They are eager to grow and develop so they can match those accomplishments. They are willing to exert great effort in their attempts.

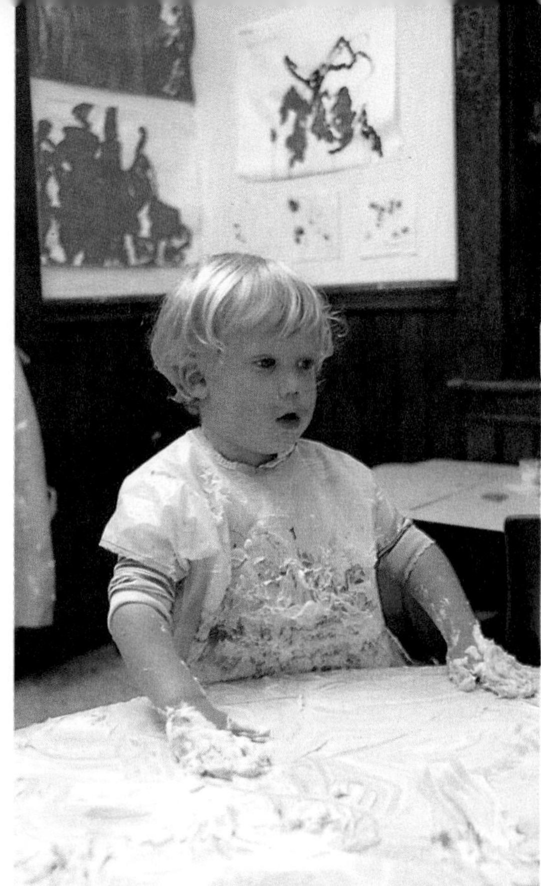

Even though they can be messy, art projects help improve small muscle skills.

Safety

While developing these large-muscle skills, accidents may occur. Children trip while running, fall while climbing, or skin their knees while riding their tricycles. Unfortunately more serious accidents happen, too. Small children cannot be expected to play safely. It is up to the caregivers to watch out for them. Caregivers faced with these risks often find it difficult to give children the freedom to play. They may be too worried about the children hurting themselves. However, caregivers must realize the importance of play in children developing skills. Children need to practice activities and learn to do things for themselves in order to gain self-confidence. Caregivers can set limits to help prevent problems.

Caregivers can protect children from unnecessary dangers by:

- Choosing clean, safe areas for children to play. A playground littered with broken glass or a busy street is not a safe area for any children.
- Guiding children as they learn new skills. For example, as young children start playing on slides, parents should help them up the ladder and guide them down the slide. Gradually helping children develop motor skills can assure their safety.
- Teaching children safety rules. Very young children cannot remember all the rules and need supervision. As they grow, though, children can learn such rules as, "Look both ways before crossing the road," etc.

Look, Listen, and Learn

Children learn through play. Play that is challenging helps children grow mentally, socially, physically, and emotionally. If a child grows without enough time devoted to play, that child may have trouble later with abstract thinking.

How can you learn to observe children at play and to evaluate their play experiences? Here are some tips for you to think about:

- Look for examples of how children take on the role of a hero or well-known personality in a dramatic play situation. Halloween offers a great opportunity to observe children portraying a hero!
- Watch how play experiences contribute to language development. There are many musical selections that combine songs with simultaneous body movements. One example is "Eeensy, Weensy Spider."
- Watch how play offers children the opportunity to learn how to get along with other children.
- Observe how play activities develop listening skills in children. ("Simon Says...Put your hands behind your back.")
- Be able to recognize types of play that develop a child's hand-eye coordination. Some examples of this are stringing beads, making potholders on a loom, or sewing simple projects.

Small Muscles

The small muscle skills are developed in the quieter activities. The arts are good examples. The use of fingerpaints, clay, children's safety scissors, paste, crayons, etc., all develop the small muscles of the arms and hands and enhance eye-hand coordination. Obviously, parents can encourage children in such activities, and doing projects together can be a source of closeness and warmth. Children profit, also, when they share these experiences with other children. The interactions can stimulate children to new levels of interest and accomplishment.

Challenging the Mental Capacity

Whether played with adults, older children, or peers, games can stimulate the intellectual development of preschool children. Simple card games and board games using dice or spinning pointers introduce young children to the concept of chance. Some children can learn to play card games like rummy in which they must understand "suits," "runs," and "three-of-a-kind." This is an introduction to the mathematical concepts of sets and groups. Such a game involves both chance and decision-making.

Many of the games that children play increase their vocabularies and their awareness of letters. Parents should be sensitive, however, to the fact that games are meant to be fun. Learning is a by-product. Pushing children to learn can lead to resistance, which has negative effects on both their intellectual development and the parent-child relationship.

Pretending, as a form of play, is important to intellectual development because imagination is the essence of creativity. Experts do not agree on whether children would pretend even if they never observed others in such games. They do agree, however, that children respond to encouragement in the use of their imaginations. Imagination, of course, uses reality and experience as a springboard. Thus, the more experiences the child has, the greater the range for pretending. Imagined experiences can be built from real experiences, the experiences of others, the experiences of storybook characters, and even other imagined experiences.

Children learn a great deal about logic by pretending. In developing their scenarios, they exercise their powers to understand cause and effect. Sometimes, a group of children may even engage in a rather sophisticated game in which they try to outdo each other with illogical events in their pretending. This usually leads to uncontrolled giggling, which some parents may consider boisterous silliness. Those parents should realize, though, the high degree of intellectual development required to play such a game and refrain from squelching the free-flowing imaginations of children.

Children love to pretend.

Choosing Toys

When selecting toys for children, caregivers should keep the following in mind:

- The toy should be interesting and appealing to the child. The price tag is not a surefire clue to a child's interest in a toy. For example, pots and pans from the kitchen make good toys as musical instruments or even for make-believe.
- Tailor the toy selection to the child's physical abilities. A child will quickly lose interest in a toy that is too easy. A toy that is too difficult will frustrate the child and give a feeling of failure.
- Toy selection should be tailored to the child's mental and social development as well.

A Matter of Fact

How would you answer this question? Who is responsible for protecting children from unsafe toys?

a) Toy manufacturers?
b) Caregivers?
c) Parents?
d) U.S. Consumer Product Safety Commission?
e) Everyone?

Answer: e) Everyone

We all have a stake in protecting children from toy-related injuries. There is no substitute for choosing toys carefully and supervising children at play. To choose toys with care, consider the age and physical abilities of the child. Toys for infants—rattles, squeeze toys, teethers—should be large enough so that they cannot enter the infant's mouth and become lodged in the throat.

Keep in mind that toys designed for older children are not meant to be in the hands of younger siblings. Age recommendations often appear on toy packaging. When you go toy shopping, follow those age guidelines. Teach older children to help keep their toys away from the younger ones. Even a broken or uninflated balloon can pose a danger. More children have suffocated on pieces of balloons than on any other type of toy.

Watch out for these toy dangers:

- Sharp edges or points can cut a child or put out an eye.
- Small parts could become lodged in a child's windpipe, ears, or nose.
- Loud noisemakers such as toy caps can damage hearing.
- Cords and strings could choke or strangle a child.
- Propelled objects such as tanks that fire missiles can cause bruises or eye injuries.

- Make sure the toy is well-constructed, durable, and safe for the child's age.

Toys for Toddlers

What toys are right for two-year-olds? At this time, the child "makes" toys carry out actions on other toys. Two-year-olds are very proud of what they can accomplish.

This age group prefers realism and bright colors. These toddlers are paying more attention to the details of toys, as well. Select ride-on toys that look realistic such as tractors or motorcycles and push toys that resemble adult equipment (vacuum, lawnmower, shopping cart). Five- to 10-piece toys that fit together, nesting toys with several pieces, matching games based on colors or pictures, and pounding or hammering toys are appropriate.

Role-play materials, play scenes, and transportation toys are good out-

Always-on-the-go children are thrilled by jungle gyms.

lets for make-believe play. Some suggestions are costumes, doll and housekeeping equipment, farm scenes, small cars, and large trucks with moving parts.

Two-year-olds can handle large markers and crayons, but they need supervision to ensure that they don't mark furniture or walls. Books for this age group should be sturdy. They should have pictures and simple stories about familiar subjects. Rhymes and repetition are favorites for two-year-olds.

Toys for Preschoolers

What's right for children three, four, and five years old? Dolls encourage make-believe play. Stuffed toys with accessories such as clothes, hats, ribbons, and animal babies attached with Velcro are favorites. Good toys for active play include balls, tricycles, rocking horses, and vehicles with steering mechanisms. Small wagons, wheelbarrows, and adult-like tools are preschool preferences. Wading pools are great fun, but adult supervision is required for safety.

For a five-year-old, a small bicycle with training wheels and foot brakes is suitable. A very well-coordinated child can master a jump rope at this age. Sports equipment is also popular with five-year-olds. They like ice skates with double blades, sleds, plastic bats, and junior-size basketballs, soccer balls, and footballs.

This age group loves play scenes. This may be the time for the child's first simple dollhouse. Make sure that there are few rooms, easy access, and that the furniture is sturdy. Five-year-old preschoolers are able to manipulate small pieces, and they pay attention to realistic detail. Space, forts, airports, and farms are favorite themes.

In the area of creative play, preschoolers show an increased interest in art products. Art supplies such as an adjustable easel, various sizes of brushes, paste and glue, and simple block printing equipment are suitable.

Select watercolor paints, a simple weaving loom, small beads to string, smaller crayons in many colors, and coloring books for older preschoolers.

To promote learning play, choose easy science models and computer programs (for teaching letters, numbers, sounds, and classification) for preschoolers from age four. From age five, consider a printing set, toy typewriter, simple calculator, or easy computer programs that teach programming. Science materials such as magnets, flashlight, shells and rocks, terrarium, and an aquarium hold the older preschooler's fascination.

The Importance of Friends

There is no question that the interactions children have with other children are among the most important factors in their emotional and social development. It is through play that children learn to be friends and to make friends.

The same pretend play that is important to the intellectual development of preschool children is essential for their development of social skills. When three neighbor children pretend to be father, mother, and child, they must interact. Each will have suggestions as to the scenario: "Get in the car. We're going to go to Grandma's house." "I'll drive!" They will work out the descriptions of the characters: "You be a little baby, Karen." "No, I want to be big, like Angie." "Okay." They will realize that if the game is to be fun, they must cooperate, take turns in leadership, and be sensitive to each other's feelings.

Dress-up is a valuable form of pretend play. It allows children to express themselves without the restriction of being themselves. The words and actions of children in dress-up play often reflect their real environments and the concerns they feel, but do not otherwise express. Family tensions, fear of death, insecurity, and aggression are just a few of the problems manifested in pretending. The interaction of children playing adult roles also helps them to establish their own identities.

One form of children's pretending that parents sometimes find troubling is the invisible playmate or pet. In fact, however, parents do not need to be concerned so long as the child recognizes the difference between reality and imagination. Perfectly normal children, who enjoy playing with friends, often will invent and name a playmate or a pet. The invisible playmate is often of the same age and sex as the child, but not necessarily. One four-year-old boy spent hours pretending he was playing basketball with the college team on which his uncle played. He would sit under the dining room table and carry on locker room conversations with each of his "teammates." During the pretend basketball games, he would shout their names when he was "open" and wanted them to pass the ball to him.

Pretend pets may be anything from tiny kittens to horses. In some cases, these may be expressions of ungranted wishes to have a pet, but that is not always the case. As with invisible playmates, children may spend considerable time talking and playing with invisible pets. There is no harm in

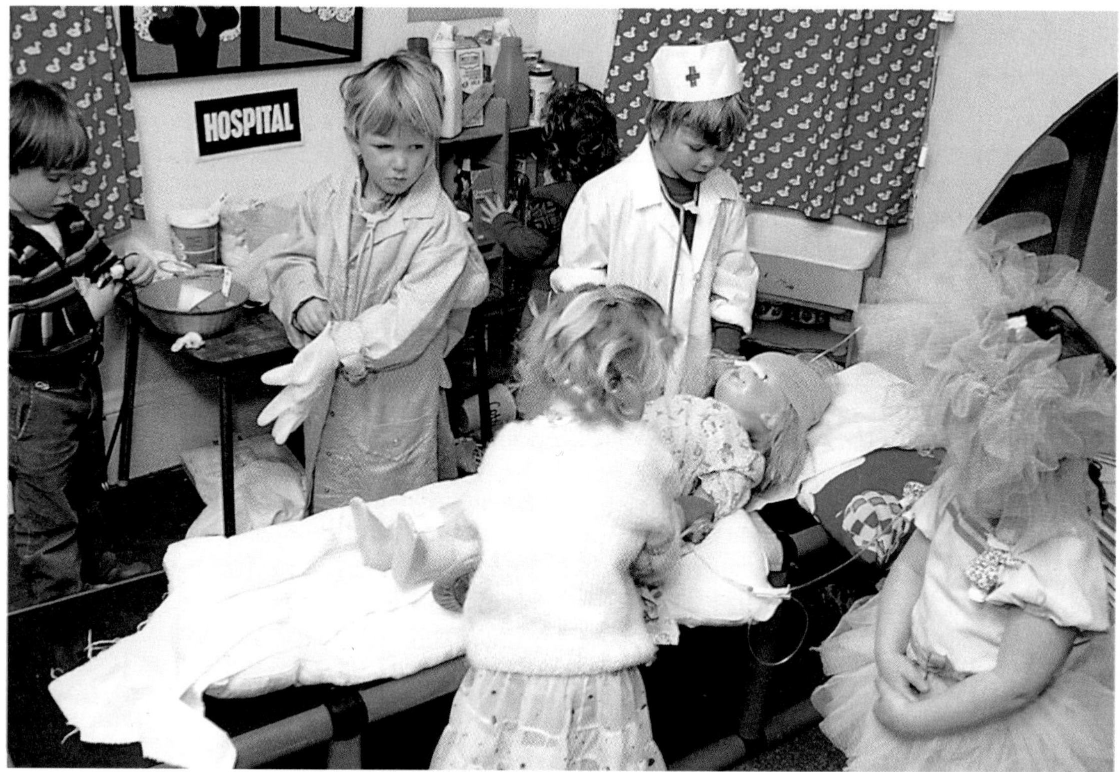

Dress-up play allows children to experience many different worlds.

parents going along with such games, or even participating. It can be good fun. On the other hand, as mentioned earlier, it is important for the child to know that the friend or pet is imaginary and not a part of our real world.

Shyness

Some small children appear to be shy toward adults other than their parents for no apparent reason. If they are equally shy around other children, their social and emotional developments are restricted. Parents of shy children need to encourage them to interact with others, but they should not push too hard. Neither should parents say to others, "Billy is really shy," when Billy is present. Once Billy's parents have categorized him as shy, he will find it difficult to behave differently.

Hosting a birthday party for 12 children probably will not help Billy get over being shy. He will simply avoid interacting. Asking Billy to interact with many children is like asking him to run before he can walk. Parents of shy children should begin by arranging play situations with just one other child. Because shyness is a symptom of restricted social development, it

A Matter of Fact

If you have trouble getting children to participate in games, here are a few tips:

- Are you sure the children are ready to participate in the game? If they are engrossed in another activity, you may want to hold off.
- Select games appropriate for the age group you are working with and their level of activity.
- After the game is complete, ask the children if they liked it or if they have suggestions on how they might change it.

might be best if the other child is a little younger so that the shy child does not feel overwhelmed at the start. It may be helpful, also, if the two children have the opportunity for parallel play, so that their interaction can begin slowly and grow.

Bullying

Bullies may seem to be just the opposite of shy children, but they, too, are restricted in their social development. Bullies have not learned to cooperate, share, alternately lead and follow, compromise, and, sometimes, give in.

Bullying is not necessarily physical, but with small children it usually is. The bully is a child who has learned by experience that size and strength can be used to gain one's way. A child can learn this just through interactions with other children, but also through interactions with siblings and parents in a home where size and strength are the sources of power. Children who are pushed around physically at home are likely to push neighborhood children around, if they are big enough to do it. They may even play with younger children so they can do it.

Parents of a bully have a responsibility to analyze their own behavior and change it when it is contributing to the problem. Other parents have a responsibility to their own children who are being victimized and to the bully, as well. We are all parents (Chapter 1). It is not fair to the bully to let such behavior go unchecked. Childhood bullies will be adult bullies unless they learn more acceptable ways. Whether adults do their bullying physically or mentally, they do it out of fear, frustration, insecurity, unpopularity, and/or other negatives in their lives. Thus, it is a sincere kindness to childhood bullies to help them become socialized. One way to do that is by offering the friendship they need, but don't know how to get. Also, recall Ben's story in Chapter 14. His playmate Ron and Ron's mother helped Ben learn how to take turns.

Ethics, Manners, and Sportsmanship

Whether children are playing board games, dress-up games, pretend games, or others, they learn ethics. **Ethics** are society's moral principles or rules of behavior. From peers, as well as from parents and older children,

Bullies don't realize that cooperation is an important part of making friends. Bullies just want their way.

they learn the value of honesty. They discover the consequence of lying or cheating. They learn respect for other children's property. They learn to sympathize with other children who are injured or who have hurt feelings. Manners, too, can be learned from other children. Those who show contempt for the rights of others probably will be scolded or banned from the group.

Children also learn sportsmanship from games and activities. Sayings such as, "It's not whether you win or lose, but how you play the game," become reality and help children learn about life. Working as a team can help children learn how to reach a goal with others.

Life's Work

Don Bothwell

- ➤Clown and Magician
- ➤Two years of college

Don's days are filled with performing, making phone calls to potential customers, mailing out flyers and brochures, and sending out contracts. He does his own bookkeeping, typing, sales, and technical stage work. Don has a "good-sized family" and spends time with them in the evening.

Don works all hours of the day. He says, "Once, when they filmed the movie *The Color of Money,* I entertained the extras and film crew for 10 days, 5 a.m. to 8 p.m. everyday."

Don says that people interested in this type of work should love to perform. They need a positive attitude and determination. Reading and writing skills are very essential. Dexterity to learn manipulation of tricks, a good memory, and communication skills are also important.

Don's advice for someone interested in this profession is, "work hard and practice hard. Get a good education. You need it to fall back on and to get you through the business end. If you grow to dislike your work, step back and reevaluate. Stay in it only if you love it."

When asked how his profession will change within the next 10 years, Don says, "I'm an optimist. Magicians and clowns have been around as long as there have been books to write about them." Sounds as if Don has confidence in the future.

In Review

Vocabulary

parallel play
cooperative play
ethics

Summary

- ✓ Children learn about the world around them through play. By playing with parents and with other children, preschoolers develop intellectually, emotionally, socially, and physically.
- ✓ Large-muscle motor skills are acquired in the vigorous types of activities engaged in by playmates of similar ages.
- ✓ Small-muscle motor skills are acquired in quieter activities that a child can share with either playmates or caregivers. The child is challenged and stimulated by the accomplishments of others.
- ✓ Many board games and card games stimulate intellectual development of preschoolers. Concepts of time, chance, and mathematics may be involved, and new words may be learned. Such games can be counterproductive, however, if the challenge exceeds the child's maturity.
- ✓ Parents should encourage the kinds of play that involve pretending, because imagination is the basis of creativity.
- ✓ Shy children and bullies are both restricted in their social development. Alert parents can help their children overcome these problems.
- ✓ By playing with peers, parents or older children, preschoolers learn ethics, manners, and sportsmanship—society's rules of behavior.

Questions

1. At a party celebrating her fourth birthday, Sandy followed her mother around and said she didn't want to play games with the other children. If you were her parent which of the following statements would you make? Explain your choice.

A. "Shame on you. It isn't nice to ignore your guests."

B. "If you don't play the games, I'm going to give you a spanking after the party."

C. "That's all right. Maybe you want to just watch."

D. "I guess you're not as grown-up as I thought you were."

2. In the situation described in #1, discuss and explain any actions you might take a week after the party.

3. List three or more ways you would try to assure the safety of your preschool children without limiting their large-muscle activities.

4. How do parents influence the play of their children in preschool even though the parents are not present?

5. Suppose that your four-year-old son, Jeff, comes home crying after being bullied by five-year-old Cindy, who lives next door. What advice would you give Jeff so he might be able to help Cindy see the error of her ways?

6. What might you say to Cindy in #5 that could help her change her behavior? Remember, she is probably already feeling insecure, so you don't want to threaten her.

7. Suppose that Ricky's friends have just told him that they won't play with him anymore because he always says they cheat when he doesn't win the games. If you were Ricky's parents, what would you say to him?

Activities

1. Write a very short story that would make a five-year-old child laugh because of its illogical ending.

Unit 5
The School -Age Child

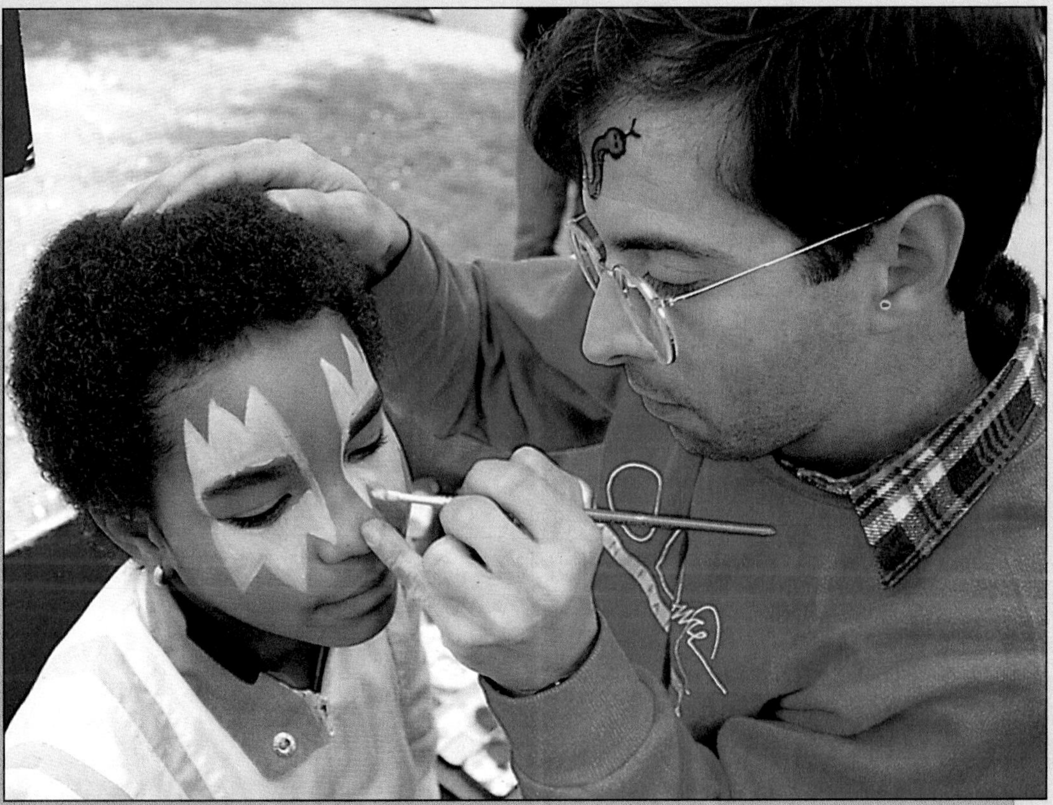

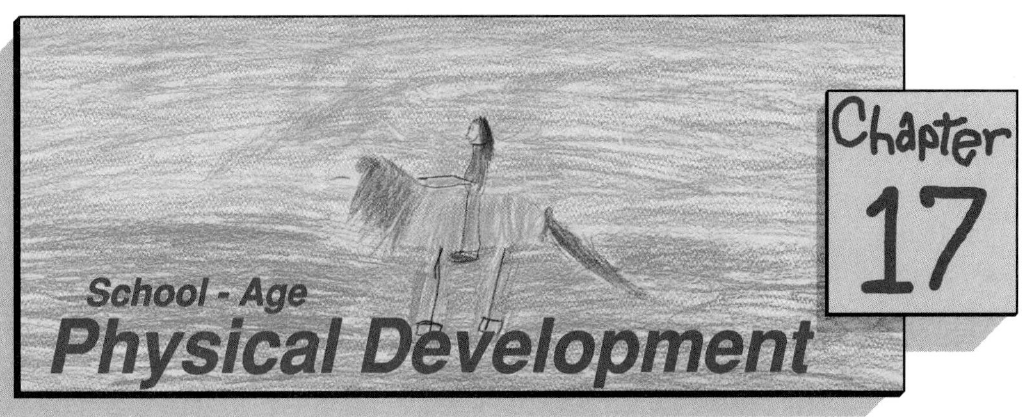

Chapter 17: School-Age Physical Development

This chapter will help you:

- recognize the importance of physical characteristics as aspects of our personalities
- understand how heredity and environment affect individual rates of growth and development
- learn how children's growth patterns influence their emotional needs and social development
- identify the principles of physical growth and motor development

Physical Changes

The term "school age" covers a wide range of developmental stages. Physically, children commonly double their weight between the ages of six and 13. During this period, they have gained 28 permanent teeth. They have come to look more like small adults than small children. Some of the girls have nearly reached their adult height. The production of sex hormones at the end of this time period has begun to change boys' voices and the body shapes of both boys and girls.

Adapting to these major physical changes presents each child with important challenges. Every parent should recognize how these physical changes relate to and affect the social, intellectual, and emotional development of children. Empathy should come easily to those parents who can remember being children themselves.

Individual Rates of Development

As you have learned throughout this book, each child develops in his or her own way. This becomes even more apparent at this period of life. For example, children who are shorter than their peers in junior high school may catch up and be taller than the others as adolescents.

Growth is stimulated and controlled by a **hormone,** a chemical substance,

Potential height of a child is determined by characteristics inherited from parents.

secreted by the pituitary gland located at the base of the brain. From birth to **pubescence,** the period of about two years prior to puberty, the rate of growth decreases steadily.

Every aspect of social, emotional, and personal development is affected by the body. First impressions are often based on people's physical characteristics and how they carry themselves. Typically, many of us describe others by their ages and physical characteristics, such as height, weight, body build, and coloring. Unusual and striking attributes such as grace or awkwardness, thinness or obesity, or very long or short hair are also commonly mentioned. Individuals' concepts of their bodies appear to be closely related to self-concept. People who think highly of themselves are likely to be accepting of their bodies. People who are self-rejecting often reject their body images.

The nature of one's body and its functioning probably has a lot of significance in the development of interests, and possibly in the selection of a career, although there is no conclusive evidence about this relationship. It is obvious, however, that the weak and awkward child probably will not become a professional athlete. The sturdy and graceful child, on the other hand, has a much wider range of possible interests, hobbies, and occupations from which to choose. Bodies and faces that are considered unattractive according to cultural standards often handicap their possessor's social life and may create additional problems with which to cope.

Some research has found that a large group of children, selected for their far-above-average intelligence, were found to be healthier, stronger, more attractive, and better coordinated than another large group of children of the same age and sex distribution selected for their far-below-average intelligence. However, many of these relations are the result, not of intelligence, but of social status. The bright children came from homes that provided them with better nutrition, better learning opportunities, and more chances for physical exercise.

Two main factors, heredity and environment, account for the individual differences among children. As you have learned, heredity is the genetic transfer of characteristics from parents to offspring. Physical traits and intellectual potential are inherited from parents. However, the environment in which a child grows affects the development of these inherited characteristics. Heredity and environment acting together influence an individual's physical and mental development. But it is heredity that limits what the environment can do in influencing children's development. For example, every child's potential height is determined by heredity. That potential height then can be achieved only if the child is raised in an environment that provides proper nourishment, exercise, and rest.

Principles of Physical Growth and Motor Development

Research on physical growth and development has disclosed certain general principles. As discussed in Chapter 12, the parts of children's bodies grow according to the **cephalocaudal principle.** *Cephalo* and *caudal* pertain to the *head* and *tail*, respectively. Thus, the upper parts of small children grow toward maturity faster than the lower parts. An adult built like a baby would be top heavy.

Motor development in small children proceeds according to the **proximodistal principle.** *Proximo* refers to *near* and *distal* refers to *far.* Thus, proximodistal development means that skillful manipulation occurs in shoulder and hip joints, which are close to the center of the body, before it occurs in hands and feet. For example, a seven-year-old child is more accomplished at jumping or throwing a ball than at small muscle skills such as writing.

Another principle is that of progression from general to specific action patterns. Motor chaining illustrates this principle. Motor chaining occurs when individuals become more efficient in a motor activity the more they practice it. An example of the chaining process is the difference in walking for children when they are one and one-half years old and when they are two years old. At the younger age, they use their whole bodies to obtain balance and to navigate. They walk for the sake of walking. At two years, they walk efficiently and easily. Rather than being perceived as a goal in itself, walking now serves as a means of getting children where they want to go.

For the school-age child, a good example of motor chaining can be observed by watching the children's swimming teams at the park district pool or the YMCA. The younger children have neither the strength nor the coordination to do the butterfly stroke successfully. But persistent practice allows the older ones to

A Matter of Fact

Have you ever watched a young child struggle to tie a shoe? This is no easy task for young learners. But when you're ready to teach this task, here are a few suggestions.

- At a children's bookstore, ask if they carry a cardboard lacing activity. The activity resembles the top of a shoe and is meant to be used as a learning tool.
- When children appear ready to start tying their own shoes, make sure the laces are long enough for little fingers.
- Give children a step-by-step demonstration by tying your own shoes. Allow plenty of time for the child to imitate your steps.
- The child might become frustrated, but don't you! Limit the amount of time you spend teaching this skill. You can always work on shoelace tying again tomorrow.
- Praise progress the child makes even if it is only getting the two laces crossed, one turned under, and then both laces pulled.
- When the child meets with success, it is cause for celebration! Treat the child to a new pair of shoes, socks, or different colored pairs of shoelaces for the child's sneakers.

accomplish the complex succession of movements involving their entire bodies.

In developing the highly complex motor skills, all the principles of learning and development just discussed do occur, and in many different sequences. Accomplished swimmers have progressed in their performance from relatively crude, gross movements to refined actions. They have learned how to combine independent movements of their feet, legs, arms, hands, and head. Chaining of responses has occurred. To achieve good performance in any physical skill, the separate movements and postures are integrated. They are changed from specific back to general, but a more complicated general. Such a process is necessary for all complex motor skills, such as dancing, boxing, tennis, and even dodging mud puddles.

Patterns of Growth

Like the different parts of the body, the various systems of the body grow at different rates and at different times. Neural growth is rapid during infancy, changing to a much slower rate during early childhood. Sexual or reproductive growth follows a dramatically different pattern. There is a slight development in early infancy, but increase in rate of growth occurs before and during puberty. The rate then slows and tapers off in late adolescence.

The most obvious physical growth is, of course, in lengths of arms and legs, the girths of the chest and abdomen, the widths of shoulders and hips, the weight, and the height. These are changing almost continuously from

Some school-age children love to participate in track and field events. What motor skills are these girls using?

birth through adolescence. This is called **somatic growth,** because *soma* means *body.* The rates of change for the various body parts are not equivalent, nor are they constant. Children who seem to be all arms and legs at one age may be perfectly proportioned at another age. Sometimes, height increases rapidly and other times growth is almost imperceptible.

In summary, one might say that the rate of growth is rapid during infancy and moderately slow during the middle childhood. Around puberty, which arrives earlier for girls than for boys by approximately one to two years, there is rapid growth, followed by slower growth in later adolescence.

Ages and Stages

In the appendix you will find general guidelines regarding the growth, behavior, and needs of school children of various ages. While these guidelines are helpful, it is important to recognize that each child develops at his or her own rate. Because children want so much to be accepted by their peers, they are apt to be very self-conscious if their development varies considerably from the average. For example, the first child in the class to lose any "baby" teeth may be embarrassed by the fact that he or she can no longer pronounce certain words. On the other hand, no one in the class wants to be the last one to reach this stage in the maturing process. Likewise, among the older

Some children seem to be all arms and legs because parts of the body grow at different rates.

school children, none wants to be the first or last to reach puberty.

At all ages, school children are sensitive to their height, weight, facial appearance, clothing, speech, intellectual ability, large motor skills, small motor skills, etc. Thus, it is important for parents to avoid hurtful comments regarding a child's individual pattern of development. An eight-year-old boy can't help it if his ears have grown faster than the rest of his head. An 11-year-old girl can't help it if her normal pubescent development has made her waist a bit larger than she'd like. Parents can be very helpful if they are understanding when children are hurt by their peers or by the teasing of insensitive older children and adults. Let's look specifically now at the physical development at various ages and stages.

Ages Six to Eight Years

When children reach the age of six years, we expect them to begin their formal education. Of course, many have already experienced daycare or preschools, and most have attended kindergarten. They have done fingerpainting, learned colors, and been introduced to the concepts of numbers and letters. Nevertheless, many first graders are not well-developed physically for the tasks they are expected to accomplish in school.

For example, for most first graders, small-muscle development lags well behind large-muscle development. In addition, the immaturity of their eyes leaves them with a tendency toward farsightedness. Thus, reading and writing are not skills easily acquired by many children in this age group—regardless of intellectual talent. Furthermore, most six-year-olds find sitting still very difficult. They are bundles of energy with rather short attention spans. Parents and teachers must be aware and accepting of children's individual rates of development. Learning opportunities must be designed to fit each child's ability as determined by his or her particular stage of physical development.

Parents must be equally aware of children's capacities for physical exercise and their need for rest. The growth *rate* for school children is slowing, but *growth* is certainly continuing. Because of the amount of energy they expend, first graders require 11 to 12 hours of sleep each night. Lack of sleep can cause nervousness, inattentiveness, loss of appetite, and susceptibility to illness.

Most six-year-olds don't eat as much as they did when they were younger. This is a natural phenomenon resulting from the fact that their growth is slowing. Obviously, it would be wrong for parents to urge a first grader to clean his or her plate by making comparisons with the hearty appetite of a younger sibling. The child will take proper nourishment when a balanced diet is available and no psychological "strings" are attached to eating. However, parents may need to make some adjustments for individual likes and dislikes. For example, if Sam dislikes lima beans, he could have green beans instead.

It is extremely important that nutritious food is offered at all three meals and as snacks. Because children this age have limited capacity, they cannot afford to fill up on calorie-rich foods having no other nutritional value.

During this period, a child's heart is growing rapidly. While most children of this age display great bursts of energy, they often lack stamina. For these reasons, many experts question the advisability of organized sports for such young children. Competition and the prodding by coaches and parents are likely to cause children to overexert.

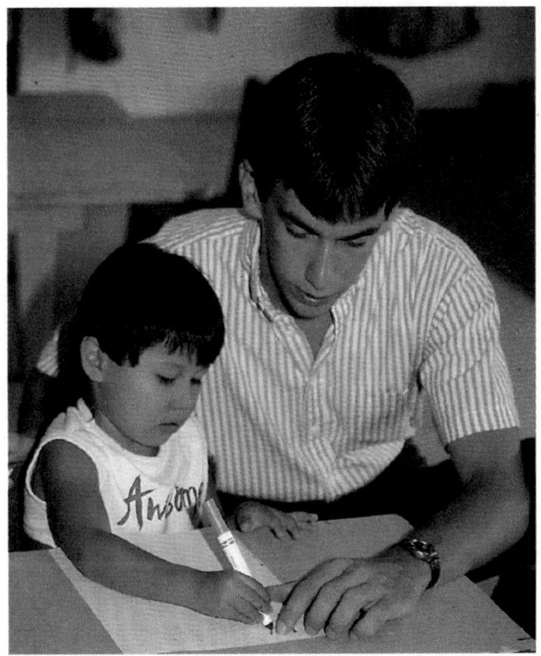

Learning how to print your name is a real challenge before small-muscle skills have developed.

Overexertion could result in damage to muscles, bones, and joints—or most importantly, the heart. In addition, children can be made to feel like failures if their limited physical development does not allow them to perform up to the unreasonable expectations of coaches, parents, or the child's peers.

At seven years, both small-muscle control and eye-hand coordination have improved. Even so, many seven-year-olds are not ready for extended periods of close work. By age eight, however, most children's eyes and small muscles have matured to the point that they are more suited to "desk" work. Throughout this period, large muscles are also growing and physical skills are developing.

A Matter of Fact

Every responsible caregiver wants to give a child a place to live that is safe and free from danger. A family's circumstances, however, will greatly affect a child's safety. Here are some situations that are accidents waiting to happen:

- when less-experienced caregivers supervise a child.
- when family members are dealing with emotional stress.
- when children are rushed into doing tasks and are not allowed the time needed to complete them carefully.
- when children are so hungry and thirsty, they'll eat or drink anything.
- when children and their caregivers are tired.

Try to avoid these situations. Here are some rules for home safety. They will reduce the chances of accidents happening in the home:

- Keep electrical appliances away from water.
- Keep the toilet cover closed.
- Keep kitchen knives and other potentially dangerous utensils out of children's reach.
- Turn the pot handles toward the back of the stove.
- Don't place a high chair near the stove or around highly trafficked areas in the kitchen.
- Cover unused electrical outlets with special plugs or electrical tape.
- Don't let children play on stairs.
- Keep stairs well lit.
- Disconnect power tools when they're not in use.
- Remove doors from stored refrigerators and freezers.
- Use nontoxic paint in a child's room.
- Don't let a baby sleep with a pillow.
- Plastic bags make dangerous toys. Don't let a child play with them.
- Never leave an infant or child home alone.

What other home safety rules can you recommend?

However, judgment does not keep up with physical development at this age, and accidents are frequent.

A Closer Look

Pat can run faster and jump farther than ever before. She thinks she can do anything. She's about to prove it by jumping off the garage roof. Fortunately for Pat, her older brother, Matthew, is working in the yard and sees her. "Pat," Matthew calls, "don't jump! Look how far down it is." Pat stops, looks, grins at him, and then climbs back down the tree next to the garage.

Ages Nine and Ten Years

Nine and 10-year-olds enjoy hobbies such as model building, sewing, and other crafts. Their good eye-hand coordination allows them to achieve satisfying results in this type of activity.

Children in this age group are teething almost continuously. When they reach age nine, they have approximately eight permanent teeth—all at the front of the mouth. In only four more years, they will have acquired 20 additional permanent teeth. When the growth of the jaw does not keep pace with the issuing of new teeth, children require the expert help of an orthodontist to straighten the teeth. This is another example of a period in a child's life when parents can play a vital role in easing the children's sensitivity to "looking different." Again, empathy and communication are important.

This is a time when many of the child's vital organs are approaching adult size. Parents must make certain that children do not overexert and that they get sufficient rest. So far as height and weight are concerned, nine- and ten-year-olds tend to grow slowly. In fact, some even seem to stop growing for a while before making a growth spurt between 11 and 13 years.

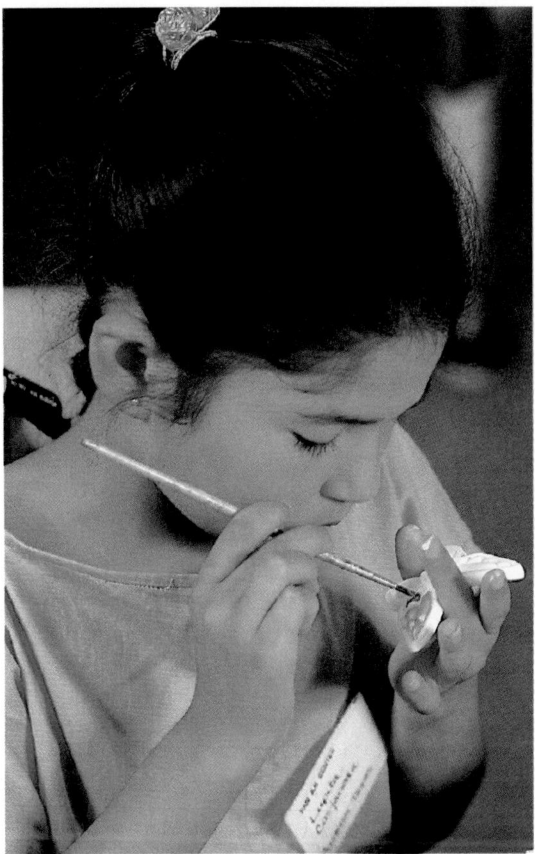

By the time children are nine years old, most have good eye-hand coordination that allows them to enjoy arts and crafts.

Ages Eleven to Thirteen Years

For the first time, the average weight and height are greater for girls than for boys. In terms of the approach to maturity, girls are as much as two years ahead of boys. This is true, not only in reaching adult height and weight, but in sexual characteristics, as well. Because of increasing bone structure, rapid muscular growth, and strenuous physical activities, youngsters have huge appetites as they approach the teen years.

Boys and girls may appear to be gangly or otherwise awkward in this age bracket because of the uneven growth in different parts of their bodies. They may have noticeably long arms or be short-waisted and long-legged. As noted earlier, they are likely to be self-conscious about physical changes. Strong support from those they respect and love will help them overcome their concerns.

In Review

Vocabulary

hormone
pubescence
somatic growth
proximodistal principle
cephalocaudal principle

Summary

- ✓ Rates of growth and development are unique to each child. Every aspect of social, emotional, and personal development is influenced by the individual's pattern of physical maturation. A child's acceptance of this pattern is closely related to self-concept.
- ✓ Heredity limits what the environment can do to influence a particular child's development.
- ✓ Physical growth in young children occurs according to the cephalocaudal principle. This means the upper parts of the body grow toward maturity faster than the lower parts.
- ✓ Motor development in young children occurs according to the proximodistal principle. This means that skillful manipulation in joints closer to the center of the body occurs sooner than in joints farther away.
- ✓ Mastery of complex motor skills is achieved through practice by a process called motor chaining.
- ✓ In school-age children, the desire for peer acceptance can cause self-consciousness for any child whose growth pattern deviates markedly from the average. Parents can play a major role in helping children to accept themselves.
- ✓ At the end of the school-age years, girls are as much as two years ahead of boys in their approach toward adult height and sexual maturity.

Questions

1. What is cephalocaudal growth?
2. What is proximodistal development?
3. What is pubescence?
4. Explain the chaining process.
5. Give an example of the transition from gross to refined control in the physical development of children.
6. If you were the coach for a soccer team of nine- and 10-year-olds, what particular concern might you have about setting up a conditioning program?
7. How does physical growth affect social acceptance?

Activities

1. The concerned parent of a six-year-old girl says to their pediatrician, "Sarah seems to tire easily, and she can never make up her mind—even about what ice cream flavor she wants. She has a vivid imagination in her artwork, but she seems to have no talent. The animals she draws don't look real at all." If you were their pediatrician, write a summary of what advice you would give this parent.
2. Interview two children in any age group about the kinds of things they like to do in their free time. List their interests. How do they compare with typical behavior characteristics for their age group?
3. Physical growth, by definition, involves change. Write an essay telling at which age it was the most difficult for you to accept your growth pattern. Explain why and tell how you dealt with your situation. Did anyone else help you in any way?

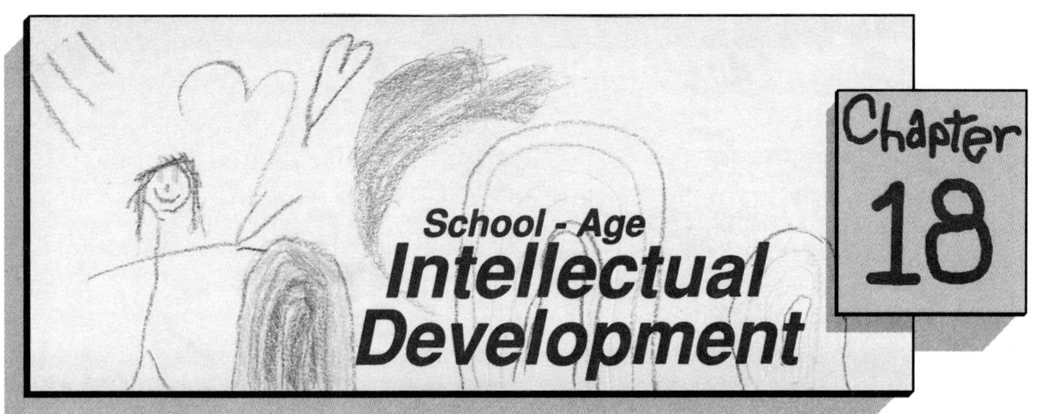

Chapter 18

School-Age Intellectual Development

This chapter will help you:

- recognize that the thought processes of young children are different from those of adults
- recognize school children's games as intellectually stimulating activities
- identify the factors that influence a child's success in school
- appreciate the importance of self-concept to intellectual development
- recognize the necessity for parental acceptance and support regardless of where a child's intellectual strengths and weaknesses may lie

A Child's Viewpoint

Children spend a lot of time trying to figure out how their world works. Their rationales are often both amazing and amusing. Sometimes they demonstrate an uncanny ability to see through the complex behavior of adults or to see simple solutions for seemingly complicated problems. This may be due, in part, to the fact that their brains are not yet cluttered with extraneous information. An example is given in the following anecdote.

A Closer Look

A truck driver made the serious mistake of ignoring the sign that said "Low Clearance. 14′." He drove his semi-trailer, which measured 14′ 1/2″, into the underpass. When he reached the midpoint of the underpass, there was a horrible screeching and scraping and the rig came to a sudden stop. Apparently, it was hopelessly wedged into this position. City police arrived to handle the traffic jam that quickly developed behind the blockage. They also radioed for engineers to come and solve the problem. After an hour of studying the problem, the engineers decided the simplest and fastest solution would be to call in crews to cut off the top of the trailer with acetylene torches. Naturally, a crowd of onlookers from the neighborhood had gathered to share in all this excitement. Just as the crews were lighting their torches, a little girl shouted, "Why don't you just let some air out of the tires and drive the truck through?"

Sometimes children are convinced of the correctness of their conclusions, even when they are not as astute as the one just presented. This is obvious to anyone who has ever tried to change a child's mind about something. There is a practical reason for this behavior. It is because children's thought processes are different from those of adults. If children cannot think on the level that is required to understand what the older people are talking about, they cannot be expected to change their minds.

Human beings acquire much of their behavior through learning. The behavior they learn is the result of experiences and negative results of their actions. Their responses may either be initiated by themselves or copied from the responses of others. In general, the facts people learn are not functional until they reflect upon them, consider how to put them into practice, and decide how to relate to them and to their behavior. This process is a vital part of learning.

Thought Processes

The leading theories on children's thinking maintain that the thought processes of children differ in quality from those of adults. Adult thought processes are more abstract. One prerequisite for abstract thinking is the ability to classify. Young children are

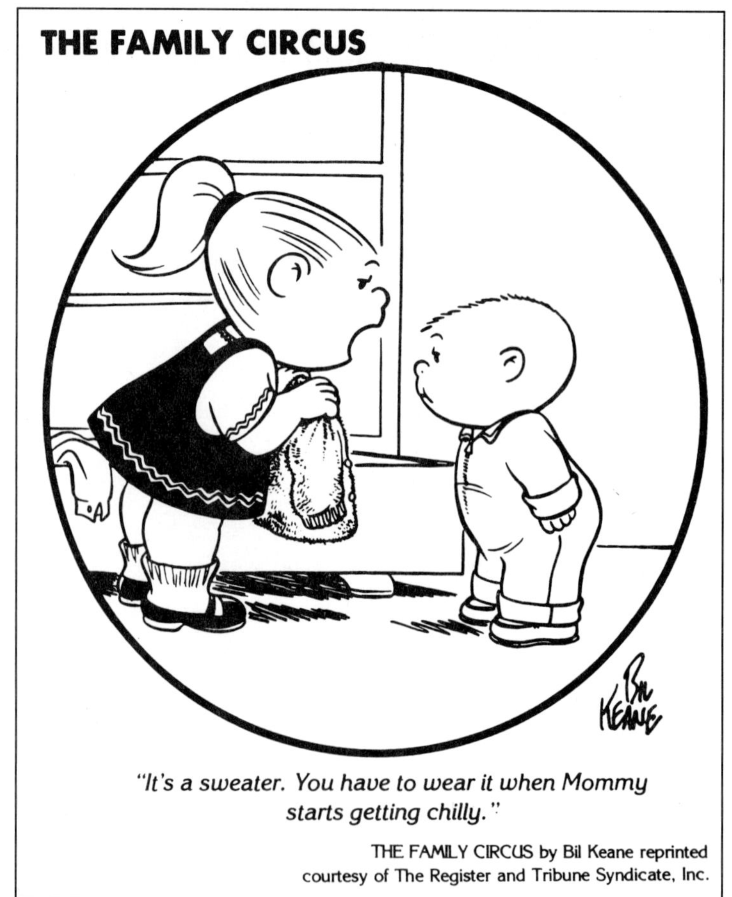

"It's a sweater. You have to wear it when Mommy starts getting chilly."

THE FAMILY CIRCUS by Bil Keane reprinted courtesy of The Register and Tribune Syndicate, Inc.

unable to use any significant criteria to put things into classifications. (**Criteria** are the standards on which a judgment or decision is based.) Their thinking is related to their own personal experience and whatever information they have acquired. At the beginning of the school-age level, children are not yet able to solve many of their problems intellectually because they do not have the necessary mental tools. For example, ask small children, "What is a father?" and they are not likely to answer in terms of the duties and responsibilities of fathers as adults might. Instead, they are more apt to respond in terms of their own observations and awareness, "Daddies drive cars and go to work."

By the time children reach school age, they are able to detach themselves from their personal and emotional framework and can focus on abstract concepts. Their systems of classification become more sophisticated as they focus on a wider range of properties. As you have learned, young preschoolers tend to classify objects on the basis of their own personal experience. They generally ignore abstract concepts and, instead, focus on family schemes and personal relations. For example, preschoolers may group building blocks into families, with large ones being the "father" and "mother" and small ones being the "babies." In a sense, they are focusing on size, but size in this case is tied to what is personally relevant to them—their families. As children progress in their ability to classify, they can separate blocks according to color and shape. They can classify things that are alike and things that do not resemble each other. They also can connect a dog with a doghouse or a bird with its nest, and they realize the humor of a dog in a nest.

How Children Think

To be effective in helping children learn and to be able to explain ideas and events to them, we must understand how they think. Psychologists Annemarie Roeper and Irving Sigel used the case study of five-year-old John to illustrate some of their research into the thought processes of children. (Reprinted by permission of National Association for the Education for Young Children.)

Frisky, the family dog, has been John's constant companion. He refers to the dog as Frisky Jones, just as he himself is known as Johnny Jones. One day the family car, parked on their sloping driveway, rolls backward and kills Frisky. John is heartbroken. His mother tries to make him feel better, explaining that it was an accident, that someone forgot to set the brakes. When she sees that John is still very unhappy, she tells him that maybe they can get another puppy just like Frisky.

How well does John understand what his mother is trying to tell him? How well is he equipped to understand the meaning of this experience? Does John know what death means? Does he know what life means? Is everything that moves alive? Then the car that killed Frisky must be alive also and must have decided to do it. Might the car decide to kill him, also? Does he think Frisky Jones was as much a

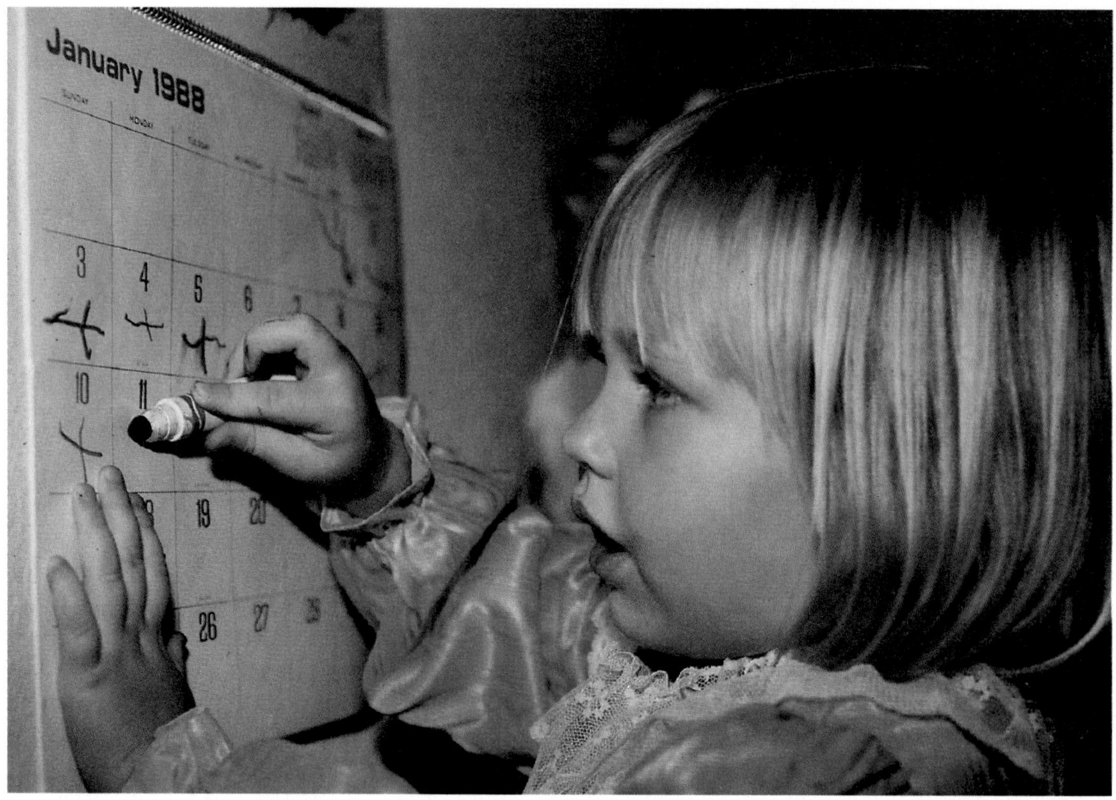

How does marking off days on a calendar help a child understand the concept of time?

member of his family as he is? In that case, would his parents soon get a new boy and forget him if he died? How much do we know of his real thoughts and concepts?

One can find great variation in children's reactions to similar situations:

1. John may think that Frisky is a true member of the family. He also may think that the car is alive and therefore may decide to run over him also, and that his parents then might easily replace him. Consequently, he feels great anxiety and grief.

2. John may have come to no conclusions, one way or another, about the identity of Frisky and of the car. (This is rare. Children want to master their surroundings. They are more likely to arrive at wrong conclusions than no conclusions.)

3. John may believe the truth and a falsehood at the same time (without being disturbed about it). He may lean more toward one concept than the other depending on his frame of mind. He might feel that Frisky was his brother, while at the same time he may be aware that this is not true.

4. John may have a true understanding of the situation. This would mean that he realizes Frisky was only a pet in the home. He also knows, then, that the car is not alive, that it was human error that caused the accident, and that there was no purpose behind the incident. In this case, he can view the incident realistically and concentrate his feelings where they actually belong, namely, in grief over the loss of his dog.

If John's standard for classification is living in the same house, Frisky can be a brother. On the other hand, through assimilation of more ideas and through accommodation of his ideas to reality, it is possible for him to correct his former idea and accept the fact that only people can be brothers. Young children function better when they focus on one idea at a time instead of focusing on the relationship of several ideas to a larger field.

As children's thought processes mature, they learn to put things together according to two or more criteria. They realize that a geometrical figure can be both blue and round. Then they can group all the blue circles together leaving out blue squares and red circles. When John reaches this level, he can classify Frisky with his family when referring to all living beings in his home, but not as part of his family when being human is the criterion.

Mastering Concepts

In time children master the concept of reversibility. As discussed in Chapter 4, this is the concept of things returning to their original condition after manipulation. A child can turn a footstool upside down and use it as a raft with four poles, but when turned back see it as a footstool. A red and blue reversible jacket is still both red and blue even though only the blue may be visible at the moment. By reversing it, the red will be seen unchanged.

Another concept that children master is seriation. **Seriation** is the process of ordering a set of objects according to some property. Size, color shade, and number are just three of the many possible common properties that a given set of objects may have.

When children have mastered all these different operations, they have reached the stage at which they can understand the concept of conservation. Conservation is one mark of the ability to think in abstract terms. Conservation refers to the knowledge that a quantity does not change even though the form in which it appears does change. In other words, if nothing is added to or subtracted from an object, the amount stays the same whether the shape is changed or the material is divided into pieces. For example, a piece of aluminum foil crumpled up contains the same amount of foil as before it was crumpled. Nothing has been added or taken away. Children who understand conservation know that the piece of foil may acquire different shapes without changing its original amount. Their conclusions are drawn according to a concept of reality. They do not let the visual change overrule their judgment.

Children achieve full understanding of conservation over a range of ages. First, they understand conservation of substance, then the conservation of weight, and finally the conservation of

It looks like a game of make-believe, but children's imaginations help them unlock the door of understanding.

volume. According to Piaget, the children he studied did not acquire these concepts until they were between eight and 12 years old. More recently, however, other researchers have reported that considerably younger children can understand conservation. One psychologist working with gifted children says they acquire the concept by the age of four years.

Space and time are two other concepts that evolve in children's minds. With all these concepts growing in their young minds, children develop a system of logic which, in many ways, bears little resemblance to adult logic. As new observations are made, however, the system evolves and allows children to formulate more sophisticated problem-solving techniques. Most of these are based on a trial-and-error method of experimentation.

Levels of Thought Processes

According to Piaget, by the time children are five or six years old, they will have advanced through several levels of representation. Let's use a puppy to explain the different stages. At the *object* level, children are reminded of a puppy only when they see one. At the *index* level, a child can visualize a puppy when one is heard barking. At the *symbol* level, the child could visualize the puppy after seeing

These children can match words, such as "cap," to a picture of the object. What level of thought process have they reached?

a picture of a bag of dog food in a magazine advertisement. At the *sign* level, children are approaching reading readiness. They are able to recognize that various combinations of letters can be used to specify objects. They can visualize a puppy when they see the letters p-u-p-p-y. As you will recall from Chapter 4, through elementary school, children are in a stage that Piaget called *concrete operational.* This means simply that children in this age group learn best by hands-on experience.

Through junior high school, children are developing their skills in abstract thinking. Piaget called this the *formal operations* stage. This is the beginning of the process by which people are able to sort and sift ideas as well as objects. Development in this stage allows people to solve many problems without previous hands-on experience. Through the remainder of the school years, and throughout all of the productive years, people build on these intellectual developments of childhood.

Games as a Means of Learning

The chief occupation of children is playing. However, time spent at play is divided between playing and arguing. Arguing whether a pitched ball was a

A Matter of Fact

Here are some games that emphasize cooperation instead of competition. Everybody wins!

"Cover Up" will amuse younger children. First, place a quarter in a bucket then fill it with six to eight inches of water. Divide 15 pennies among the players. Let each player take a turn dropping the pennies into the bucket. The object is to fully cover the quarter in the bottom. The group wins if they can do it before running out of pennies. If not, the bucket wins, and the group can try again.

"Tell Me a Picture" will develop communication and listening skills. Clip fairly simple pictures from old magazines or coloring books. Have one player look at a picture without letting the second player see it. As the first player describes the picture to the second player, the second player tries to draw as close a replica as possible. Verbal communication alone should be the guide. No hand or body signals are allowed! After one picture is done, the players can switch roles.

For the game "Machine Building," pantomime a blender, computer, or other machine for the group. Once the kids get the idea, organize them into groups of three or four. Have each group create a machine and then present it to the other groups for them to guess what it is. In this game, kids of different ages or physical abilities can participate because everyone gets to be a cog in the machine. For a grand finale, have the individual machines decide how to join into one huge, interlocking machine.

strike and whose turn it is are among the most common experiences of childhood. During these verbal battles, children acquire an understanding of the spirit of rules. Through play, they can learn fairness and taking turns, tact and diplomacy. In other words, they can begin to think on a more abstract level. If children's play is too closely controlled by adults, they lose the opportunity for this type of growth.

Children's games are not highly organized and usually are based more on competition than on cooperative effort. Games children like best are those in which they can show their skills. Children, and in particular those children who find little chance for success at meeting adult demands, can find a position of status among their peers through demonstration of skill and daring.

Children also relish the excitement of frightening games. For example, they like playing hide-and-seek at dusk so that the appearance of another child can be frightening. Often scary games can provide children with some of the information and strength needed to deal with real dangers.

Dramatic play provides the child with a rich variety of roles to explore. To be a cowboy or an airline pilot is easy. To be a parent or a teacher is not much more difficult. But to be a table, a sandbox, or another object may pose quite a challenge to a child's imagination. The ability to play a role is apparently related to intellectual ability and to adjustment.

Through play with peers, children learn a lot about themselves. Peers can be harsh critics. Any undesirable trait is quickly spotted by them and they are quite frank in ridiculing it. This frankness can hasten change in children because children rarely consider change until they become aware of the opinions of others. Through association with peers, they acquire a firmer hold on reality about themselves than is possible if they have no playmates.

Unfortunately, for some children, peer criticism may be more harmful than beneficial. For example, if children are criticized for things over which they have no control, socializing with their peers is a painful, frustrating experience. It makes them feel insecure. Even if they are criticized for their behavior, which is something they can control, they may still feel insecure if they can't figure out how to solve the problem. It is very helpful for a child to have role models who are able to help children adapt their behavior to socially acceptable standards.

Peers also provide children an opportunity for identification. Peer groups convey to their members a body of information and values. They provide a range of opportunity for the learning and practicing of social roles. Neighborhood pals may confide their family worries, explain their different religious beliefs and rites, share their observations about nature and their "theories" on reproduction, and teach how to build a kite or how to bake cookies. They learn from experience

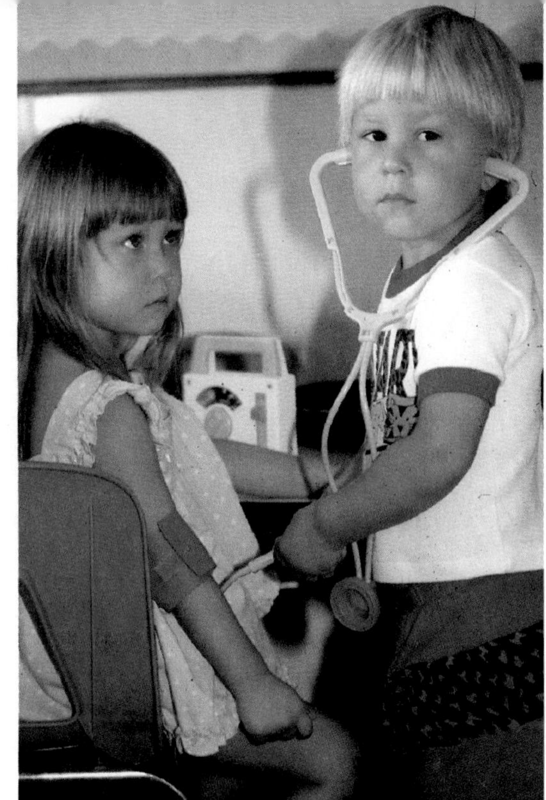

Dramatic play gives children the opportunity to explore different roles.

that "honesty is the best policy" and that "three's a crowd." They struggle to deal with problem relationships. They learn to lead, and they learn to follow.

School Success

Once a child is in school, the quality of the teacher-students relationship is critical to the child's school success. We must recognize, however, the importance of the child's attitude toward school. That attitude has been developing throughout the preschool years. It is strongly affected by the attitudes of the parents and other principal caregivers, of siblings, and neighborhood peers.

In the years past, the training of preschoolers was almost totally in the

A Matter of Fact

How can a caregiver introduce the exciting world of science and nature to a child? One of the most important things is to have an interest in the subject yourself. You can get ideas from science books in your local library. Many will contain science activities and experiments suitable for a particular age group.

With very small children, put the emphasis on having fun. Children will be entertained by a simple bubble-making activity using everyday household items such as a hanger that has been formed in a circle with a handle and liquid dish detergent. As you create the bubble magic, you may want to talk about how soap film wraps around hot air to make a bubble, bubble colors, and the shapes they make.

A nature center can be a source of family-oriented activities like flower and plant walks, animal touch-and-see programs, nature films, and bird-banding activities. Many of the programs run by nature centers are no- or low-cost.

Science activities at school and at home can provide a take-off point for further study. Older children may enjoy building models of the human body, which may lead to an interest in health and medical sciences. Growing vegetables or herbs may lead to an interest in plants and botany.

Adolescents may be interested in school science fairs, young inventors' fairs, and summer science camps. Children can learn about computers and technology at their school, in a computer camp, or, if they live near a large city, through the education department of a science museum.

But, remember, it's the attitude of the parent or caregiver that is so important in keeping an interest in science and nature alive in a child.

hands of parents. Entering kindergarten or first grade, children were exposed for the first time to the everyday influence of an adult outside their family. Today, many babies are cared for by professional "sitters." Small children are enrolled in preschool or other forms of daycare. This means that parents are entrusting some of the child-rearing responsibilities to other caregivers much earlier than before. The caregivers must be chosen wisely in order to enhance the child's likelihood of achieving success as a school-ager. If the child has spent the preschool years surrounded by role models who have little respect for the value of education, for the joy of reading, or for the other values promoted in the school setting, he or she has little chance of immediate success in school. Children in these unfortunate circumstances will succeed only to the degree that teachers can inspire them.

The teacher has the greatest impact on children's learning. Factors in the classroom that affect children are the teacher's enthusiasm, the teacher's ability to share knowledge, and psychological and emotional relation-

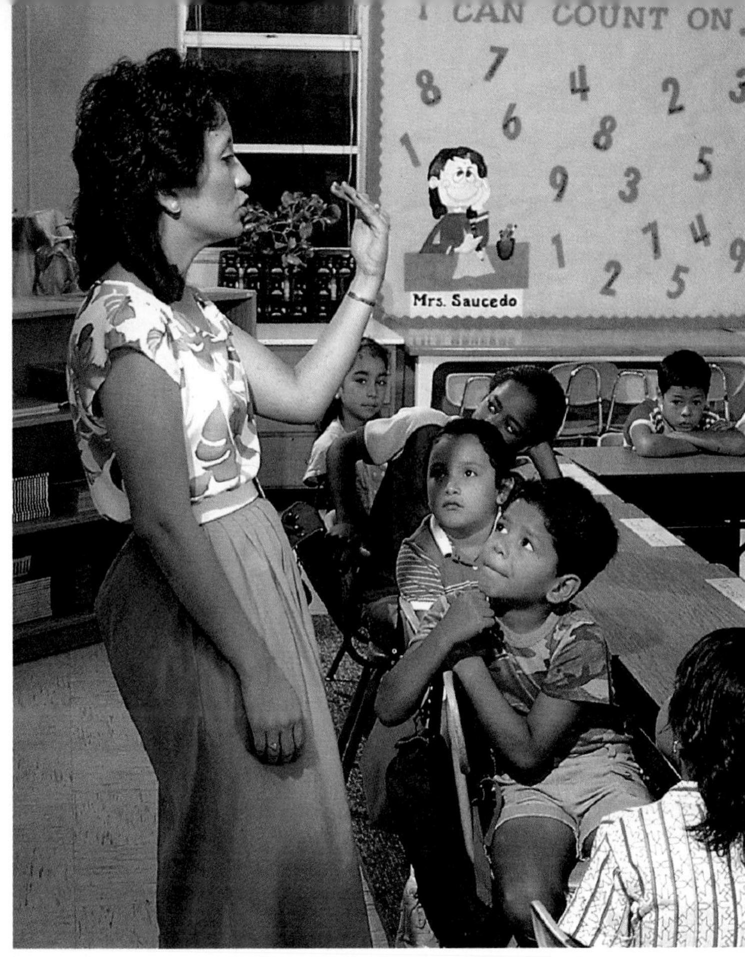

Good teachers encourage children to explore, ask questions, and seek solutions.

ships existing between the teacher and the pupils. Teachers have a significant psychological influence on children. They have a major impact on children's school adjustment, personality, and academic achievement. They may influence a student's decision about values, as well as choice of a career.

The teacher's values are communicated to the pupils directly through rules, comments, commands, and discussions. But what the teacher says is less important than what the teacher does. The teacher becomes a model for the students. Teacher approval is sought and disapproval is avoided. The first grader declares, "I love my teacher more than anyone else." The second grader says, "No, Mommy. My teacher wants me to do it this way and that's the right way." Nor is it surprising that children sometimes accidentally call their teachers "Dad" or "Mom," or that a sixth grader wants a haircut like the coach has.

The teacher actually may take the place of an absent or neglectful parent in a child's emotional life. However, teachers can never substitute fully for a parent. They can, though, create a warm and happy atmosphere in the classroom to alleviate some problems for children.

Effective teachers are those who love young people and have the desire to motivate them to explore the unexplored, seek the truth, and develop new ideas. It is unfortunate that some children need such stimulation, because it indicates that factors in their lives have stunted their natural desire to learn. Babies are born with curiosities. They want to touch, to see, to hear, to smell, and to taste everything in their environments. Curiosity is nothing but a desire to learn. Thus, when a school-aged child has little interest in learning, it seems safe to assume there have been events in that child's life that have turned off the natural curiosity. Obviously, both parents and teachers must do everything in their power to avoid causing such a tragic event.

Life during school hours can never be separated from one's experiences during the hours before or after school. A variety of parental factors influence children's achievement. These include the emotional relationship between parents and children, the attitudes of parents toward school and school achievement, and parental concern for and interest in children's performance. Some parents use the school as a threat and say, "Wait until you get to school," "The teacher will straighten you out," or "Enjoy your freedom now because you won't have any in school." Such comments create in the child a fear and dislike toward school. Parents need to avoid making negative comments about school, such as "I don't know why you like school, I hated it." Children should not be torn between two loyalties, loyalty to their homes and loyalty to their school. Each should be supportive of the other.

Children enjoy showing their parents their school papers. They hope their parents will appreciate what they have accomplished. They want their parents to be proud. For example, one evening six-year-old Dawn was showing her father her school papers. She would cheer for each star on her paper and allow her father to study the perfect papers. Those papers with errors she quickly passed over.

Many factors influence academic achievement: intellectual ability, level of maturity, relationship with parents, relationship with the teacher, emotional and personality factors, past success and failure, attitude toward school, socio-economic status, and patterns of interest. In general, the academic skills students acquire reflect the effectiveness of the school, as well as their own self-concepts. The importance of self-concept to a student's academic achievement cannot be stressed enough.

Self-Concept

How does **self-concept** (feelings about oneself) develop? Why do some children expect to fail? Why do some children expect to see a "trap door" waiting for them as they move along life's path?

Attitudes that people have toward themselves and the world around them are a very important part of their development. From their many experiences, they form ideas about other persons, about themselves, and about their expectations for personal success in the future.

If they are fortunate, they learn to feel that they are important, loved, and successful. They learn they can explore, discover, create, and enjoy. They recognize that they can have things and do things. They realize that they have their own sets of problems, but they can deal with them. They know they have their own set of advantages. In other words, they develop self-confidence and self-respect. For this reason, it is important that most of their experiences be the kind that help them to feel confident about themselves and to have trust in the people around them.

Children's views of themselves are shaped by everything that affects their development, ranging from their genetic makeup to obvious and subtle social influences in their society. One theory of the development of the self-concept is that children's views are influenced by "significant" persons, particularly their parents. Approval by others who are significant in their lives leads to self-approval. Disapproval by significant persons leads to self-disapproval. As children are thought of by "significant others," so they in time think of themselves.

Some children have a poor self-concept and they always think the worst of themselves.

The impact parents have on children depends not only on what they actually feel, think, or do, but also on the children's perception of what they think, feel, or do. The clearest testimony regarding this facet of children's experiences comes from adults who describe how their attitudes toward themselves are influenced by their parents' attitudes and intentions.

Some discrepancy between what youngsters think they are and what they think they would like to be or ought to be is probably inevitable. Even if it is not pointed out by others, they are likely through their own experiences to become aware of their limitations. They can see a discrepancy between the real and the ideal when their reach exceeds their grasp, when they fall short of achieving a goal, or when the roles they fantasize are more heroic than anything they can actually accomplish.

There always will be a gap between what is and what might be in youngsters who are seeking and striving to realize their potential. When youngsters consistently reach for the impossible, they become frustrated. If they blame themselves for limitations they cannot overcome, the situation only becomes worse. It would be absurd to think that all children have inherited the intellectual capacity to analyze Einstein's theory of relativity.

Parents and teachers can play crucial roles in helping a child to set challenging, but realistic, goals. In order to be effective, however, their own expectations for the child must be realistic. In addition, they must be able to communicate their love and acceptance to the child. Children can adapt to disappointments and develop healthy self-concepts when they feel secure in the respect of those they admire.

Dr. Howard Gardner, a noted psychologist, has stressed the importance of parents and teachers taking note of all the strengths and inclinations of children rather than trying to rate them in terms of a single criterion called intelligence. He abhors society's tendency to label children "smart" or "dumb" on the basis of IQ scores or other tests of linguistic and mathematical skills. According to his theory, there are seven areas of intelligence: linguistic, mathematical, spatial, musical, bodily-kinesthetic, intrapersonal, and interpersonal. Bodily-kinesthetic intelligence allows one to develop finely tuned motor skills. **Intrapersonal intelligence** is necessary if a person is to achieve self-identity and self-understanding. **Interpersonal intelligence** allows an individual to understand other people's motivations, feelings, and interactions. Parents are best able to help their children reach their goals and realize their potentials by encouraging them in their interests, by loving them regardless of where their strengths lie, by giving them lots of attention and praise, and by treating them with respect.

Life's Work

Phyllis Johnson Sudds
➤**Piano Teacher**
➤**M.A. Mt. Holyoke College**

Much of Phyllis's day is spent giving lessons to her students or preparing for them. The preparation includes a survey of music needed for students, an outline of lesson plans, and organization of materials in the studio. One day each week, Phyllis makes a trip to the music store or checks catalogs for new music materials. One morning each month is devoted to attendance at the local Music Teacher's Association's meetings, and each fall Phyllis attends two to three workshops conducted by well-known pianists. Phyllis also practices her own music for one hour each day and attends concerts in the local area on many evenings.

Phyllis's day starts at 7:45 a.m. by giving one to two lessons in her home studio before her students go to school. Then at 3 p.m. lessons begin again and generally continue until 7 p.m. Makeup lessons are given in the evening or on weekends. Phyllis spends 20 to 24 hours per week teaching and 10 to 15 hours preparing for lessons.

Phyllis says the skills necessary for success in her profession include an advanced proficiency on the piano as well as an education in piano pedagogy, theory, and harmony. She says, "You need a desire to teach, knowledge of child psychology, and education skills. You also need a love for children and adults and an ability to interact with them and instruct them."

Phyllis says her most rewarding job-related accomplishment is "Seeing a young child grow in musical ability—ability to perform well and acquire a love for music."

For a student considering going into her profession, Phyllis's advice is, "Obtain a solid piano background and know your materials. Learn as much as you can about teaching methods and ideas. Be a well-rounded person and obtain a good liberal arts education. Music is related to all areas of life."

When asked how her profession will change within the next 10 years, Phyllis says, "I see the introduction of more piano study using the computer programs that have been developed and increased use of electronic keyboards. The computer offers great teaching tools. Group piano lessons are increasingly popular and effective as a teaching method."

In Review

Vocabulary

criteria
seriation
self-concept
intrapersonal intelligence
interpersonal intelligence

Summary

- ✓ The thought processes of children are different from those of adults. Very young children cannot classify, so they cannot think in abstract terms.
- ✓ When children reach school age, they begin to focus on abstract concepts. They have evolving ideas about space and time. They can classify objects according to more than one criterion at a time. In the early school years, children gain the concepts of reversibility, seriation, and conservation. Even with all this development, however, a child's logic is still quite primitive.
- ✓ Through elementary school, a child's intellectual processes are in a stage that Piaget called concrete operational. This means that a child in that age group learns best by hands-on experience.
- ✓ In junior high school, children are able to sort and sift ideas as well as objects. This puts them in Piaget's formal operations stage, when skills in abstract thinking are developing rapidly.
- ✓ The teacher-child relationship is one of the most influential factors in determining a child's success in school.
- ✓ If children are to achieve up to their intellectual potential, they must believe in themselves. Parents and teachers can play crucial roles in helping a child to set challenging, but realistic, goals.

Questions

1. What is seriation? How would you test a child's ability to understand seriation?
2. What influence can peers have on the intellectual development of school-aged children?
3. What are the positive aspects of children's arguing?

4. What can parents do to help ensure that their children will enjoy school and acquire maximum benefit from their school experience?

5. Define self-concept. Why is self-concept important to intellectual development?

6. What factors influence academic achievement?

7. Vanessa, a third grader, has just moved to a new neighborhood and enrolled in a different school. Previously, her grades had been average. As part of an experiment, the principal at her new school tells the third grade teacher that Vanessa is a child with great intellectual potential. Do you think Vanessa's grades will be better or worse than they were previously? In other words, do you think that a teacher's (or a parent's) perception of a child's intellectual capacities could influence that child's academic achievement? Explain your answer.

Activities

1. Give an example of a test you might give children to learn whether they have acquired the concept of reversibility.

2. Think of games in which children can demonstrate their bodily-kinesthetic intelligence? How can games serve to develop interpersonal intelligence? Arrange to play these games with children and observe their actions.

3. Of your teachers in first through fourth grades, which do you remember best? Describe the characteristics of that teacher. How did that teacher influence your life?

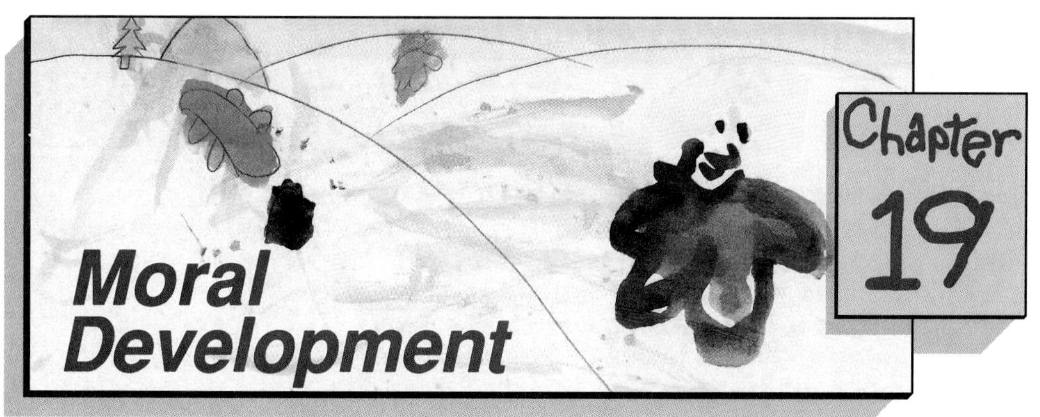

Moral Development

This chapter will help you:

- understand the relationship between morality, character, conscience, and conduct
- recognize that moral development begins at a very early age and continues to evolve throughout life
- identify the developmental stages in Piaget's theory of moral judgment
- identify the five stages of character development described by Peck
- identify the three levels and six stages described in Kohlberg's theory of moral growth
- understand how self-esteem helps children to behave in accord with their consciences

Developing Character

"Shannon, how did this mud get all over the floor?" "I don't know. I guess Skipper did it!"

It is not uncommon for children, and even some adults, to lie or blame others to avoid punishment, ridicule, or social disapproval. Shannon may not feel bad blaming the dog for her actions. On the other hand, she could feel very guilty. It depends on her moral development. **Moral development** may be defined as the growth of actions and decisions based on one's sense of right and wrong. People's **conscience** is a sort of self-censoring device that guides their behavior. **Character** is another term that refers to a person's sense of morality. In broader terms, it may be defined as moral excellence.

Although moral or character development begins long before **middle childhood** (ages six to 10) that period is especially important. Children in that age group readily adopt the values

A Matter of Fact

You have read that the average 14-year-old will have seen 11,000 TV murders, but TV in and of itself is not bad. It is simply that the tube becomes a babysitter far too often in many families. There are some terrific programs available if you know where to look. Parents and caregivers can learn to use television wisely by following these guidelines:

- Look through the television guide at the beginning of the week. Sit down with children and list the programs you want to watch. Limit the number of each child's selections.
- Make a date with the family to watch a special show together. Write it on your calendar. Pop popcorn, or put a pizza in the oven.
- If the show is about an historical event, tie it into the child's schoolwork. Do a little impromptu research on the event and share your findings with family members.
- Limit the amount of time family members spend watching TV.
- Don't let children do homework in front of the TV.
- Set priorities: homework and household chores first, TV last. If tasks aren't finished, TV privileges are taken away.
- If the child is given an assignment to watch a particular television special for a class, a parent or caregiver might let the child have a few classmates over that night as well. Parents and caregivers may be able to generate a group discussion.
- Discuss what you have seen on TV. Ask children questions. This is a good way to share feelings and transmit values between parents and children.

and attitudes of those they respect. The respected role models may be adults, or they may be peers. There is no particular age at which a child is "morally mature." In other words, there is no specific time at which children should be expected to begin exhibiting moral behavior. The approach to moral maturity is evolutionary.

Influences on Character

How does character develop? How does it all start? Early and endless training in character development is essential. Beginning very early in life, children need consistent, understandable experiences that will help them make upright and morally correct decisions. Comments by parents, teachers, grandparents, older siblings, religious leaders, and peers provide children with standards of right and wrong. Often the person's tone of voice and facial expression, as much as the words themselves, help children understand if a particular action or decision is considered "good" or "bad."

Character can be taught best by the family through example. Children may behave in a certain way in order to maintain the approval of a loving adult. Conscience begins to develop, according to researchers, in a home atmosphere when young children are reasonably emotionally dependent on their parents, when they feel accepted, and when they feel secure in their love. For moral development, it is important that this atmosphere of affection and mutual trust among family members be maintained as children grow older. In addition, children need to have explained to them the reasons the family considers certain behaviors proper and others improper. In such a home environment, children tend to adopt their parents' values and standards of behavior and make them their own.

Character development is enhanced by the simultaneous development of a positive self-concept. Parents can help their children feel good about themselves by:

- openly demonstrating that they value their children.
- placing trust in their children, and thereby encouraging trustworthiness.
- giving recognition for effort, as well as for achievement.
- recognizing and encouraging each child's interests and strengths.

Children learn more from what we do than from what we say. Telling children what's right is wasted, unless it is supported by example. For instance, a parent who fakes an illness in order to take a day off from work has little chance of successfully teaching children the value of honesty.

Children whose behavior is based on their consistent choice of right over wrong should feel good about themselves. By being supportive, parents help children develop a positive self-concept and reinforce their moral behavior. For this to occur, there must be an atmosphere of warmth in the relationship. A warm parent:

- listens to the child.
- spends time with the child in situations other than disciplinary ones, such as sharing mutual interests.
- gives more praise than criticism.

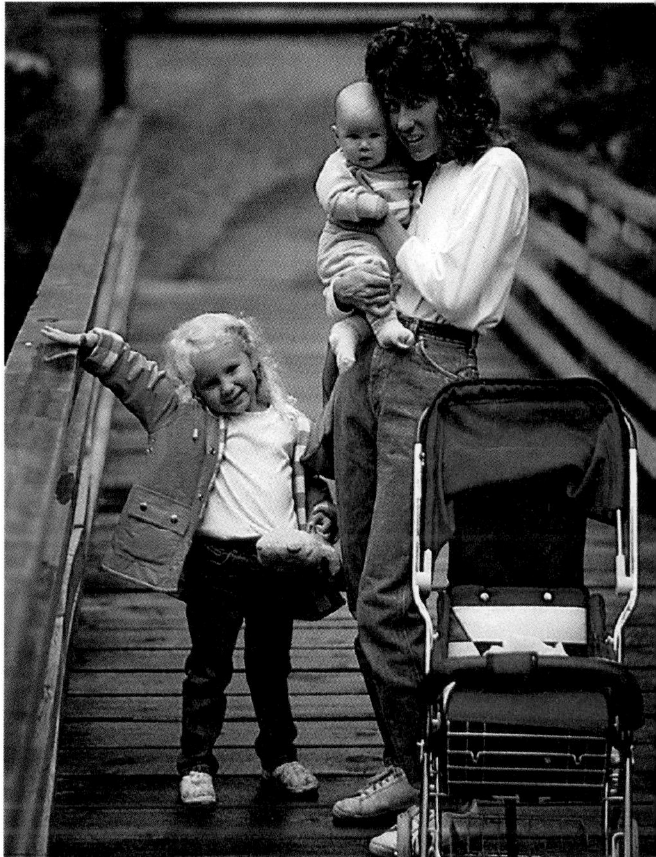

Warm, loving parents help their children develop a positive self-concept and learn appropriate moral behavior.

- is willing to give reasons and the principles basic to desirable behavior.

On the other hand, the cold parent:

- rejects, ignores, or punishes.
- fails to praise for progress.
- fails to give reasons why certain behavior is desirable or undesirable, but punishes when a child misbehaves.

A Closer Look

Kim, a nine-year-old, was the daughter of extremely permissive parents. She seemed to have no rules regarding her daily activities. Her family had very little routine. Even meals were taken at odd times, and it was rare for any two members of the family to eat together.

As long as her parents did not hear that Kim was in trouble, they assumed that everything was OK. Once, however, when neighbors complained about Kim's vandalism, her parents punished her severely. Their actions and words seemed to be revenge for ruining the family reputation. She could not understand the inconsistency of the laxity and the severity with which she was being treated. She resented the punishment.

Several months later, Kim was playing with matches in her upstairs bedroom while her parents watched television in the basement family room. She panicked when the curtain caught fire. Her first thought was to avoid punishment, so she closed the door to her room. Rather than calling for help, she tried to put out the flames herself. It was more than two minutes before the smoke alarm in the hall sounded, bringing Kim's parents to help. Fortunately, Kim suffered only first-degree burns to her hands, and the fire damage was limited to the window area. But the seriousness of Kim's misadventure and her attempt to cover it up to avoid punishment led her parents to seek family counseling. All of them are much happier since they have recognized the need for closer guidance and greater consistency.

Because young children are so dependent and trusting, it is extremely important that parents live up to that trust. Children need the guidance and safety of rules, and they need the security of consistency in rule enforcement that parents can provide.

Arbitrary rules are more difficult to enforce than reasonable rules. Parents must be thoughtful in devising rules so that the rules accomplish the goals of safety and guidance. They must also remain flexible enough to recognize the need to alter rules as children grow toward maturity in their moral judgment.

Children, at any age, learn by reward or punishment, but the accent should always be on reward. Positive parental reaction to positive behavior leads to positive self-image. When punishment is required, it should fit the wrong and never be administered in anger. Severe and abusive punishments are counterproductive in guiding children toward moral judgment. Ultimately, extreme punishment is likely to cause children to mistrust the rulemaker, the rule enforcer, and the rules themselves.

It is impossible to set forth hard and fast formulas to guide parents in their treatment of children at each stage of their moral development. A child's moral growth is unique to the individual, just as the relationship is unique to each parent-child pair.

Conscience

If we define conscience as the intellect directed toward moral behavior, then children develop moral judgment as they develop conscience. The first stage in the growth of conscience is the development of a normal emotional dependence of children on parents. Learning to accept and internalize rules—developing a conscience—is dependent upon children's ability to trust parents. During the preschool years, the conscience is fragile and delicate. At this time children waver between assuming responsibility for their behavior and letting adults decide whether their behavior is right or wrong.

During these early years it is especially important for parents not to overstress right and wrong, good and bad. Young children are freely expressing their natural impulses and desires at this time and they should not be overly suppressed. They should never be made to feel that they are "bad" people, even when their behavior is not acceptable to the parents.

Young children need to be able to openly express themselves.

A Closer Look

Andy was being raised by his grandmother. Whenever he broke one of "Granny's" rules, she told him he was a bad boy. On the other hand, she said nothing when he complied with her rules, because she simply expected his obedience. Unsatisfactory behavior gained attention for Andy, both at home and at school. The attention was reinforcing his "bad boy" image. Andy was caught up in a vicious circle. He had assumed that his respected grandmother must be correct in stating that he was a bad boy. Without being aware of his reasons, he was trying to maintain that image in order to be true to himself and to his grandmother's evaluation. Fortunately, Andy's third grade teacher, Mr.

Patterson, recognized Andy's problem in time to help him. He met with Granny, and they agreed to shower Andy with praise for any progress he made toward more positive behavior. Six weeks later, they met again when Andy played the part of Chief Massasoit in the Thanksgiving program. They congratulated Andy (and each other) on his fine performance.

When punishment is the consequence of unacceptable behavior, children can become so anxious and fearful of doing something wrong that they hesitate to do anything at all unless specifically told to do so. The people who develop a morally mature approach to conflict situations are guided by their conscience. They have been conditioned to feel guilty if their behavior is opposite to the dictates of their conscience. At the age of around four or five years, children develop guilt feelings when they do what they know they should not do. It is another step toward character development.

Child-Rearing Practices and High Conscience

Parents who are good models of moral behavior and who discipline their children with acceptance, love, patience, reasoning, and understanding have the greatest success in rearing children of strong conscience and self-discipline. Such parents set limits and standards yet allow their children to achieve a normal degree of independence. The parents' flexibility, however, does not mean permissiveness.

Some people have been reared in such a way that they are unsure of their own value systems. Parents who lack convictions of their own also lack confidence in themselves and their decisions. Children, even very young ones, sense this uncertainty, confusion, and inconsistency. This makes it difficult for the child to establish standards of right and wrong and to develop a conscience.

A Closer Look

Carla had difficulty making a decision because she didn't trust her judgment. One day she overheard her son Jamie telling a neighbor that he won first place in the school spelling contest. It was a lie. Carla called Jamie inside and scolded him for lying. Then she made Jamie go back outside and tell the neighbor it was a lie. Jamie cried for hours after that and Carla felt she had been too strict. Maybe Jamie was just trying to impress someone. A week later Carla heard Jamie tell Sheila, another child in the neighborhood, that he was going to camp that summer. It wasn't true. Jamie was going to visit his grandparents. Carla felt sorry, though, because she knew Jamie wanted to go to camp with his friends. Carla called Jamie inside. He was afraid she was going to yell at him for lying and make him tell Sheila the truth. But Carla only said, "You probably wish you were going to camp, but you know you're not, don't you?" Jamie nodded slowly. Carla left it at that. Now Jamie was confused. Last time his mother made him admit his lie. This time he got sympathy. Did that mean it was OK to lie when someone felt sorry for you? Jamie wasn't sure about how "bad" lying was.

On the other hand, if parental training is too strict, it may have either of two negative consequences:

1. The children may develop consciences that are so rigid they are unhappy because of constant feelings of anxiety and guilt.
2. The children may reject the parents' value systems.

A conscience can be rigid or too weak. A child with too severe a conscience develops values and ideals that are impossible to attain. If the conscience is too weak, the person will behave immorally. If there is no conscience at all, the person is said to be **amoral.**

Development of Morality and Character

Numerous psychologists have studied the development of morality and character. Three of the most widely accepted theories coming from this work have been proposed by Professors Jean Piaget, Robert F. Peck, and Lawrence Kohlberg. Despite the difference in terminology used by these three researchers, you will be able to detect many similarities in their descriptions of the steps and stages in the development of moral judgment and character.

Piaget's Steps in the Development of Moral Judgment

Initially, children do not obey rules because they are unable to recognize rules. According to the Swiss psychologist Jean Piaget, the child's moral judgment develops from this first stage in the following steps:

1. recognition of rules as absolute and morally correct, as given by an authority figure.
2. recognition of the arbitrary nature of rules. (Arbitrary means not based on reason.)
3. recognition of the changeability of rules.

Recognition of Rules

The development of moral judgment does not begin at one particular age for all children. Most children, however, have recognized some of the family rules of right and wrong by the age of three and have begun to conform to some degree. By the age of four or five, they are able to abide by rules, at least much of the time, even when their parents are not present.

When children have internalized their parents' rules and regulations so that they can control their own behavior, life really becomes easier for them. They do not have to wonder or worry about what their parents will do if they behave this way or that way.

Children learn how to control their own behavior by internalizing their parents' rules.

The Arbitrary Nature of Rules

As previously stated, between the ages of three and six years, children are absorbing and internalizing some of society's code of behavior. Certain concepts become part of their characters. When children first begin to recognize rules that govern behavior, they insist on following them strictly. In the second step of developing moral judgment, however, children learn that rules are not ends in themselves. At this stage, children have imagination and initiative, and are eager to explore and try out new activities. They begin to realize that some rules seem arbitrary. For example, suppose that Tyrone asks his mother, "Why can't I ever go to Willie's house after dinner?" If the reply is, "Because I said so," Tyrone probably is justified in assuming that the rule is arbitrary. Children often respond to arbitrary rules by pushing beyond the limits set by parents. Disobeying can cause children feelings of guilt. Children are less apt to disobey if they understand the reason for the rule.

In this stage, children can make many decisions for themselves, with their conscience as their guide. This is a significant step toward maturity, because eventually children must learn to guide their own actions and control their undesirable impulses.

Sometimes children disobey their parents' rules. They may be testing the limits of the rules or testing their independence.

The Changeability of Rules

In Piaget's third step, children recognize that rules may be changed. From the age of six, morality based on adult demands is firmly fixed. During middle childhood, the conscience grows at its most rapid rate. Usually children make great gains in self-control during these years. They adopt the ways of the adult society as ideals that seem to be right and best for their own personal code of behavior.

In addition, however, they recognize that rules governing their behavior at younger ages can and should be altered or dropped altogether. For example, suppose that Janet demonstrates she is a good manager of time by consistently doing her household chores and completing her homework. Probably her parents can relax the rule that limits her phone conversations to five minutes. She can be trusted to use her own judgment regarding the length of a particular conversation.

Unfortunately, some children in middle childhood experience feelings of guilt and anxiety because they cannot be as good as their conscience would like them to be. They blame and criticize themselves even when others do not disapprove. Thus, their sense of conscience is sometimes excessive. They are more severe than most adults. They want things to be either all right

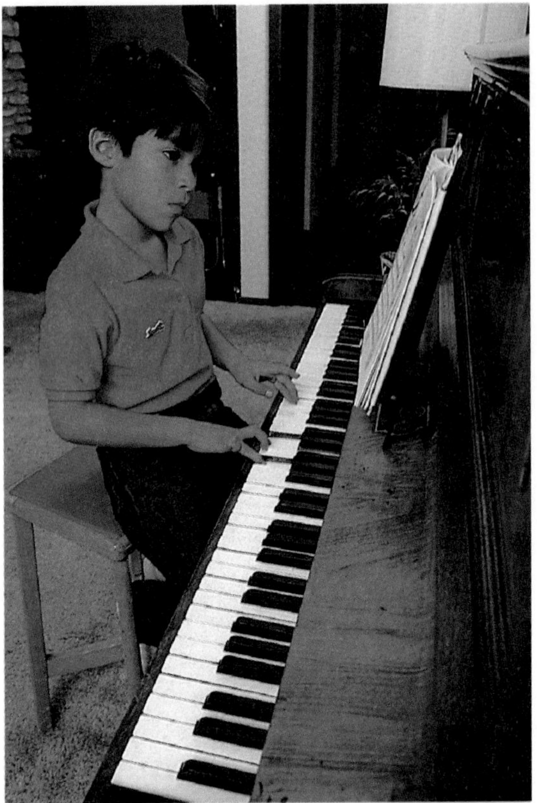

Children reach a stage in development when they are self-directed.

or all wrong. They tend to see things one way or the other. They rarely have a compromising view. They do not realize that we must make most judgments on flexible standards. Their feelings of guilt may compel them to manufacture excuses or other justifications for their behavior when it fails to meet their own inflexible standards. These children need their parents' help to guide them away from the rigidity of this early stage of development toward the more independent and responsible behavior typical of Piaget's third step toward moral maturity.

By the age of nine or 10 most children begin to be less dependent on adults for their values and ideas. They begin to look toward their peers for values. Social awareness increases by the age of 11 or 12. However, failure to learn the lessons of one period may impede growth by making it difficult or even impossible to learn these tasks at a later period. For instance, children who do not learn to distinguish right from wrong during the time when the conscience is forming may have great difficulty in doing so later.

True morality is present only when a person's behavior is guided by conscience. By the time children approach adolescence, internalized conscience, rather than environmental restrictions, should assume much of the control over their behavior.

Qualities of Moral Judgments as Described by Piaget

According to Piaget, the changes that mark the development from less mature to more mature moral judgment are as follows:

- A shift from morals based on specific rules to more general conceptions of what is right and wrong.
- A shift from a "morality of constraint" to a "morality of cooperation."
- A shift from belief in "imminent justice." That is the view that punishment for a wrongdoing flows automatically from the action, without the intervention of

a punishing person. For example, if a little girl stumbles and hurts herself after grabbing another child's hat, she might think she was hurt because she stole the hat.

- A shift from moral conduct based on external demands toward a moral code based on internal standards the child has adopted.
- An increased ability to perceive that rules of a game are not arbitrary, but instead are based on mutual respect and consent.
- An increased ability and willingness, in judging the acts of others, to take into account the circumstances in which these acts occur and the underlying motives, instead of judging them according to inflexible standards. For example, young children may voice the opinion that to steal is to steal and all stealing is bad. When they are older, they will view the theft of bread by a hungry person as a less serious offense than the theft of an apple by a well-fed person.

Along with changes in children's moral judgment, there are changes in their views regarding justice and punishment. At first, justice requires punishment and suffering for any person who has committed a wrong. This is the justice of **atonement.** This type of justice demands that if another child breaks your toy, you or an adult in authority should break that other child's toy. At a later stage, justice rests on the idea of **restitution.** In this case, the wrongdoer makes up for the loss by giving the victim a toy, or supplying the money for repairing the broken toy.

Peck's Five Stages of Character Development

Five stages of character development were identified by Professor Robert F. Peck and his colleagues. The following outlines these stages.

Amoral Stage

Amoral is an adjective that means without a sense of moral responsibility. Infants want what they want when they want it. They are not concerned that it is 2:00 a.m. and that their parents are tired. They are hungry and they want to eat, so they cry until they are fed. Infants cannot be reasoned with. The parents can't say, "Wait until 6:00 a.m. We'll feed you your favorite food then." Infants must have their basic needs fulfilled immediately. They react on impulse according to physical or psychological needs. We expect amoral behavior from infants.

Expedient Stage

The word **expedient** means that which is immediately advantageous without regard for ethics. The expedient character type develops in early childhood. Children find that their needs are better satisfied if they learn to interact with others.

A Closer Look

Sam, a toddler, tries to take a toy airplane from another toddler. The child refuses and a tug-of-war begins. Sam learns that when another toy is offered in trade, the other child gives up the plane.

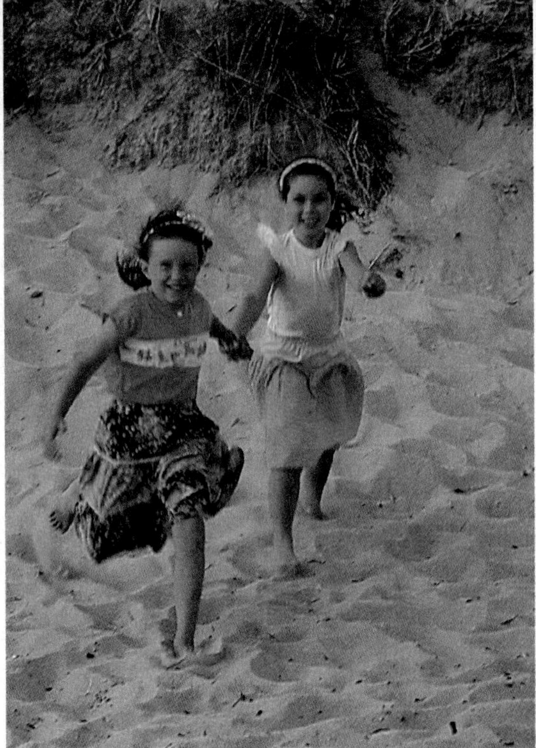

One sign of children wanting to conform to their peers is that they dress and act alike.

Parents of very young children often use this stage of development to advantage. For example, when Sue insists upon trying to touch an expensive vase, her parents may distract her by offering a suitable toy. Sue leaves the vase alone, attracted by the toy. This resolves the problem for the moment.

Conforming Stage

The conforming stage develops in later childhood when the child wants to be like everyone else. Visit a fifth grade classroom and notice the dress of the students. If it is a school where boys wear blue jeans and plaid shirts, all boys wear this outfit as if it were a uniform. Youngsters in this age group need the security of the conforming activity with their peers. They are beginning to be independent and are able to go to club meetings, baseball practice, cheerleading practice, and other events alone, without their parents. However, to take this new step toward independence from their family, they need the security of the group.

At this stage of development, the environment or the neighborhood in which children live is very influential. Children will imitate other children. They probably will use the same speech, dress, values, and habit patterns of their peer group. They thrive on conformity. Their desire for conformity includes wanting to behave the way their peers do. In this group, there seems to be an unwritten behavior code that is generally accepted. Adults often object to this stage, particularly if they feel their child is conforming to standards with which they don't agree.

Irrational-Conscientious Stage

From the conforming period, the character grows into the irrational-conscientious stage. In this stage of development, conformity to the group code is not the issue. Rather, it is conformity to a code the individual child believes in. For example, children who have been brought up to attend church may make this idea a personal belief. They may believe that all people who attend church are good and that those who do not attend church are bad. Thus they judge whole groups of people on one act that they have evaluated according to their standard of right or wrong.

The "irrational" part of this stage is apparent in the individual's rigidity. An act is "good" or "bad" depending on whether it is acceptable within the person's own rigid code of conduct,

When children know they should stand in line to wait their turn, what stage of character development have they reached?

rather than whether the act has positive or negative effects on others.

Rational-Altruistic Stage

The final stage, rational-altruistic, describes the highest level of moral maturity. People of this type think of assuring the welfare of others as well as assuring their own. Rational-altruistic people have a reasonable regard for others.

A Closer Look

Juan, a high-school student, is attending a basketball tournament. Juan really wants his high-school team to win the championship because then his school will be number one in the district. However, although he loudly cheers for the team, he does not boo the referees when they make a call against his team. Rational-altruistic persons react with emotion appropriate to the occasion. This does not mean they are unemotional. They may exhibit great excitement for activities that are going to have positive influences on the lives of others, or they may have angry "knee-jerk" reactions to injustices.

Juan is as pleasant and respectful to the custodian of the school building as he is to his friends and teachers. He tries to be honest and kind to all and to respect everyone. He respects other people's capacities and efforts to achieve, just as he does his own. He doesn't put other people into categories that he judges one way or another. Instead, he tries to treat others according to their individual merits. His interactions with other people are strongly influenced by the abstract concept of the "Golden Rule."

Juan is not hypocritical. He behaves as he says he believes. He sees himself as he really is. He does what his conscience tells him is morally right, even if his peers are doing otherwise. On the rare occasions when he behaves counter to his conscience, he feels guilty, and he changes his behavior accordingly. His sense of guilt is not irrational. In other words, when he feels guilt, he does not commit irrational acts to punish himself.

Juan has the maturity to be responsible for his own behavior. If he makes a mistake, whether important or not, he can accept responsibility for the consequences without trying to blame others. With continued growth of character, Juan will be a man who accepts community responsibilities. He will be able to give of his own time, energy, skills, and financial assets to benefit his fellow human beings.

A Summary of Peck's Five Stages

In Professor Peck's theory of character development, the stages can be summarized as follows:

- Amoral individuals disregard the effects of their acts on others. They are egocentric and strive for personal gratification only.
- Expedient individuals' behavior is more controlled. They are considerate of others, but only when it is a means to accomplish their own goals or when it is not too much trouble.
- Conforming individuals learn a role and are able to make choices acceptable in their group. Their behavior is entirely motivated by social approval. For them a choice between their judgment and the group's desire is generally controlled by the group.
- Irrational-conscientious individuals act on an emotional basis rather than a rational nature. They are dependent on rules and find self-respect in following a code endorsed by authority.
- Rational-altruistic individuals understand standards and are able to make decisions about what is important in a situation. They are concerned about the welfare of others. They are able to consider others because they also have a very deep self-acceptance.

Ideally, character development is an ongoing process, even for a person who has achieved the rational-altruistic stage. Children should progress through all five stages from infancy to the latter stages of adolescence. Unfortunately, some people's character development stops and remains at one stage or another for the rest of their lives. We may even know adolescents or adults who act according to the amoral stage of development.

Kohlberg's Stages of Moral Growth

Dr. Lawrence Kohlberg, a Harvard psychologist, is probably the most influential researcher in modern moral psychology. Because our concepts of character and morality are so closely linked, it is not surprising that Kohlberg's theories on moral growth bear a striking resemblance to the theory of character development just discussed. Dr. Kohlberg has proposed that moral growth is evolutionary and occurs at three levels called preconventional, conventional, and postconventional. Each level has two stages for a total of six stages.

Preconventional Level

The first stage of the preconventional level is one of obedience and punishment. A child is right when obeying, and wrong when disobeying. Disobedience brings punishment. For example, suppose that Jenny blows bubbles in her milk glass at dinner. Her parents ask her to please stop because she is making a mess. When Jenny tries it again, her father tells her that she will have to remain at the table for two minutes after the other children have left the table. Jenny learns that appropriate punishment is an immediate consequence of disobedience.

Some schools have children take time out to think about their misbehavior. Do you agree with this method?

The second stage is one of reciprocity. "I'll do something nice for you if you'll do something that I want you to do." Children cooperate because of rewards for their cooperation. "The sooner you pick up your toys, the more time we'll have to play in the park." Actions are right if they bring about satisfaction of one's needs.

Conventional Level

Stages three and four are in the conventional level of moral development. Stage three is one of "conformity," the same word used in Peck's theory of character development. Kohlberg called it the interpersonal concordance or "good boy—nice girl" orientation. Children seek the approval of their parents and their peers and behave to win that approval. Conflict occurs when parents and peers have values different from each other .

A Matter of Fact

What child doesn't enjoy being read to? In many households, the story before bedtime has become a ritual. It brings closeness and warmth between a parent and child, and certainly the parent looks forward to this ritual just as much as the child!

Storytelling, however, goes beyond simply reading a book. A storyteller adds a flair for drama and becomes an instant actor, actually recreating a story as it is being told. Practice using different inflections in your voice and body movement to convey excitement, suspense, etc.

If you would like to hear a professional storyteller, ask your local librarian. Libraries often have storytelling activities. They will be able to give you additional information on the art of storytelling or tell you where you can go to get further information.

Many of the stories told by storytellers are oral histories of the different ethnic groups that have settled in North America. How and where these groups of people lived, where they worked, what their traditions were, what hardships they faced, and how they prospered are familiar storytelling plots. The storyteller plays an influential role: the history of a people is retold and passed down from generation to generation. The storyteller makes people remember.

If you have ever listened to grandparents or senior citizens tell "what it was like in the old days," you might consider recording their memories on a tape recorder or a videotape recorder. Then you and your family will have a permanent record of an important part of your family history—told in a story.

Stage four is one of law and order, and Kohlberg called it society maintaining orientation. Children reach this stage when they are convinced through their own powers of reasoning that we can have no order in society without rules and laws. At this stage, people respect the rules and those who enforce them. According to Dr. Kohlberg, most adults operate at this level of morality.

Postconventional Level

The postconventional level of moral growth is also called the autonomous level or the principled level. At this level, stage five is one of social contract. People recognize that laws should guarantee rights as well as control behavior. They also can realize that right and wrong are often not clearly distinguished. Many decisions must be made "between shades of gray." At this stage, people can see the need for interpretation of rules and laws.

Those persons who attain stage six have developed a personal philosophy of life based on abstract principles of morality that they have chosen to adopt through a process of reasoning. This philosophy is comprehensive and consistent. In other words, it applies to all people and all aspects of the person's life without exception. For this reason, the stage can be called one of universal ethical principles. Persons in stage six value their philosophies so highly that they would lay down their lives to defend the principles they believe in—justice, human equality, human dignity, etc.

The Role of Families

Character development and moral growth are significantly influenced by the family atmosphere. An atmosphere with mutual trust and consistency promotes children's morality. The ultimate levels and stages of moral growth and character development will depend strongly on the parents' ability to communicate each of the increasingly more complex concepts. Parents need to communicate both by word and example. First, children must have reached readiness to understand. By having warm, open relationships with their children, parents will be able to sense each of the stages of development. Thus, they can be prepared to help their children continue to grow to the next stage.

Parents should not expect moral behavior that is beyond the comprehension of the individual child. For example, a child who happens to be in Kohlberg's stage two (reciprocity) of moral development will understand that picking up toys before naptime is "right" behavior if parents say, "If you will help me pick up your toys, I'll read you a story from your favorite book." On the other hand, a parent who was unaware of the stages of moral growth might say, "When Mickey and Sandy were your age, they picked up their toys. I expect you to do the same." Such a statement would have little effect on a child who is in stage two, because it appeals to stage three morality (conformity).

An open relationship between parent and child contributes to moral growth.

The degree of children's moral development depends on how far their parents have progressed. Parents will have trouble helping children develop beyond the stage the parents have reached. For example, parents who make the rules arbitrarily and continually enforce them by extreme punishment for disobedience might very well cause their children's development to stop at the amoral stage. As another example, adolescents raised according to rigid codes of behavior with unquestioned respect for authority might have difficulty in seeing the "gray" areas of a problem. Sensing that there are shaded areas between "right" and "wrong" could put young people in conflict with parents who believe in strictly following the rules.

Discrepancies Between Moral Concepts and Behavior

There are many gaps between a person's moral code and behavior. To follow through on beliefs requires firm conviction. This is a deeper level of conscience than can be expected of a child. Knowledge that it is wrong to cheat does not always keep children from cheating. Similarly, children who say it is wrong to fight with their classmates do not always refrain from fighting. Many times children act first and think about the results later. Most children are sometimes honest, sometimes not, sometimes helpful, sometimes not. They may not always live up to their own standards. If they do not, they may feel guilty. If caught, they may feel ashamed.

There are several reasons for differences between moral knowledge and moral behavior in childhood. Frequently children are confused about the meaning of the rules they are expected to follow. Sometimes they are confused when they have to apply a concept to a different situation. For instance, they may know that it is wrong to steal from a person, but may be confused about whether taking something from a public place falls into this category. Confusion also may arise when children see a difference between what their parents say and what they do. If it is all right for parents to preach one thing and practice another, children feel that it is all right for them to do the same. For example, Tim's parents have told him to treat everyone equally. Then a family of a different ethnic background buys a house in their neighborhood and Tim's parents get angry. Now Tim's confused. Is it OK to discriminate or isn't it?

Differences between moral code and behavior are especially likely to occur when the moral concepts of the parents differ from those of children's peers. When children must choose between what their parents think is right and what their friends think is right, they will be influenced by what is more important to them personally. If, for example, the peer group and the parents value honesty, the children will be honest. However, suppose the peer group approves of cheating because the group feels that it shows loyalty to a friend in distress. That value is more likely to be accepted as "right" by children who are more concerned with winning peer approval than parental approval.

Frequently, confusion occurs because moral concepts conflict with one another. Truthfulness may conflict with loyalty to friends or with ideals of courtesy. Ling Mei asks Paul how he likes her new dress. Paul thinks the dress does not look good on her but he doesn't want to hurt her feelings because he values being kind. He has to make a choice and decides to lie, "You look great," to spare her feelings.

Discrepancies between moral knowledge and moral behavior also

In school, children learn how to compete to be the winner yet be good sports, too.

may be due to emotional factors. For example, children may do something they know is wrong to get even with the person who has angered them. If children feel that their mother has blamed them for an incident for which she should have taken some of the blame, they may become angry and do things they know they should not do. Sometimes children intentionally misbehave.

A Closer Look

Danny has complained to his parents that his classmates call him Dumbo. He asks his parents to talk to his teacher, Ann Walker, about the problem, but they tell him, "Don't be such a baby." Despite his persistence over a period of two weeks, they refuse to contact Ms. Walker. Danny begins a campaign of classroom disruptions. His misbehavior succeeds where his requests had failed. His parents meet with Ms. Walker after she sends them a note stating, "We must discuss your son's negative attitude toward all classroom activities. Please help me to find out what is happening in Danny's life that has caused this remarkable change in his behavior."

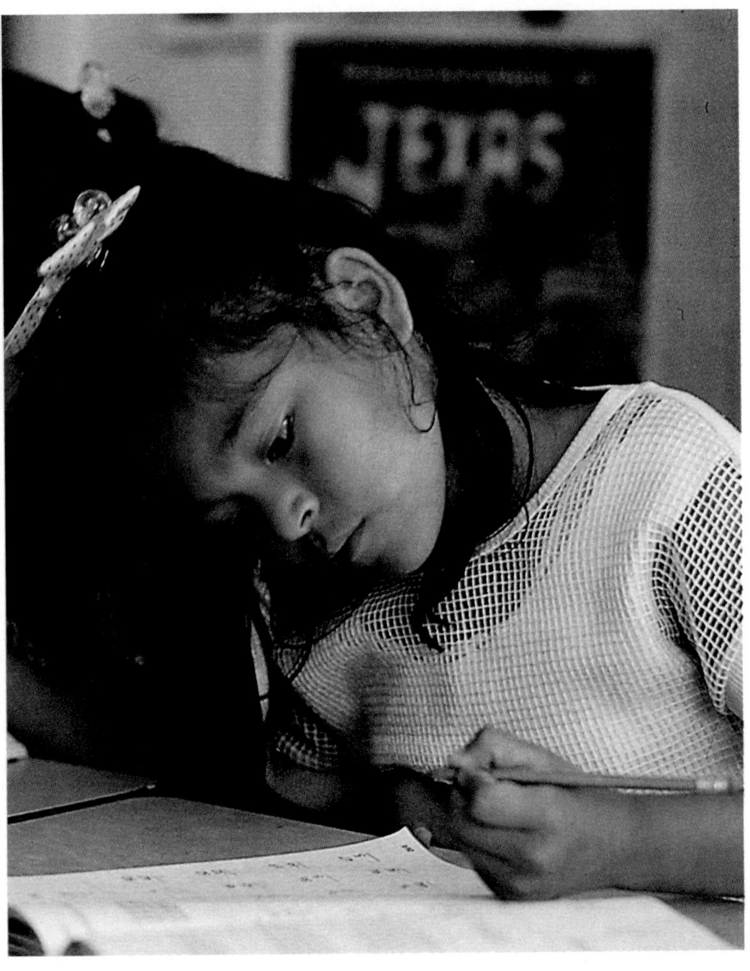

Sometimes children are so pressured to receive good grades they may feel it is necessary to cheat. What can parents do to let them know honesty is more important?

Disobedience at home or in school is often motivated by a desire for attention. Children who feel they are being ignored find that the satisfaction of being in the limelight outweighs the temporary discomfort of being punished. Children also may intentionally disobey rules and defy authority to prove to themselves and their peers that they are grown-up and independent. Many children lie or blame others to avoid punishment, ridicule, or social disapproval. In games, children may cheat because they lack the skills needed to win fairly. In school, they may cheat because parental pressures have been used to force them to get better grades than they are capable of getting without cheating. Or they may cheat to avoid being left behind.

As was stated in Chapter 1, children need to have achievable goals. A child's parents and teachers must consult with each other if they are to have mutually realistic expectations for that child. They also must understand each other's motives and techniques for helping children through the various stages of character development. For this they must know about the steps described in this chapter. In addition, they must have warm personal relationships with the child in order to recognize the child's present level of development and present needs.

Few children fail to recognize the discrepancy between their behavior and their moral knowledge. Children who are caught cheating, for example, may try to justify their acts by claiming that everyone does it. But they still know its wrong, and they feel guilty. Children who intentionally destroy the property of others may justify their action by claiming that they are getting even for the treatment they have received. If a neighbor yells at them for playing loudly, they may throw rotten eggs or garbage at the neighbor's home. They know it's wrong, but they feel the neighbor "deserves it" or "asked for it." That feeling of getting even may not stop their guilt.

Children who have a selfish attitude feel justified in their selfish behavior, even when they know their parents disapprove. On the other hand, children who disapprove of selfishness have subtle feelings of guilt when they act selfishly.

The temporary satisfaction children get from social approval from the peer group when they defy adult authority may or may not be great enough to compensate for the feelings of guilt they experience. Claiming they were ignorant of the wrong, saying that everyone else does it, or projecting the blame to a parent, teacher, or member of the peer group are common ways of trying to relieve guilt feelings. If they can convince themselves, as well as others, that there was no difference between their moral knowledge and behavior or that the discrepancy was not their fault, they then free themselves of feelings of guilt and shame.

Positive self-concept is essential if children are to behave in accordance with their moral concepts. They must feel comfortable with their values and have the self-assurance it takes to resist peers who would have them act counter to their own consciences. It takes self-esteem as well as conscience to resist peer pressure. Parents and teachers play vital roles in helping children feel good about themselves and their character development.

In Review

Vocabulary

moral development
conscience
character
middle childhood
atonement
restitution
amoral
expedient

Summary

- ✓ Moral development is learning to conduct oneself according to conscience. People of good character strive for moral excellence. Moral development begins very early in life and continues to evolve through childhood and beyond.
- ✓ A child's development of conscience is more strongly influenced by those people the child loves and respects. Parents who are warm and supportive help children develop a positive self-concept and reinforce their moral behavior. Children can learn moral behavior best when parents provide a good example.
- ✓ Permissive or inconsistent styles of parenting make it difficult for children to establish standards of right and wrong. On the other hand, when training is too strict and rigid, children often reject the parents' value systems.
- ✓ According to Piaget, there are three steps in the development of moral judgment in children. Peck described five stages of character development. Kohlberg considered moral growth as something that evolves over the entire life span.
- ✓ The effectiveness of a parent in helping children to progress to the higher levels of morality depends on the parent's ability to communicate the increasingly more complex concepts, both by word and example.
- ✓ Firm conviction is required if a person is always to behave according to his/her adopted principles. Conflicts arise for a child when parental and peer values are at odds, or when courtesy seems to rule out honesty, or when the child desires revenge for a perceived injustice.

Questions

1. What evidence can you give to support the statement, there is no age of moral discretion?

2. What kinds of parents create a strong conscience in children?

3. Give some personal evidence to support the statement, "Children learn more from what we do than from what we say."

4. Why is a rigid conscience a problem?

5. Give examples of Piaget's stages of moral development.

6. Discuss the similarities between Peck's five stages of character development and Kohlberg's six stages of moral development.

7. Which of Kohlberg's stages of moral development seems most similar to Piaget's most mature level of moral judgment?

Activities

1. Interview five children between the ages of six and 10. How do they view honesty?

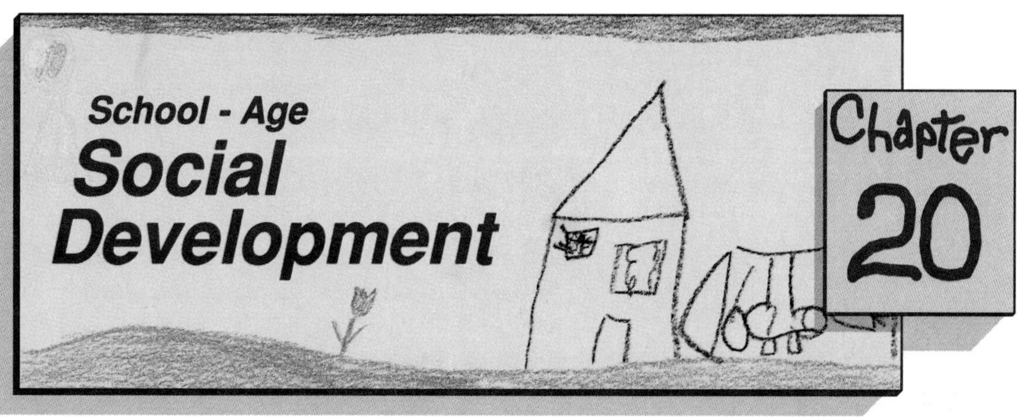

School-Age Social Development

Chapter 20

This chapter will help you:

- recognize that all school-age children require reassurance to counteract self-doubt as they undertake each new stage of social development
- understand how children make sex-role identification
- appreciate the importance of children identifying with traits of both parents
- learn the ways that families influence the social development of school-age children
- understand the influences of the peer group and significant others on the social development of children

The Effects of School

As children begin their school years, they must develop new relationships with teachers and classmates. Children in the primary grades are reaching out to find a place among their peers and elders. As they venture out among their peers, they learn more about how people work and play together. They learn how to share and how to be polite. They see that people, families, and animals vary in many ways and they begin to develop attitudes about these differences. They are concerned about their acceptance by teachers who are authority figures and by classmates who are potential friends. They are undergoing rapid changes in their physical appearance, and they wonder how these changes will affect their relationships. They wonder if other people think that their ears are too big or that they look silly without the baby teeth that have not yet been replaced. They wonder if their parents will accept a report card. Can their parents love them for the unique individuals that they are, or must they live up to their parents' notions of their potential? All children wonder who they are and who they want to be. They think about what types of behavior will gain them the social status they want and who they should use as patterns for their own lives.

Children in the upper elementary grades are strongly attached to friends of the same age. They may have a best friend and be strongly influenced by their peers. They are becoming increasingly aware of themselves and their roles as maturing individuals. They seek role models, both peer and adult, with whom they can identify and pattern themselves.

The Wish

My daughter comes to me
with her sorrow. She is
not yet ten, not yet
insistent for her father.
As if waiting out a sentence,
she sits at the round table,
her long black shawl of hair
framing high cheekbones.
She thinks she is ugly,
thinks she has no friends.

How can I comfort, what should I
try to tell this radiant
coincidence of genes?
That children can be beasts
to one another? That envy
eats us from the inside?
"All great beauties
doubted their beauty," I tell her.
But why should she believe me:
I am her mother, and asked
repeatedly for beauty,
meaning happiness.

—Ellen Bryant Voigt

Role Models and Identification

Role models are people others admire and try to imitate. **Identification** may be described as copying, modeling, or adhering to a group of which one feels a part. Human characteristics such as conscience, morality, guilt, ambition, and sex-role identity may arise through identification with one or both of the parents. For the purpose of example, three theories of sex-role identity are discussed on the pages that follow.

Social-Learning Theory

The boy who has made a male identification is one who has happily adopted maleness as his way of life. He thinks of himself as a male. He accepts his role with its advantages and disadvantages, and enjoys it. His pattern of interests, style of walking, talking, and gesturing, and his sexual behavior are male. It is assumed that the boy has learned "maleness" for various sociopersonal reasons. Ordinarily the model for his role is his father or other significant male in his life. In other words, a boy loves, respects, and in many ways, imitates the significant male in order to arrive at a male identification. However, he does not have to be just like this man to reach male identification. General modeling or patterning will have the same effect. (For a girl, the mother is the primary model for femaleness.)

The cartoon shown here is funny because surprise is one of the elements of humor. We expect boys to imitate their fathers. Thus, we are as surprised as

Hagar and Helga appear to be when their son seems reluctant to commit himself to accepting his father as a role model. Regular readers of this comic strip have laughed many times, however, at Hagar's many undesirable characteristics, which include brutishness, slovenliness, sexism, callousness, egoism, and an inclination to loot. Obviously, the boy is aware of his father's shortcomings and has set his sights on higher standards of morality.

Sex-role identification is possible even when there is little warmth toward the parent of the same sex. Identification, however, is easier and less ambivalent when accompanied by good parent-child relations. Even those who have not made an appropriate sex-role identification may assume many of the attitudes, values, and beliefs of their parents and other significant people in their lives.

Sex-role adoption and sex-role preference precede sex-role identification. This means children gain perceptions of maleness and femaleness and develop preferences before they identify with role models. Of course, these perceptions are subject to change. Also, children do not necessarily identify only with members of their own sex.

In our culture, cross-identification is important for both boys and girls. **Cross-identification** is modeling after persons of the opposite sex. For example, a boy should do at least some modeling of traits commonly labeled feminine. Girls, too, need to incorporate some traits traditionally thought of as masculine.

In general, cross-identification affords a deeper understanding of the other sex and promotes more companionable relationships between men and women. Moreover, cross-identification is advantageous because masculine and feminine roles in our culture were never absolute and are becoming even less clearly defined.

Freudian Theory

The Freudian theory, as it describes identification, is quite different from the social-learning theory just described in which the boy identifies with his father out of love and respect. According to Freud, the very young boy first identifies with his mother. At around the age of three or four, incestuous wishes toward the mother become very strong. (One way this phenomenon is manifested is when a

A Matter of Fact

You want to take a child to the movies, but you're unsure whether or not the movie you have in mind is appropriate. How can you find out?

The movie industry sets suitability ratings for its movies, but that's not the only guide available. Many parenting magazines have a movie review section and maybe even a movie reviewer on staff who can offer reliable advice on whether or not a movie is a gem or a nightmare.

You also might contact your local children's librarian or local newspaper for movie information. Other people who have already seen the movie may be good sources of advice.

Once you've decided, here are some suggestions to make the outing an economical one:

- Go to matinees.
- See if your local movie theater has regular discount nights.
- Make your own popcorn.
- Check the library. Sometimes they have special Saturday film screenings free-of-charge.
- Museums and civic organizations sometimes have children's film programs.
- Make your own "film." Borrow a video camera and learn what happens behind the scenes when you are the director.

little boy says he is going to marry his mother.) These wishes, however, are counterbalanced by the child's fear of his father's strength and the possibility of punishment. Since this fear is great and the small boy cannot hope to overcome his father and win his mother, he copes with his father's strength by unconsciously incorporating his father's attitudes into his own personality. The phrase "if you can't beat 'em, join 'em" describes this process.

Freudian theory holds that the identification process for girls is more complex than for boys. It involves first a love for the mother, then renunciation, then love, modeling, and identification again. The girl also has incestuous wishes which are later given up, and she incorporates many of her mother's attitudes into her own personality. Fear is a less important factor for girls than for boys in this process. According to Freud, at the kindergarten to first grade level, the little girl is faced with the inevitability of her femininity. If the mother is a pleasant person, she provides the best available model of the appropriate sex role for the child.

Power Theory

A third theory of identification, the power theory, is a logical extension of the Freudian and the social-learning theories. The power theory holds that identification occurs, not solely because the father is a threat and not only

A sports figure may become a role model for children.

because he is a loving model, but because he is both an effective rewarder and an effective punisher. In other words, a son identifies with him and models him because he is powerful. Children identify with strength, and parental strength is a combination of reward and punishment. A relationship in which there is more reward than punishment may be very helpful to identification.

Forces in Identification

With the high divorce rate, faulty child-rearing practices, and poor marriages as common as they are in our culture, how do so many children achieve adequate sex-typing and identification? There are at least four factors that promote identification in the absence of adequate parental figures:

1. **There are parent-surrogates.** A good kindergarten, elementary, or junior high teacher can go a long way toward providing a favorable female model for the girl whose mother is weak, vicious, or absent. The average boy, on the other hand, may not encounter a male teacher until he is in junior high school. However, other relatives, friends, and neighbors all can, and do, help provide models for the child of either sex who does not have a parental model. The Big Brother/Big Sister program offers many children a satisfying relationship with an adult.

Scouting may have resulted in part from the need for a male model for identification. The hero worship that children place on an athletic coach also

A Matter of Fact

Planning a Saturday at the zoo with a young one? Want something different to do? Here are some ideas:

- Take a ride on an elephant.
- Go to the bird show.
- Count the monkeys.
- Go to the children's zoo with your zoomate. Be patient. You may be there a long time!
- Buy a stroller-bound child a balloon and tie it on the stroller.
- Check into an adopt-an-animal program, if your zoo has one.
- Stop and have a picnic.
- Practice animal sounds.
- Find out how to become a zoo volunteer.
- Bring your favorite stuffed animal along for the trip.
- Look for information on wildlife conservation efforts.
- "Lions and tigers and bears! Oh, my!" Think of all the famous jungle beasts you know. (To get you started, Smokey the Bear, Yogi Bear.)
- Give names to your favorite animals.
- Ask a young child to name his or her favorite animal. Ask why.
- Get a map of the zoo and visit the animals in alphabetical order.
- Wear a pith helmet and a tropical shirt. Pretend you're on a safari.

may originate in this need. Traditionally, girls have had an advantage over boys in the development of identification because mothers usually were more available to them than fathers were to boys. Today, with both parents in many families working outside the home, the times children spend with mothers and with fathers may be more nearly equal. On the other hand, young sons of single mothers may be especially dependent on uncles, grandfathers, neighbors, and others as role models for sex-role identification.

2. **Passing on favorable attitudes toward an absent or deceased spouse promotes identification.** There is evidence to indicate that it is helpful for parents to pass on favorable attitudes about their absent spouses to their children. Those children's concept of and identification with an ideal father or mother is better than that of children whose parents pass on unfavorable attitudes about the absent father or mother.

3. **A general force in the culture is another factor.** Boys are rewarded for acting like boys and punished for acting like girls. A comparable process holds true for girls. Teachers, the peer group, and the community, all exert pressure for the boy to achieve masculinity and the girl, femininity. These pressures, although not necessarily completely effective, are quite powerful. However, in today's society these traits and roles overlap and some cross-identification is important.

4. **Finally, there is the factor of selective memory.** This is the process whereby we remember the good and forget the bad. Children, even when their parents have neglected, rejected,

Children learn customs from their family. These Hispanic children are celebrating Cinco de Mayo.

and punished them, tend to forget the bad times and remember the good ones. The children then create for themselves a model for identification, however flawed the original may have been. Of course, children also may unconsciously follow the inadequate pattern set by their parents because they are most familiar with it.

The Family's Role in Social Development

Of all the relationships affecting the child's development, the family is the most important force. Emotional attachments in the family are crucial in the development of all relationships in life. In this setting, children first begin to understand how human beings relate to each other. We must be aware that children, as they first observe human relationships in the home, do not have any basis for comparison. They believe that all people relate to each other in the same way. Home should be the place where children can feel unqualified acceptance. When members of their family are always after them to improve or to change, their feelings of security are affected. Their relationships throughout life will be influenced by their first interactions within the family.

Families are characterized by social status, ethnic background, religion, education, and occupations of the parents, and other factors. Together, these characteristics dictate certain rituals, customs, habits, and attitudes. While children may eventually choose which attitudes they will accept and adopt for themselves, they are originally influenced by their early exposure at home.

Unfortunately, other members of the community often have expectations of children based upon their background. Children soon realize that, in a sense, the success or failures of other members of their family influence their own development and behavior.

The decisions families make for their children also are very influential in their development. They live in a certain part of town or country. They go with the family on vacation. Certain people are invited to the house. Frequently, even the choice of television programs is supervised by parents. In this manner, families interpret the community for their children and set standards for evaluating various people, institutions, and programs. Experiences that children have within the family develop in them a sense of acceptance or rejection. If either parent rejects a child, the child is likely to be aggressive, attention-getting, hostile, hyperactive, jealous, or rebellious. On the other hand, too much attention can hinder healthy development if it prevents a child from assuming responsibility. Such parents sometimes choose children's friends or hinder them from making social contacts outside of the family. Parents also can hinder social development in subtle ways. A parent may dominate a child by demanding excessive obedience.

The size of the family also has an effect on socialization opportunities for each child. In the small family, each person's influence on the child's development becomes more significant. In a larger family, there are more people interacting.

Parents serve children and society best when they provide an atmosphere of acceptance, love, and encouragement. Parents provide children with a set of standards and security. Children need to have an opportunity to take on responsibilities and make choices at an early stage in life. They also need to be permitted to experience the natural consequences of poor choices, when these consequences are not too serious. In other words, they should be permitted to profit from their mistakes by learning how to improve. This will help them be better able to cope with the realities of life.

Parents should help children to understand that it is often desirable to say "no." Not long after children learn to speak, they test their ability to act independently by saying "no" to almost anything. In an attempt to socialize their children, many parents teach them that it is not nice to say "no." Children of all ages, however, should be counseled in the wisdom of saying "no" with determination when that is the appropriate response. Children's consciences will be tested over and over as they grow toward adulthood. If they are to have the strength of character and self-concept, they need to say "no" to activities that are counter to the dictates of their consciences. They must have warm relationships with role models who know when and how to say "no!"

Children need help in the control and direction of their drives. They look to adults for this help. Often at this time they realize that some of their drives conflict with those of others. Some families do not adequately discipline their children. The children then become spoiled and are unable to control their behavior to fit the needs of others. Children who have never come into conflict with the rights of others will be unprepared for life's con-

Siblings may develop different interests in order to maintain their individuality.

flicts. Children who do not obey certain routines in daily life also will be unprepared. For example, children who eat when and what they wish, who go to bed only when they like, and who do not know how to concentrate probably will have conflicts with others.

The Family Composition

The family make-up or composition has a marked effect upon children. Each family has a distinct structure. The first child is a new experience for the parents. Their affection is directed to the one child, and relationships are established within the family. When the second child arrives, the group immediately shifts positions. The new baby takes over the position of the older child and the older child feels dethroned, in a sense. Each succeeding baby brings about new interactions and new interrelationships. Each family member, in turn, must adjust to these changes in the family structure.

The relationships among members of the family are usually made up of alliances and rivalries. Children represent threats to each other's positions. Sibling relationships are dependent upon the meanings and interpretations that the children bring to the situation. However, sibling relationships are the first relationships children have with people who are not in authority over them. This becomes their first opportunity to cope with people at the peer level.

Sometimes family members are allies in public and competitors at home. Competition is often expressed in basic differences in interest. For example, in a family of two children where one is extremely athletic, the other may feel unable to compete. He or she consequently may devote a great deal of time to reading or mechanical skills. The similarity among siblings is an expression of the general family atmosphere. For example, if parents and children value good grades in school, or, conversely, if they give grades little importance, the scholastic activities of the children may be quite similar.

Rivalry between brothers and sisters is almost universal. It stems from wanting to be first in the eyes of one's parents. Sibling rivalry can be seen in the child who tries to break a toy of a sibling. It is clearly seen in the child who tries to hurt a younger brother or sister. Rivalry tends to be the greatest when the children are more than 18 months apart, but less than 36 months apart. Spacing children to avoid this period alleviates some problems of rivalry, but certainly not all of them. Realize, though, that rivalry is a natural part of growing up.

A Closer Look

Tom was one year older than his brother John. Tom was ambitious, tried hard to do things, and enjoyed success. John, being one year younger, couldn't compete successfully when he was young, so he decided not to compete in anything Tom could do well. Tom was a good swimmer. John didn't seem to enjoy swimming. Tom played a good game of baseball. John wasn't interested in it. Tom liked card games. John wouldn't concentrate on any games and rejected them. Later John disliked all of Tom's friends. Tom planned to go to college. John dropped out of high school only three months before graduation. Obviously, John needed encouragement throughout his boyhood to recognize his own worth, rather than becoming a "not Tom" person.

Children make decisions on how to cope with their individual situations within the family. For example, the child who is aggressive in demanding rights could stimulate aggression or withdrawal in the other siblings. Some children cope most effectively with their siblings by being the "good" child, by defeating their siblings at every turn, by being "better," and by making certain that the parents note the difference.

Peer Group

As children grow older their relationships broaden to include both the family and the peer group. The original peer group is usually composed of children in the immediate neighborhood or in a daycare setting. By the time children reach school age, they become part of a larger group. Children who have had

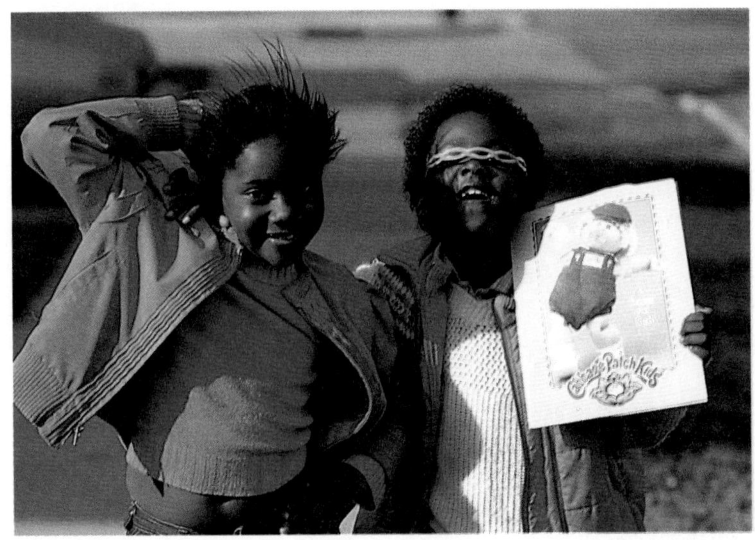

Having a best friend is an important part of growing up.

day care or preschool experiences are more socially active and progress in peer groups earlier.

In Western culture, the peer group assumes an increasingly important role in the formation of social behavior. Peer groups are really a distinct society for children. The group will have similar interests and accept members of the group on the basis of the roles they play. To ensure their acceptance by the peer group, children learn that they must accept the group's interests and values.

There are many ways in which the influence of the peer group can be positive, but it can also be negative. For example, if the children's peer group dislikes school, they must verbalize that dislike or run the risk of being rejected by the group. If their friends gripe, they will gripe. They cannot afford to be different because this might jeopardize their status in the group. Belonging is a basic need, and belonging to the peer group gives the child a social identity. However, children need to understand how to maintain their individuality in a group. They need guided practice in making minor decisions and guidance to carry through their ideas and plans. They may also need help as they try to make adjustments within themselves.

The peer group can provide children with a workshop in human relationships. It can give children contact with various religions, social classes, and ethnic backgrounds. It can help them learn to accept, work with, and cooperate with people who hold different opinions and beliefs. The peer group is important in that it provides children with a unique set of give-and-take relationships. To belong, children must live within the code of the specific peer group, keep its secrets, and be willing to meet its expectations.

Establishing peer relationships is a vital developmental task for which some children seem to have special talents. Researchers have found that

Peer groups are not always nice to other children. They may pick on someone who appears to be different.

popular children usually have realistic self-concepts. They tend to be healthy, intelligent (but not outstandingly so), athletic, physically attractive, dependable, emotionally stable, friendly, outgoing, cooperative, and socially adaptable. They show interest in the activities and ideas of their peers and are sensitive to other people's feelings. They demonstrate above average independence for their ages. Parents can best help their children to achieve satisfying social relationships by showing them acceptance from the time they are born. Children must have positive feelings about themselves before they can feel confident in their ability to develop relationships with others.

Some children are rejected by their peer groups because they tend to be demanding, arrogant, apathetic, or argumentative. They may have little interest in other people's activities. Other children may be unpopular only because they are different in some respect from most of their peers. The notable difference may be any of a large number of possibilities, of which the following are some examples:

- race
- native language
- impediment in speech, hearing, or sight
- physical—the difference could be unusual facial features, physical deformity, overweight, or others

Some children react enthusiastically to classroom discussions. Others have little interest in participating.

- lethargy—failure to participate with the expected level of intensity
- retarded motor development
- hyperactivity—disruptive of others' activities
- name—even unusual first names can set children apart from their peers.

A Closer Look

Angie is 14. Her life's goal is to be an astronomer. Of course, she must go to high school, and after school she has responsibilities at her home. She helps prepare dinner and sometimes helps her younger brother, Andy, with his schoolwork. All her other waking hours, though, she spends at the observatory. She gets along fine with the adults who supervise her activities there and can spend hours discussing the evening sky. She senses no need for friends her own age, so she does not try to develop any friendships.

Some children find group experiences unrewarding because they feel socially incompetent. Researchers have concluded that most unpopular children do not have good ideas about how to get other people to include them in peer group activities. There are a few other children who place high value on relationships or activities outside their peer group and, therefore, never attempt to develop social contacts with their peers.

Significant Others

As you've learned, children's first models for social learning occur in the family. As they grow, their world expands and they have a whole new series of models. For example, a child may try to imitate certain character traits of a favorite sitter, teacher, coach, teenager, or even a friend. If we observe young children at play, we can note the unique meanings they attach to their experiences. Through their contact with others, children come to identify and learn a variety of social roles. They may engage in exploratory activity at times, but much of their activity centers on gaining attention and approval. As children mature, they may tend to imitate and identify with those who seem to be accepted by others.

A child's sources of social identity, then, are the family, the peer group, and significant others. Through these various relationships children develop their ability to give or receive attention and affection. They learn the give-and-take of life. If the family expectations are similar to those of the peer group and the significant others, children's socialization takes place more rapidly. If there is considerable conflict in values and standards among these various groups, their social development meets with more problems.

Children's social identity is based upon the behaviors that they have observed and internalized rather than on abstract concepts that parents have tried to impose on them. School-age children encounter people who have many different beliefs, attitudes, and patterns of behavior. Children are more strongly influenced, however, in their choices of role models by their own perceptions of people than by the nature of the beliefs, attitudes, and behavior patterns that those people manifest.

In Review

Vocabulary

identification
cross-identification

Summary

- ✓ School-age children face many challenges, including adapting to the changes occurring in their own physical appearance. As a result, they need constant parental support and reassurance of their worth.
- ✓ One of the most important aspects of social development for school children is identification with role models. A child's personality and character are strongly influenced by his/her choices of models for morality, ambition, sex roles, etc.
- ✓ Many traits traditionally attributed to males are equally admirable in females. The reverse is also true. Thus, in our culture, some cross-identification is important for both boys and girls.
- ✓ Of all the relationships affecting a child's development, the family is the most important force. Children ultimately choose those attitudes and values that they want to internalize but, initially, they are influenced by the customs, habits, religion, and other factors that characterize the family.
- ✓ At its worst, the peer group persuades a child to deviate from his/her own high standards. At its best, however, the peer group provides children with a workshop in human relations. By experiment, children learn that certain types of behavior result in peer acceptance or peer rejection. Friends in the peer group satisfy a child's need to belong.
- ✓ Beside members of the family and peer group, there are "significant others" in the lives of school children. A teacher, neighbor, a police officer, and others who are respected by a particular child may serve as models for social behavior. These people may have a wide variety of beliefs, attitudes and values. A child will formulate his/her own perceptions of these and decide which to internalize.

Questions

1. Define identification. Give an example of identification from your own life experience.

2. How do children make their sex-role identifications?

3. Do you subscribe to the Freudian theory or the social-learning theory of identification, or do you feel there is value in both? Why?

4. Why is cross-identification desirable in our society?

5. What are some of the varied roles a child might play in peer groups?

6. How might different peer groups meet different status needs?

7. Give an example of how children might be willing to function outside of a peer group's demands because of other needs of greater value to them.

8. How might competition between siblings bring on unnecessary discouragement?

9. Describe the important relationships affecting a child's social development.

Activities

1. Mary is the oldest of three girls, ages 14, 11, and 9, in a family that values good scholarship. She is a "B" student, except in art, where she excels. In addition, she is very helpful around the house. Make up your own description for the characteristics of the other two girls and explain why alliances and rivalries might develop for these siblings.

2. Write a paragraph telling what you think Ellen Bryant Voigt means in the last three lines of her poem, "The Wish," that appears in this chapter. Do you agree with what you think she is implying? Explain.

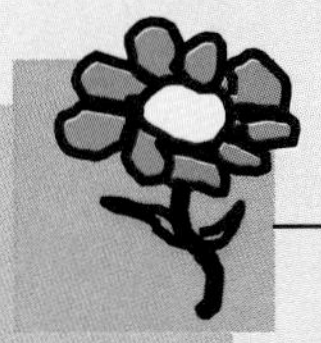

Unit 6
Guiding Children Through Change

Preschool and Day Care

Chapter 21

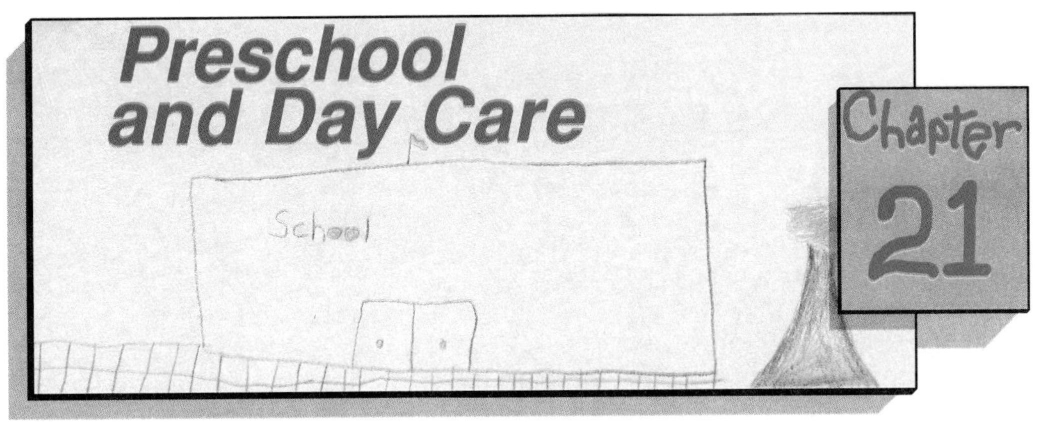

This chapter will help you:

- recognize the need for preschools and daycare centers
- identify the criteria used in selecting a preschool or daycare center
- learn the appropriate level of learning for preschoolers
- become aware of the hazards in pushing children beyond their readiness
- understand how parents can help children avoid having anxious feelings about experiences in preschools

The Need for Child Care

It has been estimated that about five million children of working parents in the United States are without supervision for significant parts of the day. There are more than eight million children under age six whose mothers work outside the home, and that number is growing rapidly. In families when both parents work outside the home and in single-parent families, often there is no choice but to seek child-care services. In fact, many parents now choose to send their children to preschools even though their work schedules do not require it. Some parents may simply enjoy a breather from the daily demands of child rearing, while others want their children to learn the give-and-take of interacting with same-age playmates. They also may want to provide their children with the environment that is available in a particular preschool, its toy and play facilities, and its opportunities to meet children of all races and backgrounds.

For families who do have the option of using daycare, they need to ask themselves what their expectations are for child care. A preschool can help a child learn to share and take turns, can provide a child with opportunities for constructive activities that help the child learn, can help the child build self-confidence, and can ease the transition to kindergarten and first grade.

A Matter of Fact

If you decide to become a babysitter, here are some points for you to remember:

- Keep safety in mind. The children you care for must be kept from harm. This is the most important part of your job.
- When you agree to accept a babysitting job for a neighbor's or relative's children, remember you are taking the place of the parent. This does not mean you become the parent.
- Ask the parents what the house rules are. You must handle the child in line with the rules the parents set down.
- As you sit regularly for children and get to know them well, you will become pretty important to them. They may imitate and look up to you. Be sure to set a good example.
- Give yourself credit for your own special skills and abilities. Your best babysitting experiences may involve caring exclusively for infants. Perhaps you are most comfortable working with older children.
- Don't accept a babysitting job if you are sick. You might suggest a substitute if you can, but don't go even if no one else is available.
- You may want to make your own toy kit. Fill an old suitcase or canvas bag with old magazines, rubber balls, crayons, pencils, notebook, pen, flashlight, storybooks, colored paper, and yarn. Fill your kit with any items you might need on the job.
- Get phone numbers from the parents in writing. Include these numbers: where parents can be reached, special emergency services, the next-door neighbor, family doctor.
- Parents will appreciate it if you ask for the following information: children's nicknames, rules for watching TV, what meals to feed, if snacks are allowed for the children, where clothing and toys are kept, what you should do if the children don't mind you, and your privileges regarding the stereo, TV, VCR, visitors, and snacks.
- Keep the phone free for incoming calls.
- Be straightforward about your rates. For example, if you charge time and a half after midnight, parents should agree to this before you accept the babysitting job.
- Show that you're responsible by being punctual and letting parents know as far ahead as possible if you can't keep your engagement.
- Nowadays people are familiar with signs of child abuse or neglect. If you notice signs of a problem, don't jump to conclusions. Be sure you are honestly concerned for the child's welfare. Talk with your parents, a school nurse, counselor, or another responsible adult who can assist children in trouble. Do not talk about it with your friends.

Types of Child Care

Child-care services can be divided into two general categories. The majority of traditional **preschools** meet for two and a half to three hours in the morning. If parents need more hours of child care, they need a daycare center. The program at a high-quality **daycare center** closely resembles that of a good preschool with the addition of lunch, a nap, and free-form afternoon activities. There are several different options available for parents looking for child-care services. Child care can be located in a person's home, in a church or community center, or a privately operated center. Some parents look for service provided by sitters who come to the children's own homes. Many parents prefer daycare with a "family" setting in a home for their babies. Rightly so, they feel infants need loving care rather than a formal education. As alternatives to family daycare options, preschools and daycare centers that offer care plus some education have become very popular.

Choosing a Preschool

In Chapter 13, we discussed the role of preschools in the intellectual development of young children. Here, we deal with the parents' decisions in choosing preschools for their children. Unfortunately, much of the daycare provided for children today is of highly questionable quality. Thus, responsible parents will need to be very selective if their children are to have positive experiences.

One thing parents can look for is a licensed home or center. However, only about five percent of the family daycare homes have been granted licenses. Many of the family daycare homes are informal, neighborhood arrangements where mothers with their own children at home take care of other children as well. Parents should judge this type of situation using the information given in this chapter. Licensed homes are inspected for health and safety. These homes are restricted in the number and ages of children they can accept to ensure that caregivers are not overburdened. They are eligible for government food programs and for training from social service agencies. Licensed daycare centers are also inspected for health and safety. Typically, the centers employ people with training in child development.

Another consideration when choosing daycare is the cost. Most daycare centers and preschools are privately operated. The costs range from $3,300 to more than $7,500 per year, unless the school is subsidized by a government agency, a church, a local public school system, or an employer. Cost for private homes ranges from $2,500 to $6,500 per year. Thus, most parents must consider cost as well as benefit when deciding whether to send their children to preschool.

How would a parent go about finding a good preschool or daycare center? The lists of licensed facilities from the local or state licensing agency is the place to begin. This list will range from caregivers who have facilities in their own homes to church-sponsored programs, school-sponsored programs in high school and college home economics/child development departments, and commercial operations.

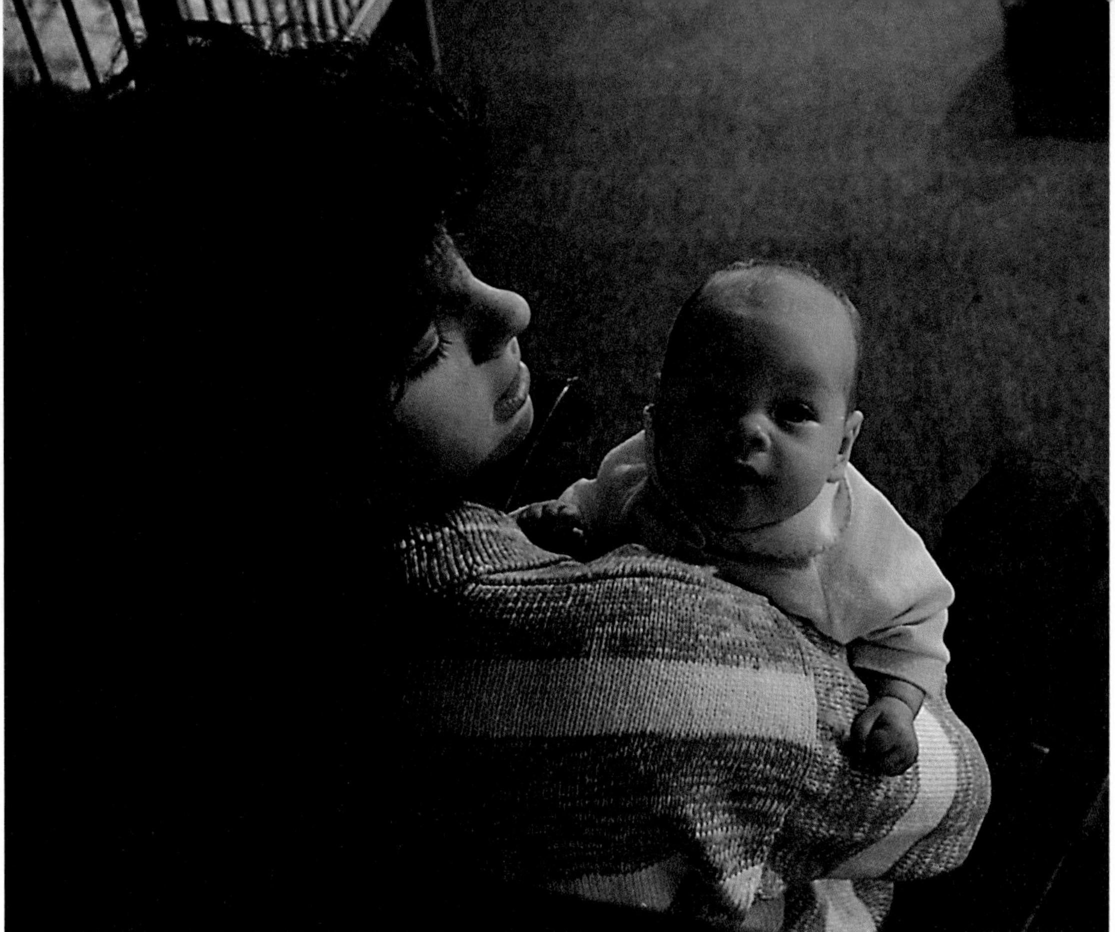

Infants require more specialized care than toddlers, so parents may want to look into having a caregiver come to their home.

Parents should talk with parents who have children enrolled in these programs. Then by telephone they can screen schools for cost and suitability. If the facility seems interesting after the telephone interview, parents should make an appointment to visit it without their child.

On the visit to the facility, parents should be ready to exercise judgment on these issues: the director or principle caregiver, the program, the staff, adult-child ratio, group size, health and safety, parent involvement, space, equipment, materials, and general atmosphere.

Here are some questions to explore:

The Director

1. Does the director or caregiver enjoy and understand children?
2. What is the director's training in the development and education of young children? In what specialties has the director received diplomas and/or certificates of achievement?
3. What does the director think a preschool should be? Do you agree?
4. Are parents given regular reports about their children?
5. Who is in charge when the director or main caregiver is ill or perhaps is on vacation?

One way to judge a preschool is by the ability of the staff. Do they like children and know how to communicate with them?

The Program

1. Which is emphasized more—creativity or structure? the group or the individual? Babies and toddlers benefit from individually structured programs tailored to their routines. Preschoolers profit from a semistructured program that allows them to interact with adults and other children as well as learn by themselves.
2. Are the children discovering new things for themselves?
3. Are there opportunities for individual response?
4. Does the program pressure the child to learn numbers, letters, etc?
5. Does the program show concern for children's feelings, interests, and attitudes?
6. Does the program recognize that children learn best by engaging in activities that involve tangible objects?

The Staff

1. How much turnover in the staff is there? Children feel more secure if the staff remains the same.
2. Are teachers trained and experienced? Have they studied child development? Do they know the principles that allow children to grow mentally, socially, and emotionally?
3. Are the teachers positive, happy individuals? Do they seem to be comfortable with the children, the program, and themselves?
4. Do the teachers understand and implement the program as defined and discussed with the director?
5. Are the teachers people parents would like to have their child imitate? Do they have mannerisms, values, and behaviors with which parents would like their child to identify?
6. Are the caregivers responsive to children's questions and signals? Do they respond quickly to babies' needs?
7. What's the pay range for the staff? How does this compare with other child-care services?
8. Do the staff members receive ongoing training?

Group Size and Adult-Child Ratio

1. Are there at least two adults in charge for every 15 to 20 children? One adult for every five children is ideal. For infants and toddlers, a ratio of four children to one caregiver is recommended.
2. Is 20 the maximum number of children?

Health and Safety

1. Is a health certificate displayed?
2. Are there fire alarms, extinguishers, fire blankets, and smoke detectors?

Children love to play outdoors, but require supervision on playground equipment. Note how this area is enclosed, too.

3. Are toilets and sinks clean?
4. Do the food handlers know sanitation? Check for sanitation certificates.
5. Do the doors open out? In case of fire or other emergency, doors must open out for quick exit.
6. Are adequate checks made on the health of the staff?
7. Is there an enclosed outside play area that's free of debris?
8. Is there an isolation room for sick children?
9. What are the janitorial standards?
10. Is the cooling and heating system working well?
11. If a child requires special medication or special care, are staff members capable of helping?
12. Do caregivers supervise toddlers around potentially dangerous places such as playground equipment, stairs, etc.?
13. Are children instructed to wash their hands before eating?
14. Do caregivers wash their hands before and after diapering a baby?
15. Is there an emergency exit plan that's practiced?
16. Are illness and accidents reported to the parent or backup person if the parent can't be reached?
17. Are caregivers trained in first aid and CPR?
18. Are electrical outlets covered and cleaning fluids and other dangerous liquids kept out of reach?

Space, Equipment, and Materials

1. Is there 35 square feet of space for each child indoors and 100 square feet of space outdoors?
2. Does each child have a place for personal belongings?
3. Is there space or a place for a child to be alone? to think? to look at a book? to paint a picture?
4. Is there big equipment for children to climb on, blocks to build with, wheel toys? (These are items needed to help motor development.)
5. Are there play props?
6. Are there natural materials such as sand and water to stimulate exploration and self-expression?
7. Are there books, poems, puzzles, pictures, and story-telling?
8. Are there opportunities for musical experiences?

A Matter of Fact

These days when the majority of parents work full-time outside the home, who minds the children when they're sick? In most homes there's a whole lot of scrambling to locate someone who's able to come in at the last second to look after a sick child. Daycare centers are out. Most won't allow sick children in the center. Some parents maintain a list of caregivers they can call on just in case. But the added stress takes its toll on caregivers. Businesses worry because the productivity of the parent-worker declines. They can't concentrate on their job knowing their child is ill, and work time is lost when the parent spends a greater than normal amount of time on the phone.

Some parents call in to work saying they are sick—when they're actually taking care of their young ones, and there's no other caregiver available. Some parents are able to take work home with them, come in late, or make up the lost time on their own.

In some areas, special centers have helped to meet this need by caring for children with the sniffles and sneezes, mild colds, and sore throats. One thing is certain: parents desperately need this kind of assistance. Businesses are listening and beginning to show concern.

What kinds of solutions can you think of?

9. Are there plants and animals for children to enjoy?
10. Are there construction sets and other toys to promote problem-solving?
11. Are the children required to share and to take turns?

Parent Involvement

1. Is visiting encouraged?
2. How often will parents get reports?
3. What chances do parents have to make suggestions?

General Atmosphere

1. Does the school smell good?
2. Are the children happy?
3. What are the expressions on the faces of the children? the adults?
4. Is the background noise the hum of absorbed children?
5. Do parents and children feel at home here?

Overall Considerations

Children in daycare need quality care from individuals who care about them. Parents are concerned with having consistent, dependable care they can afford. Caregivers are concerned with wages, working conditions, and meeting the needs of children and parents. The right daycare system satisfies all those needs.

Appropriate Level of Learning

Beware of the preschool that promises your child will read, count, and play a musical instrument before the year is finished. Don't hurry children! The hurried child is deprived of childhood. Parents hurry children

Learning opportunities need to be available to children, but children should not be forced into achievement by pushy daycare directors or parents.

when they insist that they acquire academic skills, such as reading at an early age. This pressure by parents reflects parental needs, not the children's needs or inclinations. Children forced to try to read before they are ready may feel like failures. They could develop long-term learning difficulties, too.

Good preschools and daycare centers provide the benefits of healthy interactions with other children and with adults other than parents. Whether children are with their parents, with sitters, in preschools, or daycare centers, they need to have opportunities to learn. On the other hand, children should not be pressured to grow up and stop acting like children while they are still children. Hurrying a child's growth process is an abuse. Children tend to see hurrying as rejection. When parents want their children to read before they are ready, or to take on adult types of relationships, the children see this as rejection—rejection of their intellectual abilities and rejection of their emotional and social maturity. Hurrying children into relationships with several different caregivers, into academic achievement, or into making decisions they are not really able to make is rejection. It is rejection of children as they see themselves, of their ability to cope, and of their ability to achieve.

Helping Children Adjust

When parents must, by necessity, seek child-care services before the child is completely ready for this new arrangement, they need to be sensitive to the child's feelings. They need to do everything they can to prepare the child by talking enthusiastically and in detail about everything that is going to happen. They also should explain why this new arrangement is necessary. Children are quite capable of understanding and accepting rational explanations. A parent might say, "I'm really going to miss you today. I wish you could be with me, but I have to work to earn money so I can pay the rent and buy our food and clothing. You go to preschool and have a busy day. I'll go to work and have a busy day. I'll pick you up late this afternoon, after you've had your nap and your play time. You are going to help me so much by playing nicely and having fun with your playmates and your teacher."

Parents should try to arrange to spend time with the child at the preschool or daycare on the first day in order to help the child adjust to the new situation. Just dropping a child off in a rush and expecting the child to "jump in with both feet" is unfair. Children will feel more comfortable with the new situation if their parent takes them in, introduces them to the director and staff, and then stays with them for awhile. Once the child is interacting with others and feeling comfortable, the parent can say, "I need to go to work now. I'll be back to get you after lunch. You go ahead and play now." Parents should avoid slipping out unnoticed. The child may feel deserted.

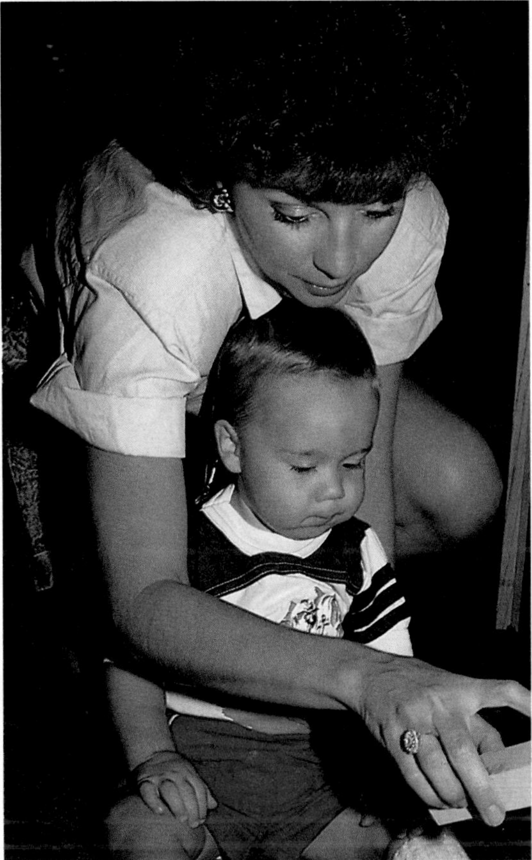

Playing together is a good way for parents and children to interact.

When together at home, parents need to spend time playing with their children. By playing together, parents can help to relieve the stresses that the children feel when they are being pushed. Play gives children and parents the opportunity to relax together, laugh together, and create together. Parents should approach playtime not with a sense of duty, but with as much anticipation as the children feel. Whether they are going to build with blocks, play word games, or

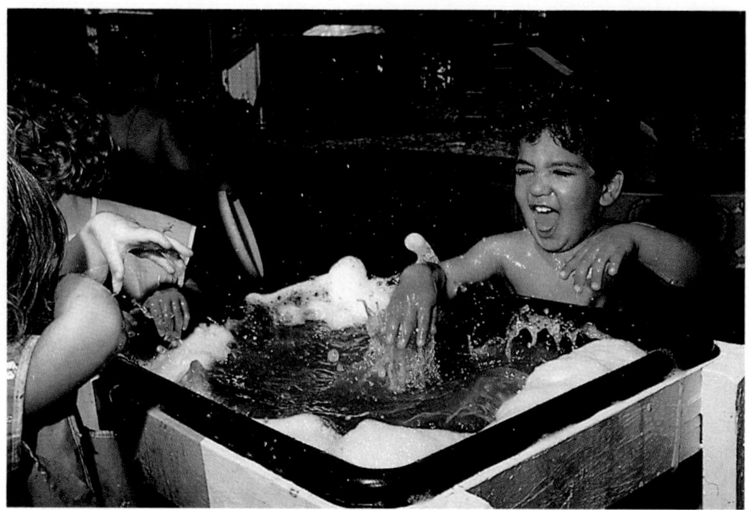

Play is important to children because it gives them a chance for self-expression and an opportunity to exercise their imaginations.

create with pencils, crayons, paints, clay, or Playdough, parents are sharing an experience of personal expression with their child.

Play Schools

The term **play school** has been criticized and gone out of use with the terms "preschool" and "daycare" as replacements. Play school, however, may be the most productive, imaginative, and motivated of all possible schools. Play is a chance for self-expression. Children need time for activities that enhance learning and development, that give opportunities for exercising imagination, and that give relaxation and humor. Valuing childhood does not mean seeing it only as a happy, innocent period, but rather as an essential period of life in which children develop in ways that lead to fuller and richer adult lives.

Life's Work

Lisa Incopero

➤ **Puppeteer/Pero Puppets**

➤ **B.S. in Accounting and Marketing**

Lisa's day starts with her packing equipment, puppets, and props into cases, loading it all up, and then driving to the place of performance for that day. She sets up the equipment and stage. When the audience arrives, she performs a 45 minute puppet show and afterward answers questions. Then she packs up everything, drives to a second show, and repeats the process before driving home and putting away all her equipment.

On the day of a performance, Lisa averages four hours depending on the number of shows, length of the show, and the distance from home. In addition, there are many hours spent working on developing new shows, making puppets, rehearsing, marketing, doing contracts, bookkeeping, writing stories, and making props and costumes.

Lisa says the skills necessary for success in her profession include, "A knowledge of all aspects of the theater from acting, art, lighting and sound, costuming, and scriptwriting to a sense of how to entertain people—especially children. Determination and dependability are important. I think a sense of fun, flexibility, and performing help to make a successful show. Manipulation and choreography are most important in a puppeteer and show."

Lisa feels the most rewarding part of her job is, "Having both adults and children tell me they enjoyed the show very much and a child hugging me after the show to thank me."

For a student considering going into Lisa's profession, she recommends, "Practice, practice, practice—all parts of your performance from your introduction to your bows. Explore different ways to make puppets and storylines to find your own unique combination. Watch and study other puppeteers."

When asked how her profession will change within the next 10 years, Lisa says, "There will be more types and uses of puppetry. The shows will continue to expand with television. School and community programming for children will contain more puppet shows and workshops."

In Review

Vocabulary

preschool
daycare center
play school

Summary

- ✓ There is an increasing demand for preschools and daycare facilities. Responsible parents must be very selective. In addition to cost, parents should consider licensing, health conditions, safety, food service, and staff training. Also important are space, physical equipment and materials, group size, and the general atmosphere. Parents should talk with preschool directors and caregivers about their philosophy regarding the training of young children.
- ✓ Children of preschool age need consistent, quality care from people who love them. Providing that kind of care should be the goal shared by parents and other caregivers, whether they are in preschools, daycare centers, or private homes.
- ✓ The programs in preschools should provide children with challenging opportunities to learn at their individual levels of readiness. They should not be pressured, because children perceive pressure as rejection.
- ✓ Many children need parental help to adjust to preschool or other types of daycare. They need simple explanations of why this alternate child care is necessary, and they may require time to adjust to new people and surroundings.

Questions

1. If your financial situation allowed you the option of caring for your only child yourself, would you choose to send the child to preschool? Explain your answer.

2. What are the eight aspects of preschool that parents should try to evaluate? Which three would you rate to be most important? Why?

3. What is meant by the general atmosphere of a preschool?

4. What is the role of play in child development?

Activities

1. Using the criteria for choosing a preschool, visit a preschool and write up the philosophy of the director and the emphasis of the program.

2. Mrs. Jones is sending her son Kevin to preschool so that Kevin will be able to read by age four. Write a report describing what kind of advice you would give Mrs. Jones. What do you predict for Kevin?

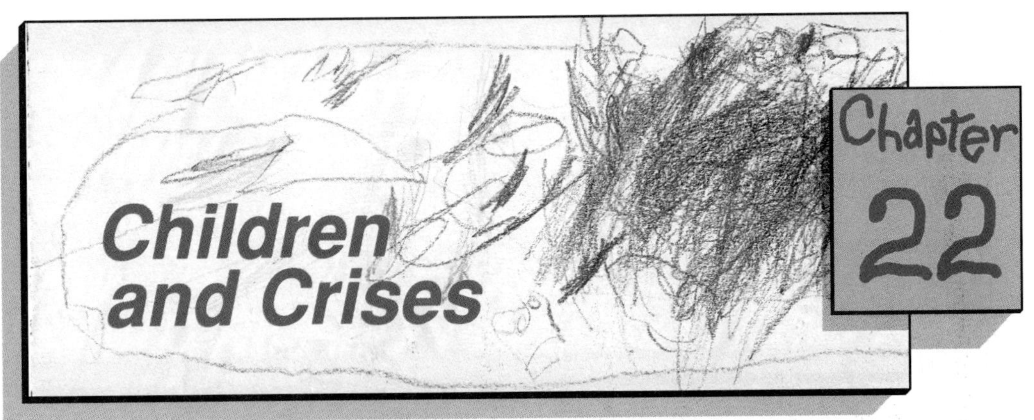

Chapter 22: Children and Crises

This chapter will help you:

- recognize the relationships between crisis, stress, and strain
- identify certain characteristics that allow families to cope effectively with crises
- learn how parents can help children to cope with crises arising from moving, divorce, child abuse, drugs, and death
- identify the five stages of dying described by Kübler-Ross

Crisis or Not

A **crisis** is a turning point—a time when we must make a decision that will influence the course of our lives. At such a stressful time, it may seem that we have no way to turn.

All forms of abrupt changes are likely to cause crises. (Crises is the plural form of crisis.) We may bring on crises by our own actions or they may be brought on by the actions of family members, outsiders, or natural forces.

A similar event may be a crisis for one family, but not for another. There are three variables that help to determine whether an event becomes a crisis for a family. They are:

1. the hardship of the situation or event itself.
2. the resources of the family: its structure, flexibility, and previous history with crises.
3. the family's view of the event, that is, whether the family does or does not treat the event as if it were a threat to their status, goals, and objectives.

While the three variables are closely related to each other, the first focuses on the event or social and physical situation. The second concentrates on past and present family functioning. The third focuses on the psychological reactions of individual members and the family as a group. Some families are known to be crisis-prone. **Crisis-prone** means that almost any out-of-the-ordinary event causes great stress in the family.

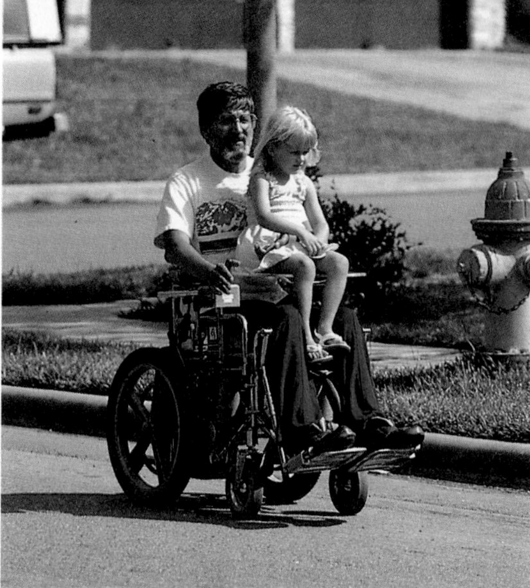

A physical handicap doesn't have to be a crisis. This family has turned it into a positive experience.

Relief of Stress

Crises cause stress. Undue psychological stresses can cause family relationships to be strained or broken. If those stresses are to be relieved, the family must change its course of action. Roles need to be defined and communication between family members needs to be improved or better understood. Perhaps the family needs to acknowledge the presence of a problem. Often problems cause stress because they are never allowed to surface. The ways of solving problems and conflicts vary from family to family.

Positive Response to Crisis

Families that can cope with crises seem to have three features in common. These features are involvement, integration, and adaptation.

- **Involvement** refers to commitment to and participation in family life by the members of the group.
- **Integration** has to do with the interdependence or interchange between the roles in the group. The family members give support to each other and receive support from each other.
- **Adaptation** refers to the ability of the family group and each of its members to change their responses to one another and the world around them as the situation demands. Another word for adaptation might be flexibility. Family members must be flexible in times of crisis.

Crises are not necessarily bad for the family or the family members. A crisis may prompt the family to develop new ways of handling problems, new role definitions, and new insights into themselves and others. Out of a crisis situation, a family may become more insightful, more understanding, and stronger.

Sources of Crises

Some of the natural forces that can produce personal or family crises are earthquakes, floods, tornadoes, hurricanes, fires, auto accidents, and mudslides. Many more crises, however, are precipitated when human relationships are strained or broken. For example, an unwanted pregnancy, a mental breakdown, or alcoholism cause much heartbreak and strained, if not broken, family relations. Unexpected changes in the family makeup through the loss or gain of a member are also sources of crises.

The loss of a family member may be the result of divorce, desertion, running away, commitment to an institu-

A Matter of Fact

It's a fact that an increasingly large number of children spend a part of the day home alone without adult supervision. Because of this, it is important that latchkey children know how to treat minor cuts and burns, insect stings, and nosebleeds. But in a real medical emergency, children may actually have to call an ambulance. Caregivers may want to prepare the children in advance.

- Make sure the children know their home address. In addition, the house number should be seen clearly from the street, day or night. Some areas have the house number painted on the street curb.
- Post ambulance, police, and fire emergency telephone numbers by each phone. Some emergency services provide stickers for the phone.
- In an area with a 911 emergency system, teach children to dial 911.
- Teach the children not to get upset when a dispatcher asks questions and to speak as specifically as possible about the emergency. Role playing with children using a similar scenario will help them understand what to do.
- Keep the name and phone number of the family doctor in a convenient location, preferably near each phone.
- Teach children to turn on the porch lights and extra inside lights if it is dark. This will help providers of emergency services locate the house.
- It's a good idea if children can lock up pets in another room before emergency-service providers arrive.

tion, imprisonment, or death by illness, accident, or suicide. It also may create a family crisis if a grandparent comes to live with the family, if an adolescent daughter expects her parents to raise her child, if a son brings his new bride home to live with his family, or if a family member divorces and returns to the parents' home. Often one crisis precipitates another, unless appropriate steps are taken to relieve the stress. Let's take a look at some of these crises.

Moving

Moving often creates stresses and family crises. Parents get caught up in the numerous decisions that have to be made in selling a home, buying a house or finding an apartment, arranging for the family's furnishings to be moved, choosing new schools for their children, etc. They also may be emotionally drained by saying good-bye to friends and family. It is a time that requires both psychological and physical stamina.

Along with all the other responsibilities, parents must be sensitive to the needs of their children during the decision-making process, during the move, and throughout the adjustment period. The reasons for a move should be discussed with children in advance,

A move that means leaving behind relatives and friends can be traumatic. Parents need to be sensitive to children's feelings and help them adjust.

so they can adjust to the decision. It may take great patience, understanding, and detailed explanation to convince children that moving is the right thing to do. After all, leaving friends, teachers, home, and other familiar places is never easy. It can be even more difficult if the move means leaving cherished grandparents, aunts, uncles, and cousins.

In addition to helping children adjust to the idea of moving, parents need to do everything they can to help children fit into their new situation. Parents should find out what activities are available for children in the new location and help their children get involved. By joining a parent-teacher organization, parents can familiarize themselves with the school system. Knowing the system, parents can communicate more effectively regarding any problems that arise. Children should be encouraged to invite new friends into the home. By being good listeners, parents can be aware of their children's concerns and, thereby, lend support when and where it is needed.

Divorce and Children

Divorce occurs in three phases, all of which can be very troubling to children. The **pre-divorce phase** starts when incompatibility, unfaithfulness, or other causes become evident to the couple. This is the period of waiting to see if the problem will be resolved and to determine if the marriage is still workable.

During the pre-divorce phase, parents often try to keep children ignorant of the problem. Their wish to protect children from unneeded worry is commendable if they are actively seeking solutions to their differences. If both parents really want the marriage to work, a marriage may be saved in the pre-divorce phase. However, sometimes one partner wants the marriage to be saved while the other would just as soon see it dissolved. When this is the case, children should be kept somewhat aware of the problems so that they are not totally surprised and shocked by the divorce. Children should be assured at the outset, however, that they are in no way to blame for the marital problems of their parents.

Many spouses admit they feel great relief when the decision to divorce is finally made. This is the time the **divorce phase** is set in motion. Other spouses who want reconciliation, but feel that the decision to divorce is final, feel hopeless and may become severely depressed. This case is particularly trying for both parent and child. Whether or not children know exactly what is happening, they feel the tension in the home and react to it.

Even though they do not remain husband and wife, parents remain parents. Thus, during the divorce phase, children take their cues from the attitudes of both parents, not just the one with whom they happen to be living. If this phase becomes a time of fights over child custody, the child's welfare and development are hampered. If parents never cooperated before in rearing their children, they should start trying during the divorce phase. Some divorced people are bitter, but others are more agreeable than they were in marriage.

The quality of the **post-divorce phase** for children again depends mainly upon the quality of the parents' attitudes, personalities, activities, friendships, and financial conditions. For the parents, the post-divorce phase is the time of greatest loneliness and anxiety. After having been intimately associated with another person for a significant part of a lifetime and after sharing with the person in the creation of other human lives, that person is gone. One may feel abused, abandoned, empty, and relieved at the same time. After all, it's over now. The acute anger and psychological suffering of the pre-divorce phase and the divorce phase are in the past. Still, the future holds so many unknowns that anxiety dominates the emotions. The parent with whom the children reside will be the focus of the children's interest. Often the children's moods, attitudes, and feelings will reflect those of the parent.

The parent who does not live with the children may have a legal responsibility to provide for them financially. This parent must also be emotionally supportive of the children to avoid letting them feel any sense of rejection. Each parent should respect the love the children have for the other parent. When one parent makes negative remarks about the other, children are placed in the middle of a dispute they did not create. If parents sincerely love

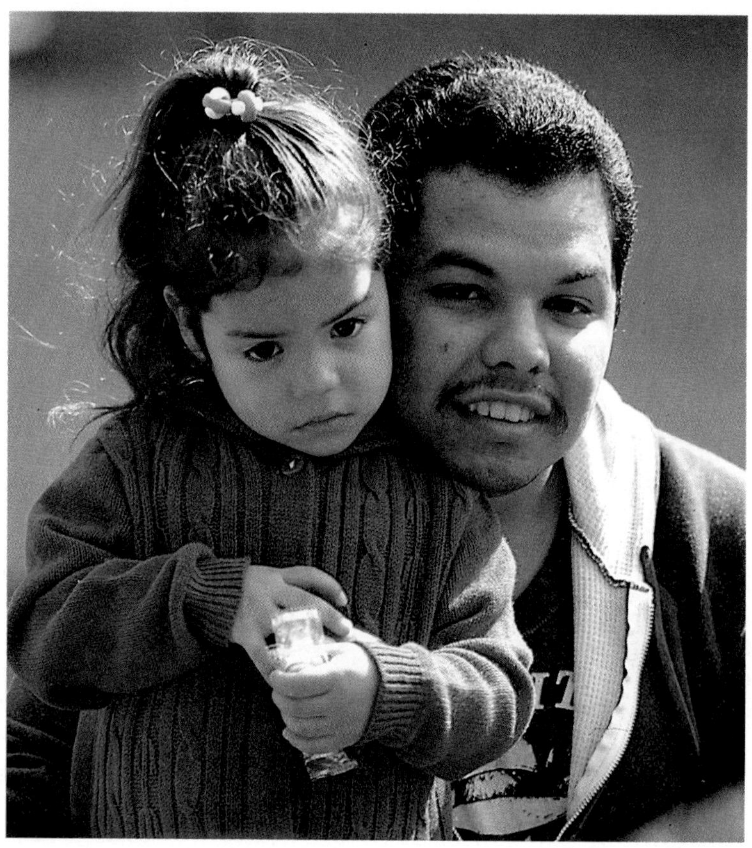

A divorce is hard on all of the family. It is important for parents to make sure that the children do not feel abandoned.

their children, they will not try to put them in such uncomfortable and precarious positions.

Unemployment

The loss of a job can be devastating, especially if it was a job that provided a sense of accomplishment and security. The individual and family need to work through the stages of "mourning" the job loss. Each family member must adjust to a new identity or role. The wage earner must accept that he/she has not successfully maintained that role. The unemployed person may also have to recognize his or her skills are no longer marketable.

Besides causing loss of self-esteem, unemployment can alter the family lifestyle in many ways. Family income is lower, so adjustments in spending patterns are required. The former wage earner spends more time in the home. This may change his or her role as an authority figure and as a contributor toward home management and maintenance. Another family member may be forced to seek employment.

Like most crises, unemployment is a challenge to the entire family. It can be dealt with by cooperative effort. Everyone must give reassurance and support to the unemployed family member. He or she must be included in the family's daily activities, and his or her talents appreciated. Self-confidence and self-esteem must be regained. Unemployment need not be overwhelming if the family faces the problem squarely with empathy, mutual respect, patience, encouragement, and flexibility.

Child Abuse

For one year in the 1980s, records of the American Humane Association show that 851,000 cases of child abuse and neglect were reported. The number of *unreported* cases could be even higher.

As you read in Chapter 3, child abuse takes many forms. Some children are physically battered. Many of them suffer permanent internal injuries, brain damage, or paralysis. Some die from their injuries.

Verbal abuse is also extremely harmful to children. Adults who continually criticize, demean, reject, or ignore a child inflict an especially destructive, psychological kind of hurt. Maltreated children are starved for love, for the sense of being wanted, and for self-esteem.

Child abusers are often people who suffered abuse as children. Thus, child abuse is a self-perpetuating problem. It is a training ground for general violence. In some cases, child abuse can be linked to the stresses created by societal problems: addiction to alcohol or other drugs, unemployment, poor health, inadequate housing, etc. On the other hand, child abuse can occur when none of these obvious societal ills are present. Some researchers are becoming convinced that the explanation lies in the fact that many people accept corporal (physical) punishment as a means of disciplining children.

As discussed in Chapter 3, corporal punishment is an ineffective means of helping children to learn self-discipline. Infractions that provoke the parent into giving a child a "smack on the backside" may be thought to deserve a "good licking" the next time. Continued infractions may bring "belt whippings" and then "beatings." The entire progression may be perpetuated by a well-intentioned but misinformed and misguided parent who "only wanted to make the child behave."

According to researchers, there are three main patterns for physical child abuse. The first has to do with the way the adult was reared. If as a child the adult was abused, he or she can sincerely believe that abuse is a necessary part of child-rearing. Because their basic needs were not met when they were children, these child abusers have severe emotional problems. Some of these child abusers may have temporarily or permanently lost contact with reality.

The second pattern may occur if the adult does not understand the ages and stages of children and perceives a child as a very small adult. In this case, the adult has unrealistic expectations. Potential abusers may expect a baby to love them, to care about them, to obey them. Babies are incapable of loving others or caring about others. They cry when they have needs and they can't obey when adults demand that they stop crying. If the adult has unrealistic expectations, conscious or unconscious resentments grow and may be

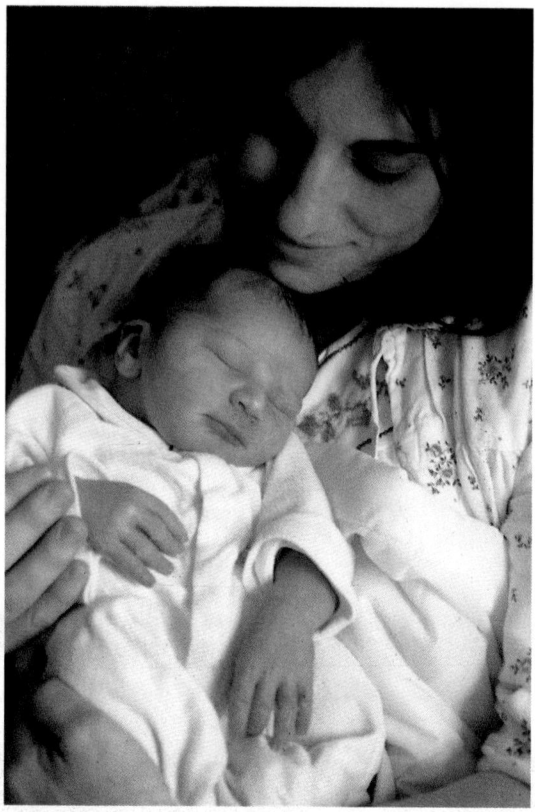

Parents are responsible for meeting all the needs of their children, including their need for love.

manifested in explosive acts of violence. Approximately one-third of all types of physical child abuse affect babies under one year of age. Abuse may result from an adult's unrealistic expectations for children of any age, including adolescence.

The third pattern of physical child abuse occurs in crisis situations. The types of crisis situations that provoke the abuse are widely varied because individual's stress levels are so different. A situation considered a crisis in one household may go unnoticed in another. Even in a given family, spilt milk may be a trifle on one day, but may provoke physical abuse on another day when other crises are being experienced by the parent.

Sexual abuse of both male and female children is recognized today as a problem of great magnitude. It has been estimated that 25 to 30 percent of all females and 10 percent of all males have been the victims of some form of sexual abuse by the time they are 14 years old. Researchers report that the harmful psychological effects of such encounters are long-lasting.

Today, physicians are required to report any suspected cases of neglect, sexual abuse, or physical abuse to government authorities. Also, state welfare agencies have experts who investigate such cases and counsel family members. Other organizations, such as Parents Anonymous, help parents deal with their frustrations associated with child-rearing or with any personal problems that may lead to child abuse. In severe cases of child abuse, a child may be temporarily put in the custody of a child-protection agency and then placed in a foster home. Child protection agencies, however, prefer to maintain the child's family unit. When the situation has improved, the child is reunited with the family. Review Chapter 3 for other ways children may be helped.

Special Needs

Every pregnant couple expects to have a healthy baby. They dream of a child who will live a normal, happy life. Unfortunately, for some, that dream is not realized.

As was pointed out in Chapter 6, most genetically defective embryos and fetuses are lost by miscarriage. Some,

Like all children, special needs children want to be included and have friends. Parents should not shelter them from participation with others.

however, survive the full gestation period and are born with one or more handicaps. In addition to genetically defective babies, of course, there are those whose impairments arise during the pregnancy or birth. Prenatal drug use, anoxia, and brain damage by birthing instruments are examples of the many possible causes. The list of possible impairments is long. It includes the following categories: sight, hearing, speech, emotional, orthopedic, health, and learning. Within each category, one can specify numerous types of impairments.

A handicapped baby is of immediate concern to the parents and family. The severity of the handicap determines the degree of concern. First, of course, there is shock and disappointment along with sympathy for this new loved one. Some parents are forced to recognize that the child cannot receive proper care at home and must be placed in an institution. Other parents must face the child's imminent death. Still others must accept the long-term responsibility of nurturing the impaired child to adulthood and beyond.

We have discussed the need for parents to recognize that each child is different from every other child. For special needs children, the differences are more extreme, and the needs may be extraordinary. One of the most important, and often most difficult tasks is to satisfy the child's basic need for acceptance.

Special needs children are no different from other persons in their need to achieve good self-concepts. They need to be included, they need friends, they need time with their loved ones, and they need to be encouraged to participate and perform up to their capabilities. Some parents of special needs children make the mistake of being overprotective. Special needs children, like all other children, need to face the real world and adapt, cope, and develop whatever degree of independence is possible. We help special needs children to attain these goals by stressing what they *can* do, not what they can't do.

Whatever the special need of a child, it will require extra expenditures of money, patience, creativity, and energy by the family. Parents are well-advised to work closely with professionals who understand the problems of special needs children. The earlier the impairment is discovered, and the earlier the extra help begins, the greater the advantage is to the child and the family. With specialized education and training, the children have the best opportunity for reaching their potential.

Caring for a special needs child can put great stress on family relationships. Parents must be attentive to each other's needs as well as the needs of other family members. It is fair to expect family cooperation to meet the needs of the special needs child, but it would be unfair to demand so many sacrifices that other siblings cannot lead normal lives.

Children and Drugs

When the drug problem exploded during the 1960s, many people thought it was a problem for a rather small group of "disturbed" college students, and that for a few others it was a fad. Drugs were something new, to be tested and tried. But drugs caught on and spread through colleges. The users ranged from youths who may have been disturbed to those who were, by our standards, normal, sociable, and well-adjusted. From colleges, drugs seeped into high schools, and from high schools into elementary schools.

The impact of drugs is staggering. It has affected the international economy. It has affected children of political leaders and millionaire business people as well as children from middle- and low-income families. The impact and pervasiveness of drugs are now apparent to all people. In one way or another, drugs have affected virtually everybody's lives. The wide use of illegal drugs has affected the functions of government, medicine, law, law enforcement, education, and parenthood.

The reasons for drug use are varied. Some young people are pressured by peers into experimenting with drugs. Other young people learn by example from parents or other adults. Some adolescents want to escape from inner turmoil or emotional problems. Yet others are simply bored or just curious.

Society as a whole may be partly to blame for present-day attitudes toward mind-altering drugs. Martini lunches and cocktail parties are standard for many people in government, business, and industry. Drugs are used widely by dieters for weight loss. Tranquilizers,

Drugs hurt all of us. When you consider that children learn so much by example, what is the potential effect of witnessing a drug purchase?

sleeping pills, and pep pills are prescribed on a regular basis for millions of people. If children are identifying with their parents, maybe it is not surprising that many youths are not averse to experimenting with chemical substances.

Regardless of the reasons for experimentation and use of mind-altering drugs, they pose a serious danger to our society. Drugs can create the illusion of intense and immediate experience that is self-oriented and exclusive of the troubling outside world. The great danger is that young drug users will lose a sense of their capacity to experience reality, and that they will abandon what could be influential roles in our society. If so, they may simply drift toward a totally isolated existence.

The drug problem is a practical one that demands practical solutions. More theoretical solutions, such as honest communication between youths and adults, are important, but the problem must also be dealt with in concrete terms. For prevention, of course, we need education of our youth and the public on the dangers involved in the use of mind-altering drugs. After the fact, however, we somehow need to rehabilitate those who have become addicted.

It is usually extremely difficult for abusers to understand the dire consequences of continued use of alcohol or other drugs. Obviously, the earlier they

A Matter of Fact

Do you know what emergency action to use for poisoning? Symptoms that signal poisoning include vomiting, diarrhea, burns around the mouth, convulsions, empty containers nearby, and signs of ingesting poisonous plants. If caregivers suspect poisoning, call the number for poison control or 911. Keep a sample of the suspected poison or the bottle so the poison can be identified.

If the child has swallowed medicines, don't give anything by mouth until you have called for medical advice. If the child has swallowed household products or chemicals, unless the child is unconscious, having convulsions, or cannot swallow, give milk or water immediately. Then call for medical advice about whether you should make the child vomit or not. Chemicals that burn going down will burn coming up.

Rule of Thumb: Keep on hand a one-ounce bottle of syrup of ipecac for each child in the home. Ipecac is a drug that is extracted from the South American Ipecacuana plant. It is a natural irritant to the stomach that safely induces vomiting within a short time. Ipecac is available without a prescription at any pharmacy. Use ipecac only on the advice of a poison control center, emergency department, or physician.

can be convinced to seek treatment, the less permanent damage will be done to their minds and bodies. Their rehabilitation will be easier as well.

The abusers of alcohol and other mind-altering drugs create serious problems for their families and friends, as well as for themselves. Family members often need to seek out support groups or professional counselors for help in rebuilding strained or broken relationships with the abuser and, sometimes, even with other members of the family.

Death

Despite the naturalness of death as the conclusion of life, death is a source of crisis because it brings about drastic changes in the lives of those who remain. Facing the fact that death is inevitable can make life more meaningful. Confronting the idea of death is one of the most challenging ways to consider the meaning of our activities in life. Are we leading a life that we can look back on with satisfaction?

Fears Associated with Death

There are many thoughts that enter our minds as we confront our own death and the death of others. Some of the thoughts are listed here.

1. Impact on family and friends. What will happen to my family and friends when I am no longer living? How will they face the change either emotionally, socially, or financially?

2. Interruption of goals, dreams, plans. People fear that death will keep them from achieving their plans, goals, or dreams. The last words of Alexander Graham Bell sum up this attitude, "So little done. So much to do."

3. Fear of death of others. How will I cope with their illness? How will I cope with the pain of death? How will I live without my parent or my friend or my relative? How will I cope with the pain of death?

4. Fear of not being. The idea that death could come at any moment makes some people worry about the purpose of their lives.

5. Fear of embarrassment. Some people fear that when they have to face death they may find themselves cowards.

6. Fear of suffering and pain. It is difficult to think of one's body or mind deteriorating.

Children and Death

When a child asks, "What is dead?" the simplest sort of factual answer may be all that is needed. It is not so much what we say as how we say it. The following excerpt elaborates on this problem of helping children cope with and understand death.

A Closer Look

When Donna's mother told Donna that her grandmother had died, the little girl showed no sign of emotion. Although she had loved her grandmother dearly and had spent a fair amount of time with her, Donna seemed almost unaffected by the news. Awkwardly, as if she were embarrassed, Donna said, "Grandma was very old, wasn't she?" Then she looked away and said, "Janie is waiting for me outside." She ran out to play with her friend.

Donna's response to the news that someone she cared for had died was altogether normal. Indeed, Donna's reaction, though not the only kind children are likely to make, was more typical than not. As a first response, it was a healthy one.

Though parents are likely to feel that a lack of expressed feeling on a child's part indicates a callous and uncaring attitude, this is by no means true. Children are not indifferent to death or uncaring about such a loss. A lack of concern such as Donna's is only apparent, not real, and serves an important purpose. The fact is that death, particularly the death of someone's parent, is very threatening to children. It is so threatening that they can't take it in all at once. The death of Donna's grandmother—her mother's mother—signified to Donna that mothers can die. What if her own mother, whom she needed more than anyone else in the world, were to die? It's more than likely that the one spoken response Donna made was an effort to quiet her instant fear. "Grandma was very old, wasn't she?" meaning, "My mommy won't die. She's not old."

Fortunately, Donna's mother wasn't hurt or angered by her daughter's apparent indifference. She understood that the meaning of the event which was so painful to her the—realization that she would not see her mother again—was not yet a reality to her daughter. Even more than adults, children need time to absorb a grave shock such as this one. They need time to come to accept it and understand it.

Emotions and Death

There has been a great deal of research during the past 30 years devoted to understanding the meaning of death and seeking ways to help people cope with loss. Many psychiatrists believe that there are three stages of mourning that need to be lived through if the person is to regain equilibrium after suffering a deep loss. During the first stage, the bereaved person gradually absorbs the shock of the loss. In this stage, some people deny the facts. Donna's blankness and her running out to play were expressions of denial, of pushing the facts away from her for the time being, and pretending that everything was just the same as always.

More commonly, during this first stage, both adults and children find themselves flooded by feelings of disbelief from time to time. "I can't believe he's gone" or "It's impossible to take it in." By expressing such feelings and talking about them, grieving persons gradually permit the terrible fact to become real to them.

The second stage of mourning is the active, open expression of sorrow. The admission of the loneliness that lies ahead. It is the acknowledgement that one feels anger and bitterness.

Finally, a person reaches the third stage of mourning, which is the beginning of healing and the return to emotional stability. This is the time when bereaved persons accept death and the fact that it has touched their lives closely. They think about the meaning of this painful event, the lessons to be learned by those who are still alive. They begin to regain a sense of independence and self. For most adults this process may take a year or two. For children, who are more vulnerable to loss, it may take longer.

Most adults instinctively recognize the wisdom of openly facing this kind of hurt and, therefore, friends and family members encourage the person most deeply involved to talk about feelings and memories of the person who has died. The customs found in all countries that bring friends and relatives to visit with those who are bereaved help the person through this necessary act of grieving.

Children who have suffered a loss need even more encouragement than adults to begin the process of mourning. Being more needy emotionally and more threatened by death, they are likely to try to cover up their sorrow.

If young children have suffered the loss of a parent, they may be fearful. They may think, "What will become of us?" In addition, they are likely to be overwhelmed by feelings of guilt and anger. Often, children believe that bad things can happen to them for bad things they have done. Perhaps in the past they said to their parent, "I hate you. I wish you were dead." Now, superstitiously, they believe this is their punishment for having had such a wish. Beyond this they may feel great anger because their mother or father abandoned them. They are likely to be ashamed of their anger and in turn feel guilty about that, too.

Children need help to recover from the deep shock of losing a parent or a brother or sister (which tells them that children die, too). They need patient and loving encouragement to enable them to express their feelings, overcome them, and gradually gain the courage to make new attachments. Children are helped to deal with their feelings by having a model to follow, by seeing how adults whom they trust handle sorrow. This is why they should not be "protected" from all participation in the events following a death in the family. They should be permitted to take part in sorrowful family gatherings, and they should be treated naturally.

Unfortunately, many adults are not prepared to help children handle tragedy. Many aspects of our culture teach us to control ourselves in the face of heartbreak. Lots of men and women believe that to break down and cry or give way to feelings of despair at the time of a tragedy are signs of weakness. On the contrary, the expression of such feelings is necessary to emotional strength.

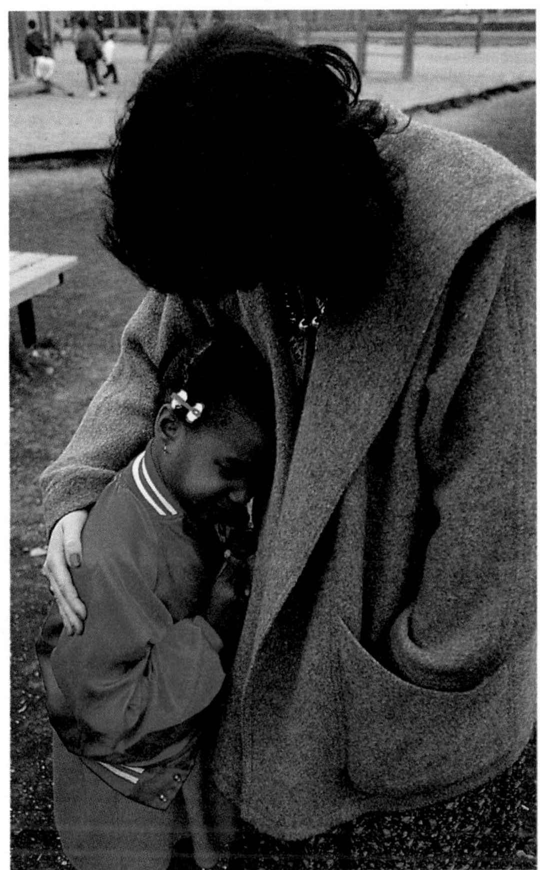

The death of someone in the family or a friend is a painful experience. Caregivers can help children cope with their grief.

Death of a Child

As the death of a parent or parents is the most terrible loss to a child and the most difficult to overcome, so the death of a child is the hardest loss for parents to sustain. Yet when parents lose a child they must not only cope with their own shock, they must also help their other children express their feelings.

The most comforting thing parents and children can do is to talk together, unhesitatingly referring to the child who has died whenever it is natural to do so. "Remember how funny Johnny looked when he caught the frog?" or "There's the teacher you and Johnny both had when you were in fourth grade." Trying to avoid this painful topic can only keep the pain alive. Talking about the many things one remembers doesn't immediately diminish the sorrow of losing a child, of course, but it does gradually make the loss more bearable.

Sometimes, before children can talk about their feelings, they act them out.

A 12-year-old boy whose older brother was killed in an accident became quarrelsome with almost everyone. The patience his parents and teachers showed him helped him cope with his anger at his loss, enabling him gradually to express his feelings directly, and to talk about them openly.

Helping Children Understand Death

To prepare children in a general way to accept death as they will one day have to do, we need to help them understand the naturalness of death and its simplicity. Frequently, of course, children learn this important lesson about death as the natural conclusion of life in a way they can comprehend and accept. This happens when they are able to experience some of the sorrow that death brings without being excessively threatened by it. Typically for children, this happens when a pet dies. Youngsters (as well as adults) feel keenly the loss of an animal companion. They say sadly that they'll never be able to love another dog or cat or rabbit again. No matter how sad they feel however, they know their security, safety, and well-being are not threatened by such a loss. After a while they succumb to the charms of another puppy or kitten or bunny. They are able to love and take care of a pet again.

If children sense that their questions do not trouble you too much, they will know it is all right to think and talk about death. It is a matter of such prime importance that children's genuine searching deserves encouragement. Moreover, children will gain much strength from the realization that the subject of death can be talked about without fear.

As children grow older, they learn that both life and death raise questions that are worth asking, whether they can be answered completely or not. Recognizing that many questions cannot be answered, we gain a reverence for both life and death. Children should be made to feel comfortable, emotionally and intellectually, about the changes in their lives, including those brought on by the deaths of loved ones. In the lyrics of a song, Mike Nobel has expressed one parent's attempt to answer his child's questions about death. (Reprinted with permission.)

The Valley On One Side Is Green

by Mike Nobel

One day my daughter and I took a hike
On a summer mountain,
Searching as we sometimes do
For the perfect view
And we came to a hillside,
Filled with flowers, that
Looked out over so many
Rivers and valleys, it seemed like the
Whole world was in our gaze

And there, with the sun on our backs,
And the colors in our eyes
My daughter turned to me and said,
Daddy, where do I go when I die
And I smiled, and looked
Straight up into the sky
And though I didn't have an answer,
I gave it a try

I said, the valley on one side is green
And the banks all ablaze with life
And the birds sing a soft song of hope
To the birds on the other side

And in the floor of the valley
Flows a laughing river

Under a bridge called the bridge of no cares
And the bridge on this side is made of gold
On the far side, it's made of air

And you'll cross that bridge, and hear the
Laughing voices of a million souls
Who crossed before you
And they'll take you in their arms,
And teach you their songs, and fill you
With the joy of love

And your voice will join with theirs
In the roar of the oceans, and in
The music of the skies
And all the wonders, and all the
Mysteries of life will be clear
Before your eyes

And here, in this field
There will grow a young flower
As sweet as your laughter
To smile for your friends
Who remember your songs
And they can hear you, though you're gone
And you'll be gone, but you'll be here

Concept of Death at Age Five to Six Years

The young child begins with a matter-of-fact orientation to death. The child believes that death is deliberate and planned. Death is not viewed as an inevitable occurrence. Young children assume that death will not occur if they are good. Children see themselves as all powerful. For this reason, children may believe that they are responsible for the death of a loved one. Because of their natural self-centered focus and limited understanding of cause and effect relationships, young children of five or six years of age do not clearly comprehend the finality of death.

"What makes people die?" asks the young child. It is important to find out why the child has asked this question. An effective response is to give a simple physical reason for the particular death, explaining that we do not yet know how to cure some diseases or heal the injuries of some accidents. If the child expresses guilt feelings about the death, adults should help the child develop a new set of perceptions by discussing the positive aspects of the relationship. Children need to be told that they were loved by the deceased, but that the deceased cannot come back to life.

Children should not be told that death is like sleep or a sickness. Thinking death is like sleep may cause a fear of bedtime. Comparing death to sickness causes children to be fearful when they or loved ones become ill.

Concepts of Death at Age Seven to Nine Years

Young school children are aware that death is the common finality for all living things. They associate death with the disintegration of the body. Many children up to age 10 visualize death in various forms, that is, as a bogeyman, a skeleton, or a ghost. To children of this age, death still seems to occur mostly to the old, but they are beginning to sense that it can occur to adults like their parents and possibly even to children like themselves.

Many children of elementary school age who suffer a loss do not show their grief verbally but display their feeling in other ways. Since school is their natural habitat outside home, the school situation becomes a main focus for such displacement. Many bereaved children cannot concentrate on their school work and have no desire to play with friends.

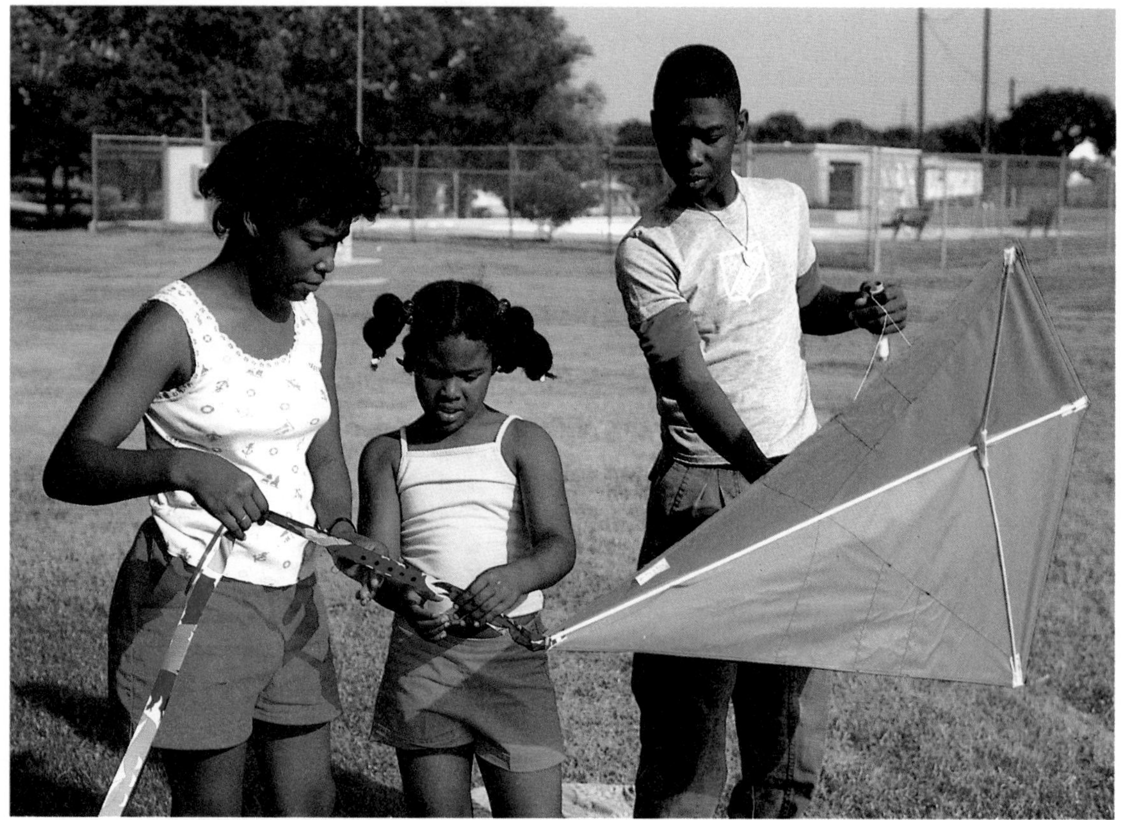

In a family crisis, it is important for the children to be able to depend on each other.

It is important for children to realize that weeping is not a sign of immaturity or weakness. Adults can assist children to understand that sorrow and tears are not for the person who has died, but are expressions of our own sorrow at having lost a loved one. Sorrow and tears show our recognition that we are going to miss that loved one very much. The vocabularies of children in this age group may not allow them full expression of their intense feelings. Creative play with clay, crayons, or paints can be helpful forms of expression.

If a child tells the teacher that a significant person in their lives has died, the teacher may ask the child to tell about the happy and not-so-happy times they had together. Adults can help a child realize that no two people can always have happy times together and that the angry feelings do not lessen the love and strength of the relationship.

Concept of Death at Age 10 to 12 Years

By the age of 10 years, most children have the concepts of time, matter,

Some parents hide their grief over the death of a loved one from their children. However, adults can help children understand that the person will be missed and that crying is an expression of that sorrow.

cause, and effect that allow them to understand that death is final and inevitable. Nevertheless, the desire for self-preservation is so strong that children who are faced with death will fantasize an alternative. They will try to mentally find some way they can continue to exist after death.

Coping with Death and Dying

Some children are unable to put their understanding of death into words. Elisabeth Kübler-Ross, psychiatrist and world-renowned authority on death and dying, suggests that these children can often express their feelings through art. When a child is given crayons and paper, he or she often draws a picture of a huge tank, a huge cannon, or a large fire. These objects signify death as the destructive and unstoppable force that the child feels. The child also draws a stick figure of a child holding a stop sign or a white flag signifying a fruitless attempt to halt the force. A child's counselor, who wants to share in this nonverbal concern, may draw a large stick figure standing next to the small stick figure with a hand on the small figure's shoulder. This picture would say to the child, "I cannot stop death, but I can be here with you to comfort you." Dr. Ross says that after several such drawing sessions, the child often draws a large

Creative art projects can help children express their emotions.

bird. This is a bird of peace flying away from the destructive scene. The child is expressing acceptance of the inevitability of death.

A different kind of indirect communication came from a terminally ill eight-year-old who was in an oxygen tent. She had not spoken of illness or death to anyone. She asked a nurse, "What happens if my oxygen tent catches on fire?"

The nurse replied, "It won't. We don't allow anybody to smoke in here." The reply was understandable, but the nurse recognized that the child was reaching out for help. So, the nurse sat down beside the child's bed and said, "What do you really want to ask about a fire?" The child cried, "I just know I am going to die and I've just got to talk to someone about it."

Many people try to keep terminally ill children ignorant of their condition. These youngsters often sense the concerns of adults and feel that questions about their illnesses are not permitted. Some children who are terminally ill are not old enough or mature enough to understand or to cope with information about their situation. However, children are very curious. They have questions and concerns. Some children benefit by having their questions answered and their concerns shared. It is not uncommon to learn that children have sensed the terminal nature of their illness, but have failed to discuss their own concerns for fear of upsetting their families.

A Closer Look

The parents of 12-year-old Billy knew that he had leukemia. They asked the doctor to withhold the facts from the child. The doctor agreed. Billy's questions about his illness were answered with assurance that he would soon be feeling better.

After a while Billy did not ask questions about his health. As he came closer to death, the seriousness of his condition was still kept secret. Both of his parents and the doctor felt that Billy would suffer needlessly if he knew how little time he had to live. Billy asked no questions. He kept all of his conversations cheerful.

After Billy's death, his close school friend said that he knew what had been wrong with Billy. Billy had told him, but had made him promise to tell no one. The doctor and the parents then realized that because they had not been willing to discuss the truth with Billy, they had forced him to face death alone.

Children with terminal illness search continuously for verbal as well as nonverbal clues that can help them to cope with isolation. They listen for changes in tones of voices, sounds of footsteps, and parents' expressions. Their first feelings may be those of isolation and loneliness. The concept of death is the same as separation. For this reason, parents of fatally ill children should be allowed to be with them as much as possible. In this way, the child is comforted and the parents can face the serious illness of their child.

When a child is terminally ill, the emotional strain on the family is great. The family goes through the same five stages that a dying adult does—denial, anger, bargaining, depression and grief, and acceptance as outlined here.

The five stages just referred to are the "stages of dying" expressed and described by Dr. Ross in her book, *On Death and Dying.*

1. **Denial.** "No, not me." This is the typical first reaction when a person learns of terminal illness. Denial helps to cushion the impact of the patient's awareness that death is inevitable.
2. **Anger—rage.** "Why me?" The patient resents the fact that they must die while others lead healthy lives.
3. **Bargaining.** "Yes, me, but...." The person thinks, "Maybe a cure will be developed next week, maybe the tests are incorrect, maybe if I do something a miracle will happen."
4. **Depression.** "Yes, me." Initially, this is a time of mourning past losses, things not done, and wrongs committed. Later, the person enters a state of "preparatory grief," getting ready for the arrival of death.
5. **Acceptance.** "My time is very close now and it's all right."

Suicide

For about a month, John had been rather moody, but then he changed. For several days he seemed happy, eager to talk, glad to be with his parents, and especially kind to his brother Tom. Before John's mother took Tom to his piano lesson, she asked John to turn on the oven in 25 minutes and to boil water for spaghetti. She said they'd be home for dinner after they picked up Dad at the train station.

When they arrived home, John was dead. The water was boiling, and the meat balls were warming in the oven, but John was dead. Why? Why had John committed suicide?

Suicide has been called the last statement of anger. Others have labeled it the permanent solution to a temporary problem. Suicide knows no boundaries. It can occur in any neighborhood. Its victims belong to all races, religions, age groups, ethnic groups, and economic classes. They have no particular psychological makeup.

What was John's problem? Why was he angry? Often, for those left behind, there are no ready answers. They often need counseling to help them through their grief. It is common for them to blame themselves or others. There are guilt feelings to be dealt with, along with feelings of anger and betrayal. Beside the crisis of losing a family member, there is the crisis of losing esteem because of failed relationships.

Teenage suicide is a growing problem. According to William Steele who is Clinical Supervisor of the Suicide Prevention Center, some teenagers are deeply concerned with threats and social problems that were almost unknown in earlier generations. Among these are the threat of nuclear devastation, fear of not finding a job, fear of moving to a new location, and the difficulty of trying to find new friends. Youngsters today are bombarded with violence in movies and on television. In many areas, street violence is common. When such problems weigh heavily on a person's mind, he or she may feel that nothing has stability or positive purpose. Youngsters are at a disadvantage in dealing with their concerns because they have a very limited concept of the future. They think what they're feeling today is what they will feel for the rest of their lives.

Can suicide be prevented? The answer is a qualified "yes." Friends and family can help someone who is contemplating suicide if they are aware of certain signs

- Excessive worry, loss of appetite, changes in habits and behavior, sleepless nights.
- Excessive generosity—giving away prized possessions.
- Sudden relief of tension, a newly acquired relaxed attitude.

Here are some suggestions to help teenagers cope with the stresses they may be feeling:

- Keep a happy, open interchange in the family.
- Don't expect perfection.
- Realize that tomorrow may very well be a better day.
- Don't make an exaggerated effort to hide errors.
- Let the child share in the family ups and downs.
- Reinforce positives at all levels.
- Share in joys. Spend time together in a positive, restful manner.
- Recognize that there is no need to keep up with anyone else.
- Applaud the self.
- Remember that almost all problems are temporary, but suicide is permanent.
- Be aware that help is available. The Crisis Intervention Service and The Suicide Prevention Service are listed in the Yellow Pages of many phone books. If you find neither "crisis" nor "suicide" in your phone book, your police, county health agency, library, or phone operator can tell you who to call for guidance.

Life's Work

Melissa Orcutt

➤Teacher of the Severely Handicapped
➤Elementary Teaching Credential and Specialist Credential

Melissa says that her day starts at 8:15 with preparation of the classroom and materials for the day's work. The students arrive at 8:45. From that point on her day is divided into 30-minute segments that stress a specific skill area such as dressing, fine motor and large motor skills, speech, and language. She has a 30-minute lunch break and a 30-minute preparation period during the day. With other staff members, she rotates yard, lunch, and bus duty. The students leave at 2:30. Then she has meetings with the staff or parents. Extracurricular activities such as Special Olympics can extend the day.

Melissa says the skills necessary for success in her profession include, "A sense of humor, organizational skills, effective communication skills, a solid background in methods and techniques for teaching special needs children, patience, and the ability to see growth in small increments."

Melissa's most rewarding job-related accomplishment is "Watching my 'special' students blend into a 'regular' school program so effectively that no one could point them out—not parents, teachers, or other children."

For a student considering going into Melissa's profession, she recommends, "Visit special education classrooms to make sure you can handle the sights, sounds, and smells of that type of room. Volunteer your time with special needs individuals. Examine your motives. You will not be an effective teacher because you pity your students, rather you need to respect them."

When asked how her profession will change within the next 10 years, Melissa says, "Unfortunately, there will always be a need for special education teachers. But I do see technology coming more and more into the classroom. This includes more sophisticated computers to assist in speech and language areas, braces, chairs, toys, and books that the child can maneuver independently."

In Review

Vocabulary

crisis
crisis-prone
involvement
integration
adaptation
pre-divorce phase
divorce phase
post-divorce phase

Summary

- ✓ A crisis is a turning point. Crises require decisions that influence the rest of a person's life. A crisis may result from actions of that person, the family, outsiders, or nature.
- ✓ Whether a situation becomes a crisis for a family depends on its severity, the family's perception of the situation, and the family's ability to cope.
- ✓ Moving is a stressful time for families. Along with all the details that parents must deal with, they must also be sensitive to children's concerns. Children need to understand why the family will benefit from the move, and they need parental guidance in adapting after the move is made.
- ✓ Divorce occurs in three phases, all of which can be very troubling to children.
- ✓ Child abuse is a self-perpetuating problem. Abused children often become abusive parents. Abuse, whether it is verbal, physical, or sexual, leaves psychological scars on children.
- ✓ Raising a special needs child can present a family with many crises. The welfare of special needs children is best served when their individuality is accepted, and when their talents are stressed, challenged, and reinforced.
- ✓ Almost every family has been affected directly or indirectly by drug abuse. Drug prevention through education is important, of course, but rehabilitation is also required for those who have been hurt.
- ✓ Like many adults, children have fears associated with death. Their questions require answers at a level they can understand. They need frankness, even when they are terminally ill themselves.
- ✓ After a death in the family, children need to go through the stages of mourning, just as adults do. Parents should not try to hide their grief or shelter children from its reality.

Questions

1. Without using names, discuss a circumstance that appeared to be a crisis for one person you know, but was treated as insignificant by someone else in the same situation. What characteristics of the two people caused them to react so differently?

2. Give a one-word answer to the following question: What is most important for the relief of stress in families? Explain your answer.

3. List three fears that a seven-year-old child might express about an upcoming move to another state. If you were the child's parent, how would you help the child deal with these fears?

4. In question 3, substitute "high school sophomore" for "seven-year-old child."

5. Discuss at least three points that you would stress in telling your five-year-old child that you and your spouse have decided to separate. Explain why each point is important for the child's well-being.

6. Describe the stages of the mourning process.

7. How can a child be helped to understand and cope with death?

8. When answering a child's questions about the death of a loved one, how can you avoid causing the child undue fear? Discuss your thoughts about the lyrics of "The Valley on One Side Is Green."

Activities

1. Look up "death" in *Bartlett's Familiar Quotations.* Write down three quotations and discuss why they are the most meaningful to you.

2. Imagine yourself in the following situation: For the third time in a month you have lost patience with your little girl and struck her hard and repeatedly, leaving her bruised. In a calmer moment, you remember the advice contained in a few lines of Mike Nobel's lyrics, "Take a Step Back from Anger" below, and you decide to seek some help. What steps would you take to find appropriate counsel?

Just trying to be a good parent
Can be the hardest job in your life.
You know, kids can make so many demands
On your energy and your time.

But when you feel that old volcano of
Frustration is gonna go off,
Please take a step back from anger
And try to solve the problem with love.

a Child Restraint Device

Agencies Working for Children

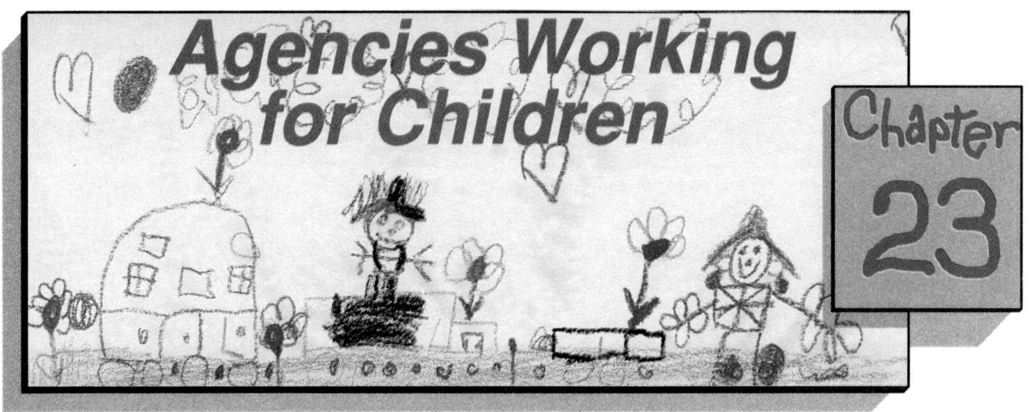

Chapter 23

- recognize that outside help is available for seemingly overwhelming family problems
- understand that families should not feel ashamed to seek help when they cannot find solutions to their problems from within themselves
- identify sources of professional and volunteer family services for various types of family problems
- understand the need for and the purposes of foster care

When We Need Help

At times, our lives may seem more like mazes than open paths to the goals we seek. We may need a helping hand to find our way. It can happen to anyone.

When we marry, we marry with great expectations. We hope that our love will grow, that our health will continue, and that we will be able to handle our problems. We expect to be financially independent, to be happy, to have many friends, and to be able to solve our problems together. Yes, we all have great hopes as we start out on the adventures of married life.

When we embark on the adventure of parenthood, we also picture in our mind an ideal situation. We hope for a healthy, happy, normal child. We also see ourselves as very successful in our parenting role. How often we think, "When I'm a parent, I'll do such and such.... I'll be a really super parent." We hope that all these expectations will come true.

What do we do when our hopes and dreams do not materialize? What do we do if our baby is not what we had expected? What if our baby is deaf, blind, or physically or mentally handicapped? What do we do if we find that we must support a child and ourselves without help from our family or a partner? What do we do if we face housing problems?

The loneliness, the disappointment, and the frustration when our hopes and dreams are crushed are difficult to

A Matter of Fact

The term "displaced homemaker" is becoming more familiar to American families. A displaced homemaker is an individual, in most cases a woman, who has lost her primary source of income because of divorce, separation, the death or disability of the spouse, or the loss of public assistance.

Today, there are more than 11 million displaced homemakers in the United States, and 9 million of these are over the age of 45. Statistics reveal more than half lack a high school diploma, and two-thirds of displaced homemakers are unemployed.

Although we live in an era when women have entered the paid labor force in record number, the stories of millions of displaced homemakers tell of a different life pattern. These are the women who stayed home and raised their families.

Displaced homemakers have a common need—jobs. But frequently they face a double barrier when forced to enter the job market, their age and lack of paid employment history. These women need counseling and support systems in order not to fall through the cracks in society.

There are more than 900 programs geared toward displaced homemakers. The clearinghouse for information on displaced homemakers is the Displaced Homemakers Network, 1411 K Street, NW, Suite 930, Washington, DC 20005.

consider. In times of trouble, stresses build up and troubles seem to multiply.

Sometimes, families cannot solve their own problems. Families with problems should not feel alone. There are agencies at local, state, and federal levels, that can help them with their troubles. There are also local support groups that provide assistance. By seeking the proper agency, council, counselor, service, or support group, families can come to grips with their problems.

Families should not feel ashamed to seek help nor should they expect to be able to find solutions to all their problems from within themselves. Most people would not expect to grind their own lenses for their glasses or fix a broken refrigerator. People often seek help with their problems. A difficult family problem, like any other problem, may be solved with some outside help that provides valuable insights and fresh perspectives.

Where to Find Help

Help for many family problems may be as close as the Yellow Pages or Blue Pages in your phone book. Most county and city governments provide many **social services** and can steer families to volunteer and support groups for many other kinds of help. By calling the general information number listed for the county, a family can obtain the numbers of agencies providing the services they'll need. Cities and counties are organized differently, so these agencies may be listed under Health Services, Human Services, or some other department.

Usually, city and county agencies dealing in human services are aware of all the volunteer organizations and support groups in the county. Thus, even if a family does not feel the need for the professional expertise directly available through the agency they contacted, the agency can put them in touch with the appropriate group for their particular needs.

Many of the volunteer organizations have religious affiliations, such as:

- Interfaith Family Life Centers
- Catholic Charities
- Church Women United
- Churches United—Youth Service Homes
- Combined Jewish Philanthropies
- Salvation Army
- FISH

DENNIS the MENACE
'WHY ARE CATS AN' DOGS SO EASY TO UNNERSTAND... AN' PEOPLE SO HARD?'

DENNIS THE MENACE® Cartoon used by permission of and © by Field Enterprises, Inc.

FISH is an organization founded in England in 1961. It now has a total of 1000 chapters in the United States and several other countries. There is at least one chapter in most urban communities of the United States. This volunteer service provides emergency transportation, clothing, and babysitting when needed for individuals and families in crisis. More information is available from The Anchor Society, 2398 Pine Street, San Francisco, CA 94115.

There are now support groups for nearly every imaginable family concern. Look in the Yellow Pages under Social Service organizations for such groups as:

- Alcoholics Anonymous
- Association for Children with Learning Disabilities (for children and their parents)
- Emotions Anonymous
- Families Anonymous (for families of youth with behavior problems)
- Narcotics Anonymous
- Parents Anonymous (for parents of abused children)
- Parents without Partners

More information on mutual-help groups can be obtained from the Con-

A Matter of Fact

It is a sad fact of life that many children diagnosed with a life-threatening disease will not live to see their dreams realized. However, many organizations throughout the United States and Canada try to see to it that no child dies without having her or his wish come true. The Make-A-Wish Foundation, headquartered in Phoenix, is just one organization that grants wishes to terminally ill children, up to age 18, regardless of the family's emotional or financial circumstances.

In most cases, the parent or guardian of the terminally ill child must contact the organization in order to get the wish fulfillment process started. The child's doctor may be asked to confirm the diagnosis before the child can qualify, and the family may fill out an application or be asked for an interview. Most wish fulfillment organizations handle the process rapidly, because they realize these children simply can't wait.

What do children wish for? One of the most popular wishes is a trip to Disneyworld or Disneyland. Some children wish for a personal visit from famous athletes or movie stars. Many organizations recognize the importance of keeping the family together—and wish fulfillment organizations make it possible for immediate family members to participate in the child's dream as well.

Wish fulfillment organizations are able to grant the wishes of terminally ill children through the goodwill of volunteers and donors who give their time, money, talents, facilities, and equipment to help bring some child's dream to life.

To find out more about these types of organizations, you can contact the American Cancer Society.

sumer Information Center, Pueblo, CO 81009.

Your public library can provide you with more human-service information including names of agencies, their objectives, addresses, telephone numbers, and fees. One reference book is the *Medical and Health Directory*, which is a guide to professional and nonprofit organizations, government agencies, educational institutions, and health-care delivery agencies.

Pamphlets and information on a variety of topics relating to parenting can be obtained from The National Committee for Prevention of Child Abuse (NCPCA). One of their pamphlets, for example, is entitled, "You're Not Alone: Kids Book on Alcoholism and Child Abuse." Write or call NCPCA, Publishing Department, 332 S. Michigan Avenue, Suite 950, Chicago, IL 60604-4357, (312) 663-3520.

Another guide to organizations is the *United States Government Manual*. This reference book, published each year, describes the purposes and programs of most federal government agencies and lists key officials. Some of the agencies and departments that deal with problems of children and youth are:

- Action (Administration for Children, Youth, and Families)
- AFDC (Aid to Families with Dependent Children)
- Department of Human Resources
- Department of Social Services
- Department of Welfare
- Employment and Training Administrations
- Family Service Agency
- Food and Nutrition Service
- Health Services Administration
- National Institute of Health
- Office of Child Support Enforcement
- Office of Human Development Services
- Office of Juvenile Justice and Delinquency Prevention
- W.I.C. (Women, Infants, and Children)

The *Encyclopedia of Associations*, usually available in your local library, also provides detailed descriptions of over 13,000 national and international nonprofit organizations. It contains information on social welfare, health and medicine, public affairs, and religious organizations. Listed under **social welfare organizations,** for example, are agencies concerned with adoption, foster care, daycare, child development and education, child abuse, etc. The *Encyclopedia* is especially useful because it refers people who need information on highly qualified sources. By making phone calls or sending letters to the appropriate organizations, people usually can obtain the information they need.

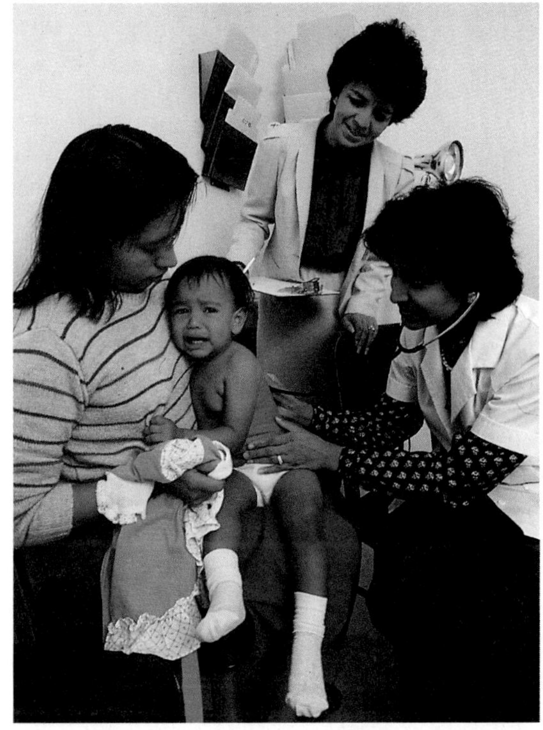

Human service agencies provide help to families in need of health care.

Some counties have compiled their own *Who's Who in Human Services.* Your library may have a copy of this and/or a social services directory for your area.

Agencies and Foster Care

Agencies that place children in foster homes have a great responsibility. They play an important role in the lives of the children and the parents. Foster parents are paid by the agency to provide temporary care for children while their parents work out financial, emotional, or medical problems.

Because they have a well-rounded education, these deaf students have the ability and confidence to perform in a concert.

The placement a foster care agency makes for children definitely affects their emotional development. If the agency places children in a family with whom they feel comfortable and compatible, they may thrive. If the placement is a poor match for a child and the family, the child may suffer emotional damage. Frequently foster care children have been shifted from one unhappy placement to another. This instability has traumatized many children and made them unable to make emotional attachments to others.

Kinds of Placement

There are different kinds of placement for children. The outcome of foster care for a child could be:

1. a long period of placement (more than three months, less than total childhood), terminating in a return home
2. a long period of placement, terminating in adoption
3. placement for the duration of childhood with minimal change
4. repeated placements for the duration of childhood.

The first possibility represents the most desirable outcome for the child, while the last represents the least desirable one. The second and third possibilities lie between the two extremes.

Foster care agencies make an effort to support the natural family unit. They set a high value on the reunion of children and their parents. When these agencies find, however, that the parents' circumstances do not improve, they do not want to return the child to the parents. The agencies, in this case, give full support to the foster home relationship as long as the foster parents want to continue in that role and are able to do so.

In a sense, the agencies recognize and favor the "psychological parents," who best serve the child's interests and fulfill the child's emotional and physical needs. The natural parents, however, may insist that their child be returned to them. Courts and legislators generally support the parents' rights, even when there is some evidence of abuse, neglect, or indifference. There is much pressure against government agencies taking children away from their parents.

Agencies responsible for foster care affect people's lives significantly. They help parents who can't or won't provide care for their children. They try to rehabilitate biological families. They provide services in times of crisis. Most importantly, they give children a chance for a happy home life and a chance to feel loved.

In Review

Vocabulary

social services   social welfare organizations

Summary

- ✓ Embarking on the adventures of marriage and parenthood, couples have expectations and dreams that sometimes don't come true. When seemingly overwhelming problems arise, we should feel no shame in seeking the help of support groups or professional counseling.
- ✓ There is help available from outside the family unit for virtually every type of family problem. In seeking the appropriate assistance, a good place to start requesting information is a local county government.
- ✓ The goal of foster care agencies is to support the natural family unit by providing temporary care for children while their parents work out financial, emotional, medical, or other problems.

Questions

1. How do human service agencies serve all of us, even if we do not personally seek their help or counsel?

2. Suppose that your spouse was killed in an auto accident two months ago. Grief, financial problems, and single parenthood are creating more stress than you can handle by yourself. Outline a positive approach for dealing with this crisis in your life.

3. Three children were placed in a foster home because their natural parents abused them. Six months later, the parents appeared before a judge to demand the children's return to their custody. If you were the judge, what questions would you ask the parents and the children?

Activities

1. Go to your local library and discover what kinds of information you can obtain on family support groups in your community.

2. Call or visit an agency, a volunteer organization, or a support group that deals with children-related family problems. Report to the class on your findings or ask a staff person at the agency to speak to your class on their professional duties.

This chapter will help you:

- understand that a child's education in family living begins at birth
- appreciate the importance of family-life sex education
- identify the ways that children's attitudes toward their sexuality are influenced
- learn how to deal honestly with children's questions about their bodies and about reproduction
- identify children's six stages in understanding matters of sex and reproduction

The Importance of Family-Life and Sex Education

Human beings do not have built-in knowledge of how to solve the problems of family living. This knowledge must be acquired. **Family-life education** provides training in human relationships to help people cope with such problems.

Family-life education has three main purposes.

- One purpose is to develop emotionally stable children and adolescents who can make decisions about their conduct without being carried away by their emotions.
- Another purpose is to provide sound knowledge not only of the physical aspects of sex behavior, but also about the psychological aspects.
- A third purpose is to develop attitudes and standards that will ensure responsible sex behavior in young people and adults.

Family-life education is training in human relationships. Teachers, peers, religious leaders, and community leaders play an important role in developing standards of family living. Parents, however, are the major educators in this field. More important than any influence on children is the continuous experience of being part of a family. Parent's attitudes toward each other and their children, and their conduct with friends and other relatives all serve to teach a growing child about human relationships. It is not important for parents to protect their children from every type of setback. After all, a child's character and personality develop from the totality of his or her experience. Often we can learn and grow as the result of a setback. However, the persistence of such experiences over a long period of time is cause for concern. Normally it is the recurrence of similar experiences, whether they be good or bad, that has a great influence on children's feelings about themselves and about others. On the other hand, certain types of single events also may be extremely important. For example, witnessing a murder or being a rape victim can certainly have lasting effects on a person, regardless of age.

As part of a family, children learn about members of their own sex and the opposite sex, and the interaction between the two. Parents who trust and respect each other, who show that they value and hold equal the complementary roles of husband and wife, are worthy models for their children. In turn the children will have a good feeling about their future as adults.

The home is a kind of school in which the parents teach their children many lessons simply by being themselves. This is why knowledge of self and perception of self are so important. In order to understand a child's needs, likes, and dislikes, parents must understand their own needs, likes, and dislikes. In order for parents to achieve their goal of raising independent but socialized children who will accept and respect others rather than leading a life of individual isolation, they need to be sensitive to their own deepest feelings. It is these feelings that determine the quality of their actions, which in turn teach children the most lasting lessons of life.

The Family as Educators

Parents are children's first and most lasting educators. Education in family living begins at birth. The way children are held, fed, spoken to, bathed, and diapered gives them their earliest clues as to how people interact. It is not surprising, then, that children's parents are their first source of knowledge about interpersonal relationships. As children mature, the peer group, church, school, and mass media also influence their views. Their parents, however, remain their most enduring educators in family living. Education in family living continues throughout life. Adults, as well as children, are constantly gaining new insights.

Sex education is part of family living. Children learn about **sexuality** gradually. They learn from everyday experiences. Those children who feel comfortable about themselves, their home life, and their peer group will likely develop healthy attitudes toward sex. Sexuality is more than just physical aspects. It also includes masculine and feminine personality traits and behavior.

It is important to the long-term relationship of parent and child that lines of communication be kept open. Children need to ask questions. If they feel that their questions will not be answered openly, they will avoid asking them. Children can sense adults' emotional reactions. Parents who show uneasiness or embarrassment in response to questions will find that their child asks fewer and fewer questions. Parents who are receptive to what the child is asking, and who answer simply and honestly, are likely to receive more questions in the future.

Parents who avoid children's questions about sexuality do not dampen their curiosity. Children will learn that it is a forbidden subject with their parents and will seek information elsewhere, usually from peers. Unfortunately, peers are often sources of misinformation that can result in poor attitudes toward human sexuality. Many parents don't realize that informal sex education by peers begins in the middle of the preschool period.

Attitudes Toward Sexuality

The attitudes children acquire about their bodies during infancy and early childhood are responsible in part for their future attitudes toward sexuality. If parents scold or shame children for wetting or soiling themselves in infancy, they may develop unhealthy attitudes. Parents who treat the organs of excretion as dirty and shameful are likely to raise children to view those areas of their bodies similarly. If parents consider the names of the genitals to be dirty words, their children's attitudes toward sex will be influenced accordingly.

Children turn to their parents for guidance about many subjects. Parents need to let them know they are always there to help.

During their early development, children discover their fingers, toes, and genitals. It is natural and normal for small children to play with their genitals, so parents need not be upset when they observe this behavior. Children are usually easily distracted when parents suggest another activity. If a child persists, however, in excessive genital play, the parents should look for reasons. Some children simply may be bored and need challenging toys. Others may feel lonely or unloved.

All children are likely to be curious about the bodies of others, particularly those of the opposite sex. When parents find children of the late preschool or the primary school period exploring each other's bodies, they should not be upset. Parents should treat such an incident in a matter-of-fact way. They should try to satisfy children's curiosity by giving them information. At the same time, they should tell them that privacy and modesty are desirable, but sex experimentation with other children is not.

Introducing Sex Education

It is important that parents impart sex information before the child acquires misinformation from others. Sex information needs to be taught as honestly as possible. If parents are going to answer a child's questions about sex, they must first have worked out their own feelings about sex so they can discuss the subject with candor and sensitivity. Parents need to be able to put sex in proper perspective. Luther G. Baker, professor and author, believes that we have gone from an era of sexual restrictiveness to an era in which hustlers and advertisers have distorted the value of sex. Too many people equate sex and intimacy. They mistakenly seek to find the intimate love that they need through sexual encounter. They do not recognize that true intimacy is psychological, not physical.

Besides having the proper perspective, parents need to know the facts and how to present them. If children do not ask questions about sex, it may mean they sense their parents' embarrassment with the subject. Information can be given to them in an informal manner. An approach used by some parents is, "I used to think that doctors brought babies in their black bags. What did you used to think?"

When discussing sex with children, a parent should not overwhelm them with information. Children should be told what they want to know in terms that they can understand. By letting children's curiosity be a guide, a parent can judge how much information is necessary to impart. By realizing that children's thought processes are not the same as adults', the parent can be careful to provide information that matches the child's level of mental development. For example, three-year-old Karen might point at her new baby brother lying on the changing table and ask, "What's that?" The response should be, "That's Bradley's penis." Karen has discovered that her brother is different from her. Because she received a matter-of-fact answer to her first question, she will not hesitate to ask, "Why is Bradley different from me?" whenever her natural curiosity brings this next question to mind. The "why" question may occur to Karen immediately, or it may not occur to her for days or weeks. She may even assume from her first observation that babies have penises, but three-year-olds do not. At any rate, it would be a mistake for Karen's parents to overwhelm her with a complete description of the reproductive process when she asks her first question about the male genitalia. Through open interchange she will eventually assimilate all the facts over a period of years.

Quite often children manage to twist the information they have received into their own amazing versions of creation. Their explanation of reproduction can be quite humorous and fanciful. To determine whether misunderstandings exist, a parent should ask children

Filling children's minds with stories of the birds and bees only confuses them. Parents should give straightforward answers about human reproduction.

questions about reproduction after they have enough time to process the information they have received.

Where Do Babies Come From?

In answer to children's questions as to where babies come from, the parents may want to explain that the baby grows in a special place inside the mother. This place is called the womb or uterus. It is near the stomach but not in the stomach. The place is comfortable and warm. It protects the baby until he or she is big enough to be born. Talking about the birds, the bees, and the flowers may confuse children. This study is of interest to them later, but not in answer to the question concerning where babies come from.

Preschool children are likely to ask how the baby gets out. All they need to know is a simple straightforward answer: There is a special passage called the vagina, which stretches so that the baby comes out between the mother's legs. The child needs to know that this passageway is different from the openings for the bowel movement and for urine. It may be necessary to explain that people do not usually display these parts. This can be carried out as a part of teaching modesty. However, parents should not imply that there is anything shameful about this part of the body.

Preschool children may want to know how a baby gets started. A simple explanation that a cell from the father's body joins a cell from the mother's body and from this the baby starts to grow may satisfy them.

If children feel free to ask questions, they will eventually ask, "How did the tiny cell from the father get into the mother?" Many parents find this difficult to answer. Young children ask out of simple curiosity. They have no great feelings about sexual union. It may be enough to say, "The father's penis, which contains the sperm cells, fits in the mother's vagina. A special fluid called semen carries the sperm cell until it meets the special cell inside the body of the mother." It is usually necessary to tell the child that semen is something quite different from urine.

As mentioned before, preschool children are likely to ask why they differ from their brother or sister. They can be told that boys have a penis because they may be fathers and girls have a vagina because they may be mothers when they grow up.

There is no cut-and-dried technique for child-rearing or for giving specific sex information. Each parent is different and every situation is different. The ideas presented here can be adapted by parents to fit their needs and those of their children.

Six Stages of Understanding

According to Dr. Anne Bernstein, who is a clinical psychologist, current research indicates that children have six stages or levels of understanding sex. These levels of understanding reflect differences in children's problem-solving abilities. They also can be correlated with Piaget's stages of intellectual development.

To determine children's levels of understanding, a parent can ask questions to elicit children's beliefs. Some questions that can be asked are: How do people get babies? How do mommies get to be mommies?

- Level-one children believe that babies have always existed.
- Level-two children, on the other hand, believe that babies have not always existed. They believe babies have to be made. They view making a baby, however, in terms of manufacturing. They believe that babies can be built just like dolls, cars, or houses can be built.
- Level-three children know the major aspects of reproduction. However, they have difficulty putting the concepts into a coherent framework. Often they take adults' explanations quite literally. For example, they may think that the father actually plants the seed as one would plant a flower. At the end of this stage, children are beginning to recognize some of the weakness in their explanation.
- Level-four children know the physical facts of life, but they do not understand why genetic material must join for conception to occur. For example, they may believe that the sperm exists to provide an escort service for the egg. In general, they know the facts, but the reasons for the

A baby manufacturing plant with storks delivering the finished product may be one misconception that level-two children hold.

facts are beyond their level of understanding.

- Some level-five children attempt to explain why the egg and sperm unite. However many believe that one of the cells, either the egg or sperm, actually contains the whole baby, in miniature form. That cell simply grows to full size in the uterus. These children can explain sexual intercourse, but have difficulty defining fertilization. Level-five children, about 11 to 12 years old, tend to be embarrassed about discussing sexual behavior.
- Level-six children have a clear understanding of reproduction. They understand why the genetic material must unite for a baby to develop. They can explain the process of reproduction in a coherent and logical way. Children at this level also understand the moral and social aspects of sexual behavior. They know that pregnancy can occur without marriage.

When explaining sex and reproduction to children, the adult should provide information the child can understand. Generally, children are able

Sharing a parent's attention with a younger brother or sister can be difficult for older children. Parents need to give all of their children constant love and support.

to understand explanations of sex in terms that are one level beyond their present level of understanding. For instance, a level-two child may be told, "Making a real live baby is different from making a doll, a car, or a teddy bear. Parents make babies from special cells, tiny things, in their bodies." The child will process this information and eventually restructure his or her understanding when the new information does not fit into his or her old view of the world.

Concerns of Children at Various Ages

The following overview of the general characteristics of children may help parents to cope with the concerns of each age group.

Lower Elementary, Grades K-2

Children in the primary grades are already aware of some of the physical differences between men and women, and they have begun the process of adopting traits that have been traditionally identified with maleness or femaleness. Early elementary children will naturally have numerous questions regarding human reproduction in the months before and after the addition of a baby to the family. They expect and deserve forthright answers.

Children in this age group also will have to make many adjustments when a new baby arrives in the home. They need steady assurances of love and security from their parents. They need to feel comfortable as they go out into the world. They also need to know that they can return to the safety of home. They need guidance from adults to help them understand what behavior is appropriate.

Upper Elementary, Grades 3-5

At this time, children should learn about the physical changes which they will soon experience. Their questions should be answered frankly and honestly. As they become aware of their changing bodies, they require privacy and dignity.

Junior High, Grades 6-8

Junior high youngsters strongly identify with members of their own sex, but they are also increasingly aware of the opposite sex. Their feelings of identification lead them to accept group standards of dress and behavior. Their emotions are likely to be strong and variable. They may be ecstatic one moment and deep in gloom the next.

It is important for them to understand the many ways in which they are maturing. They should understand that they are maturing both physically and emotionally. They also should know that growing up is an ongoing process. At times it may involve returning to childish ways, in addition to becoming more and more adult. It is important that they feel secure fluctuating between roles of childhood and adulthood as they mature.

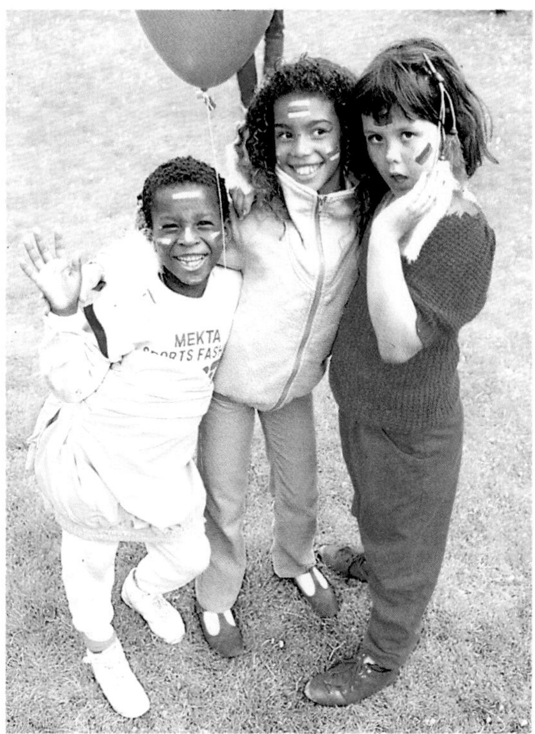

Older children develop an increasing self-awareness and may feel a strong need to be part of a group.

Senior High, Grades 9-12

Young people also need to understand and deal with their sexuality. Mature behavior is responsible behavior, and irresponsible behavior is immature behavior. Responsible behavior depends on intellectual, emotional, social, and moral maturity.

Life's Work

Dana and Carl Selin

➤**Camp Directors**
➤**Ph.D. and M.S. in Education**

The Selins start their day at 6:30 a.m. They first talk with the counselors about daily trips and routine. Breakfast is at 8 a.m. with campers and the staff. At 9 a.m., they check to see the daily schedule is being followed. Next they handle the accounting and follow up with a trip to town to run errands. At 11 a.m., they have a meeting with the staff on camper problems. After lunch with the campers and staff, they make phone calls to parents of campers to keep them up-to-date. In the afternoon, they check on the activities and they have a daily swim with the campers and staff. Supper is at 6 p.m. Evening activities run from 7 to 9 p.m.. The Selins round out their day by having a staff meeting until 11 p.m.

The Selins are on call 24 hours a day to solve problems, handle emergencies, and meet the needs of campers and staff. There is almost no free time from June through September. During their off-season, they plan an eight-hour workday.

What skills are necessary for success in their profession? Dana and Carl answer, "Getting along with people is by far the most important. Problem-solving ability and marketing and promotion are essential. Financial aptitude is extremely necessary." People in this area also need sports skills. For the Selins it is water-related skills.

For a student considering going into this profession, they advise, "You've got to love camping and the out-of-doors." For experience they suggest, "Work in a variety of camps and study successful camp managers. Learn financial skills. Use of a computer is now essential. You have to love to work with people. Learn as many skills as possible that will be taught in your camp."

When asked how their profession will change within the next 10 years, the Selins say, "Camping will include more 'Adventure Camping.' Computer use will play an ever increasing part as will marketing with videos. Teaching outdoor skills and especially protection of our environment will be more important each year."

In Review

Vocabulary

sexuality family-life education

Summary

✓ Family-life education is far more than sex education—it is training in human relationships. Responsible sexual behavior is only one aspect, and it includes psychological and sociological effects encompassing values, feelings, and attitudes.

✓ Family-life education begins at birth. As children mature, their attitudes are influenced by other people, but the parents remain the most enduring educators.

✓ Sex education is a part of family living. Children learn about sexuality gradually. By answering children's questions about sex and sexuality with openness and honesty, parents can engender healthy attitudes in their children.

✓ Parents need to recognize a child's stage of understanding in order to give appropriate answers to questions regarding sex and reproduction.

Questions

1. Who are the most influential family-life teachers? Explain your answer.
2. What factors affect children's attitudes toward their own sexuality?
3. What are the main purposes of family-life education?

Activities

1. Imagine that you are the parent of a normally curious seven-year-old child who has never asked you any questions about human reproduction. What questions might you ask the child to initiate a dialogue? What might you say to demonstrate your willingness to answer questions?

2. Discuss the applicability of the following statement to sex education: "It is not so much what you say as how you say it."

3. Give your interpretation of the statement, "Mature behavior is responsible behavior, and irresponsible behavior is immature behavior." What does the statement mean as applied to adolescent sexuality?

This chapter will help you:

- recognize the transition from childhood dependence to adult independence as one of the most important tasks for adolescents
- identify some of the introspective questions that adolescents ask themselves
- identify ways that parents can help adolescents to meet their basic needs
- appreciate the importance of a high school education that provides preparation for life
- understand that as individuals we are in control of our own futures

Gaining Independence

Possibly one of the most difficult tasks facing adolescents is that of gaining independence from their parents while maintaining working relationships based on mutual respect. The adolescent must move from the dependence of childhood to the independence of adulthood. This transition period brings many questions to mind. Some of the questions are:

- How can I feel comfortable in my new adult body?
- How can I gain independence from my parents?
- Can I trust myself to make decisions?
- What can I do to earn enough money to support myself?
- What do I want to do with my life?
- What do I value?
- Who do I trust?
- How can I share in making the world a better place?
- Can I find a friend who will really be true?
- Can I be a valued friend?
- What is love? truth? honesty?
- What do I really believe?
- Do I want to marry? Do I want to have children?
- How can I tell people what I really believe and stand for?
- How can I help others reach their potential?

The list can go on and on. Younger adolescents are concerned with identity—who they are as individuals. Older adolescents are trying to decide about their future. They need to learn about the options open to them after graduation. These include a job or career, further education, and/or marriage. They need to learn more about their options so they can make satisfying choices for themselves. They are preoccupied with setting goals and deciding how to achieve them. These goals are accomplished over a number of years. For some individuals, they may not be achieved until the late 20s. In reaching each goal, young people are brought closer to the adult roles they will someday assume. Parents can be very helpful in this transition period if they recognize the basic needs of adolescents.

Adolescents and Needs

Adolescents need friends their own age who share with them ideas, ideals, dreams, and goals. They need friends who will take part in daily activities with them and help them assume responsibility. They need friends with whom they can trust their deepest secrets. Adolescents also need encouragement in independence. They need encouragement to succeed. They need a chance to demonstrate and develop their skills. They need the chance to prove themselves by making increasingly more important decisions and then having the opportunity to understand the outcomes of their decisions. Adolescents need opportunities to develop a sense of responsibility, a sense of self-esteem, and a sense of importance. In short, they need to be needed. And yet, at the same time, they need to be encouraged to become independent.

Youths need adult models. They need parents and other adults who set high standards. Parents can teach concepts of values, morals, and acceptable behavior. Some adults, however, are not suitable models because they are still struggling with their own identity.

A Closer Look

When her family living class was discussing the importance of discipline, Karen wondered why she seemed to be able to discipline herself, even though she did not think of her parents as strict disciplinarians. In answer to her teacher's questions, Karen said that her parents were very patient and thoughtful, and they had always been willing to talk about making decisions and judgments. She loved her parents dearly, so she always tried to please them. They often told her they were proud of her responsible behavior. Obviously, Karen's parents believe that the most effective way to discipline children is to act as responsible models, to encourage moral development, and to stress self-discipline, rather than parental discipline.

Young people at this age also should be able to act less mature at times without being chided for it. They are actively seeking freedom with responsibility, but they must realize that they

Young people need older role models. Some schools offer a buddy program that teams up teens and youngsters.

are not quite ready to accept it completely. Adolescents need patience, understanding, and time to grow. They need adults who can help them achieve self-identity. They need the opportunity to play roles, to share ideas and ideals, and to be involved in plans and goals from start to finish. Adolescents need adults who will provide them with positive experiences. They need adults who will respect them and understand they are changing, maturing human beings on their way to adulthood.

The transition from adolescence to the independent state of adulthood can be traumatic for the child as well as for the parents. If parents have prepared themselves and their children for this step, it can be a rewarding time. In some families independence is resisted by parents who refuse to cut the apron strings and by children who don't want to let go of them. One is reminded of the man who built a boat in his shop. When he finished he found that he could not get the boat through the door. He was left with three alternatives: the boat could remain inside the shop, the shop could be torn down, or the boat could be taken apart and built elsewhere.

Parents who have more foresight than the boatbuilder can avoid having to face alternatives as drastic as his. The initial steps in the process of "letting go" should begin early in a child's life. The transition during adolescence should be the culmination of a purposefully gradual evolution toward independence, rather than a distinctly new phase.

Having a job helps students gain independence. Besides earning an income, they can learn many interpersonal skills.

Adolescents and School

Is it possible to drop out of school and drop into society? Do some young people drop out of school mentally but remain in school physically? The answer to both questions is yes. Perhaps the emphasis on the school dropout problem is misplaced. It may be that society should focus on the school and not on the school dropout. How relevant is the school experience?

Many frustrations of today's young people result from extended periods of education that keep them in a state of dependency long after they have reached physical maturity. This was not always the case. For example, only 2% of the 17-year-olds graduated from high school in 1870. One hundred years later, 76% graduated.

To help young people cope with the frustrations of dependency, we must provide opportunities for them to contribute to their school and community. Adolescents need opportunities to demonstrate their skills and receive recognition. They need positive experiences to help them develop a positive self-image. Adolescents need to feel that they are valued for themselves and for their unique contributions.

Almost every school's statement of education objectives includes at least two sections. The first talks about academic excellence, subject mastery, and getting into college or finding a job. The other discusses the human purpose of school—values, feelings, personal growth, and leading a full and happy life.

What students learn and what they become depends to a large degree on how they feel about themselves, their classmates, and their teachers. Thus, the second set of educational objectives may significantly influence the first. The school dropout is the pupil for whom neither set of objectives is being met.

Many students see school as a place to "learn stuff." They sit in the classroom, regurgitating answers, anxiously waiting for the bell to ring. They are frustrated by the mindless lessons, the memory and boredom, and the rules in cafeterias and study halls—no talking, sit up straight, get a pass, etc. For some students, English, mathematics, history, and science seem irrelevant. From class to class, from school to home and back again, they pass the time. What they learn is to submit—to time, to authority, to events.

Parents know that their adolescents should stay in school. They know that young people need to "get an education" and acquire skills if they are to support themselves someday. Parents may not realize, however, that schools do not necessarily do an effective job of educating all types of students. Parents must, therefore, familiarize themselves with the schools in their communities. They should know whether the curriculum includes course work for both the students who are college-bound and those who will be seeking full-time employment when they leave high school. It is important for the schools to emphasize preparation for life, as well as preparation for college and/or a job. Parents must do their utmost to ensure that their children are provided with the best possible opportunities for physical, intellectual, emotional, social, and moral growth in their schools, as well as in their homes.

Sexual Responsibility

The control of sexual behavior is a major challenge for young people. Adolescents reach the age of sexual maturity long before they are able to assume the responsibility for the possible consequences of their sexual activity. Thus, adolescents' sexual responsibility is of utmost concern to both the family and society.

Irresponsible sexual behavior causes much heartbreak and shatters many dreams. Venereal diseases, AIDS, and unwanted pregnancies are major social and medical problems. The Statistical Abstract of the United States reports that each year there are about 900,000 new cases of gonorrhea

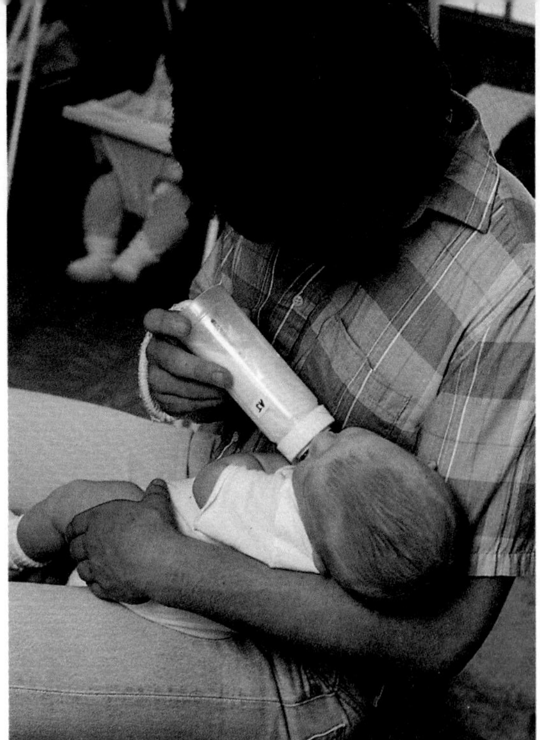

Too many teenagers become sexually active before they are prepared to take on all the responsibilities that result.

and 70,000 new cases of syphilis. Genital herpes for which there is treatment but no cure, strikes 500,000 new victims annually, according to the Center for Disease Control in Atlanta.

Despite all the publicity about the deadly AIDS virus, the number of cases reported each year is still growing rapidly. For several years after the first diagnoses of AIDS in North America, almost all cases were limited to homosexual men or intravenous drug users. Now, however, increasing numbers of women are contracting the disease through sexual intercourse with infected men. In those countries of the world where AIDS has reached epidemic proportions, there are about equal numbers of male and female victims. Obviously only sexually responsible behavior can prevent the same

A Matter of Fact

Can a baby have the AIDS virus? Yes, if the mother is infected with AIDS, the virus can be passed on to the baby before it is born or during birth. Her baby has about one chance in two of being born with the AIDS virus.

If a woman is considering having a baby and thinks she may have been at risk of being infected with AIDS, she should receive counseling and be tested before she gets pregnant.

from happening in this country. The lack of sexual responsibility that results in AIDS brings a very heavy emotional burden to the family—the loss of a family member. AIDS kills.

Experts are in general agreement that adolescents are not ready psychologically, physically, financially, or emotionally to handle birth and child care. Yet each year, more than one million American teenagers become pregnant.

Some of the crises faced by families were discussed in Chapter 22. The lack of sexual responsibility by adolescents that results in pregnancy may bring a loss of status for family members, a challenge to the family's sense of identity in the community, and the emotional burdens of shame, guilt, and doubt. The family also may feel threatened by the additional burden of rearing a grandchild. Furthermore, helping the adolescent member achieve a more positive self-concept may be difficult and stressful for the family. The enormity of the psychological stress imposed on an unwanted child was discussed in Chapter 5.

In addition to all of the other problems, adolescents should be aware of the severe financial realities of parenthood. A large majority of teenage mothers do not finish high school. Few finish vocational school or college. This means that their earning power is minimal throughout their lives. The younger a teenager is when she gives birth to her first child, the more likely it is that she and her child will live in poverty. The lack of sexual responsibility creates problems for unwed mothers and unwanted children who become dependent upon society for financial support. Teenage fathers may not be able or willing to lend any support. Those who do support the mother and baby find the financial burden is very great for them as well. They may drop out of school in order to support the family. Then their lack of a high school education will always hinder their earning potential.

Making an adoption plan for a child is extremely difficult. Birth parents who choose this alternative do so because they love their child and want a better life for him or her than they can provide at this time. If this option is chosen, the birth parents and their families are likely to face intense grieving for the child being reared in another family.

Traditionally, the family and the place of worship had the most responsibility for teaching control and direction of sexual behavior. These institutions were the source of most adolescents' values but, of course, the peer group also has been influential. Today, increasingly free sexual expression in books, magazines, movies, television, and advertising strongly influences the attitudes and sexual behavior of adolescents. Sex is used to sell commercial products. Sex is used as a source of humor. Sex is used as a cure-all for the release of tension. Sexual techniques and problems are discussed in household magazines and on television talk shows. Unfortunately, the message that is often conveyed is: To break with sexual tradition is to be modern, free, and alive.

In spite of all these influences on sexual behavior, adolescents are the ones left with the awesome responsibility of controlling and directing their own sexual behavior. Moreover, this responsibility is given to adolescents at a time when they have little training or preparation for decision making. Individuals at this stage lack the experience and social maturity that are necessary to function as adults and take full responsibility for the consequences of their actions. Many teens try to ignore the consequences. Remember, pregnancy, venereal disease, and AIDS are all very real.

Genuine love is built on respect for the other person.

When young persons consider the sexual decision-making process, they face a sequence of choices. The first choice is whether to engage in sexual intercourse or not. The decision made by the individual concerning this choice will determine subsequent issues and choices. It is clear that the decision that will be most trouble free is to postpone sexual intercourse until marriage. This decision eliminates all the other decisions. Thus, the adolescent postpones decisions concerning pregnancy and children until marriage, a time when the individual can accept full responsibility for his or her actions. To protect against AIDS, safe behavior again is postponing sexual activity until after marriage. If adolescents are to be sexually responsible, they must know more than the "facts of life." They must understand that they alone are in control of their futures. Their own decisions regarding sexual behavior will influence all the remaining days of their lives.

Life's Work

Edward Poole

➤**Guidance Counselor**
➤**M.A. from Northwestern University**

In a typical day, Edward confers with teachers, administrators, and parents. Of course, he also counsels students. He is a member of the school's Special Services Team comprised of a psychologist, a learning disabilities teacher, administrators, counselors, etc. He gathers information and writes a report for that team. In addition, Edward teaches classes in guidance on drug abuse prevention.

When asked about his most rewarding job-related accomplishment, Edward says, "Junior high students have a positive outlook and are willing to try things to improve themselves. Little things said or done mean so much to them. I really enjoy making a meaningful contribution to these young people's lives."

For a student considering becoming a guidance counselor, Edward advises, "After college, the prospective counselor should teach for a number of years. The years spent in the classroom will better equip you to relate to the unique pressures and problems of the classroom teacher. You also should have a thick skin about the problems you are going to be dealing with. If you tend to overly worry about the students' problems, you are not going to have the objectivity to help them with those problems. (Remember reading about empathy in Chapter 3?) Trust your intuition. All the books and theories in the world cannot explain that 'sixth sense' counselors develop. Learn to trust it. Above all, be morally upright. Trust and confidence are essential ingredients for a counselor."

When asked how his profession will change within the next 10 years, Edward says, "I believe the need for counselors will increase. As more and more parents enter the job force and are returning home later and later, more problems will arise and students will need someone to talk to. When I started in the profession, I was talking to students about study skills, peer pressure, etc. Nowadays we occasionally get a case dealing with drug abuse or suicide. I would guess that the seriousness of the problems presented to the counselor will increase. Because of the response to our parent seminars, I feel that they will become the job of counselors. The parents are hungry for ways to get their children through the adolescent years successfully."

In Review

Summary

- ✓ Adolescence is a transition period. In attempting to move from the dependence of childhood to the independence of adulthood, teenagers are forced to seek answers to many questions about themselves. For younger teens, the questions are concerned with identity. Older teens are making decisions about their future.
- ✓ Parents have a responsibility to know the objectives of their children's schools and to be involved in helping children achieve those goals. At the high school level, much of the coursework is aimed at subject mastery in preparation for a job or college. A well-balanced curriculum includes, also, emphasis on preparation for life.
- ✓ Adolescents must recognize that each individual is responsible for his/her own sexual behavior. Irresponsible sexual behavior causes heartaches and shatters dreams. The decisions made by teenagers regarding sexual behavior influence all the remaining days of their lives.

Questions

1. Why is the control of sexual behavior one of the most important challenges of adolescence? How could irresponsible sexual behavior on your part affect the remainder of your life?
2. The lack of sexual responsibility by an adolescent creates problems for society and the family, as well as the adolescent. What are these problems?
3. What are some of adolescents' needs?
4. How does the statement "Adolescents need to be needed" apply in your life?

Activities

1. Without using names, describe someone you know who is in school physically, but who has dropped out mentally.
2. Who played the most important role in influencing your attitude toward school? Was it a parent, a teacher, or someone else? How old were you when their influence came into play? Write a brief summary of this person's influence on your life.

Appendix

Examples of Ages and Stages

While we cannot expect all children to develop at the same rates, there are general guidelines that are helpful. The following charts outline rather typical physical development, patterns of behavior, and special needs at various age levels. These suggest to parents the types of guidance that children need in order to accomplish their developmental tasks.

How Needs Change With Growth

Infant	Preschool Child	School Child	Adolescent
	Significant People		
Family, especially primary caregiver	Two or three playmates and family	Many companions and family	Friends of own age group
	Types of Contact		
Solitude and one or two at a time	Parallel play	Group games, active play	Boy-girl activities
	Requirements from Others		
Nurturing care	Supervision	Guidance	Encouragement in independence
	Response		
Receiving	Exchanging	Sharing	Accommodating

Runabouts

(from 2 years through 4 years)

Physical Development

- motor skills unevenly developed—marked development in large muscle coordination, but small muscles and eye-hand coordination still not well developed
- full set of temporary teeth by three years
- gradually acquire ability to feed and dress themselves with greater skill
- rapid language development—from a few words to an average of 2000
- change in sleep pattern—12 hours needed at night with daytime naps gradually given up, but still need rest period because they tire easily
- toilet habits acquired—usually take care of their own needs by end of period

Characteristic Behavior

- learning to understand their environment and to conform to many of its demands
- often do the opposite of what caregivers want at beginning of this period, but gradually become able to accept necessary limits and restraints—want adult approval
- like to be close to parents and caregivers
- like to help around the house
- imitate language, manners, and habits
- constantly active, but capable of longer stretches of quiet activity toward end of period
- show fatigue by being irritable or restless
- gradually learning what is acceptable behavior and what is not
- great curiosity—ask countless questions

Needs

- security of love and affection from parents
- guidance and a pattern of behavior to follow
- time, patience, understanding, and genuine interest from adults
- simple, clear routines with limited choices
- opportunities to learn to give and take, to play cooperatively with other children
- wider scope of activity with limited freedom to move about and to move away from immediate home environment by end of period

About Five

Physical Development

- period of slow growth—body lengthens out and hands and feet grow larger; girls usually about a year ahead of boys in physical development
- good general motor control, though small muscles not so fully developed as large ones
- sensory-motor equipment usually not ready for reading
- eye-hand coordination improving, but still poor—apt to be far-sighted
- activity level high
- attention span still short, but increasing
- some remaining infantile articulation in speech
- handedness established (right or left hand preference)

Characteristic Behavior

- stable—have good balance between self-sufficiency and sociability
- home-centered
- beginning to be capable of self-criticism—eager and able to carry some responsibility
- noisy and vigorous, but activity has definite direction
- purposeful and constructive—example, know what they are going to draw before they draw it
- use language well—enjoy dramatic play
- can wash, dress, eat, and go to the toilet by themselves, but may need occasional help
- individuality and lasting traits beginning to be apparent
- interested in group activity

Needs

- assurance that they are loved and valued
- wise guidance
- opportunities for plenty of activity—equipment for exercising large muscles
- opportunities to do things for themselves—freedom to use and develop their own powers
- background training in group effort, in sharing, and in good work habits that they will need next year in first grade
- opportunities to learn about their world by seeing and doing things
- kindergarten experience if possible

About Six

Physical Development

- growth proceeding more slowly
- large muscles better developed than small ones
- 11 to 12 hours of sleep needed
- eyes not yet mature, tendency toward far-sightedness
- permanent teeth beginning to appear
- heart in period of rapid growth
- high activity level—can stay still only for short periods

Characteristic Behavior

- eager to learn, exuberant, restless, over-active, easily fatigued
- self-assertive and aggressive—want to be first, less cooperative than at five, keenly competitive, boastful
- whole body involved in whatever they do
- learn best through active participation
- inconsistent in level of maturity—regress when tired, often less mature at home than with outsiders
- inept at activities using small muscles—relatively short periods of interest
- have difficulty making decisions
- group activities popular—boys' and girls' interests beginning to differ
- much spontaneous dramatization

Needs

- encouragement, ample praise, warmth, and great patience from adults
- ample opportunities for activity of many kinds, especially for use of large muscles
- wise supervision with minimum interference
- friends; by end of period, a best friend
- concrete learning situations and active, direct participation
- some responsibilities, but without pressure and without being required to make complicated decisions or achieve rigidly set standards
- help in developing acceptable manners and habits

About Seven

Physical Development

- growth slow and steady
- annual expected growth in height—2 to 3 inches (5 to 7.5 centimeters); in weight—3 to 6 pounds (1.25 to 2.70 kilograms)
- losing teeth—most seven-year-olds have their six-year molars
- better eye-hand coordination
- better use of small muscles
- eyes not yet ready for much close work

Characteristic Behavior

- sensitive to the feelings and attitudes of other children and adults
- especially dependent on approval of adults
- interests of boys and girls diverging—play less together
- full of energy but easily fatigued; restless and fidgety; often dreamy and absorbed
- little abstract thinking—learn best in concrete terms and when they can be active while learning
- cautious and self-critical, anxious to do things well—like to use hands
- talkative, prone to exaggeration, may fight verbally instead of physically, competitive
- enjoy songs, rhymes, fairy tales, myths, nature stories, comics, television, movies
- able to assume some responsibility
- concerned about right and wrong, but may take small things that do not belong to them
- basic understanding of time and monetary values

Needs

- the right combination of independence and encouraging support
- chances for active participation in learning situations with concrete objects
- adult help in adjusting to the rougher ways of the playground without becoming too crude or rough
- warm, encouraging, friendly relationships with adults
- acceptance at their own level of development

About Eight

Physical Development

- growth still slow and steady—arms lengthening, hands growing
- eyes ready for both near and far vision—near-sightedness may develop this year
- permanent teeth continuing to appear
- large muscles and small muscles developing—manipulative skills are increasing
- attention span increasing
- poor posture sometimes

Characteristic Behavior

- often careless, noisy, argumentative, but also alert, friendly, interested in people
- more dependent on their parents again, less so on their teachers
- sensitive to criticism
- new awareness of individual differences
- eager, more enthusiastic than cautious—high accident rate
- peer groups beginning—best friends of same sex
- allegiance to other children instead of to an adult in case of conflict
- greater capacity for self-evaluation
- much spontaneous dramatization, ready for simple classroom dramatics
- understanding of time and use of money
- responsive to group activities, both spontaneous and adult-supervised
- fond of team games, comics, television, movies, adventure stories, collections

Needs

- praise and encouragement from adults
- reminders of their responsibilities
- wise guidance and channeling of their interests and enthusiasms, rather than domination or unreasonable standards
- a best friend
- experience of belonging to peer group—opportunities to identify with others of same age and sex
- adult-supervised groups and planned after-school activities
- exercise of both large and small muscles

About Nine or Ten

Physical Development

- growth slow and steady—girls forge further ahead; some children reach the plateau preceding the preadolescent growth spurt
- lungs and digestive and circulatory systems almost mature—heart especially subject to strain
- teeth may need straightening—first and second bicuspids appearing
- eye-hand coordination good—ready for crafts and shop work
- eyes almost adult size—ready for close work with less strain

Characteristic Behavior

- decisive, responsible, dependable, reasonable, strong sense of right and wrong
- individual differences and distinct abilities now apparent
- capable of prolonged interest—often make plans and go ahead on their own
- perfectionistic—want to do well, but lose interest if discouraged or pressured
- interested less in fairy tales and fantasy, more in their community and country and in other countries and peoples
- loyal to their country and proud of it
- spend a great deal of time in talk and discussion—often outspoken and critical of adults, although still dependent on adult approval
- frequently argue over fairness in games
- wide discrepancies in reading ability

Needs

- active, rough-and-tumble play
- friends and membership in group
- training in skills, but without pressure
- books of many kinds, depending on individual reading level and interest
- reasonable explanations without talking down
- definite responsibility
- frank answers to their questions about coming physiological changes

The Preadolescent

Physical Development

- a "resting period," followed by a period of rapid growth in height and then growth in weight—this usually starts sometime between 9 and 13—boys may mature as much as two years later than girls
- girls usually taller and heavier than boys
- reproductive organs maturing—secondary sex characteristics developing
- rapid muscular growth
- uneven growth of different parts of the body
- enormous, but often capricious, appetite

Characteristic Behavior

- wide range of individual differences in maturity level
- peer groups continue, though loyalty to the group stronger in boys than in girls
- interest in team games, pets, television, radio, movies, comics
- marked interest differences between boys and girls
- teasing and seeming antagonism between boys' and girls' groups
- awkwardness, restlessness, and laziness common as a result of rapid and uneven growth
- opinion of own group beginning to be valued more highly than that of adults
- often become overcritical, changeable, rebellious, uncooperative
- self-conscious about physical changes
- interested in earning money

Needs

- understanding of the physical and emotional changes about to come
- skillfully planned school and recreation programs to meet needs of those who are approaching puberty as well as those who are not
- opportunities for greater independence and for carrying more responsibility without pressure
- warm affection and sense of humor in adults—no nagging, condemnation, or talking down
- sense of belonging, acceptance by peer group

The Adolescent

Physical Development

- rapid weight gain at beginning of adolescence—enormous appetite
- sexual maturity, with accompanying physical and emotional changes—girls are usually about two years ahead of boys
- sometimes a period of glandular imbalance
- skeletal growth complete, adult height reached, muscular coordination improved
- heart growing rapidly at beginning of period

Characteristic Behavior

- going to extremes, emotional instability with "know-it-all" attitude
- return of habits of younger child—nail biting, tricks, impudence, day-dreaming
- high interest in philosophical, ethical, and religious problems—search for ideals
- preoccupation with acceptance by the social group; fear of ridicule and of being unpopular; oversensitiveness and self-pity
- strong identification with an admired adult
- assertion of independence from family as a step toward adulthood
- respond well to group responsibility and group participation
- groups may form cliques
- high interest in physical attractiveness
- girls usually more interested in boys than boys in girls, resulting from earlier maturing of the girls

Needs

- acceptance by and conformity with others of own age
- adequate understanding of sexual relationships and attitudes
- kind, unobtrusive adult guidance that does not threaten the adolescents' feelings of freedom
- assurance of security—adolescents seek both dependence and independence
- opportunities to make decisions and to earn and save money
- provision for constructive recreation—some cause, idea, or issue to work for

Estimated Safe and Adequate Daily Dietary Intakes of Selected Vitamins

Age	K (micrograms)	H (micrograms)	B-5 (milligrams)
0-6 mos.	12	35	2
7-12 mos.	10-20	50	3
1-3 yrs.	15-30	65	3
4-6 yrs.	20-40	85	3-4
7-10 yrs.	30-60	120	4-5
11-17 yrs.	50-100	100-200	4-7
18+ yrs.	70-140	100-200	4-7

Estimated Safe Daily Dietary Intakes (in milligrams) of Trace Elements and Electrolytes

Age	Trace Elements						Electrolytes		
	Copper	Manganese	Fluoride	Chromium	Selenium	Molybdenum	Sodium	Potassium	Chloride
0-6 mos.	0.5-0.7	0.5-0.7	0.1-0.5	0.01-0.04	0.01-0.04	0.03-0.06	115-350	350-925	275-700
7-12 mos.	0.7-1.0	0.7-1.0	0.2-1.0	0.02-0.06	0.02-0.06	0.04-0.08	250-750	425-1275	400-1200
1-3 yrs.	1.0-1.5	1.0-1.5	0.5-1.5	0.02-0.08	0.02-0.08	0.05-0.1	325-975	550-1650	500-1500
4-6 yrs.	1.5-2.0	1.5-2.0	1.0-2.5	0.03-0.12	0.03-0.12	0.06-0.15	450-1350	775-2325	700-2100
7-10 yrs.	2.0-2.5	2.0-3.0	1.5-2.5	0.05-0.2	0.05-0.2	0.1-0.3	600-1800	1000-3000	925-2775
11-17 yrs.	2.0-3.0	2.5-5.0	1.5-4.0	0.05-0.2	0.05-0.2	0.15-0.5	900-2270	1525-4575	1400-4200
18+ yrs.	2.0-3.0	2.5-5.0	1.5-4.0	0.05-0.2	0.05-0.2	0.15-0.5	1100-3300	1875-5625	1700-5100

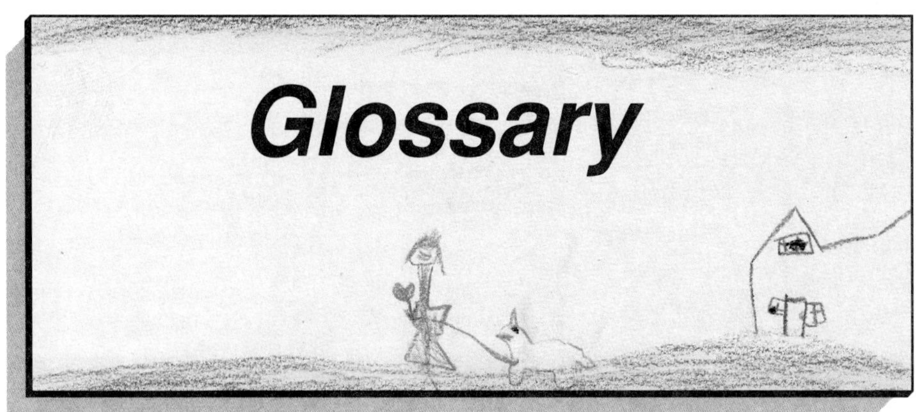

A

accommodation A term used by Jean Piaget to indicate a child adjusting his or her knowledge of a situation to external reality. Accommodation demonstrates that a child understands a situation as it relates to earlier experiences.

adaptation The ability of people to change their responses to one another and the world around them when the situation demands.

aggression The actual attack that accompanies anger.

ambidextrous The ability to use both hands equally well.

amoral Having no conscience.

anger A feeling that accompanies being restrained or blocked in progress toward some sort of fulfillment.

anoxia Failure of the fetus to receive enough oxygen during birth resulting from damage to the placenta or umbilical cord. It can destroy brain cells and also may be fatal.

anxiety A worry or deep concern about possibly impending danger or misfortune.

Apgar score An assessment of physical health resulting from tests given to newborns one minute after birth.

artificial insemination A procedure whereby a doctor inseminates a woman using sperm from a donor.

assimilation A term used by Piaget to describe a child incorporating new elements into existing thinking. The child experiences an event as he or she perceives it, but not necessarily as it actually is.

atonement A type of justice that requires punishment and suffering for any person who has committed a wrong.

autonomy A feeling of self-reliance.

B

Babinski reflex The automatic response of newborns that causes them to fan up their toes when the sole of the foot is stroked.

behavioral events of emotion The emotions that are reflected in changes in one's feelings and emotional reactions.

birth defects Abnormalities present at birth that affect the baby's well-being.

birthing center A facility, which may or may not be associated with a hospital, that tries to maintain a family atmosphere. Labor and birth occur in the same birthing room.

blended family A family formed by joining the children from two different families into a new family when their parents marry.

body language Communication by gestures, physical movements, and facial expressions.

bonding A strong emotional attachment that forms between parents and their children.

breech position A birth in which the baby's buttocks or feet are first in the birth canal, rather than the head.

C

Cesarean birth A birth in which the baby is delivered through a surgical incision in the mother's abdomen.

cephalocaudal principle The principle of development that states that the upper parts of small children grow toward maturity faster than the lower parts.

cervix The opening between the uterus and the birth canal.

character A person's sense of morality.

child abuse Psychological, physical, or sexual mistreatment of children.

chomosomes Genetic material in the nucleus of cells that controls hereditary characteristics.

cognitive development Intellectual growth.

colostrum Fluid secreted from a mother's breast for the first few days after giving birth. This fluid contains antibodies that help the baby become immune to many forms of infections.

communication A two-part exchange that involves both sending a message and someone receiving it.

competence Having adequate ability.

compromise A means by which two or more people agree to a solution based on ideas from both sides. Each side gives in a little to reach an agreement.

concept of analysis A process in which people separate a whole unit into separate parts so as to understand its workings.

concept of synthesis A process in which people put together individual objects or facts to create a functional entity.

conception The union of sperm and egg that results in a new life.

conscience A person's self-censoring device that guides behavior.

cooperation Working together for common benefit.

cooperative play The type of interaction in which children enjoy playing together.

crisis A decisive moment when some event, person, or action causes a turning point.

crisis-prone When almost any out-of-the-ordinary event causes great stress.

criteria Standards on which a judgment or decision is based.

cross-identification Modeling after persons of the opposite sex.

culture The values, attitudes, knowledge, and skills of a society.

D

daycare center A facility that provides daylong care for children before they reach school-age.

democratic parents Parents who believe that their children should be allowed to have a voice in making the rules and choosing the limits for their behavior.

developmental theory A theory of socialization that states the seeds of socialization are present in all people and will come to maturity in an accepting and rather passive environment.

discipline Setting and adhering to standards of behavior.

divorce phase The second stage in the dissolution of a marriage in which the married couple decides to obtain a divorce.

E

ego integrity A result of an individual's ability to look back on life with a sense of satisfaction.

egocentrism A type of thinking in which a child is unable to see a situation from any point of view except his or her own.

embryo From two weeks to eight weeks after conception the mass of cells developing in the uterus is called an embryo. After that it is called a fetus.

embryo transfer A medical procedure in which sperm from the husband is used to artificially inseminate a woman other than his wife. After several days, the embryo is transferred to his wife's uterus.

empathy The ability of a person to sense, appreciate, and understand the feelings of another person.

environment One's surroundings, including people, places, and things.

episiotomy Minor surgery performed prior to the birth of a child to avoid tearing the distended issues at the end of the birth canal.

ethics Society's moral principles or rules of behavior.

expedient Seeking that which is immediately advantageous without regard for ethics.

F

family-life education Training in human relationships to help people solve the problems of family living.

fetal period The period of development of the fetus from two months after fertilization through birth.

fetus The developing unborn baby from two months after conception to birth.

fine prehension The ability to pick up and hold small objects.

G

generativity A concern for people beyond the immediate family group.

genetic counseling Scientific advice based on medical studies and family histories concerning heredity and the risks of hereditary abnormalities.

grasp reflex The automatic response of newborns to close their hand when the palm is touched.

H

heredity Traits passed on genetically from parents to their offspring.

hormone A chemical substance produced by the body that has a specific effect on the body, such as growth.

hypothesis Unproved guess about the solution of a problem.

I

identification Copying, modeling, or adhering to a group of which a person feels to be a part.

immunization Injections or medications that provide protection against disease.

in-vitro fertilization An embryo from the woman and sperm from the father are united in a petri dish. The embryo grows in an incubator for two to three days and is then implanted in the mother's uterus.

incubator A highly sheltered crib with a controlled environment to protect premature babies.

individuation A stage of development in which babies learn that they are people separate from their caregivers and their caregivers are persons separate from them. Compare to symbiotic period.

infertility The inability to conceive a child.

integration A term used to describe the interdependence or interchange between the roles in the group.

internalize To incorporate values or patterns within the self.

interpersonal intelligence The type of intelligence that allows a person to understand other people's motivations, feelings, and interactions.

intrapersonal intelligence The type of intelligence that allows a person to achieve self-identity and self-understanding.

involvement A term used to refer to

commitment to and participation in family life by the members of the group.

J

jealousy An angry feeling that results when individuals are frustrated in their desire to be loved the most.

L

Lamaze A training method that is an approach toward natural childbirth. In Lamaze classes, the mother learns breathing techniques and exercises that will be useful during labor. The father learns how to assist during labor.

latchkey children A term used to describe children who come home from school to an empty home because their parents are working. They are so-called because many of them carry their own key to their home.

lightening A transition toward the final stages of pregnancy when the head of the baby moves down into the pelvic cavity relieving some of the pressure the mother has felt.

locomotion The power of moving from place to place.

M

maturation The process of coming to full development. Involves emotional, social, intellectual, and physical growth.

middle childhood A child from ages six years to ten years.

midwife A person trained to assist in the birth. May be licensed through nurses' training or unlicensed, having learned through experience.

moral development The growth of actions and decisions based on one's sense of right and wrong.

Moro reflex The automatic startle response in newborns that causes them to spread their arms apart and then bring them together when set off by a loud noise or a tap on the abdomen.

N

negative reinforcement The discouragement or punishment of a child for undesirable behavior. Telling children what they may not and should not do.

neglect A situation in which parents do not provide food, clothing, shelter, safe conditions, or emotional caring for their children.

nurturing A willingness to promote well-being and development of a loved one.

O

object-permanence A stage of development in which children are aware that an object exists even though they cannot see it.

obstetrician A medical doctor specializing in the care of pregnant women and birth.

ova Female reproductive cells or eggs contained in the ovaries.

ovaries Female reproductive organs that produce the ova.

ovulation The process of the female body releasing an egg from an ovary.

P

parallel play The type of play in which children enjoy playing next to each other but not together.

parenting roles Being responsible for the welfare of children and other people.

pediatrician A medical doctor who specializes in children's health.

permissive parents Parents who expect their children to exhibit independent behavior and be responsible for the consequences of their own decisions.

person-permanence A stage of development in which a child is aware that people exist even though they are out of sight.

personality The totality of a person's appearance, unique behavior, and emotional temperament.

placenta The tissue structure by which the fetus is nourished in the uterus. It separates from the fetus at birth.

play school A term used to describe a daycare center or preschool. ·Not often used now.

positive reinforcement Rewarding particular behavior in order to encourage it. Telling children what they may or should do.

post-divorce phase The phase after the legal dissolution of a marriage in which the family adjusts to its new status.

pre-divorce phase A phase in the dissolution of a marriage that starts when incompatibility, unfaithfulness, or other causes becomes evident to the married couple.

preschool A facility that provides for care of children before they reach school-age. It is for approximately three hours a day.

proximodistal principle Principle of growth that states that skillful manipulation occurs in parts of the body closer to the center of the body such as shoulder and hip joints before it occurs in such parts as hands and feet.

pubescence The period of growth during the two years prior to puberty.

R

rejection A situation in which the parents do not accept responsibility for the welfare of their child

restitution A type of justice in which the wrongdoer makes up for a loss by trying to make amends.

reversibility The ability to understand that a completed process also can be performed in the reverse order so that the materials used are returned to their initial state.

rivalry An angry feeling toward another person that results when individuals are frustrated in their desire to do their best, to win, or to place first.

role model A person another person patterns his or her life after.

rooting reflex The automatic response of newborns to turn in the direction in which their cheeks or corners of their mouths are touched.

S

schemas A term Jean Piaget used to describe patterns of action.

self-concept Feelings about oneself.

self-discipline Children's ability to guide and control their own behavior.

seriation The process of ordering a set of objects according to some property.

sexuality Sex and gender role.

sibling rivalry Competition between children in a family for their parent's approval, attention, and love.

social learning theory A theory that states children become social and self-confident to the degree that they learn they must adapt themselves to others in order to have their own needs satisfied.

social welfare organizations The agencies concerned with adoption, foster care, daycare, child abuse, family counseling, etc.

socialization The process of training individuals for their particular social environment.

society Any group of people that follows a generally accepted code of behavior.

somatic growth Observable changes in physical growth.

space concepts An understanding of spatial relationships that indicates a lessening of egocentrism.

sperm The male's reproductive cell.

stillbirth The birth of a dead fetus.

strict parents Parents who take an authoritarian posture regarding their responsibility as guardians of their children. They make and enforce all the rules.

surrogate mother A volunteer substitute mother who agrees to carry to term an embryo/fetus fertilized by a wife and husband. This procedure is utilized when the wife is unable to carry a fetus to term.

symbiotic period A stage of development in which babies experience oneness with their primary caregiver.

T

time concepts An understanding of time that indicates a lessening of egocentrism.

toddler The term used to refer to children from the time they start to walk until around three years of age.

traditional family A family consisting of a biological father who earns an income to support the family, a biological mother who is a full-time homemaker, and their children.

U

umbilical cord The cord that connects the placenta to the unborn baby and through which the baby is nourished.

unequivocally Leaving no doubt, being very clear.

uterus The womb. The female organ in which the fetus develops.

V

vaccine An injection or medication that contains a small amount of disease germs. The body systems fight the germs in the vaccine and thereby develop a resistance to the disease.

W

water sac The balloonlike sack filled with amniotic fluid in which the fetus floats.

Z

zygote The growing mass of cells from conception to two weeks later when it is called the embryo.

Index

C

D

E

F

G

H

I

J

K

L

M

N

O

P

R

U

V

W

Y

Z

Credits

Acknowledgements

The authors and editor would like to express their gratitude to the following people who were instrumental in creating this book: Terry Boles (illustrator), Colleen Haas (the art teacher at Wooddale Montessori Academy who arranged to have her students create artwork), and Rose Boelke (who also arranged for children's art).

Photo Credits

Andrew Brilliant, 3, 15, 37, 46, 50, 56, 68, 82, 112, 117, 215, 260, 272, 278, 330, 395

Bob Daemmrich, vi (middle), vii (bottom), x, 4, 12, 24, 26, 28, 31, 33, 35, 39, 42, 53, 57, 65, 80, 81, 83, 85, 87, 91, 95, 107, 118, 120, 126, 143, 144, 146, 151, 166, 178, 186, 206, 207, 222, 244, 246, 252, 274, 281, 289, 300, 305, 309, 312, 319, 323, 335, 340, 349, 350, 354, 376, 388, 392, 401, 404, 406, 412, 417, 418, 423, 428, 435, 436, 437

Robert Fried, vii (top), 89, 184, 236, 253, 266, 268, 270, 279, 286, 291, 299, 343, 359, 361, 371, 378, 386, 429

Cindy Garoutte, ix, 116, 121, 123, 129, 149, 152, 153, 177, 193, 195, 214, 229, 230, 235, 237, 251, 256, 276, 307, 316, 321, 345, 347, 381

Images Included/Steven Ruehle, 55, 188, 201, 202, 216, 333, 420

March of Dimes, 104

Lennart Nilsson, 96, 101

Carol Palmer, vi (top), 6, 8, 13, 14, 18, 20, 43, 59, 66, 67, 86, 103, 133, 140, 168, 194, 197, 209, 212, 238, 248, 249, 261, 284, 287, 293, 342, 367, 372, 377, 382, 394

Frank Schroder/Tannenblick Studio 233

Dave Simson, 432, 439

Slater Studio, vi (bottom), 60, 78, 102, 164, 365

Vanderbilt University, 106

David York, 134

Children Artists (and age)

Ashley Cheney (2), 1
Erika Latham (4), 7
Karine Feldman (4), 25
Jennifer Sherry (3), 51
Sam Parara (5), 79
Karington Brown (5), 97
Jennifer Smolley (6), 113
Brett Mitchell (5), 127
Danny Lichtblau (5), 141
Stephanie Li (5), 165
Eric Bryan (3), 185
Andrea Arnoldi (7), 203
Sean Sullivan (6), 223
Nikki Petter (4), 245
Elisabeth Renner (8), 267
Rachel Lynae Tholen (6), 285
Maureen Perry (7), 301
Amanda Herring (7), 313
Erika Bereuter (7), 331
Sarah Hanson (5), 355
Shawna Larson (8), 373
Adam Miles (3), 387
Lyncee Davies (5), 413
Adam Boelke (2), 421
Kiersten Fure (6), 433
J. R. Lamettry (8), 442
Courtney Shackleton (6), 452
Johnny Swon (9), 460
Lee Grunwald (6), 469